THE WORKS OF SRI CHINMOY

POETRY
VOLUME III

THE WORKS OF SRI CHINMOY

POETRY

VOLUME III

TOME I

★

TWENTY-SEVEN THOUSAND
ASPIRATION-PLANTS

PART 1 TO 64

LYON · OXFORD

GANAPATI PRESS

LXXXVI

© 2016 THE SRI CHINMOY CENTRE

ISBN 978-1-911319-02-3

See appendix for notice regarding this edition.

FIRST EDITION WENT TO PRESS ON 13 DECEMBER 2016

POETRY

VOLUME III

TWENTY-SEVEN THOUSAND ASPIRATION-PLANTS

PART 1 TO 64

1.

Twenty-seven thousand
Aspiration-plants:
Indeed, the distance is too long.
But my Beloved Lord Supreme
Says to me,
"My child, the distance is too
    short.
In top secrecy I am telling you:
I shall walk with you
All the way."

2.

Every day my entire being
Receives a blessingful Boon
From my Lord Supreme,
And that boon is
A beauty-flooded dawn of joy.

3.

Choice is my unnecessary
    imperfection
In my desire-life.
Choice is my indispensable
    perfection
In my aspiration-life.

4.

I am a chosen instrument
Of my Lord Supreme
Not because I have done
Something great for Him,
Not because I shall do
Something good for Him,
But because He wants to do
Something divinely great
And supremely good
In and through me.

5.

I shall become a purity-prayer
So that my heart
Can safely climb up to God.
I shall become a luminosity-
    meditation
So that God's Delight
Can easily enter into me.

6.

Since God has not given up
His Vision-Transcendence-Dance,
How can you give up
Your God-manifestation-song?

7.

You are useless!
Therefore you do not fight
Against ignorance the intruder.
You are stupid!
Therefore you do not want
God the Lover to fight for you.

8.

A soulful cry, where is it?
Inside my heart.
A powerful smile, where is it?
Inside my soul.
A bountiful blessing, where is it?
Inside my life.
And where am I, myself?
Inside God's unknowable Vision-Eye.

9.

If you and your mind are afraid
Of a silence-life,
That means you are nowhere near
God's Transcendental Throne.

10.

Yesterday
My mind was fond of
God's Greatness.
Today
My heart is fond of
God's Goodness.
Tomorrow
My life shall be fond of
God's Oneness.

11.

My Lord, how can I be pleased
   with You
When You do not give me
What I want?
"My child, I cannot be cruel to
   you.
You want from Me
The bondage of the finite.
I want to give you and I shall give
   you
Only the freedom of the Infinite."

12.

O Inspiration-Runner,
I love your running.
It is so beautiful.
O Aspiration-Climber,
I love your climbing.
It is so soulful.
O Realisation-Diver,
I love your diving.
It is so powerful.

13.

In the morning
My Lord gives me
A powerful concentration-arrow.
In the evening
My Lord gives me
A beautiful meditation-bow.
At night
My Lord asks me to kill
My ferocious ignorance-tiger.

14.

My mind's brooding doubt-sea
Versus
My Lord's ever-illumining
   Patience-Sun:
Who can unmistakably
Predict the result?

15.

God and His Infinity's Power
My mind wants.
God and His Immortality's Love
My heart needs.

16.

O my mind,
Do unlearn quickly!
O my heart,
Do learn soulfully!
O my soul,
Where are you hiding
Sleeplessly and calmly?
O my God,
I am here!
I need You only,
Desperately!

17.

The Vision-Eye
Of my Beloved Supreme
Thinks of me.
The Compassion-Heart
Of my Beloved Supreme
Loves me.
The Forgiveness-Life
Of my Beloved Supreme
Immortalises me.

18.

My prayer-cry is making my heart
Beautiful and soulful.
My meditation-smile is making
   my life
Powerful and fruitful.

19.

My Beloved Supreme never reminds me
Of my tiny ant-promises.
Alas, why do I remind Him every day
Of His mighty Lion-Promises?

20.

O my stupid mind,
Do not dare to challenge
My heart's sleepless
And breathless faith
In my Lord Supreme.
Also, do not dare to challenge
My soul's birthless
And deathless oneness
With my Lord Supreme.

21.

During my morning God-Hour meditation,
My Beloved Supreme said to me:
"My child, your heart-ecstasy's
Fountain-Source
Is not a secret treasure
But always a sacred,
Supremely sacred, treasure."

22.

When I am inside my mind,
I am a helpless sigh
Of utter failure.
When I am inside my heart,
I am a mounting flame
Of divine love.
When I am inside my soul,
I am a translucent smile
Of my Beloved Supreme.

23.

Yesterday my success-life
Made me godless.
Today my progress-heart
Has made the world speechless.
Something more,
My Beloved Supreme now tells me
That my life has become totally flawless.

24.

You have blindfolded your vision-eye
Completely.
Yet when, out of His boundless Bounty,
God comes to your rescue,
You blindly refuse to accept
His unconditional Help.

25.

I call it life.
My soul calls it beauty's temple.
I call it death.
My soul calls it purity's shrine.

26.

You are a chosen child of God,
Yet you envy.
Whom do you envy?
You envy your own totally
   forgotten
And astonishingly unrecognised
Boundless oneness-self.

27.

In my life's battlefield,
At long last my world-division-
   mind
Has unconditionally surrendered
To my God-oneness-heart.

28.

If you do not become
A conscious God-lover,
Then you will always remain
A stranger to your own
Absolute vision-heights.

29.

Do you know that I am
A very special member
Of God's immediate family?
Do you know that at every
   moment
I am being guided, moulded,
Perfected and liberated
By God's fondest instrument-
   child:
Compassion?

30.

What is my human mind
If not a life of sheer nothingness?
What is my human heart
If not a life of fragile littleness?
What is my divine soul
If not a life of supernal newness?
Who is my Supreme Lord
If not the Life of Universal
   Oneness
And Transcendental Fulness?

31.

The God-lover who prays
With a sincere mind,
Meditates with a soulful heart
And serves with an unconditional
   life
Is a hero-warrior
Of God-Immortality's infinite
   Delight
Who is journeying home.

32.

You know that it takes time
For the mind to become
Sincerely spiritual.
How is it that you are unwilling
To give your life the needed time
To become perfectly perfect?

33.

Right from the day I was born
I have been maintaining a very
  strict diet
Of God's very special food:
His Eternity's Compassion
And
His Immortality's Love.

34.

Secretly you enjoy climbing
The staircase of despair.
Openly you enjoy gathering
Your life's incapacity-sighs.

35.

My prayer wants to conceal
The impurity of my unnatural
  sound-life.
My meditation wants to reveal
The beauty of my Lord's
Natural Silence-Life.

36.

Your aspiration tells you
That God you can have.
Your dedication tells you
That God you already have.
Your realisation tells you
That God you always have been.

37.

My constant happiness entirely
  depends
On the quality of my gratitude-
  heart
And on the quality of my
  surrender-life
To the Will of my Inner Pilot.

38.

Nothing is as eternally beautiful
As my life's surrender-dance.
Nothing is as infinitely fruitful
As my heart's gratitude-song.

39.

I deeply admire
Your three astonishingly
Sincere confessions:
You have not prayed to God
Even once in your entire life
Unconditionally.
You speak ill of God the creation
Secretly.
You serve God and help man
Quite unwillingly.

40.

You do not want to live for others.
That is fine with me.
You do not want to live with
  others.
That is fine with me.
You do not want to live for me.
That is fine with me.
You do not want to live with me.
That is fine with me.
But if you do not want to live
For God's full Manifestation on
  earth,
I shall never be pleased with you.
And if you do not want to live with
God the Lover and God the
  Beloved,
I shall not only be displeased with
  you,
But I shall never forgive you,
Never!

41.

O my heart,
Can you not become
A climbing sun?
O my life,
Can you not become
An expanding sky?

42.

As a doubting mind
Finds no comfort on earth,
Even so, a loving heart
Finds no comfort in the grave.

43.

My Lord Supreme,
You are both
The Creator and the creation.
Why is it so difficult for me
To thank You as the creation?
"My child,
Because of the capacity
I have given you
To serve My creation,
You are thanking Me, the Creator.
Because of the opportunity
My creation has given you
To serve Me,
Can you not thank Me, the
  creation?"

44.

You are not
What others think you are.
You are not
What you claim to be.
Others think of you
As a useless human being.
You claim to be
A perfect human being.
Now I shall tell you
What you actually are.
You are an eternal pilgrim
Walking along the road of
   aspiration
Towards the destined goal:
Perfection.
And your perfection is another
   name
For God's complete Satisfaction.

45.

My Lord, every day I see those
Who are creating so-called
   happiness
Through self-deception.
They think and feel
That they are absolutely perfect.
What can I do with them?
What can I do for them?
"My child, you do not have to do
Anything with them or for them.
Just remain silent.
Your silent indifference
Will be the most severe
   punishment."

46.

Only a mind
That has learnt a bitter lesson
Realises what an extraordinary
   sacrifice
The aspiring heart has already
   made for it
And how many more sacrifices
Are yet to follow.

47.

A mind of wandering thoughts
Will sooner or later have to face
Life-devouring worries and
   anxieties.

48.

My Lord, do not tell me
What Your Will is.
Without knowing Your Will
I shall try to fulfil it.
Why?
Because, my Lord,
If I first learn Your Will
And then execute it,
Who knows,
I may not be as happy.

49.

My Master's race
Has already begun,
And I shall make
The perfect choice:
My heart shall be with him
And my life shall be for him alone.

50.

I may not be
A great truth-seeker.
I may not be
A great God-lover.
But not to tell the world
About God's Compassion-Eye
And Forgiveness-Heart
Would be a destructive
And unfortunate mistake.

51.

My Lord, do examine me.
Do examine the extravagance
Of my doubting mind.
Do examine the sincerity
Of my heart's climbing cry.

52.

Your heart lives
In a remote land
Of hope.
Your mind lives
Inside a devastating flood
Of fear.
But yours is the soul
That will never give up
Until it has indisputably won
The God-manifestation-race.

53.

My Lord Supreme,
This time I shall be
A good seeker.
I shall definitely
Spare You the torment
Of waiting for me any longer.

54.

Mind, my mind,
Are you not ashamed
Of walking every day
Along the stupidity-street?
Heart, my heart,
Are you not tired
Of walking every day
Along the insecurity-path?
Soul, my soul,
I definitely know
You will accompany me
When I start walking consciously
Along Eternity's Road.

55.

To consume the poison
Of your suspicion-mind,
What you need
Is a new inspiration-start
And a new aspiration-journey.

56.

God is not ashamed
Of what you say and do.
Therefore,
You do not have to be ashamed
Of what you are.
Just give God cheerfully
As many chances as He needs
To correct and perfect you.

57.

The universal discovery
Of all God-lovers:
God's Compassion-Height
Is God's Vision's
Transcendental Justice-Light.

58.

The winter of my life's lethargy-night
Is over.
The spring of my soul's action-delight
Has come.
Now God has given me
The capacity to reveal His Satisfaction
Through my perfection-life.

59.

My mind is always unwilling
To ask God
What He thinks of it—
For fear of the answer.

60.

Each day
Is a hopelessly futile day,
And each day
Shall remain a hopelessly futile day,
If I cannot cheerfully cast aside
The impurity-ink
Of my mind.

61.

Who asks you to remain
Buried beneath the soil
Of self-indulgence?
Tell me, who?
Nobody!
I am ready to guide you
Along the age-old path
Of self-discipline –
But are you ready?

62.

When you are trapped
Between your mind's disbelief
And your heart's belief,
Invoke your Lord Supreme
To rebuke you sharply.
You will before long
Swim in the sea of wisdom-
   delight.

63.

My Lord Supreme,
There was a time when I did many
   things
To please myself.
Now I am doing only one thing,
Not for me but for You.
I am watering my life's
Gratitude-plant
With my gratitude-tears.

64.

My eyes are so blind
That they do not see
My Lord's Compassion.
My heart is so dull
That it does not feel
My Lord's Compassion.
My mind is so arrogant
That it does not care for
My Lord's Compassion.
My vital is so stupid
That it thinks it does not need
   compassion
Either from earth or from Heaven.
My body is so lethargic
That it enjoys ignorance-sleep
All the time.
Therefore, it does not even know
What compassion is.
But my soul is fully awakened.
Therefore, it unmistakably knows
That the breath of my perfection-
   life
Lives inside my Lord's
Compassion-Heart.

65.

You are unwise
If you are satisfied
With today's inner flames,
And do not try to increase
Your receptivity-light,
For, who knows,
Tomorrow's outer sun
May not rise at all.

66.

What is it like to be another God?
It is like attaining
Not only your unattained self
But also your unattainable Self.

67.

God has made many roads
Leading to Him
Since God wants to please
Each individual in his own way,
As He Himself wants to be pleased
In His own Way.

68.

A cheerful self-giving
And a powerful God-becoming
Are the obverse and reverse
Of the life-perfection-coin.

69.

No outer aptitude can ever equal
The inner aptitude for self-
   transcendence
And God-Satisfaction.

70.

O my doubting mind,
Let us say a final farewell
And invoke Eternity
To appreciate our stupendous
   parting.

71.

My proud mind
Does not stop talking about God.
Alas, alas!
My timid heart
Has not started talking about
   God.
Alas, alas!

72.

If your eyes want to see the world,
Then do it, but measure.
If your heart wants to love the
   world,
Then do it, but don't measure.

73.

You have installed
Teeming fears and doubts
In the confusion-chamber
Of your mind.
How then can you install God
And His Infinity's Splendour-
   Delight
On the illumination-throne
Of your heart?

74.

Before you dare to analyse God,
You must tranquillise your mind,
Organise your life
And sensitise your heart.

75.

Your only complaint against me
Is that I am incapable
Of being false,
Even when necessity demands.
My only complaint against you
Is that you are incapable
Of being indifferent,
Even when necessity demands.

76.

Do you know
What failure has taught you?
It has taught you
Not to make any compromise
With ignorance-night.

77.

Soul, my soul,
You save me from constant
Invasions of death.
Soul, my soul,
You welcome the teeming
Sighs of my life.
Alas, I do not consciously
Love you
And yet I desperately
Need you.

78.

The outer sun is not new every
   day,
But the inner sun is.
The outer sun
Asks me to climb up
To the Himalayan heights.
The inner sun
Tells me to remain sleeplessly
On my Himalayan peak.

79.

The human in me foresees my life
As a hopeless battle.
The divine in me foresees my life
As a peerless God-victory.
It is I who have to make
The correct decision.
I shall either allow myself
To be discouraged by giant fears,
Or I shall prepare myself
For God's God-Embrace.

80.

My inspiration-smile
Is my secret power.
My aspiration-cry
Is my sacred power.
My realisation-song
Is my God-manifesting power.

81.

Mine is the mind that wants to be
Reunited with ignorance-power.
Mine is the heart that wants to be
Reunited with wisdom-king.
Mine is the life that wants to be
Reunited with perfection-
   emperor.

82.

Your life is invaded
By uncertainty-truths
Because your mind is reluctant
To enjoy the sun-vast dreams
Of God's world.

83.

Every morning
I faithfully do three things:
I climb far above
The clouds of my mind.
I master my despair-life.
I try to become a champion
   instrument
Of my Lord's Satisfaction-Delight.

84.

A single breath
Of impurity-night
Can fell the hope-tree
Of your outer life
And the promise-tree
Of your inner life.

85.

He is at once
The professor of his desire-life
And the student of his mind's
Illusion-prison.

86.

Do not try to conceal
What your mind has.
You will badly fail.
Try to reveal
What your soul has and is.
You will speedily succeed.

87.

Every door can be shut —
But not death's door.
Every room can be ignored —
But not life's room.

88.

A true God-lover's aspiration-
   heart
And dedication-life
Can and will enjoy
The beauty-hours
Of Heaven-days.

89.

You are your burdened life.
You are your sense-hunger.
How then can you expect your
   heart
To liberate you?

90.

Your life has teeming problems.
Your mind has become
A chain of falsehood-mountains.
But God knows and tells the world
That He will transform your
   earth-life
Into His own Heaven-Home.

91.

Yesterday I was sincere.
Therefore, I admitted
That I have human weaknesses.
Today I am again sincere.
Therefore, I am admitting
That my Lord Supreme
Is transforming me
Fast, very fast,
Into His divine instrument
Unparalleled.

92.

Now that your mind is totally
   shattered
By its own absurd pretensions,
Your life will soon have
The capacity to reveal
God's self-transcending Vision-
   Light
In and through you.

93.

Because you approach every situation
With your heart's moon-white poise,
God is granting you
His own Eternity's universe-feeding Voice.

94.

What is sleepless self-giving
If not the flowering of God-Delight
Inside your heart's aspiration-garden?

95.

Yesterday
God most compassionately told me:
"Attachment-night
Is quenchless thirst
In the desire-world."
Today
God most satisfactorily tells me:
"Detachment-light
Is endless nectar-delight
In the aspiration-world."

96.

I keep on praying and praying to God
For His Forgiveness.
God keeps on forgiving and forgiving
My entire existence-life.
God's Heart and my soul feel
That this is an extremely charming
And illumining game.

97.

Do not sink into despair!
Your obedience-light
In the heart of your aspiration
And in the life of your dedication
Is your highest victory
And God's boundless Delight.

98.

The day I threw myself
On God's side,
God secretly granted me
Three world-loving, world-illumining
And world-fulfilling lessons:
How to cry for the world
Sleeplessly,
How to smile at the world
Soulfully,
How to serve Him in the world
Unconditionally.

99.

My Beloved Supreme,
I shall without fail
Tame everything in my life
Save and except
My heart's sleepless tears
To realise You.

100.

Are you absolutely sure
That your heart cries for God
    only?
If so, then rest assured,
God will before long give you
His Eternity's GOLDEN ALL.

101.

Each aspiring life
Is a Dream-Wave
Of the Lord Supreme
Which will eventually
Break upon the blue-gold shore
Of God's Vision-transformed
    Reality.

102.

Definitely there is nothing new,
Beautiful, soulful,
Powerful or fruitful
Inside your proud mind.

103.

My Lord Supreme,
How can I make lightning
    progress
In my spiritual life?
"My child,
Do the right thing
And become the perfect thing
With a nameless life
And an expectation-empty
    breath."

104.

Keep your mouth
Always shut
And keep your ears
Always open
If you want to be wise.

105.

Everyone gets Compassion
From Him.
Everyone is perfect
In Him.

106.

The world's oldest wisdom:
Each evil thought
Infuses the mind,
Sooner or later,
With an unholy fear.

107.

His Himalayan realisation
Dwarfs all mankind's
Present and future
Earthly pride-towers.

108.

Look what your self-binding mind
Has done to you!
It has taught you
Cleverly and quickly
How to suspect yourself.

109.

One of my constant problems:
I always think
About others
But never care
For others.

110.

If your mind lives
Inside your heart's golden flames,
Then your life will not be found
In an abysmal abyss.

111.

So far you have made no attempt
To climb up your inner life-tree.
How, then, can you expect
To enjoy most delicious fruits
From your outer life-tree?

112.

Two difficult things to achieve:
A gratitude-heart
And
A surrender-life.

113.

His heart of tear-filled years
Is sleeplessly looking for
Only one thing:
A newborn hope.

114.

If you want to think of God
Everywhere,
Even inside the supermarket,
Then you must first think of God
At home.

115.

My rich heart is always ready
To give my poor mind
What it has in abundant measure:
Peace.
But my blind and unreceptive mind
Will never accept
Its generous and unconditional offer.

116.

Your division-mind may deceive
My sleeping mind,
But your oneness-heart can never deceive
My searching mind
Or my aspiring heart.

117.

God loves me,
But I do not have the time
To love God.
God speaks to me,
But I do not have the time
To speak to God.
God knows who I am,
But I do not have the time
To know who I am,
Whose I am
Or why I am.

118.

O my inner life,
Do not weep for me,
For I do not deserve it.
O my outer life,
Do not smile at me,
For I do not need it.

119.

My yesterday's resolution:
I shall change earth's face.
My today's resolution:
I shall grow into
God's infinite Grace.

120.

God creates each human being
With His Heart's
Translucent Hope
And His Soul's
Transcendental Promise.

121.

Something has to die immediately
Inside my mind.
Ah, I know what it is!
It is my monster-ego.
Something has to blossom immediately
Inside my life.
Ah, I know what it is!
It is my flower-heart.

122.

The lethargic body collapses —
The aggressive vital follows.
The impure mind collapses —
The insecure heart follows.

123.

Since the beginning of creation
The soul and the heart
Have been singing the same songs
While travelling along
Eternity's Road.
The heart sings,
"So much to do on earth,
But where is the time?"
The soul sings,
"So much to do in Heaven,
But where is the time?"

124.

Your life of noise must love
The Voice of God.
Your life of noise must love
The Life of God.
If not, you are bound to see
Your life unfinished,
And therefore unrecognised
Here on earth.

125.

You were a thinker
Of the past.
You are a lover
Of the present.
You will be a fulfiller
Of the future.

126.

You are imperfect,
But you can easily become perfect.
You just need a head that bows,
A heart that loves
And a soul that dreams.

127.

My Lord,
I would like to express
My gratitude to You,
But I am groping for words.
"My son,
Do not waste your precious time
Learning the art
Of gratitude-expression.
Just learn to tell Me
Only one thing:
That you are happy,
Forever happy."

128.

A crying heart and a smiling life
Are the direct descendants
Of God the Dreamer
And God the Lover.

129.

When I speak to you about God,
You don't believe me.
When you speak to me about God,
I don't believe you.
Therefore, what is the use
Of our talking to each other
About God?
The best thing will be for us
To pray for God to speak,
For He is the only One
Who can talk about Himself
With inner Illumination
And outer Compassion.

130.

There is and there can be
Only one age-old question:
Can anyone realise God?
There is and there can be
Only one answer:
Yes, certainly,
Anyone can realise God.
Why?
Because that is what God wants.
How?
By constantly singing
The song of surrender
On the summit-height
Of one's own realisation-
 mountain.

131.

Those who do not believe in God
Are self-styled gods.
Those who believe in God
Are being moulded by God
 Himself
To become exact replicas
Of His Vision-Eye,
Compassion-Heart
And Satisfaction-Life.

132.

He who prays unconditionally
For God's transcendental
    Satisfaction
And he who meditates
    unconditionally
For God's universal Manifestation
Is the God-man of tomorrow.

133.

The line of those
Who do not want to transcend
Their earth-bound bondage-life
Is endless.

134.

A God-searching mind
Does not know
What outer frustration is.
A God-loving heart
Does not know
What inner stagnation is.

135.

Today I have made
Two decisions:
From now on
I shall love God
Consciously;
From now on
I shall obey my Lord Supreme
Sleeplessly.

136.

My Lord,
You know that I do not want
To disappoint You.
How is it then
That You are not willing
To appoint me
To serve Your Feet,
Love Your Heart
And manifest Your Vision-Eye
Here on earth?

137.

My Lord,
You have given my heart
The capacity to wait for You
For Eternity.
Will You not give my mind
The capacity to wait for You
Even for a fleeting second?

138.

My soul-bird needs two wings,
An aspiration-wing
And a dedication-wing,
To fly the highest
In the firmament of Eternity's
    Peace,
Infinity's Love
And Immortality's Delight.

139.

My Lord Supreme,
Please tell me how I can stop
Deceiving You.
"My sweet child,
You can and will stop deceiving Me
Only when you stop
Deceiving yourself.
You deceive yourself when you mix
With those time-wasters
And life-killers:
Your unconscious body
And your impure mind."

140.

God tells me that if I agree with Him
At every moment,
Then He will grant me
His own Satisfaction-Love
To use in His Eternal Now.

141.

If you can feel
That your heart's inner cry
Is the only thing you have,
Then God will grant you
The thing He treasures most
In His own Life:
Sweetest Oneness-Satisfaction.

142.

Your God-manifestation-dream
Will definitely come true,
But before that you must have
Another dream:
A God-realisation-dream.

143.

If there is a tug-of-war
Between your heart's faith
And your mind's doubt,
Which side will you join?
Or will you be afraid
To join either side,
And embrace the life
Of indifference?

144.

Insincerity,
I do not want to have you any
  more.
It is you who have carried me away
From the Mind
Of my Beloved Supreme.
Impurity,
I do not want to have you any
  more.
It is you who have carried me away
From the Heart
Of my Beloved Supreme.
Jealousy,
I do not want to have you any
  more.
It is you who have carried me away
From the Vision-Eye
Of my Beloved Supreme.
Insecurity,
I do not want to have you any
  more.
It is you who have carried me away
From my oneness-life
With my Beloved Supreme.

145.

My prayer is worth infinitely more
With my sacrifice-flames.
My meditation is worth infinitely
  more
With my silence-perfection.

146.

My worst enemy is not
My hopeless unworthiness.
My worst enemy is
My constant unwillingness.
My best friend is not
My heart's aspiration-cries.
My best friend is
My life's surrender-smiles.

147.

If I want to be
A prominent guest of God,
My ignorance-sleep
Must soon expire.

148.

Your sweet Lord wants from you
Only four things:
Your regularity-drop,
Your punctuality-flame,
Your sincerity-cry
And your spontaneity-smile.
With these four invaluable
  treasures,
You will be able to walk along
The road of your perfection,
And God will be able to walk
  along
The road of His Satisfaction.

149.

God is keeping His Victory-Crown
Ready for you to wear.
Once He offers it to you,
He will feel that He has placed it
On His own Head.

150.

The more the unaspiring life
Wants to possess you,
The more you should love
Your sleeplessly aspiring heart
And your extraordinarily
Self-giving life.

151.

"I want God."
This, everybody says.
"I need God."
This, how many are ready to feel?

152.

Your body is not graceful.
Your vital is not faithful.
Your mind is not prayerful.
Your heart is not grateful.
Your life is not soulful.
How, then, do you expect to be
A useful instrument
Of the Supreme?

153.

I shall no longer swim
In the ignorance-sea.
I shall throw my heart and soul
Into the spiritual life.
Right from this moment
I shall inundate my life
With the most powerful faith
That I will succeed
Inwardly and outwardly.

154.

Each human being
Has a higher life and a lower life.
The lower life
Is the life of division.
The higher life
Is the life of oneness.

155.

When your lower life attacks me,
My higher life feels miserable.
Why?
Not because it is angry with you,
But because it has compassion
For your own higher life.

156.

Your deliberate destruction
Is now causing you sorrow
Because your higher life
Has come forward
To teach you that destruction
Belongs to the lower life.

157.

If you are devoted
To your daring heart,
Then you are bound to be blessed
With a liberated life.

158.

You can challenge death's dominion
If you travel with your heart
Towards Immortality's Sun.

159.

When my heart cries,
God compassionately feeds my heart.
When my life smiles,
God lovingly feeds my life.

160.

The mind enjoys
The newness-game.
The heart enjoys
The soulfulness-game.
The soul enjoys
The oneness-game.
God enjoys
His Fulness-Game.

161.

If I approach God as a beggar,
I will have to wait forever
To see Him.
If I approach God as a divine lover,
I can see Him
At my sweet will.

162.

My mind needs
Purity's new creation.
My heart needs
Beauty's new revelation.
My soul needs
Duty's new satisfaction.

163.

Sometimes you have to fight,
If God does not want you
To be humiliated by your enemy.
Sometimes you have to forgive,
If God wants you
To illumine your enemy.

164.

By exercising his will-power
A seeker, with his finite life,
May enter into
The infinite Life,
But only at God's choice Hour.
By exercising His Will-Power
God, with His infinite Vision
And infinite Reality,
Not only touches
But lives inside
The breath of the finite.

165.

A surrender-heart cannot die.
It always enjoys
Immortality's oneness-
   satisfaction.

166.

My Lord,
Do take from me
What I have:
Hope.
My Lord,
Do give me
What I do not have:
Surrender.

167.

Between your justice-light
And God's Forgiveness-Light
I shall have to make a choice.
Am I such a fool
That I will take your side?
God's Forgiveness-Light
Not only do I long for
But one day I would like to grow
   into.
Indeed, this is my only goal.

168.

A tough old lie:
I have not cared for mankind.
A tough old truth:
God Himself has sent me
Into the world
To manifest Him
In a most remarkable way.

169.

You will without fail collect
A harvest of sorrow
If you deliberately refuse to know
Who you truly are.

170.

The waves of hatred-night
Can easily be dissolved
In the sea of oneness-love.

171.

My heart's iota of suffering
Can never, never equal
The Compassion-Flood
That descends from Above
Not only to console me
But also to illumine
And satisfy me.

172.

Hell has captured my mind.
Despair has captured my heart.
Alas, before long,
Failure shall capture my life,
My poor life.

173.

If you are ready to give up
Your sadness-face,
Then God is more than ready
To grant you His Gladness-Heart.

174.

My mind is now willing
To become God's choice
    instrument.
My heart is now ready
For God to accept
Either its soulful cries
Or its powerful smiles.

175.

Unless you practise
Your heart's peace-songs
Every day,
You will be compelled to watch
Your vital's frustration-dance
Go on and on.

176.

Do not allow your mind
To wrestle with uncomely
    thoughts,
For it will unmistakably fail.
Just ask your heart
To illumine your thought-world.
It will instantly change
The face and fate
Of each and every thought.

177.

What is success?
My need for expression-voice.
What is progress?
My need for God's Satisfaction-
    Choice.

178.

Never again shall I miss
My appointment with God,
Never!
Not even when doubt-clouds
Cover my entire being.

179.

Earth, my earth,
What do I owe you,
If not my concern?
Heaven, my Heaven,
What do I owe you,
If not my compassion?
God, my God,
What do I owe You,
If not my satisfaction?

180.

He is trying hard to forget
His former freedom,
The freedom that taught him
To be only for
His own pride-bound self.

181.

If you uncover
Your wild ignorance-laughter,
God will surely cover
Your soul's sweet smile.

182.

If you explore
Your heart's silence-garden,
You are bound to discover
Delight's fragrance-buds.

183.

How can you breathe
A breath of hope,
When you yourself have tightened
The tangle of perplexities?

184.

If you can kindle
Your heart's cry,
Your entire being
Will soon be aflame
With beauty's light
And duty's delight.

185.

Your promised
God-manifestation on earth
Must not fail
While performing
Its divine task supreme.

186.

If anxiety is your real name,
How can you expect purity
To be with you,
And how can you expect divinity
To be for you?

187.

Your life-boat
Is bound to capsize
Because your mind is still attached
To its anxiety-shore.

188.

Your life is shunted about
By ceaseless fears, doubts
And other anxiety-accumulations.
How, then, do you hope
To recognise your self-form
In this lifetime?

189.

Relinquish your confusion-mind
As soon as possible
If you really want your heart
To soulfully and unreservedly
   enjoy
God's Compassion-Satisfaction-
   Game.

190.

My heart has the inner purity-cry
To challenge and overrule
The authority-frown of my outer
   world.

191.

The mind thinks
It is a very difficult task
To approach the Truth.
The heart feels
It is an extremely easy task
Not only to approach the Truth
But also to become the Truth
Transcendental and Universal.

192.

If ignorance has the capacity
To damage my heart,
Then God's Compassion has the capacity
To cure it,
And God's Oneness is the capacity
To transform it
And to radiate God's Vision-Light
Through it.

193.

My mind begins to work
And then gives up.
My heart begins to work
But does not know
Whether it will continue.
My life begins to work
But does not care to finish.
My soul begins to work
And wants to continue
Throughout Eternity
To manifest tomorrow's beauty-heart
And divinity-life.

194.

God is desperately looking
For your purity's soulful devotion.
You are deliberately looking
For your mind's bewildered
Death-bed devotion.

195.

Mind the lawyer
Has never won a case.
Heart the lover
Has not only won all its cases
But has also become
The colossal Smile
Of God's Compassion-Eye.

196.

An ignorance-lover
Promptly closes his ignorance-
   eyes.
A God-lover
Not only immediately opens
His aspiration-eyes
But also silently begs God
To secretly open
His Eternity's Eye.

197.

If you even dare to think
You belong to God,
Then the distance between you
   and God
Becomes not just short
But non-existent.

198.

It is easier to have faith in God
Than in myself,
For time and again
I have overestimated my capacity
And found myself caught
In a strange self-deception-net.

199.

If anything has to pray,
Then it is my mind
That has to pray first.
If anything has to obey,
Then it is my heart
That has to obey first.
If anything has to surrender,
Then it is my life
That has to surrender first.
If anything has to preach,
Then it is my soul
That has to preach first.

200.

My Supreme Lord
Has placed His Eternity's Lamp
Right before me.
Placing the Lamp
Inside the depths of my heart,
I shall illumine my inner life.
Carrying the Lamp
Along with me,
I shall guide my outer life.

201.

My Lord,
I simply do not know how to
   thank You
For Your sleepless Compassion-
   Flood.
"My child,
You do not have to know
How to thank Me.
Just try to remain all the time
Inside your breathless receptivity-
   heart."

202.

I have been loving God
   unconsciously
For millennia,
But I shall love God consciously
From this moment on.

203.

The sound that never fails
Is the sound that is cradled
In tranquillity's oneness-vision.

204.

God has only one simple need:
Your inner and outer obedience.
If you can fulfil His need,
You will be able to make Him
   happy,
And He will be able to make you
   happy.

205.

He reluctantly obeyed God.
Even so, his obedience saved him.
Darkness-night did not last
And a spiritual dawn he saw.

206.

Meditate soulfully.
Even if an earthquake takes place,
You will not be afraid,
For you will be safely sheltered
In God's own Heart.

207.

You ask who is right
And who is wrong.
Who cares,
As long as you have established
True oneness?

208.

Although you surrendered to him
In the battlefield of life,
Hidden inside your surrender
Was the thought of revenge.
When will you learn
That who is stronger or weaker
Is of no importance?

209.

The day he became a God-seeker
Was the beginning of his
    conscious
Feeling of Immortality.
On that day he came to know
That he is part and parcel
Of Immortality.
On that day he realised
That he represents Immortality
On earth.
On that day he became
A pathfinder and harbinger
Of Immortality
For those on earth who will accept
The spiritual life after him.

210.

Today you are seeing your Master
As another runner
Just ahead of you
As you run faithfully
Along the inner road.
Tomorrow you will see your
    Master
Not only as the road
But also as the goal itself.

211.

If you see good qualities in others,
Then claim them as your own,
For who knows when you will find
Those same qualities
In your own nature?

212.

The Vedic seers tell us
The entire world is ours —
Everything, inside and outside,
Belongs to us.

213.

Your country has peerless
    qualities.
My country needs them badly.
Let us share
Our great God-given gifts.

214.

I am an open-hearted soul.
Therefore, even my worst enemy
May claim at will
All my inner treasures.

215.

Upon his world-carrying
  shoulders
Rests the completely lost
New generation.

216.

When I see the fountain of purity
Inside you,
I become the beauty and divinity
Of soundless silence.

217.

My Supreme Lord,
I know, I know,
I have a strong weakness.
Do give me the sincere
  determination
Which is infinitely stronger
Than my weakness.

218.

God will grant you
The willingness-capacity
To change your life
The day your lip-deep prayer
Becomes heart-deep.

219.

At all the precious moments
Of humanity's life,
The mind is tormented
By uncomely thoughts.

220.

The ordinary human mind
Is a container.
You can fill it
With good thoughts
Or bad thoughts.
It is up to you.

221.

Life plays the union-game.
Death plays the division-game.
Life thinks it is beautiful.
Death thinks it is powerful.
Life comes from the abode of
  aspiration.
Death comes from the abode of
  illusion.

222.

Silence-sky
Around me glows
When realisation-tree
Within me grows.

223.

Not to renounce
And not to enjoy.
Not to be an ascetic
And, again, not to be
The world's greatest epicurean.
This is the path
To true happiness.

224.

Do not go to extremes.
Accept the body
And the five senses.
Only use them spiritually,
Divinely and soulfully.

225.

When something is without form,
We may feel it has no life.
But should our Beloved Supreme
Come to us without form,
We must cultivate the same kind of
Faith, love and devotion
For His formless aspect
As we have for His physical form.

226.

Easily you can count the miracles
That you have seen or heard of
During your entire lifetime.
But even a so-called miracle-man,
Who himself is as stupid as you,
Will not be able to fathom
The abysmal abyss
Of your stark stupidity.

227.

If you want to succeed,
Then allow not your mind
To experience others' experiences.
Allow your mind
Only to sit at the foot
Of your own realisation-tree.

228.

If someone comes to me for
    knowledge,
How can I refuse to teach him?
What little wisdom-light I have
I shall gladly offer.

229.

If you aspire
Soulfully and powerfully,
Your climbing aspiration-plant
Will grow into a fruitful
Aspiration-tree.

230.

I may say
That my possessions are my own.
But can my possessions
Not also say
That I am theirs?

231.

Uninvited he came into the world
To cry with humanity's
Sacred sorrows.
Uninvited he will go back to
  Heaven
To drink deep Divinity's
Secret Delight.

232.

O my heart-flower,
If you are truly and unmistakably
  mine,
Then I would like you to smile
At everybody,
Not only today
But every blossoming day.

233.

I do not give up,
I never give up,
For there is nothing
In this entire world
That is irrevocably unchangeable.

234.

God's Body knows
How to shine.
God's Heart knows
How to give.
God's Life knows
How to love.
God's Vision knows
How to become.

235.

Surrender practised,
Gratitude lived,
Perfection received,
Satisfaction achieved.

236.

He has fallen victim
To the false criticism
That he has copied
Everything from others.
I declare
That he is simply unveiling
The qualities he himself had
All along.

237.

Since he has learnt about God
Before you,
There is nothing wrong in
  accepting
His higher wisdom.

238.

My heart says,
"O my Eternity's Beloved
   Supreme,
I shall not blame You
If You do not love me any more.
I shall not blame You
If You do not need me any more."
My mind says,
"My Lord, I shall certainly blame
   You
If I cannot smile at You every day.
I shall certainly blame You
If I cannot cry for You every
   night."

239.

When I was a God-dreamer
My Lord said to me,
"Come, come, it is getting late!"
When I was a God-seeker
My Lord said to me,
"Run, run, I want you
To be on time!"
When I was a God-lover
My Lord said to me,
"Fly, fly, I have so many things
To tell you!"

240.

My Beloved Supreme,
Is there anything
You will not allow me to be?
"My child,
There is only one thing
I shall never allow you to be."
What is it,
My Beloved Supreme?
"My child,
I shall never, never allow you
To be unworthy of My infinite
   Love."

241.

Now is the time for me to do
Two most significant things:
I must say good-bye
To the failure-centuries
Of my life
And increase my God-hunger
Immeasurably.

242.

The divine meaning of
   competition
Is the manifestation of soulfulness
In the outer life.
The supreme meaning of
   competition
Is the perfection of oneness
In the inner life.

243.

The seekers of the hoary past
Prayed mostly for the inner
  strength
To realise God.
The seekers of today
Are praying mostly for the outer
  strength
To manifest God.
The seekers of tomorrow
Will pray soulfully
For the inner strength
And the outer strength
To both realise and manifest God.
When God sees they have realised
  Him
And manifested Him,
He will grant them a very special
  boon:
God will transform
The entire earth-consciousness
In and through these
Specially selected instruments
Of His.

244.

My heart cries
To see Infinity's God-Beauty.
My soul smiles
Because Immortality has chosen it
As its own Eternity's child-friend.

245.

My soul knows
Where God is.
My heart longs to know
Where God is.
My mind does not care to know
Where God is.
My vital feels that God is
Wherever strength is.
My body thinks it is all the same
Whether God exists or not.

246.

You long for inner opulence.
Do you want to know
Where it can be found?
It can be found deep inside
Your speechless and sleepless
Soul-eloquence.

247.

A gratitude-heart
Receives from God
Infinitely more
Than it can ever imagine.
A surrender life
Plays with God's
Omnipotent Vision-Smile.

248.

Desire tells the mind,
"O mind, you are extremely
    powerful."
Aspiration tells the heart,
"O heart, you are extremely
    soulful."
Realisation tells the life,
"O life, you are extremely
    fruitful."
I tell the soul,
"O soul, you are always
    bountiful."

249.

You tell me
That you cannot cry for God.
In that case,
Can you not smile at God?
You tell me
That you also cannot smile at God.
In that case,
Can you not at least feel
That God definitely loves your
    company?

250.

Look and see
Who is inside your life-boat!
Do you know who it is?
It is God's authentic
    representative:
Your ever-sympathetic soul.

251.

My mind suffers
Because it is sumptuously fed.
My heart suffers
Because God is not sleeplessly fed.

252.

Because of my stupid mind,
Today I am a beggar.
Because of my sincere heart,
Today I am a seeker.
Because of my illumining soul,
Today I am a genuine God-lover.

253.

Because of your doubt-thunder,
God does not want me to befriend
    you.
Because of your aspiration-tower,
God wants me to be your
    Eternity's
Oneness-friend.

254.

My mind is satisfied
With its imperfection.
My heart is satisfied
Only with perfection.
My soul is satisfied
Only with God's Satisfaction.
I am satisfied
Only with God's Vision-Beauty
Within me.

255.

O my mind,
There is no way
For me to make you feel
That you are fooling yourself
All the time.
O my heart,
There are so many ways
For me to make you feel
That God loves you dearly,
Needs you unmistakably
And is proud of you powerfully.

256.

I tell my desire-mind
That God is not pleased with us
Because we want to possess Him,
But my mind does not believe me.
I tell my aspiration-heart
That God is extremely pleased
    with us
Because we want to be possessed
    by Him,
But my heart does not believe me.
I tell my illumination-soul
That God is extremely pleased
    with us
Because we are manifesting Him
In a remarkable way,
But my soul does not believe me.
O my Lord Supreme,
Nobody believes me.
Do You think that at least
You can believe me?
"My child,
Not only do I believe you,
But I also appreciate your
    mounting
And illumining wisdom-flames."

257.

I do not know
And I do not want to know
What God has done for my mind.
Who knows, like my mind,
I may not be pleased with God.
But I do know
What God has done for my heart
Out of His infinite Bounty.
As my heart is pleased with God,
Even so, I am more than pleased.

258.

Before my heart,
My mind does not want to admit
Its inferiority.
Before my soul,
My heart does not want to admit
Its insecurity.
Before God,
I do not want to admit
My stupidity.

259.

I am keeping my doubting mind
Behind me.
I am keeping my aspiring heart
With me.
I am keeping my illumining soul
Ahead of me.
This is how I am completing
My Heavenward journey.

260.

I have enjoyed the company of
    ignorance
For such a long time,
Yet I am not tired of it.
My soul has been asking me
For my companionship
For such a long time,
Yet my soul is not tired
Of my incapacity,
Not to speak of my unwillingness.

261.

Why do you want to hypnotise the
    world
With your mind's outer smile?
If you have nothing else to do,
Try to immortalise the world
With your heart's inner cry.

262.

My sweet Lord,
Do make my life into a constant
    sacrifice.
I wish to sacrifice my life
For You.
I wish to sacrifice my life
For those who love You.
I wish to sacrifice my life
Even for those who think and feel
That they love You.

263.

My sweet Lord,
You are fond of me
Not because I have already become
Great and good,
Not because I shall become
Great and good,
But because You and Your
   Fondness
For me, Your creation,
Are always inseparable.

264.

My sweet Lord,
You have given me what You have:
Compassion.
I shall give to mankind what I
   have:
Concern.
My sweet Lord,
You have given me what You are:
Oneness.
I shall give to humanity what I
   am:
Service.

265.

My sweet Lord,
I need two things from You badly:
Speed and time.
If You cannot give me both,
At least give me one!
Give me either Your fastest Speed
Or Your eternal Time
As Your Boon supreme
To please my aspiration-heart.

266.

My sweet Lord,
You have given me a purity-heart.
What I need now
Is a sincerity-mind
And what I shall always need
Is a dedication-life.

267.

My sweet Lord one day said to me,
"My child, can you not give Me
Your best possession
If I give you Mine?"
I said to my sweet Lord,
"I can easily give You
My best possession:
My restlessness-noise."
My sweet Lord was highly pleased
   with me
And immediately granted me
His Immortality's Oneness-Voice.

268.

My sweet Lord,
Do tell me when You love me
　　most.
Do You love me most
When I pray soulfully?
Do You love me most
When I meditate sleeplessly?
Do You love me most
When I consciously surrender
　　myself
To You entirely?
Do You love me most
When I become a gratitude-heart?
"My child, no, no, no!
I love you most
Only when you declare
Your inseparable oneness with
　　Me,
Not only in your inner world
But also in your outer world.
Your conscious feeling of oneness
　　with Me
Shall always please Me most."

269.

My sweet Lord,
Do tell me when I shall be able to
　　see
That dear deer of Yours
Which You have kept secretly
Inside my heart-garden.
I am eagerly looking forward
To seeing my precious deer,
For I want to feel that someday
Its inner speed and beauty
Shall be mine.

270.

My sweet Lord,
You have given my soul-bird
The capacity to fly
In the Heaven-free sky.
My mind-bird does not have
That capacity.
It is compelled to fly
In the earth-bound sky.
My sweet Lord,
Do give my mind the capacity to
　　fly
Like my soul-bird
In the blue-vast sky
Where there is no fear,
No doubt, no death
But only the dawn
Of an ever-blossoming
　　Immortality.

271.

My sweet Lord,
Do tell me how I can be
Always faithful to You.
"My child,
If you want to be faithful to Me
All the time,
Then you must remain cheerful
All the time."
My sweet Lord,
How can I remain cheerful
All the time?
"My child,
You can remain cheerful
All the time
If you can only make yourself feel
That I am always pleased with
   you.
This is not a false belief
But the sincere awakening
Of your true life
Deep inside My Heart."

272.

My sweet Lord,
Do tell me how old You are.
"My child,
I am very pleased with your
   question.
I shall answer your question
And also answer one more
   question
Which you may want to ask Me
Some other time:
How young I am.
My child,
I am as old
As your heart's inner cry
And as young
As your life's outer smile."

273.

My sweet Lord,
Do You want me to learn
The art of concentration?
Do You want me to learn
The art of meditation?
Do You want me to learn
The art of contemplation?
"My child,
I want you to learn them one by
  one.
If you learn concentration-art,
Then you will be able to enter
Into the end of time.
If you learn meditation-art,
Then you will be able to bring
Right in front of you
The birthless and deathless Time.
If you learn contemplation-art,
Then you will see that you are at
  once
The birthless, deathless and
  endless Time
And the Time
Of the ever-transcending
  Beyond."

274.

My sweet Lord
Do You want me
To conquer the world
Or do You want the world
To conquer me?
I shall be equally pleased
In either case.
"My child,
I do not want you either
To conquer the world
Or to be conquered by the world.
I want you to conquer
Your own outer world
And your own inner world.
Finally, I want you to conquer Me
Once and for all.
To conquer your outer world
What you need
Is a volcano-will.
To conquer your inner world
What you need
Is an aspiration-mountain.
To conquer Me
What you need
Is your soul-beauty's gratitude-
  heart."

275.

O my doubting mind,
You only know how to boast.
You never dare to defend me
When I vehemently argue
With the boatman of ignorance.
But my loving heart always
    defends me.
It immediately comes to the fore
To protect and fulfil me.
O my doubting mind,
I do not need you any more.
O my loving heart,
You and I are for each other
Always.

276.

Who invented me?
God the Vision.
Who discovered me?
God the Compassion.
Who fulfilled me?
God the Love.

277.

Who is my coach?
He who inspires me
Before I run.
Who is my coach?
He who aspires in and through me
During my run.
Who is my coach?
He who corrects and perfects me
For a better future run.

278.

"Come back to Me, My child,
Come back."
Father, how can I?
Do You not see
That I have become inseparably
    one
With ignorance-prince?
"My child,
This is not your realisation.
This is the realisation
Of ignorance-prince
That you are conveying to Me.
My child,
Do you not realise
That I shall remain incomplete
Unless and until you consciously
    declare
Our inseparable oneness?"

279.

O Father, my Father,
Do not be displeased with me!
I am staying in my temporary
    home:
Doubt.
Before long I shall dive
Into Your Ocean of Love
And that will be
My permanent home.

280.

His soulful heart
Does not want to remember
That his body walked across
The barren fields of yesterday.
His fearful mind
Not only remembers
But also does not want to forget
That his body walked across
The barren fields of yesterday.

281.

My sweet Lord Supreme,
I have failed You time and time
　　again
Not because I am ignorant,
Not because I am impure,
Not because I am insecure,
Not because I am unwilling,
But because I have never dared
To claim You as my own,
Very own.

282.

Divinely beautiful
Is the imagination-bird.
Supremely soulful
Is the aspiration-bird.
Eternally bountiful
Is the realisation-bird.

283.

You want to know the secret
Of my progress-light.
I just do not allow my life
To be cluttered
By attachment-night.

284.

Human love begins
With imagination-hope.
Divine love begins
With aspiration-promise.

285.

I cannot and I shall not
Be able to see God
Face to face,
For I am extremely impure
And totally imperfect.
Indeed, this is the realisation
Of an unparalleled non-believer.

286.

O outer world,
Do not poison
My inner hopes.
O inner world,
Do not laugh
At my outer promises.

287.

Allow not your anxiety-mind
And frustration-vital
To crowd together
Inside your God-fulfilling heart.

288.

Since there is no silence-delight
Inside your mind,
How can you expect to see
Eternity's Vision-Perfection-Sky?

289.

Yours is a doubtful mind.
Yours is a sorrowful life.
Just conquer one.
Lo, the other also is conquered!

290.

You pay so much attention
To your problem-making mind.
Can you not pay a little attention
To your problem-solving soul?

291.

Do not be hypnotised
By your past failure-life.
Make fresh attempts!
A success-life
Is definitely planned for you
In God's Vision-Calendar.

292.

During the day
When I pray,
I have a witness:
Sound-beauty.
During the night
When I pray,
I have a witness:
Silence-purity.

293.

Yesterday my faith was watchful.
Today my faith is prayerful.
Tomorrow my faith shall become
Not only bountiful
But also fruitful,
And so it will remain forever.

294.

His mind has committed him
To dire uncertainties.
His heart has committed him
To powerful certainties.
His soul has committed him
To Infinity-manifestation
In the finite.

295.

My Lord Supreme will teach me
The necessary and indispensable
Inner exercises
To conquer the unconquered
King of body-torture.

296.

If you are afraid
Of saying good-bye
To your teeming bad thoughts,
Do you not think
Your blossoming good thoughts
Will be hesitant to touch
And play with your mind?

297.

God calls it His Vision.
I call it my inspiration.
God calls it His Satisfaction.
I call it my perfection.

298.

Heaven is indifferent to me.
That is no reason
Why my soul shall not go back
To its celestial abode.
The world does not appreciate me.
That does not mean
I shall not unreservedly
Give to the world
What I have
And what I am.

299.

When my heart soulfully cries,
I clearly see
That my emptiness-life
Is totally destroyed.
When my soul proudly smiles,
I unmistakably see
That my fulness-divinity
Is totally pleased.

300.

This time definitely
I am going to please my Lord
    Supreme
In His own Way
Because I have realised the secret
That He alone
Is my Eternity's Lord Supreme.
This discovery of mine
Is my illumination
And my Lord's Satisfaction.

301.

My Lord,
Do allow me to do
Only one thing:
I wish to spread
My soul's dream-stars and planets
At Your infinite Compassion-Feet.

302.

Now that your hopes
Are shooting only upward,
Each day will come to you
With perpetual morning-delight.

303.

Slowly, steadily and
    immeasurably
A true God-seeker's and God-
    lover's
Excellence-gratitude-flames
Mount and spread
And spread and mount.

304.

I shall definitely not mind,
O my Lord Supreme,
Even if my worst foe pleases You,
As long as You are highly pleased.

305.

As you stretch out your beggar-
    arms
To receive from the world
Its glittering but fleeting riches,
Even so, you can lift your heart
    upward
To receive from Above
Light and Delight in infinite
    measure.

306.

The world applauds
Only your manifestation-drops.
But in silence God applauds
Your aspiration-dedication-sea.

307.

He was not afraid of making
Bold decisions.
Therefore, today he is blessed
With a new future:
Life-perfection in God-
    Satisfaction.

308.

O my heart,
I am all gratitude to you,
For your flower-fragrance-purity
Is a most blessingful and powerful
    assault
On my ego.

309.

In the morning I shield myself
From the jealousies of my mind.
In the afternoon I shield myself
From the frustrations of my vital.
In the evening I shield myself
From the imperfections of my
    body.
At night I shield myself
From the failures of my life.

310.

My Lord, You please me
Either by fulfilling my desires
Or by not fulfilling my desires.
What will happen, my Lord,
When I do not have any desires?
"My child,
When you do not have any desires,
Then I shall be able to plant
My own Eternity's Aspiration-
    Plants
In your supremely fertile heart-
    soil."

311.

My Lord,
You have temporarily saved me
By Your strong refusal
To satisfy my mind's desires.
Will You not permanently save me
By taking away once and for all
My desiring mind?

312.

Ignorance-night and I
Weep together.
Knowledge-day also weeps.
It weeps for my illumination.
I will now change my partner
And stay with knowledge-day.
My Lord Supreme is smiling
At my decision
And at my new partner's
    compassion.

313.

When I am inside my heart,
I love my green plants of hope.
When I am inside my soul,
I love my blue trees of promise.

314.

My past, present and future
Are persecuting me —
My yesterday's failure-life,
My today's indecision-life
And my tomorrow's fear-life.

315.

If you know everything,
Then answer two questions
That have been torturing me
For a long time:
Is God really superior to me?
When am I going to be
Another God?

316.

Be a little more careful
With your heart's spirituality
If you really want your life
To become richly fruitful
And remain so forever.

317.

A single breathless act of
   surrender
Has granted him
A beautiful dream-tree,
A soulful truth-tree
And a fruitful love-tree.

318.

My mind never took insincerity;
Insincerity took my mind.
My heart never took insecurity;
Insecurity took my heart.
My body never took impurity;
Impurity took my body.
I never took divinity-cry;
Divinity-cry took me.

319.

Heaven is speaking to you.
Listen carefully!
God is inviting you
To His special Heart-Room.
Delay not!

320.

His heart of aspiration
Is on intimate terms
With Eternity.
His life of dedication
Is on intimate terms
With Infinity.
His soul of vision
Is on intimate terms
With Immortality.

321.

My mind has discovered
The torture of failure.
My heart has discovered
The rapture of success.
I have discovered
The satisfaction of God's own
　Progress
In and through me.

322.

I tell you,
The more your mind is informed,
The less you will understand.
The more your heart feels,
The less will be the distance
Between you and God.

323.

His aspiration-heart
And his dedication-life
Are crying for him,
And he is crying to see
The world's worry-free God-
　embrace.

324.

You tell me
That you have failed
In your spiritual life.
I tell you,
It is not hard to start again.
But this time start
With your unconditional
　surrender-heart.
You will definitely succeed!

325.

Your songs need only
Two divine qualities
To please your Beloved Supreme:
Soulfulness and dynamism.
Offer these two supremely
Divine qualities
In abundant measure
To your Inner Pilot.

326.

When I want to know something,
I go and live inside
My Lord's Mind-House.
When I want to become
　something,
I go and live inside
My Lord's Heart-Home.

327.

I shall soon start dancing
On the waves of time,
Now that my Eternity's dream-
    boat
Is repaired
And I am all ready to sail it
Across Infinity's ocean-sky.

328.

Ambition is bondage
When I want to sit
On humanity's head.
Ambition is freedom
When I wish to sit
At the Feet
Of my Beloved Supreme.

329.

Just because I am old,
Do you think I shall not
Be able to fulfil
Humanity's necessity?
Just because he is young,
Do you think he will not
Be able to carry
Divinity's message?

330.

Everything is changeable.
Therefore, protest
The seemingly unchangeable
And make it not only changeable
But also extremely lovable.

331.

His soul's light
Powerfully shines.
His heart's love
Unreservedly gives.
Therefore his life's breath
Has consciously become one
With God's Breath.

332.

God wants to hear
Your prayers now.
He will have no time to listen
To your deathbed prayers.

333.

Man the lover
Will never become a beggar
In the inner world.
Man the seeker
Will never become a loser
In the outer world.

334.

If ignorance has the capacity
To close your eyes,
Do you not think
That God has the capacity
To open your eyes?
Just give God a chance!

335.

Why is it so easy for me
To have faith in God
But not in myself?
Either because I
    disproportionately
Extol myself to the skies
Or because I foolishly
Belittle myself.

336.

If God the Vision
Has started working in you,
Then rest assured,
God the Compassion
Will complete the task.

337.

There was a time
When I used my mind-telescope
To see God's Compassion-Eye.
Now I am using my heart-
    microscope
To see God's Satisfaction-Heart.

338.

Do not try to possess
The binding body of the world.
Only prepare yourself to be
    claimed
By the illumining soul of the
    world.

339.

Even when the mind surrenders,
Its unwillingness-breath
Does not surrender.
But when the heart surrenders,
Its willingness-oneness-life
Also surrenders.

340.

If your eyes are made of hopes
And if your heart is made of
    promises,
Then there shall come a day
When your life will be made
Of God's Vision-Delight.

341.

I am smiling
Because today I have discovered
My old friend doubt
Caught in the act
Of hypocrisy.

342.

I tell my mind's oblivion,
"I have no time to wait for you.
My heart and I are now on our way
To Heaven's Delight supreme."

343.

How can your life succeed,
How can your heart proceed,
If you always beg God
To grant you the experiences
That He has kept aside for others?

344.

In the beginning it seems
That even God the Compassion
Is not approachable.
But after you make
Considerable inner progress,
Not only is God the Compassion
Approachable,
But so is God the Justice.

345.

Certainly the mind is a road.
But if this road does not lead me
To my choice destination,
Then for me this road
Is worse than useless.

346.

O my confusion-mind,
Slow down, slow down!
Let my aspiration-heart
Come to the fore
And catch up with you.

347.

Because of the severe pressure
Of his inner weaknesses,
He no longer sees
His mountain peak of hope.

348.

If you want to become
God's ambassador,
Then the most important thing to do
Is to watch the quality
Of your thought-life.

349.

When God invites you,
Go to Him
Not with the dead leaves of desire
But with the fresh plant
Of aspiration.

350.

If you want to master
The length of ignorance-night,
Then you must live
In the depth
Of Wakefulness-God.

351.

The delight of the morning sky
Is welcoming you.
No more can the tears of sorrow
Shatter your heart.

352.

I am glad
That you have
Broken completely
The chains of intellect.
I am glad
That your mind-energy
Is no longer enslaved.
I am glad
That you are
No longer possessed
By a stone-hearted life.

353.

If you are always
In love with tears,
How can you ever enjoy
The vision of God's
Constant Self-Transcendence?

354.

What my mind needs
Is a promising hope
And not a tempting desire.
What my heart needs
Is a loving God
And not a binding world.
What my soul needs
Is man's satisfaction-delight
And not man's perfection-
   promise.

355.

Your conscious mistakes
Have the power
To show you the giant footsteps
Of your spiritual death.

356.

Your soul still loves you
Although you are a slave
Of envy-passion.
Your God still needs you
Although you deliberately
Try to avoid Him.

357.

Today if your mind enjoys
An iota of darkness,
Then tomorrow your life
Will be mercilessly forced to enjoy
A sea of misery.

358.

Alas, how can my Lord Supreme
Enjoy His birthless and deathless
Satisfaction-Delight,
Unless I totally give up enjoying
My age-old oblivion-night?

359.

Do not fill your life
With self-accusations.
Just look at your endless
Inner self-transcendence-light.

360.

Each human life abides
Between the cheerful question of
   life,
"Who am I?"
And the powerful answer of death,
"I am all."

361.

Each good thought
Is a small heaven.
Ask your heart if I am correct.
Each bad thought
Is a big hell.
Ask your mind if I am correct.

362.

Since your mind is only dreaming
And your heart is not loving,
How can you expect to change
   your face?
How can you?

363.

Your life's uncertainties
Vanished away
The moment your mind
Stopped seeking dominion
And started seeking liberation.

364.

Unbelievable but true:
My confusion-mind is longing
For liberation
To see God enjoying
His Infinity's Delight.

365.

I am not going to listen
To your wild arguments,
O my stupid mind.
From now on I shall listen
To the ocean-deep wisdom
Of my soul
For my fast-approaching
  enlightenment.

366.

You tell me
That you are enjoying
The absence of desire-forest
Inside your mind.
But you have forgotten
To tell me something else.
I am sure you are also enjoying
The presence of aspiration-
  mountain
Inside your heart.

367.

Now that you have learnt
The invaluable art of whispering
To God,
Your life will soon become
A panorama of divine perfection.

368.

Heaven's unanswerable "Why"
Will now surrender to you
Because the Absolute Supreme
Is smiling through your heart-
  tears.

369.

Do you remember
That once upon a time
You were a flaming torch of love?
Do you remember
That once upon a time
You constantly flew upward
To your Beloved Supreme?
Do you remember
That once upon a time
You pleased God unconditionally?

370.

You tell me
That God is not always needed,
But can your mind dare to say
That God the Compassion
Is not always needed?
Can your heart dare to say
That God the Forgiveness
Is not always needed?

371.

God has given you
The power to choose,
But what have you chosen?
You have chosen
To grovel in darkness,
You have chosen
To live in appalling ignorance.

372.

You have chosen to live
In ignorance.
Ignorance has chosen to live
In temptation.
Temptation has chosen to live
In deathless frustration.

373.

Do you really want
The highest illumination
In your life?
Then keep yourself always free
From the false bubble of
    reputation.

374.

There is an absolute
God-perfection-room
Inside my heart,
But my mind never dares
To enter there.

375.

You have already become
An observing eye
And a remembering heart.
Can you not also become
A self-giving life?

376.

Ask your mind not to sink
Into the sleep of despair.
Ask your heart not to rest
Until it has discovered
The ultimate meaning
Of human life on earth.

377.

My Lord Supreme,
By praising You,
Not only do I get deep joy
But also invaluable self-
    confidence
In measureless measure.

378.

I use the ears of my heart
To hear my Perfection-Lord
    Supreme.
I use the eyes of my heart
To see my Satisfaction-Lord
    Supreme.

379.

He conceals humanity's
   imperfection
Inside his heart.
He reveals divinity's satisfaction-
   promise
With his illumination-soul.

380.

As I believe in the emptiness
Of desire-possession,
Even so, I believe in the fulness
Of ignorance-renunciation.

381.

Since you have developed
The inner courage to correct
   yourself,
God is now all ready to dance
His Satisfaction-Dance
Inside your heart
And before your mind.

382.

You have now started
To experience envy,
God has now started
To experience sorrow
And I have now started
To experience complete
   bewilderment.

383.

God is waiting
For the revelation
Of my powerful potentialities.
I am waiting
For the completion
Of God's bountiful Vision.

384.

God has three very special friends:
My soulfulness-life,
My willingness-mind
And my oneness-heart.

385.

Mine is the mind
That likes fantastic minds.
Mine is the heart
That loves ecstatic hearts.
Mine is the soul
That becomes inseparably one
With God-intoxicated souls.

386.

The eye of my soul
Threatens ignorance.
The mouth of my soul
Frightens ignorance.
The life of my soul
Transforms ignorance.
The Pilot of my soul
Illumines ignorance.

387.

His heart was extremely grateful
To those who came forward
To sing his aspiration-realisation-
Manifestation-songs.

388.

What can the absence
Of desire do?
It can make you see
That you are a meditation-river
Running into the realisation-sea.

389.

My sound-life means nothing
To you,
But your silence-life means
   everything
Not only to my aspiration-life
But also to my desire-life.

390.

Although my vital does not know
   it,
There is a secret joy
In serving.
Although my mind does not know
   it,
There is a great power
In unlearning.
Although my life does not know
   it,
There is a supreme satisfaction
In surrendering.

391.

There is no such thing
As might is right or right is might.
Wisdom-light is both right and
   might,
And this wisdom-light
Is nothing other than
Our heart's love-oneness-
   perfection.

392.

My dependency
On my Lord's Compassion-Eye
And Forgiveness-Heart
Is not my helplessness
But my perfect wisdom-light.

393.

If you keep your mind-door
    closed,
You can easily go in and out
Through your heart-door,
For that door is always kept wide
    open
By God's own Satisfaction-Heart.

394.

I have two friends.
One is my mind's
Unconscious teacher:
Ignorance.
The other is my heart's
Conscious tutor:
God.

395.

Nobody can force you
To be the author
Of your own despair.
Nobody can prevent you
From being the fulfiller
Of your golden dreams.

396.

No, human life is not
An endless limitation.
Human life is the breathless
And deathless Vision-Light
Of our Pilot Supreme.

397.

As God's Compassion
Is a definite necessity
In my outer life,
Even so, God's Satisfaction
Is a supreme necessity
In my inner life.

398.

If you demand,
You are a fool.
Why?
When you demand,
You try to force others
To give you joy.
With force you cannot conquer
    the heart,
And if you cannot conquer the
    heart,
Then there is no true joy.

399.

For him to reach the highest
    height
Of his realisation-tree
Was an extremely easy task.
For him to bring down its fruits
Was a harder task.
For him to distribute these fruits
To the world in abundant measure
Was an extremely difficult task.

400.

Do not recognise any defeat!
Recognise only one thing:
Your own soul's omnipotence
In your life.

401.

My Lord,
Your morning Smile
Is my breath
During the entire day.

402.

I call it a sacred thought.
My Beloved Supreme calls it
A Satisfaction-Smile
From His own Manifestation-Life.

403.

As beauty's dawn does not last
Longer than a few moments
In man's ugly mind,
Even so, purity's evening
Does not last
More than a few fleeting seconds
In man's impure heart.

404.

In the inner world
You are a spiritual failure
Not because God has
No special love for you
But because you do not want
To meet with God's Justice-Light.

405.

When I hear
The song of your eyes,
I enter into
The world of beauty.
When I hear
The song of your heart,
I enter into
The world of purity.
When I hear
The song of your soul,
I enter into
The world of sweetness
   unknowable.

406.

There was a time
When you used to feel
God's loving Heart,
But now you are only seeing
God's ruling Hand.
I tell you,
Do not be confused or frightened.
God's ruling Hand is only
   showing you
How to return home
Safely, soulfully and richly.

407.

I am here, my Lord,
Waiting for Your Compassion-
   Heart.
I am here, my Lord,
Waiting for the embrace
Of Your infinite Freedom.
I am here, my Lord,
Waiting for You to come
And take my broken heart
To Your celestial Abode.

408.

Give yourself only once
An unconditional chance
And then remain completely
   silent.
Your Lord Supreme will sing
His Immortality-Song
Through your beauty's silence-
   perfection.

409.

If you allow yourself
To be fettered by the world's
   opinions,
God will never grant you
His Vision-Life-Pinions
To carry you into His Eternity's
Delight-flooded Sky.

410.

Beauty and purity
Are Heavenly possessions.
If you want to own them,
Your mounting aspiration-heart
Must increase its height
And your growing dedication-life
Must increase its length.

411.

My heart and I
May not be ready to say
We owe everything to God's Love,
But my life and I
Are more than ready to say
We owe everything
To God's Forgiveness.

412.

A messenger from the morning-world
Has given me
A very special message:
God will before long
Capture my heart
With His Soul's Smile
And capture my life
With His Heart's Cry.

413.

In this lifetime of yours,
Can you not become
A dancing hope,
A singing promise
And a transcending perfection?

414.

You will remain
With your unborn dreams
Because you always forget to smile
At Heaven's wealth
And always forget to cry
With earth's poverty.

415.

Do you not realise
That you are your heart's
Short-lived devotion?
Do you not realise
That you are your mind's
Completely forgotten inspiration?
Do you not realise
That you are your life's
Unconditionally accepted failure?

416.

The latest news from God:
His Compassion-Height
Is not going to fight any more
Against His Justice-Light
Because it is tired of fighting
For the ever-ungrateful
And ever-unreceptive humanity.

417.

Do not stop smiling
If you want to become as beautiful
As a child's heart.
Do not stop crying
If you want to become as pure
As a saint's life.

418.

My impurity-mind
Does not surprise God.
My insecurity-heart
Does not puzzle God.
But my unwillingness-life
Definitely amazes God.

419.

Since you are living inside
Your doubting mind's hopes,
How can you see
Your faithful heart's promises
Or feel the Oneness-Love
Of God's bountiful Heart?

420.

My Lord Supreme,
My eyes live
For Your Compassion-Eye,
My heart lives
For Your Satisfaction-Eye,
My life lives
For Your Self-Transcendence-Eye.

421.

Everybody tells you
That you will fail,
But do they help you
To succeed?
Do they pray
For your victory?
Therefore, why do you need
Their stupid and proud comments
On your success-failure-life?

422.

God is man,
Man is God.
Man is God's hope.
God is man's promise.

423.

Your Master is at once
God's Silence-Whisper
And
God's Sound-Murmur.

424.

Every potential God-server
Lives inside the breath
Of your sleepless selflessness.

425.

You can conquer fear
Just by turning your life
Into a happy song
Of happy oneness.

426.

Man is the challenger
Of yesterday's frustration
And tomorrow's hesitation.

427.

If you forget something divine,
Then your conscious oneness
With God's Will
Is not sufficiently developed.
If you forget something undivine,
Then it is a great blessing,
For there are many things
That should be forgotten!

428.

When God asks you
To do something for Him,
Before thoughts enter your mind,
Cry and try,
Try and cry
To consciously establish
Willingness inside your heart.

429.

How to dissolve yesterday's anger?
Just inundate it
With today's peace of mind!

430.

Pray to God to grant you
More purity in your mind.
Pray to God to grant you
More sweetness in your heart.
Pray to God to grant you
More humility in your life.

431.

You can overcome resistance
By exercising the power
Of insistence.
Insist on doing the right thing.
Lo, the power of resistance
Will disappear.

432.

You can love more
Only when you feel the necessity
Of becoming more useful
To your Beloved Supreme
In your inner life of aspiration
And in your outer life of
    dedication.

433.

Look around at those who worry
And see if they are able
To save themselves
From unwarranted suffering.
When you see their foolishness,
You will be wise
And not enter into
The sea of worry.

434.

Your past is a devouring tiger.
You should not only
Forget your past
But also annihilate it.

435.

You will stop hesitating
When your inner heart
Becomes stronger
Than your outer mind.

436.

To become nicer
Than you are now,
Offer the beautiful rose
Inside your heart-garden
To your Beloved Lord Supreme.

437.

Great people live and die
Only to make you their slave.
Good people live and die
Only to help you become
Another God.

438.

I know You, my Lord:
This is my illumination.
I love You, my Lord:
This is my perfection.
I follow You, my Lord:
This is my satisfaction.

439.

Just call Me
Secretly.
Just say My Name
Soulfully.
I shall grant you
The richest harvest
Of My Vision-Eye.

440.

You are a useless fool
If you imitate others.
Do you not realise
That their stupidity, like yours,
Beggars description?
Imitate God!
First try to imitate His Signature.
Then try to imitate His Voice.
Finally try to imitate His Silence-
    Smile.
God-imitation is not imitation;
It is the revelation
Of your inner illumination.

441.

A single "Yes" from God
Is all he needs
To destroy the exorbitant pride
Of his ignorance-night.

442.

On the way to his earth-home
From Heaven,
God advised him to specialise
In only one thing:
Self-giving.

443.

When the heart is unemployed,
The mind's doubt-treachery
Runs riot.

444.

My Lord,
Your Compassion-Sea
Is my capacity.
Your Love-Sky
Is my divinity.
Your Satisfaction-Sun
Is my Immortality.

445.

A songless day
Is ruthlessly compelled
To voyage to the despair-shore.

446.

As they want the Buddha
To be for the East
And the Christ
To be for the West,
Even so, they want your one
    shoulder
To liberate them
And your other shoulder
To save them.

447.

The motto of the human race:
The life of division
Must not last.
The motto of the divine race:
God's and man's oneness-song
Will last eternally.

448.

You pray early in the morning
And meditate early in the evening.
Indeed, this is your conventional
    approach
To the spiritual life.
But if you feel that this approach
Is not offering you
Satisfactory results,
Then try an unconventional
    approach:
Pray and meditate
Any time of the day or night
Until God-hunger tortures
Your entire being.

449.

Alas,
My heart-temple is always empty
Of worshippers.
My body, vital and mind
Are always absent.
Now I have decided
To have a new temple,
My soul-temple,
And I shall urge my heart
To come and worship there.
I am sure my heart
Will always abide
By my soulful request.

450.

Power,
Do not claim me!
Love,
Let me claim you!
Delight,
Let us claim each other!

451.

O my mind,
You are completely mistaken
When you tell me
That my heart is eclipsed
By your unlit presence.
No, my heart is illumined
And shall always remain so,
For my soul has befriended my
  heart
And this friendship
Forever shall last.

452.

My Lord,
Do not bind me to You
With my victory's height.
Do bind me to You
With Your invisible
Embrace-Delight.

453.

Yesterday I prayed to God,
"My Lord, give me, give me."
Today I am praying to God,
"My Lord, take me, take me."
Tomorrow I shall pray to God,
"My Lord, may Your Vision-Eye
  smile
Inside Your creation-heart."

454.

Unless and until my mind
Measures my Lord's Newness,
I shall never be happy.
Unless and until my heart
Measures my Lord's Sweetness,
I shall never be happy.
Unless and until my life
Measures my Lord's Oneness,
I shall never be happy.

455.

If you are a saint,
You will discover purity
Inside nothingness.
If you are a yogi,
You will discover fulness
Inside nothingness.
If you are another God,
You will discover that
  nothingness-dream
And oneness-reality
Are extremely fond of each other.

456.

The newness-love of silence
Illumines the human in me.
The fulness-silence of love
Fulfils the divine in me.

457.

The day I lost
My complaining mind,
Something extremely significant
Took place.
My Eternity's Beloved Supreme
Showed His explaining Heart
To the world at large
To reveal my perfect perfection-life.

458.

Right now I may not know
Where God is
Or who God is,
But one thing I do know:
I know that I am going to be
The satisfaction-fruit
Of my Lord's Compassion-Seed.

459.

My mind thinks
That it has already become
   something.
My heart feels
That it will never become
   anything.
My soul knows
That God has already become
   everything
To make my life worthy
Of His Compassion-Company.

460.

O my mind,
Are you trying to tell me
   something
That I do not know as yet?
"Yes! I am trying to tell you
That my very existence
At long last is caught
By God's Compassion-Smile."

461.

He who is worth possessing
Can never be possessed,
But He who is worth loving
Can always be loved.

462.

By way of joke
I tell my Lord Supreme
That I do not need Him.
But my Beloved Supreme
Has not yet mastered
The art of joking.
In all sincerity He tells me
That He needs me sleeplessly
And that someday,
Somehow, somewhere
He will place me
On His transcendental
Trance-bound Throne.

463.

You have not studied enough
In the mind-school.
Therefore, you may not be
A chosen instrument of man.
But you have definitely studied
For many, many years
In the heart-school.
Therefore, you are well-qualified
To become a chosen instrument
Of your Inner Pilot.

464.

If you pierce the world
Of frustration-night
With the arrow of your heart's joy,
Then God Himself will proclaim
Your Himalayan victory
An unprecedented achievement
For the world.

465.

O earth-consciousness,
I die for you to receive
More Light and Delight from
   Above.
O Heaven-consciousness,
I live for you to manifest
More Light, more Delight
Plus more Satisfaction
Here on earth.

466.

There was a time
When my life was divinity's
   perfection
And my heart unconditionally
   lived
Inside my Lord's Compassion-Net.
Alas, that time is no more!

467.

A God-realised soul
May have a free access
To God's Heart-Home,
But he quite often
Finds it difficult
To secure a free access
To man's mind-room.

468.

He who is raised
On God's constant and infinite
   Grace
Will eventually become
Humanity's totally transformed
   face.

469.

Never, never give up
Your faith-life.
There shall come a time
When you will definitely be able
To reap the bounty
Of God's Pride in you.

470.

Now that he has passed through
Ignorance-tunnel,
He can easily change
His life's erring course.

471.

My sweet little soul-bird,
I feel extremely sorry for you.
I do not know how long
You can go on living
Inside my fettered hopes.

472.

I am fully acquainted
With my death-door,
But I am still trying to become
    acquainted
With my life-door.
Why?
Because my Beloved Supreme
Every day knocks
At my life-door
And, alas, returns home every day
Unanswered.

473.

If you are unaccustomed
To fear and doubt,
Then rest assured,
Endless happy hours
Are being born inside you
To live with you and for you.

474.

In my outer life,
Service-perfection
Is my whole dictionary.
In my inner life,
Oneness-love
Is my whole dictionary.

475.

My Lord,
Yesterday my only desire
Was to love You.
Today my only desire
Is to live inside You.
Tomorrow my only desire
Will be to be exactly like You.

476.

O onlookers of greatness,
You are the students
Of power.
O lovers of goodness,
You are the students
Of God's secret and sacred
Temple-School.

477.

The smoke of ideas must
    disappear.
The birth of new ideal-flames
Must become our reality's
    perfection.

478.

My Lord,
Each time I forget
My self-imposed earth-bondage,
You make me a channel
For Your perfect Love.

479.

To bridge the gulf of ignorance,
Every day I must accelerate
My aspiration-speed.

480.

My Lord Supreme,
How can I please You every day?
"My child,
You can please Me every day
By feeding your aspiration-
    strength
And increasing your dedication-
    length."

481.

Each individual
Is a favourite child of God.
To each of His children
He has given the capacity
To conquer Him with oneness-
    truth.

482.

He has cultivated sincerity-flower
Inside his heart.
Therefore God calls him
His own Beauty's
Illumination-Joy.

483.

My Lord,
Give me speed!
Give me purity!
With speed I shall win
My long-lost inner race.
With purity I will be able to see
Once more
Your Infinity's immortal Face.

484.

To live inside my Lord's Heart
Consciously, soulfully and
    perfectly,
I need a sprinter's
Concentration-power
And a runner's
Dedication-power.

485.

In my heart's secret depth,
There is always a poignant cry
To destroy the disharmony
That fetters and bruises
My outer life.

486.

He has the skill
Not to forget God's Name.
He has the thrill
Of loving God's Heart
Sincerely,
Soulfully,
Sleeplessly
And
Ceaselessly.

487.

My inner voice
Is my dear friend.
I hear it
In every heart
Singing the song
Of God's Oneness-Victory.

488.

My prayer is to think
Only of Him
With my purity-mind.
My meditation is to love
Only Him
With my aspiration-heart.

489.

Every second counts.
Therefore, I must listen to my
   soul-tutor
And learn my life-transforming
   lessons
And my Lord's Heaven-
   manifesting-lessons
As soon as possible.

490.

My soul lavishes the boundless
   bounty
Of its love on me.
Its smile of grace
Every day shines on my face
In bright multiplied bliss.

491.

His smile wins
A thousand hearts a day.
His cry wins
Only one heart a day
And that heart is his own
Infinity's God-Heart.

492.

There shall come a time
When peace-diamond,
Joy-diamond
And perfection-diamond
Will all be in your satisfaction-
   safe.

493.

My mind is waiting
For my heart's absurdity-dream to
   end.
My heart is waiting
For my mind's hallucination-
   dream to end.
My life is waiting
For my impossibility-dream to
   end.
My soul is waiting
For my ignorance-dream to end.

494.

Immortality is not of the body.
Immortality is in
The consciousness-seed,
Immortality is of
The consciousness-flower
And Immortality is for
The consciousness-fruit.

495.

His purity-heart is trying to smile
Inside his uninspiring eyes.
His divinity-soul is trying to dance
Inside his unaspiring mind.

496.

It may be very easy
To surrender what we have:
Ignorance.
But it is very difficult
To surrender what we are:
Unwillingness.

497.

What does my gratitude-heart do?
It takes me directly
To God's Heart-Home.

498.

O remembrance-night,
Do not persecute me.
I wish to be
A purity-flame
Of my heart's mounting cry.

499.

He knows how to love
The Eternal in himself.
He also knows how to serve
The Absolute in himself.
But something more he has to
    learn:
How to treasure sleeplessly
The Beloved Supreme in himself.

500.

My Lord,
Your first Smile is still singing
Inside the very depth
Of my gratitude-heart.
My Lord,
Your last Smile
Will safely return my soul
To its celestial abode.

501.

O my life's surrender-tears,
You are beautiful,
You are sweet,
You are pure,
You are perfect.
Because of you,
God every day grants me
His Infinity's Smile.

502.

The repetition of a doubtful
   thought
Can mark the very beginning
Of a self-deception-life.

503.

Try to be aware of the wealth
In your life's security-bank.
Then you will not have to camp
In the desert of stark insecurity.

504.

A life of unconditional surrender
Is at once the seeker's life-saver
And God's Life-fulfiller.

505.

My today's dedication-song
Will tomorrow be transformed
Into my life's perfection-dance,
And the day after tomorrow
My perfection-dance will be
   transformed
Into God's Satisfaction-Smile.

506.

Try every day
To paint your life of dynamism
With purity-brush.
You will definitely be chosen
To run the victory lap
In your Godward race.

507.

Your life hears
The clang of failure
Because your mind consciously
   enjoys
The tremors of doubt.

508.

Now that he has liberated himself
From self-doubt-prison,
His life has become a hope-
   blossom
In his heart-garden.

509.

Every day he waters
His heart's aspiration-plants
With his soul's fruitful tears
And with his life's powerful
   smiles.

510.

Not my Master's smile,
Not my Master's blessings,
Not my Master's compassion,
But my Master's forgiveness
Is my life-breath,
My only life-breath.

511.

My life's soulfulness-shield
Always protects me
From the world's doubt-arrows.

512.

Knowing perfectly well
That your mind is a circus
Of confusion,
Why do you live inside your
    mind?
Knowing perfectly well
That your heart is a garden
Of illumination,
Why do you not live inside your
    heart?

513.

Your life is now
A sinking raft of emotions
Because you are not allowing
Your soul's wisdom-buoyancy
To come to the fore.

514.

If you do not love the world
Sleeplessly and unreservedly,
Your inner world and outer world
May eventually become
Smouldering hate-ashes.

515.

The message from your vital:
Temptation-tiger is very beautiful
And not so powerful.
The message from your soul:
Temptation-tiger is not only
    dangerous
But also voracious.

516.

Unless you continuously climb up
The aspiration-tree,
You may disappear in the
    quicksand
Of the desire-world.

517.

In the morning
He sees his mind's doubt-shadows
Vanishing.
In the evening
He sees his heart's beauty-flames
Rising.

518.

Do you know what you actually
     need?
You need God's Compassion-
     Splashes
On your heart-lawn
And God's Forgiveness-Showers
On your mind-desert.

519.

The human mind is so foolish!
Not only does it allow
But it even enjoys
The company of a host
Of doubt-convicts.

520.

If you do not love
The beauty and purity
Of what you already have,
Then you will not be able
To sever the bondage-chains
Of your self-torment.

521.

Your body was not meant
To saunter down lethargy-lane.
Your body was meant
To challenge death to a constant
     duel.

522.

In his outer life
He is happy because he keeps pace
With his mind's inspiration-
     rabbit.
In his inner life
He is happy because he keeps pace
With his heart's aspiration-bird.

523.

Try to move forward
Out of the aspiration-blocks
As powerfully as possible
If you want your life
To breast victory's tape
As quickly as possible.

524.

Your mind's jealousy-dagger
Has severely wounded you.
If you want to be healed,
Try to discover as soon as possible
The flames of your aspiration-
     heart.

525.

As God wants to tame me
With His Love-Power,
Even so, He wants me to tame
     Him
With my surrender-power.

526.

Unless a seeker is consciously and constantly
Walking along the avenue of perfection-life,
He will not be allowed to reach Heaven's supreme Illumination-Gate.

527.

A true God-lover is he
Who at the end of each day
Soulfully and selflessly sees
How high he has built
God's Kingdom here on earth.

528.

Each thought is a world.
This world has no meaning
If it has no purity of purpose.

529.

Because your heart has accepted
The aspiration-life as your only life,
God has asked your soul to cancel
Your immediate appointment with death.

530.

Now that your God-hunger-life
Has safely coasted through
The dark ignorance-tunnel,
Your heart can reap the Bounty
Of God's Satisfaction-Delight.

531.

Not the cosmic gods,
Not even God Himself,
But man alone
Has to rectify
His own teeming blunders.

532.

Each human mind
Is ultimately changeable.
Each divine heart
Remains eternally unchangeable.

533.

Self-conquest means
The manifestation of
God's Satisfaction-Dance
In a seeker's life.

534.

Each man has to know
That he is Eternity's forgotten
   thirst
For his own Infinity's lost
   excellence.

535.

In the spiritual life,
To doubt is to meet with
A great disaster,
To lose faith in one's Inner Pilot
Is to meet with
A greater disaster
And to go back once more
To the ordinary life of pleasure
Is to meet with
The greatest possible disaster.

536.

Unless you love the invisible God
Within you,
How can the visible God
Love you and bless you
And give all He has to you?

537.

The hand of man wants to touch
The Power-Head of God
Before it has touched
The Forgiveness-Feet of God.

538.

Each soul bravely and smilingly
Comes into the world
Carrying a perfect cargo.

539.

Unless the mind destroys
Its own anxiety-army,
How can it be blessed with
Divinity's peace-troops?

540.

Because his heart has the
   munificence
Of self-offering,
His life has become the
   magnificence
Of perfection-beauty.

541.

If your life sleeplessly ventures
Towards the ever-transcending
   Beyond,
Then who can deny you the
   summit
Of perfection-peak?

542.

If you can align your mind
With wisdom-beauty,
Then God will never hesitate,
Even for a fleeting second,
To share with you His Majesty-
    Kingdom.

543.

My Beloved Supreme has
    appointed
My life's unconditional surrender
As His Eternity's housekeeper.

544.

If you want to remain always
    happy,
Always perfect and always
    fulfilled,
Then always keep inside your
    heart
A pocketful of sweet dreams.

545.

The difference between
The pebble-mind and the
    mountain-heart
Is this:
The pebble-mind wants to
    challenge
The strength of God-Power.
The mountain-heart sleeplessly
    longs for
The embrace of God-Hour.

546.

God's imperial Love-Treasure
You can own
Only after you have impeached
The uncomely thoughts
Of your unaspiring mind.

547.

With indomitable power
A oneness-heart constantly zooms
Towards the ever-transcending
Satisfaction-Goal.

548.

No brutal power
Can ever successfully challenge
The dark callousness
Of the mind's indifference.

549.

You must shorten your vacation
In your body's lethargy-land
If you want not only to lengthen
    your stay
But also to have a permanent
    residence
In your soul's happiness-
    manufacturing
Energy-land.

550.

God will allow you to officiate
In His Perfection-Palace
If you are ready to abdicate your
    throne
In your long-treasured ego-palace.

551.

You always tell me
That you do not want to be bitten
By doubt-mosquitoes.
Why then are you not willing
To come out of the swamp
Of your doubting mind?

552.

If your heart is a true seeker,
If your life is a true server,
If your soul is a true dreamer
And if your God is a true Lover,
How can you ever be a quitter?

553.

You have unconsciously chosen to
    be
A lifelong prisoner
In your insecurity-prison.
God has consciously plus
    unconditionally
Chosen you to be
The quintessence of
His Immortality's Breath.

554.

If you are ready to wrestle
With your ambition-bull,
Then God will allow you to play
With His Illumination-Lamb.

555.

The strength of man's faith-bridge
Can smilingly and perfectly hold
The weight of God's entire
    universe.

556.

God does not want your mind
To be crushed
Under your own impurity-boot.
He wants your mind to wear
The same purity-shoes
That your heart has been wearing
For a long time
And the same divinity-sandals
That your soul has been wearing
Throughout Eternity.

557.

You can enjoy
The flowering of your divinity
Only after you have offered earth
What it needs,
Your heart's sleepless cry,
And offered Heaven what it wants,
Your soul's fruitful smile.

558.

My heart's prayer-letter to God
Tells about earth's hunger
For news of Heaven.

559.

If you stay under the hope-
    umbrella,
Before long you will be able
To speedily run towards God.

560.

If your mind is flooded
With ego-pride,
Then your life, without fail,
Will be mangled
By confusion-tiger.

561.

Enthusiasm and self-offering
Are fertile ground
On which to sow the perfection-
    seeds
Of the satisfaction-tree.

562.

If your mind is clogged
With thick impurity-dust,
How can your life become one
With other lives
Inside the purity-temple?

563.

In the morning
My heart sings with my Lord
His Eternity's Song.
In the evening
My life dances with my Lord
His Immortality's Dance.

564.

If you are a genuine seeker,
Then every day watch carefully
To see if the leaves
Of your aspiration-tree
Are increasing or decreasing.

565.

Every day my thought-world
Performs its circus-life-act
Inside my Lord's
Compassion-Forgiveness-Tent.

566.

Unless you expel your division-life
Through your aspiration-life,
How can you climb the stairs
To satisfaction-peace?

567.

Your heart cannot do
And does not want to do
What your mind always does:
Live comfortably in the pleasure-vital
Of self-deception.

568.

His life's oneness-heart-smile
Is every day electrified
By God's God-Love-Power.

569.

No difference between
The mind's hatred
And the life's hopelessness.
No difference between
The heart's love
And the life's God-Fulness.

570.

His heart is a most powerful
And soothing murmur
Of his soul's dream-river.

571.

The satisfaction-life-field
Can be furrowed only
By the soul's perfection-plough.

572.

A true God-lover
Does not find his life
Snared in ignorance-trap.
Therefore, his face wears a
 divinity-smile
Painted with the colours of
 delight.

573.

As Compassion-Forgiveness-Suns
Are my Lord's Love-Toys,
Even so, surrender-gratitude-
 flames
Are my love-toys.

574.

As his life is inching
Towards perfection,
Even so, his heart is inching
Towards satisfaction.

575.

The favourite dessert
Of my Beloved Supreme
Has always been
My satisfaction-smile.

576.

Weep not, weep not!
The vast immortal sun
Is going to teach you
How to unlearn
The knowledge of death.

577.

Shut not your heart-door.
God wants to come in
And sing His Delight-Songs
To turn your life
Into an ecstasy-sea.

578.

My Lord Supreme,
Even my undivine mind
Receives peace and light
From Your Smile.

579.

If you can make your heart
Into a flower of purity,
God will make your life
Into a pillar of divinity.

580.

My Lord,
I pray to You and
I try to glorify Your Name.
Which of the two do You like better?
"My child,
Praying and glorifying
Are not two separate things.
You pray to Me
Because you have faith in Me.
You glorify Me
Because I have faith in you."

581.

My life's dedication-heart
Is all Yours, my Lord.
My world's desire-mind
Is all Yours, my Lord.

582.

Quench my thirst, my Lord.
I wish to come and sit at Your Feet.
"Quench My Thirst, My child.
I wish you to keep your heart-door
Wide open all the time
For Me, only for Me."

583.

My Lord Supreme,
Why is it that I do not listen to You?
"You do not listen to Me, My child,
Because you do not consciously feel
That you need Me.
There is no other reason
And there can be no other reason."

584.

Those who believe and then see
Are infinitely better instruments
Than those who must first see
Before they believe.
Believe and become one
With your Master's vision.
Then you will easily be able to see
Your own progress
And God's Manifestation.

585.

Beauty upon beauty
Descends from Heaven
When my heart becomes the receptivity
Of luminescent stillness.

586.

Alas, he does not realise
What is flowing
From his own heart.
His own soul-radiance is flowing
From his heart
To help him sit at the mystic Feet
Of his Beloved Supreme.

587.

Only inspiration born on high
Can whisper with words
Of pure delight.

588.

Be a true truth-seeker,
Be a true God-lover.
The multi-winged goddess of
   truth
Will gladly appear before you.

589.

I have drunk from the depth
Of my splendour-spangled soul.
No more can my mind sink
In the quicksand of ignorance.

590.

O my vital,
You have been giving me
The same experience
For so many years!
When will you put an end
To the tyranny-experience
Of my pleasure-life?

591.

The capacity of the body is
   limited —
Yours, mine, everybody's.
But the capacity of the soul is
   unlimited —
Yours, mine, everybody's.

592.

In his inner life
He has been transcending himself
Faster than the fastest
Right from his childhood —
Of course, all due to
The infinite Compassion and Love
Of his Inner Pilot.

593.

My Lord Supreme,
Will I ever please You
In Your own Way?
"My child,
The very fact that you have asked
This soulful question
Means that there shall come a time
When you will definitely please Me
In My own Way,
Not only sleeplessly
But also unconditionally."

594.

In the outer world
You may see how limited and useless
Your physical body is.
But in the inner world
Countless times
Your Inner Pilot will prove to you
That your speed is absolutely the fastest.

595.

To bear sleeplessly
The world's unbearable pain
Is the fate of a great inner champion.

596.

The pain he endured
On the physical plane
Was beyond earth's imagination.
But the joy and delight he experienced
On the psychic plane
Was also beyond earth's imagination.

597.

As the Absolute Supreme has the hope
That His chosen children will realise Him,
Even so, His children have the dream
That they will be able to prove to the world
That the inner and the outer life
Are complementary realities.

598.

Someday the body will give to the soul
What it has:
Its aspiration-hunger.
Someday the soul will give to the body
What it has:
Its realisation-smile,
A divine meal.

599.

Your self-transcendence-goal
Is not something
That you have to achieve.
It was already given to you long
   ago
By your Beloved Supreme.
You have only to believe it.
You have only to receive it.

600.

My Lord Supreme,
How can I make the fastest
   progress?
"My child,
Pray to Me
For a purity-flooded mind.
Pray to Me
For a beauty-flooded heart.
Pray to Me
For a dedication-flooded life.
Pray to Me
To give you the capacity to see
That your inner voice
Is your only choice."

601.

My heart does not know
How it can ever live
Without the daily
Compassion-Consolation-
   Embrace
Of my Beloved Supreme.

602.

Because your mind sincerely
   needs
Illumination,
Because your heart soulfully needs
Liberation,
Because your life desperately
   needs
Perfection,
God is going to give you, before
   long,
His own Credit Card.

603.

Who else is a real fool
If not he who does not ask God
For anything
For fear of His Answer?

604.

He is not suffering
From his disbelief.
He is suffering
From the extravagance
Of his self-styled faith.

605.

My heart needs only one thing.
It needs to be guided
Along the age-old path
Of life-blossoming self-awareness.

606.

Allow me, O Lord,
Immediately to stand
For the God-realisation
    examination.
I wish to be spared
The torment of waiting.

607.

Self-indulgence means
The extinguished flame
Of hope for God-realisation.

608.

Expectation
Is the beginning of temptation
In the outer life.
Dedication
Is the beginning of satisfaction
In the inner life.

609.

I have opened up an account
With God's Heart-Bank.
Therefore, I see nowhere
The battering waves of poverty-
    thoughts.

610.

When are you going to realise
That you are living in the dark
When you live in the great maze
Of tormenting thought?

611.

A single breath of purity
Can fell the hurtful
Division-tree.

612.

Since you have survived
The countless attacks of
    ignorance,
For you there can be
No illusion-prison of false dreams.

613.

Bitter failures have taught you!
Therefore, you do not have to
    remain
Any longer a stranger
To your pure self-insight.

614.

Since temptation-life has failed
To bind your mind,
Fear-cramps cannot grip
Your heart.

615.

A seeker's humility-heart
Knows how to become
The Smile of God.

616.

If you start now,
You will have plenty of time
To convince God to grant you
His immortal Smile
Before death forces you
To enter through its door.

617.

If you constantly indulge
Your incapacities,
You will be forced to climb
The stairway of despair.

618.

Do not bury the world
With your indifference-eye
If you want to see
The beauty-hours of Heaven-days
On earth.

619.

If you find fault
With God the Compassion,
How can you expect to see
The death of your desire-life?

620.

If you can have patience
As your inner breath,
Then you will have fortitude
As your outer body.

621.

To feed my mind
My Lord has become great.
To feed my heart
My Lord has become good.
To feed my soul
My Lord has become perfect.
To feed my life
My Lord has become
His humanity's cry
And His Divinity's Smile.

622.

Because your mind
Lives on stupidity-street,
Your heart's divinity-flames
Are all extinguished.

623.

I foresee a hopeless battle
Inside you
Between your mind and your heart.
Your mind wants to poison your heart
So it cannot pray to God.
Your heart wants to unburden your mind
So it will not put unnecessary
And unwanted pressure on the heart.
Indeed, this will be a hopeless battle.
God alone knows whether either party
Is going to win.

624.

I do not want to remember
My unaspiring heart,
Complacent mind
And strangling vital.
The very act of remembering
My past weaknesses
Can destroy me.

625.

Imagination
Is the beauty of power.
Aspiration
Is the power of purity.
Realisation
Is the oneness of divinity.

626.

His ego has been bluntly
And mercilessly assaulted.
Therefore, the human in him
Is heaving a sigh of remorse,
The divine in him
Is heaving a sigh of relief
And the Supreme in him
Is celebrating his new birth.

627.

Your desire-lives
Are your own history's dust-heaps.
Your aspiration-lives
Are your God's Heaven-climbing
And earth-illumining Towers.

628.

Allow failure to teach you
A supreme lesson:
Each sunset is the beginning
Of a very, very bright
And powerful sunrise.

629.

If you want to succeed
Divinely and supremely,
Then every day you must water
The green plants of your heart-
 garden.

630.

The winter of your body's lethargy
Can immediately be over
Only if you are ready to welcome
The spring of your soul's
 dynamism.

631.

Do not be afraid
Of your teeming weaknesses.
Brook no compromise with them!
Wrestle with the task
Of divinising them
With your soul's wisdom-light.

632.

Tame everything in your life
Save and except
Your heart's soulful tears.

633.

Be not discouraged!
Be only determined!
The Golden Shore is eagerly
 waiting
For the arrival of your silver
 dream-boat.

634.

No wonder your hope-rainbow
Has completely vanished!
You have allowed your mind-sky
To be eclipsed by the darkness
Of countless doubt-clouds.

635.

Unless you release
Your heart's hidden tears,
You will not be able to see
The beauty and divinity
Of your life's improvement-sky.

636.

O mountains of
 misunderstanding,
I am praying to God
While, at the same time, waiting
For your life-stories to end.

637.

My mind tells me
That God's Timetable
Does not change at all.
My heart tells me
That God's Timetable
Changes very slowly.
My soul tells me
That God's Timetable
Changes not only speedily
But also perfectly.

638.

You call it
A tiny disobedience.
I call it
The unmistakable beginning
Of your life-destroying
Spiritual downfall.

639.

Two things must live together
Inside a seeker:
His heart's absolute truth
And his life's grateful obedience.
Then alone can he be
A supremely chosen instrument
Of God.

640.

Each soul
Is an accomplished interpreter
For the unknown worlds
Of unmanifested divinity-flames.

641.

If you really want
To succeed in life,
Then do not allow
Your aspiration-heart to waver
Between wisdom-hope
And ignorance-despair.

642.

My mind calls it complacency,
My heart calls it carelessness,
My soul calls it blindness,
My God calls it uselessness
And I call it
My God-forgetfulness-life.

643.

If your mind was born
To inspiration,
If your heart was born
To aspiration,
If your life was born
To dedication,
If your soul was born
To illumination,
Then you were definitely born
To realisation.

644.

One little act of selflessness
Is the magnet
That draws both God's Perfection-
    Eye
And God's Satisfaction-Heart.

645.

The loser's inner speed
Is lethargy.
The loser's outer speed
Is unwillingness.
The winner's inner speed
Is self-offering.
The winner's outer speed
Is self-perfection-smile.

646.

Do not accept any substitute
For God.
God has asked me to inform you
That He never liked the idea
Of having a substitute for
    Himself.

647.

To whom does the world belong?
Certainly it does not belong
To my self-sufficient mind.

648.

You have now become
A supremely chosen instrument of
    God
Because you were ready to risk
The world's dire disapproval.

649.

Look what the dark impurity
Of your mind
Has done to you!
It has given birth
To a giant rascal-ego.

650.

How can you expect to find any
     proper cure
For your chronic depression-
     night,
When you were not even alarmed
By the early death
Of your faith-plant-life?

651.

When your winning-life
Ceases to matter,
God's loving Heart will grow
Quickly, proudly and
     unconditionally.

652.

Since your mind is invaded
By uncertainty,
Your heart is bound to be caught
In a web of sorrow.

653.

At the end
Of its unimaginably long journey,
Intellect said to intuition:
"I am very sincerely yours."

654.

Always say a willing "Yes"
To God
If you want Him to liberate you
From the prison of self-
     indulgence.

655.

You have uprooted your faith-
     tree.
Therefore, your God,
Unlike mine,
Has now become very small.

656.

The shadow of a deep sorrow
Is crossing your heart-path
Because you do not care
To shake ignorance-dust
From your two little eyes.

657.

Yesterday I was happy
Because God's Eye was watching
     me.
Today I am happy
Because my eyes are turning
     towards God.
Tomorrow I shall be happy
Because my eyes and God's Eye
Will together dine.

658.

As God the Heart-Searcher
Is very careful,
Even so, God the Life-Saviour
Is very powerful.

659.

How can Heaven be near your
   heart
When you so deeply enjoy your
   stay
In the house of indulgence-
   luxury?

660.

What can the body-bound nature
Of man's mind do?
It can only remain imprisoned
In its own low and abysmal life.

661.

His heart is a born God-seeker.
His life is a born God-lover.
His soul is a born God-distributor.

662.

This world lives
In a totally false peace.
Therefore, my heart longs
To be left alone for Eternity.

663.

His life is too pure to play
With the world's temptation-
   flames.
His heart is too sure to play
With the world's frustration-fires.

664.

Where does he live?
He lives on the altar
Of his heart's sacred song-flames.

665.

Truth does not know
How to transcend,
But God knows!
Truth is old,
But God is at once
Eternally new
And eternally old.

666.

When I open my eyes
I see God,
The Beauty of the finite.
When I close my eyes
I see God,
The Divinity of the Infinite.

667.

My heart's willingness
Has the capacity to open
My life's locked limitation-doors.

668.

If you keep your faith-treasure
    safe,
Your doubt-mind cannot decide
The course of your life.

669.

O my backward-thinking mind,
How will you ever feel
The delight-touch
Of my soul-light?

670.

Because you offer God
Only imitation prayers,
God is not liberating you
From your swarm of wild
And dangerous worries.

671.

What is an unaspiring life
If not an unbearable agony
Of self-deception?

672.

A disturbing thought:
This is what your mind
Can any time be.
An illumining oneness:
This is what your heart
Forever shall remain.

673.

Unless your heart becomes
A constantly spinning hope-top,
How can your life set an abiding
    trend
Of success-smile and progress-
    dance?

674.

What was I doing?
I was hunting my mind's
Dangerous thoughts.
What am I doing now?
I am obeying my soul's
Precious will.

675.

If you want to prove
Your unparalleled capacity,
You will end up exhibiting
Your unparalleled incapacity.

676.

Twice I was awestruck.
Once I was awestruck
By the imperfection-night
Of my life,
And once I was awestruck
By the Compassion-Sun
Of God's Heart.

677.

Do you want to know
What I am missing?
I am missing my heart's
God-loving orphan-sorrow.

678.

There can never be any difference
Between the haughtiness of
A self-sufficient mind
And the emptiness of
A God-deficient life.

679.

My life of dedication
Cheerfully owns
Only what God has
   unconditionally sown
Inside my aspiration-heart.

680.

The mind is
Its own nonsense-cleverness.
The heart is
Its own wisdom-oneness.
The soul is
Its own perfection-fulness.

681.

If you do not make
The people around you happy,
Your heart's inner shrine
Will be without God.

682.

What is life
If not a longing for
The blossoming of an opportunity
To become an integrally perfect
   man?

683.

Today before the sun sets
I must realise that my mind
Is only a fleeting thing
And that my heart
Is an abiding treasure-gift from
   God.

684.

My prayer-life
Powerfully awakens me.
My meditation-life
Richly rewards me.

685.

Nobody, not even God,
Enjoys the confrontation between
Light-beauty and darkness-
    ugliness.
How, then, can you enjoy it?

686.

My tiny gratitude-plant
And God's huge Compassion-Tree
Are inseparably growing together.

687.

A life ruled by
The laughable certainty
Of the finite mind
Is even worse
Than a life hopelessly lost
In a labyrinth of possibilities.

688.

So simple a thing as love divine,
Alas, nobody wants.
So sweet a thing as oneness
    perfect,
Alas, nobody needs.

689.

Victory over the mind
Helps you become
The partner of God the Liberator.

690.

Experience is the miracle
Of transformation.
Realisation is the natural
    awareness
Of oneness-perfection.

691.

To establish your reign
In every atom,
You must scatter the seeds
Of universal oneness-love.

692.

My Beloved Supreme,
I shall gladly allow You
To steal my heart
Only on one condition:
That You do not return it.

693.

Because of your impure mind,
Yesterday you were tempted to take.
Because of your pure heart,
Today you are prompted to give.

694.

What I know
And what I do not know:
I know the abyss of hell,
And I do not know
The transcendental heights of Heaven.

695.

If you think
You are God's slave,
Then beg Him slavishly
To give you an iota of Love.
If you think
You are God's child,
Then ask Him soulfully
To give you His infinite Delight.

696.

Alas, when will life's
Treacherous vanity
Be illumined by the soul's
Sleepless God-loving thirst?

697.

His heart has become as generous
As a fountain of art.
Therefore, his life is becoming
Humanity's precious journey's start
To Heaven's unmeasured
And unscaled heights.

698.

Enslave your ambition-horse
If you want to become
God's fondness-lamb.

699.

Do you not see
That your life's excessive hope
And your mind's possessive nature
Will before long destroy you
Completely?

700.

My Beloved Lord Supreme,
Your Justice-Flames may not know,
But Your Forgiveness-Sun does know
How to make me Your own, very own.

701.

When I pray,
My Lord Supreme tells me
That in Heaven He will grant me
A most beautiful place to live.
When I meditate,
My Lord Supreme tells me
That I have found on earth
The most perfect place
For Him and His Satisfaction to live.

702.

Ignorance-pirate has captured you
Because you did not go to enjoy
Your oneness-picnic
With God's other seeker-children.

703.

You have been persuaded
To the false conviction
That God does not want you
Or need you.
Therefore, your entire life is haunted
By doubt-phantom.

704.

Every day my soul visits
My Lord Supreme
And brings down faith-medicine
From His Salvation-Pharmacy
To cure my insincerity-mind,
Impurity-heart
And insecurity-life.

705.

The donkey inside my mind
Lives an indecision-life.
The deer inside my heart
Is always ready with decision-speed.
The lion inside my soul
Enjoys immediate God-ordained
Satisfaction-action.

706.

Your heart's God-reliance
Is a powerful shaft
Of God's death-silencing Truth.

707.

God does not allow my mind
To give talks on perfection
In His Amphitheatre,
But every day He invites my heart
To give talks on aspiration
And dedication.

708.

Now that you have become one
With your soul's silence-light,
You can easily depart
From the doubt-madhouse of
   your mind.

709.

O my life,
Do not aim for anything else
Save and except
My Lord's Satisfaction-
   Permanence.

710.

The human mind finds it
Quite impossible to believe
That it is an immigrant
From the ignorance-world.

711.

Now that your heart
Is no longer petrified
By insecurity-monster,
Your life can enjoy
The towering tallness
Of satisfaction-house.

712.

Alas,
My mind has destroyed itself
By thinking.
Alas,
My heart is looking for a hope-
   plant
Inside my barren life.
Alas,
My soul has become a complete
   stranger
To satisfaction-delight.

713.

His is the formless God.
He meditates and meditates
On God the Light
To illumine him.
Mine is the personal God.
I meditate and meditate
On God the Supreme Beloved
To fulfil me.

714.

Now that you have launched
Into the spiritual life,
Just remain faithful.
You will definitely reach
Your golden destination.

715.

My Beloved Supreme,
I may not have many things to
  give You,
But I do have two things to give
  You:
A heart of gratitude
And a life of surrender.

716.

Your self-reliance
Is nothing short of God-defiance.
Therefore, you will always be
  denied
Infinity's blue-gold ecstasy-
  dreams.

717.

If you want to be perfect,
Then what you need is
Minute-to-minute aspiration.
If you want to be satisfied,
Then what you need is
Year-to-year dedication.

718.

Your mind has been stung so
  mercilessly
By jealousy-bee
That you are not able to see
Your heart-bird
Inside God's Love-Nest.

719.

Who says you have become
  nothing?
You have become the dead-end
  road
Of self-styled satisfaction.
Perhaps you do not realise it,
But that is something —
Something absolutely intolerable.

720.

What am I doing?
I am building my silver dream-
  boat
To sail my earth-bound human
  life
To the liberation-shore.

721.

To see God the Light,
To feel God the Light,
To become God the Light:
This is the only goal
Of my meditation.

722.

When he meditated on light,
Inside light he saw peace.
When he meditated on peace,
Inside peace he saw
The liberation of the world.

723.

O my soul,
Can you please tell me a few words
About God's Eye and God's Heart?
"God's Eye
Is His Eternity's Newness.
God's Heart
Is His Eternity's Fulness."

724.

If every day you put on
The armour of faith,
God will grant you
His most precious gift:
Satisfaction-Delight.

725.

Yours is a life
Of self-contradictory hungers.
Yours is a mind
Of continual hallucinations.
Yours is a heart
Of helplessness multiplied by
   weakness.
What then can anybody expect
   from you?

726.

He who conquers his mind
Is invited by God
To be a co-sharer
Of God-Immortality's infinite
   Treasure.

727.

There can be no greater absurdity
Than to think that your life
Will no longer be able to succeed
And that your soul
Will no longer be able to proceed.

728.

Give your heart's beauty and life's
   duty
To the world's tremendous
   necessity.
You will enjoy swift and lofty
   flights
To your Immortality's self-
   transcendence.

729.

Only an aspiring heart can feel
That God's Vision-Eye
Is all promise
And that God's Reality-Heart
Is all fulfilment.

730.

When I pray soulfully,
My Beloved Supreme gives me the
   capacity
To love my inner life infinitely
   more
Than I love my outer life.
When I meditate sleeplessly,
My Beloved Supreme grants me
   the capacity
To love Him infinitely more
Than I love my outer life of hope
And my inner life of promise.

731.

The heart's purity
The human hand cannot pollute.
The soul's divinity
The human heart cannot grasp.

732.

Because his heart is perfected
By gratitude,
He is now blessed
With a liberated life.

733.

If you are not ready to accept
Suggestion-light
From your heart's Heavenly
   realm,
Then how do you expect to receive
Nectar-delight
From your soul's unparalleled
   height?

734.

You must expose yourself
To only one thing
And that thing is
The divinity-world
Of Heaven's infinite Love.

735.

His life is hopelessly wavering
Between the world
Which wants to devour him
And his Beloved Supreme
Who wants to be devoured by him.

736.

The visible God daily invites you
To come and eat with Him.
The invisible God silently asks you
To invite Him to eat with you
At least once in your entire life.

737.

If there is no purity of purpose
In what we say and do
God will never be able to dance
His Satisfaction-Dance before us.

738.

My Lord Supreme,
Where can I find You
    immediately?
"My child,
You can find Me immediately
Inside the hearts of those
Who are selflessly and untiringly
    building
My Kingdom of Heaven
Here on earth."

739.

What you are doing is ridiculous!
On the one hand
You are looking at your life
Through the maze of
    discouragement.
On the other hand
You are expecting the advent
Of a new saviour.
I have a new name for you:
Absurdity!

740.

How can you see the bright hue
Of your happiness-dawn,
When you sleeplessly enjoy
Your self-taught ignorance-game?

741.

When are you going to learn
That you need to completely
    abandon
Your life's monstrous insecurity-
    queen?

742.

He who is sustained
Only by his faith-force
Is cherished
By God's transcendental Pride.

TWENTY-SEVEN THOUSAND ASPIRATION-PLANTS

743.

Only the unflinching
   determination
Of your heart
Can save you from your mind's
Aching loneliness.

744.

There can be no dead end
Not to speak of a U-turn
For a genuine seeker-traveller
Of the Absolute Supreme.

745.

Your mind is totally lost
In academic confusion.
Your vital is completely lost
In ruthless frustration.
Your heart is absolutely lost
In shameless unwillingness.
Alas, how then can you expect
Happiness from your life?

746.

Do you want to keep your mind
   free
From the debris of impurity-
   thoughts?
If so, appoint your heart
To be your mind's regular
   housekeeper.

747.

Every day adhere to your
   convictions!
Your mind's brooding doubts
Are the worst enemies
Of your heart-life.

748.

If your mind is devoted
To perfection-revelation,
Then your soul can dynamically
   activate
Your useless lethargy-body.

749.

His soul is so kind to his mind.
Every day his soul enters into his
   mind
And prescribes a new
And effective prayer-medicine
For its lingering doubt-disease.

750.

If you enjoy sitting
On the bench of contentment-
   luxury,
Then how do you expect to
   complete
Your Godward race?

751.

Personal and impersonal,
With form and without,
God the Supreme
Encompasses all.

752.

When I pray,
I feel that I am a beggar
Looking at a rich man's house.
Perhaps, out of compassion,
The rich man will give me alms.
When I meditate,
I feel that I am waiting for
My dearest friend
To do me a special favour.
Since we have established our
 oneness,
My Beloved Friend will definitely
Do the needful.

753.

Why must you always ask,
"When will I become beautiful,
When will I be free from
 ignorance?"
If you think that you are ugly,
All your joy disappears,
And ugliness becomes your name.
If you think that you are caught
In the meshes of ignorance,
You become bound, totally bound.

754.

You want to secretly go up
And not look back at anybody else
Once you have reached your
 height.
But I tell you,
Both realisation and
 manifestation
Are absolutely necessary
In God's divine Game.

755.

There is no other power
Except the heart-power
To tame man's
Dark-energy-flooded animal life.

756.

Since you must rely on the world
To sustain your body
While you strive
To attain God,
Can you not offer the world
A little peace, light and joy
In return?

757.

What is my earth-bound mind
If not a daily
And regularly false promise
To itself?

758.

Do not allow your life
To be lured into complacency-
   sleep
If you want to see and enjoy
The panorama of your heart's
Beauty-perfection.

759.

Death is flying on silence-wings
Right above you.
Be careful!
As soon as possible invite your
   soul-bird
To come to the fore
And chase away this death-bird.

760.

Before my life-journey's close
I shall realise God.
Indeed, this is not a matter of
   chance
But of unmistakable choice.

761.

My Lord Supreme,
May my flower-life grow
Inside Your Heart Garden,
And may my existence be offered
On the shrine of Your Life-Breath.

762.

I always pray to God for
   forgiveness
When I do something wrong.
If God forgives me,
Then who can punish me?

763.

Since it is with yourself
That you must live,
You must teach your heart
The art of sacrifice
And you must teach your mind
The art of forgiveness.

764.

With your life
An innocent heart was born.
With your life
A complicated mind will die.

765.

The Master's eye says,
"The search begins here."
The Master's heart says,
"The search shall forever
   continue."

766.

The separation-clouds between
   you and God
Will disappear only when
You are ready to accept cheerfully
Everything from God's
   Compassion-Sky.

767.

His life is running towards
The Infinite
And his heart is transfixed
In ecstasy-sky
Because his soul
Is a God-tuned lover.

768.

Each seeker must become
A lion of self-control
Before he can dream of turning
   into
A selfless saint.

769.

He has left the path
Of divine love,
And now his life has become
A completely withered tree.

770.

He is incapable of saying "No"
To the outer life.
He is incapable of saying "Yes"
To the inner life.
Every day problems appear to
   him,
But solutions never.

771.

If you allow your heart to stand in
   the Light
Of God's blessingfully
   unchanging Eye,
Then your imagination-life
Will be totally satisfied.

772.

My Lord Supreme,
How can I achieve wisdom?
"My child,
You can achieve wisdom
Only through an obedience-life
And a surrender-heart."

773.

God wants you to know Him
As your Eternity's Friend.
He does not like you to think of
   Him
As your Eternity's Sovereign.

774.

There was a time when my life
Held my heart's rainbow-dreams.
Alas, my life has now become
A blazing fire of false hunger.

775.

You are your mind's
Quenchless attachment-thirst.
Therefore, your life has become
A godless poison-drink.

776.

Let us try to recapture
Our lost time
If we really want not only to see
But also to expedite
The arrival of God's Hour.

777.

I am just learning to feel
That I do not have to actually
    catch God,
But that someday God will catch
    me
And pour into my heart
A flood of ineffable Delight.

778.

He is eternal and immortal.
He is within this world and
    beyond it.
He is the Creator,
Both universal and
    transcendental.

779.

If you are a sincere seeker
But have not prayed and
    meditated
For a long time,
Then your heart's utopia-dream
Is fast turning into
Your mind's autocracy-nightmare.

780.

Loneliness has mercilessly
    attacked mankind
And made half the world suicidal.
Alas, when will each human soul
    realise
That its inner and outer
    nothingness
Can easily be transformed into
Plenitude without and infinitude
    within?

781.

There are many marathon-
  questions
In life,
But the only sprint-answers are
  these:
A hopeful heart
And a purposeful soul.

782.

The mind is painfully running
Towards death,
Whereas the heart is powerfully
  denying
The very existence of death.

783.

Since your life has become
A loud self-proclamation-drum,
How will you ever feel the joy
Of a transcendence-satisfaction-
  life?

784.

Your own sincere search
For yourself
Will become a synonym
For perfection-happiness.

785.

Your mind's only business
Is to stop torturing God.
Your heart's only business
Is to please God.
Your life's only business
Is to become another God.

786.

Mine is the mind
That is tired of losing,
Yet mine is the heart
That enjoys frequent competition.

787.

You tell me
You are a noble-minded soul.
Then show me
Your ignorance-renouncing life!

788.

His every breath is an ascending
  prayer
For God to stop the tug-of-war
Between his insecurity-mind
And his impurity-vital.

789.

The mind-knowledge travels
To the moon.
The heart-wisdom not only travels
To the sun
But also brings down the sun's
Silent flame-smiles.

790.

Do you know what is going to
   happen
Eventually
To your suspicious mind?
It will collapse in a house
Of wild madness.

791.

Unconsciously you cherish
A chain of falsehood-mountains.
Consciously you would like to
   cherish
The advent of beauty's skies.
Alas, you have become a life
Of sorry contradictions.

792.

If you consciously throw yourself
On God's side,
God will grant you
The Concentration-Arrow
Of His Eye
And the Meditation-Bow
Of His Heart.

793.

Truth tells you
When your mind will wake up.
Peace tells you
When your heart will wake up.
God's Satisfaction tells you
When your life will wake up.

794.

Instead of always saying,
"God, I need You to please me,"
Can you not only once say,
"God, I love to please You"?

795.

If you want to better your inner
   life
Of aspiration and dedication,
Then uproot the long-cherished
Unwillingness-tree
That is growing in your mind.

796.

No wonder the nebulous clouds
Of uncertainty
Are torturing your mind
Constantly!
Do you not realise that your mind
Lacks even a trickle
Of sincerity-determination?

797.

O my mind,
Are you not sick of losing
Time and again
In the battlefield of life?
When are you going to claim
The marvel of faith divine
As your birthright?

798.

God is inviting you
To share His Life.
But before you do,
He expects you to do Him a
    favour.
He wants you to ruthlessly destroy
Your desire-thoughts.

799.

Every day
During his morning prayer,
He enters into his heart's hope-
    meadow
To enjoy God's Company,
Even if only for a few brief
    moments.

800.

My Beloved Supreme,
You are my real Friend.
I do not have to ask You
For anything,
For You know all my needs.

801.

The heart of man sighs
For beauty-wings
So it can soar like a bird
In the vastness-height of the sky.

802.

If you study the world
Of your heart,
God will bless you
With His Life's Sunrise.

803.

If you want to be
A perfect instrument of God,
Then never overestimate
Your mind's wisdom
And never underestimate
Your heart's obedience.

804.

Because you are completely lost
In the jungle of impurity,
You cherish the audacity
To deny God's unconditional
Compassion-Existence
In this world.

805.

When man is his own revelation
And not God's,
What can poor God do?
He simply retreats
To His secret and sacred Confines.

806.

Purity is a soulful beauty
Which is long-lost and forgotten
Inside the mind's confusion-
   jungle.

807.

The ghosts
Of my past failure-life
Are still torturing
My tiny, delicate plant-heart.

808.

I do not want to hear from
Your God-thirsty lips.
I want to feel
Your God-hungry heart.

809.

The clouds of separation
Between you and God
Will before long disappear
If you are careful how you spend
Your waking hours.

810.

Do not pray to God
To take you away from this world.
Pray to God
To change your nature here on
   earth.
What you need is transformation
And not escape.

811.

The greatest tragedy is my own
   life.
Although I am God's choice son,
I deliberately do not listen
To God's Voice.

812.

Because of your sincerity-mind,
Purity-heart and luminosity-soul,
You are being carried
By the Compassion-Current
Of God's Heart-River.

813.

O world,
I have this to say to you:
My heart shall never
Run out of aspiration,
My mind shall never
Run out of inspiration
And my life shall never
Run out of dedication.

814.

His cry stole my heart.
His smile stole my soul.
His love stole my life.
His oneness with God
Stole my all.

815.

Hope never deceives me.
Hope is a divine instrument
Which aspires to achieve and
   reveal
God-manifesting beauty.

816.

I wish to be one of the few,
Very few,
Who can sincerely feel
That God is responsible
For my success
And that I am responsible for His.

817.

Yours is the divinely created
Aspiration-blossom,
Permeated with sincerity's
Divinity-fragrance.

818.

Faith knows no tension,
For it knows that God
Is always with it
And always for it.

819.

During my morning talk with God
He told me that there is no crisis
In any human life
That cannot be resolved
By a divinely sunlit smile.

820.

On the way home
From earth to Heaven,
He brought along with him
Earth's hope-sea
To play with Heaven's fulfilment-sun.

821.

When my soul is in Heaven,
It whispers a prayer
For compassion.
When my soul is on earth,
It whispers a prayer
For peace.
When my soul is with God,
It whispers a prayer
For God-satisfaction.

822.

I feel such purity
When I gaze at the moon.
I feel such power
When I gaze at the sun.
But, alas, I feel such uncertainty
When I gaze at myself.

823.

Yours is a world
From which God is always absent,
Do you know why?
Because you are always fond of wandering
In your mind's wasteland.

824.

God will definitely rescue you
From your anxiety-emergency
If you do not waste
Your heart's obedience-breath.

825.

In the heart of each struggle
There is always
A sun-vast victory-crown.

826.

Sadness-purity is my life's
Fleeting voice.
Gladness-divinity is my soul's
Eternal voice.

827.

My Lord Supreme,
Do widen the narrow rivulet
Of my life
So that I can forever surely flow
Into Your Heart's Ecstasy-Ocean.

828.

If your rebellious mind is
   unwilling
To admit defeat,
Your heart is doomed to carry
The stupidity-freedom of your
   life.

829.

God's ultimate Miracle
Shall secretly blossom:
You will become the perfection-
   beauty
Of your own soul's
Stupendous God-discovery.

830.

Responsibility cannot weigh you
   down
If you take responsibility
As a God-approved opportunity.
It can only lift you and your life
To the higher worlds.

831.

His is the magic smile
That every day eclipses
My heart's excruciating pangs.

832.

Since Buddha did not come
For the East alone
And Christ did not come
For the West alone,
You should know
That you have not come
For yourself alone.

833.

You are always allowed
To come near God
And play with Him,
Not because you live
In a great reality-world
But because you constantly
   cherish
God-dreams.

834.

God's Compassion-Sun is not
  invisible;
My heart is just blind.
God's Forgiveness-Sky is not
  invisible;
My mind is just blind.
God's Assurance-Ocean is not
  invisible;
My eyes are just blind.

835.

The animal in me says,
"Why is there a God
When I do not need Him?"
The human in me says,
"Where is God
When I do need Him?"
The divine in me says,
"Whether I need God or not,
He eternally is."

836.

Alas, you have placed your
  happiness-life
Not only in the hands of others
But also at their giant feet.

837.

If you do not have surrender-tears,
Then try to create them.
If you do have surrender-tears,
Then soulfully treasure them
And try to increase them.

838.

There should not be any weakness
In your thought-life
Or any carelessness
In your heart-life
If you care for
The transcendental Smile of God.

839.

If you fear to aspire,
Do you not realise
That you and your life
Will very soon
Expire with fear?

840.

The difference between
  involvement
And commitment is this:
If you are involved,
You are a problem-maker.
If you are committed,
You are a problem-shooter.

841.

O my soul,
Did you ask God
When my suspicion-mind
Will be unquestionably defeated
By my aspiration-heart?
O my soul,
I hope you have not forgotten
This time also.

842.

The dust of the past
Has soiled his heart.
Therefore, he cannot win admission
To God's pure Heart-Home.

843.

To have your desires
Fulfilled for the asking
Is to be forced to dance
With your life's inner failures.

844.

Instead of creating self-styled fantasies
To decorate your life,
Why do you not become a translator
Of God's Vision-fulfilling Silence-Message?

845.

When I walk,
I walk prayerfully
So that I can have
A soulful heart,
A powerful life
And a fruitful vision of God.

846.

My heart's dawn has come,
My heart's dawn has come.
Inside my heart
I see only one thing:
The happiness of a God-intoxicated
Beauty-life.

847.

O my body-dungeon,
Even you can be full of God.
Just do not mix with the mind.
Do not even listen to the mind,
For it is drunk
With egotism-night.

848.

Since your heart was awakened,
You have been praying and
   meditating
To see divine light,
And this light itself wants you to
   see
That there is another world
Where truth, peace and bliss
   abide.

849.

O my soul,
Each time you come down
Into the world-arena,
You bring with you the promise
To offer light to the world at large
And to manifest God in God's own
   Way.

850.

Inwardly and outwardly
Your Beloved Supreme
Is pleading with you
To listen to all His Requests
Cheerfully and soulfully.

851.

If you do not make progress
In God's own Way,
Then what you call progress
Will be only the aggrandisement
Of your ego.
If you make progress
In God's own Way,
Then you are bound to feel
God's Love, Peace and
Satisfaction
Inundating your life.

852.

The thunder of sound
Is God's ambassador to earth.
The beauty of silence
Is God's ambassador to Heaven.

853.

My Lord Supreme,
Why do I feel insecure?
"My child,
You feel insecure
Because you are afraid of vastness.
Try to claim the vastness
Of the ocean and the sky
As your own, very own.
Then you will never be insecure."

854.

My Lord Supreme,
How can I maintain my inner
    strength?
"My child,
You can maintain your inner
    strength
Only by having peace of mind."
My Lord Supreme,
How can I have peace of mind?
"My child,
To have peace of mind
What you need
Is purity in the body, the vital
And the mind itself."

855.

His prayerful mind and soulful
    heart
Have made his life
A shadowless illumination-sun.

856.

The East is for realisation.
The West is for manifestation.
The East cares mainly
For height.
The West cares mainly
For length and breadth.

857.

Your mind does not want
God's loving Heart.
God's Heart does not want
Your doubting mind.
Unless and until you change your
    mind,
God is not going to change His
    Heart.

858.

God has revealed His infinite
    Light
Through your glowing eyes.
Can you not reveal your soulful
    delight
Through God's ever-fulfilling
And ever-transcending Heart?

859.

Every day God and I
Exchange our dreams.
I share with Him
My mind's frustration-dreams;
He shares with me
His Heart's Satisfaction-Dreams.

860.

Because your heart has become
A God-pleasing prayer,
Your life has now become
God's secret and sacred
   powerhouse.

861.

If you live in the dark cave
Of blind individuality,
How can you expect God
To grant you an interview?

862.

Indeed, he is a chosen instrument
   of God,
For his heart is aspiration-
   intensity,
His life is dedication-luminosity
And his breath is perfection-
   divinity.

863.

Your desire-life will never desert
   you
Of its own accord.
It is your aspiration-life
That has to discipline, illumine
And liberate your desire-life
From its sleepless ignorance-
   hunger.

864.

Futile fears and doubts can never
Impose themselves upon him,
For he lives in his heart-life,
And his heart-life is always
Flooded with God-Light.

865.

Every time he sails the boat
Of confidence-light
He is befriended
By God's Satisfaction-Delight.

866.

An unexpected Compassion-
   Touch
From Above
Can transform the absurd
   inventions
Of the intellect
Into God's all-satisfying
Intuition-Treasures.

867.

Your mind foolishly tries
To fathom God.
Your heart soulfully waits
For God's Compassion-Light
And Forgiveness-Height
To measure your life.

868.

Your mind-conquest
Is yesterday's forgotten
   resolution.
Therefore, how can you conquer
Today's desire-hunger?

869.

God does not need your mind's
Partial insecurity-surrender.
God needs only your heart's
Inseparable oneness-hunger-
   delight.

870.

My aspiration-days and devotion-
   nights
Have successfully and
   permanently removed
My life's ego-mask.

871.

Your soul has been hiding
For centuries.
But rest assured,
It will not remain hidden forever.
Someday, somewhere, somehow
It will reveal
Its God-manifesting perfection-
   delight.

872.

You do not want to remove
Your ego-mask,
Yet you wonder why yours has
   become
An upside-down life-view.

873.

Your heart-compass does not
Always point to God.
How then do you expect
Your life-star to ever rise
In Eternity's Infinity-Sky?

874.

Your mind-land neither loves you
Nor needs you.
Alas, even so, you are not willing
To go back to God's Heart-Land.

875.

Alas, right now
You are your own vital-fury.
Do you not realise that before long
You and nobody else
Will become your own heart-
   injury?

876.

I am glad that you like
Your heart-beauty's friend:
Life.
I am glad that you like
Your life-warning friend:
Death.

877.

You have abandoned
Your heart-shrine,
Yet still you are looking for
The presiding deity of your life.

878.

Jump over your limitation-
   hurdles
And become a bold bondage-
   breaker!
Then your life will not remain
A drooping question mark.

879.

Love makes all human beings
   equal.
Oneness makes all human beings
   perfect.
Satisfaction makes all human
   beings
Exactly the same as God.

880.

Since God is
His own Patience-Light,
Can you not become
Your own obedience-delight?

881.

Your aspiration-crisis has alarmed
Not only Heaven's mounting
   heights
But also earth's crying lengths.

882.

His is an unusual interpretation
Of spiritual awakening.
He thinks that first man shakes
   God,
And then God wakes man.

883.

You will be caught
In time's clutches
If your dedication-life
Does not grow into a surrender-
   heart
To please God in His own Way.

884.

My best speciality is this:
I never allow my life
To be caught
In my mind's confusion-net.

885.

If you go on placating
Your screaming vital,
How will you ever see
Your life's sunrise?
Will you not always remain
In your death's moonless night?

886.

If your love is in transit
To devotion
And your devotion is in transit
To surrender,
God will cheerfully and proudly
Tell you His Code-Name
So you can invoke Him
At any time you want.

887.

O stupid world,
Why should my soul be
    responsible
For piercing your thick bravado-
    shell?
My soul is accountable
Only to God the Justice-Light.

888.

Every day you are trying so hard
To discover your guardian angel.
I tell you,
Your aspiration-dedication-faith-
    flames
Can easily do the work
Of your guardian angel.

889.

An insecurity-heart
Hears a loud shout
In every feeble whisper.

890.

Until a better dream begins,
His heart will be longing
For only one thing:
God's Compassion-Smile.

891.

Darkness will arrive
Without any warning
If love is not found daily
In your life's dictionary.

892.

Truth can live only with right.
Falsehood can live only with
  wrong.
Ask your mind and heart
To make their choice.

893.

His unquenched thirst
For greatness-height
Has fallen under
The inescapable thumb of death.

894.

The past tense of hope
Is promise.
The future tense of hope
Is dedication.

895.

Because of your complacent mind,
You are now lost
In a lifeless desert
With an endless inheritance
Of sorrow.

896.

Do you think that God
Does not want to retire?
He does want to retire!
He has time and again asked
The cosmic gods
To arrange His retirement party,
And each time the cosmic gods
Are obliged to refuse.
But the more God asks them
For this special favour,
The stronger become their hearts'
Failure-pangs
For not having transformed
Humanity's life.

897.

Unless you give up
The shameless tricks
Of your mounting pride,
Death will hasten
Its impending visit to you.

898.

When you soulfully become,
What do you become?
You become God's partner.
When you unreservedly give,
To whom do you give?
You give to God.

899.

Nothing can help
And nothing will help
Steer God's Boat
Save and except your sleepless life's
Cheerfulness-breath.

900.

When my Lord plays upon my life-flute,
He gives me the boundless capacity
To walk along His royal Road
To reach His Immortality's Heart-Kingdom.

901.

Claim God's Delight-Fountain
With your heart's
Purity-flooded innocence-cry.
God has been waiting for you to do so
For a very, very long time.

902.

A prayer-mountain:
This is what my mind urgently needs.
A meditation-fountain:
This is what my heart sleeplessly needs.

903.

Even a segment of a sincerity-heart
And the firmament of a divinity-soul
Are extremely fond of each other.

904.

Even if I remember God too late,
God will not hesitate
To give me a beautiful flower
From His Heart-Garden.

905.

This moment my mind
Is a pathless forest.
Next moment my mind
Is my heart's silence-devouring tiger.

906.

When God's Heart
Is my only choice,
God not only fulfils my prayers
But also grants me
His Rainbow-Voice.

907.

A life that does not aspire
Is indeed a failure-life
That returns again and again
Through Eternity's revolving
  door.

908.

When I soulfully love God,
I consciously become
A God-taught student
Of God-Satisfaction.
When I do not love God
But only love myself,
I helplessly become
A self-taught student
Of deathless dissatisfaction.

909.

Do you know what my mind
Has done?
It has tapped my heart's
Telephone line to God.
Why?
It suspects that my heart
Is speaking ill of it secretly
And that God is powerfully
  encouraging,
Appreciating and loving my heart.

910.

My mind becomes familiar
With the word "No"
When God speaks to my mind.
My heart becomes familiar
With the words "Yes" and "No"
When God speaks to my heart.
My soul remains familiar
With the word "Yes" – always
  "Yes" –
When God speaks to my soul.

911.

O my mind's stupid anger,
Can you not see what you have
  done?
You have chained me
To my worst enemy: doubt.

912.

My mind, heart and soul
All work for my Lord Supreme.
My mind demands a high salary.
In order to keep peace,
My Lord grants my mind
A high salary.
My heart needs only a low salary.
God grants my heart a low salary
And thus satisfies my heart.
My soul does not want any salary.
It works for God for free
And is all gratitude to Him
For using it as His instrument.
God says to my soul,
"You are My Eternity's Pride,
My Infinity's Joy
And My Immortality's Love."

913.

He does not hate God any more
Because he now wisely knows
That he depends on God.
He does not hate the world any more
Because the world finally realises
That it helplessly depends on him.

914.

I have locked
Inside my body-prison
Two things:
God's morning Smile
And
Man's evening cry.

915.

My heart tells me
That God the Lover
Is a sprinter.
My soul tells me
That God the Smiler
Is a middle-distance runner.
My body tells me
That God the Dreamer
Is a long-distance runner.

916.

Your beauty-spreading life-flower
Is bound to fade
If you do not soulfully offer
Your heart-tears
To your Beloved Supreme.

917.

My mind says to my Lord
   Supreme,
"Please do not fire me,
Although I am not working hard
For You."
My heart says to my Lord
   Supreme,
"Please do not employ me
Until I can become a good
   instrument
Of Yours."

918.

When he searched within
He discovered two things:
A silver purity-sky
And a golden divinity-sun.

919.

If you can play
On your heart's gratitude-flute,
Then God will definitely grant
   you
His Vision's unhorizoned Smile.

920.

My Lord,
You have severely scolded me
Not because I love You
Less than before,
Not because You love me
Less than before,
But because I have started
Loving excessively
My frustration-generating desire-
   life.

921.

As long as God is on my side,
I shall not care
Whether or not this world will
   ever be
On my side.

922.

You know perfectly well
That what you have
Is a good-for-nothing mind.
Why, then, do you spend so much
   time
With your mind, in your mind
And for your mind?
You know perfectly well that
   yours
Is a good-for-everything heart.
How is it, then,
That you always act like a stranger
Towards your heart?

923.

O my uncooperative mind,
What you need from my Lord
Is a powerful Kick
And not a blessingful Touch
For your illumination.

924.

My Lord,
I shall no more give You
My mind's despair-tears.
I shall give You only
My heart's aspiration-smiles.

925.

Your life has become
A difficulty-mountain
Because you feel that God is
Neither His Compassion-Eye
Nor His Forgiveness-Heart.

926.

If you regularly fly
In your aspiration-plane,
God will definitely invite you to
  fly
In His Satisfaction-Plane.

927.

When you fell from your pride-
  tree,
Did you not see God standing
On your heart's oneness-lawn,
Looking at you with His
  Compassion-Eye?

928.

My heart's aspiration-road is
  paved
With God's ever-blossoming
  Beauty.
My life's dedication-road is paved
With God's ever-illumining Duty.

929.

Your vital is on strike!
But alas, your vital is not suffering
From the strike.
It is your heart that is suffering
Endlessly.

930.

If you live in the cramped room of
  fear,
How can you ever be
A choice instrument of God?

931.

Between my present happiness
And my future happiness,
Two divine things exist:
My promise-divinity
And
My faith-beauty.

932.

He who thinks
That he does not know
What truth is in the inner world
Is an illegal alien there.

933.

Long before my heart's
Little light grows dim,
I must capture the vast Light
Of my Lord's infinite Heart.

934.

In the outer world
I have buried
My inferiority complex
To become great.
In the inner world
I have buried
My superiority complex
To become perfect.

935.

Your stupid and ungrateful mind
Is not ready to pay
Even a courtesy call on God,
Whereas your heart every day pays
A devoted and surrendered visit to
   God.

936.

The mind that does not want
To change
And the life that does not want
To grow
Have already contracted a deadly
   disease:
Suspicion.

937.

In your spiritual life
Drive forward fast, very fast.
If you cannot do that,
At least drive forward slowly.
But never, never
Drive in reverse!

938.

If you live a life
Of loveless duty,
How can you experience
The divinity of a day
Freed from endless ordeals?

939.

My Lord,
I cannot separate
Your Heart of Tears
From Your Eye of Scoldings.
To me they are absolutely the
    same.

940.

When you are your heart's
Diamond calmness,
God becomes His thousand Smiles
And million Dances.

941.

His newly illumined life-boat
Plies between his mind's silver
    trance
And his heart's golden dance.

942.

Unless you challenge
The age-old victory of ignorance,
Your life is doomed to remain
A failure-sigh.

943.

My Lord gave me
His magical Vision-Eye
And now I am giving Him
My radical reality-life.

944.

Yesterday's stupidity-life
I gave up.
Today's insecurity-life
I am giving up.
Soon I shall start enjoying
Tomorrow's practical God-life.

945.

My mind is satisfied
Being God's tortoise.
My heart is satisfied
Being God's deer.
My soul is satisfied
Being God's lion.
And I am satisfied,
Completely satisfied,
Being God's lamb.

946.

Each hope-blossom
Is a God-sent messenger
From Heaven's God-distributing
Delight.

947.

Your division-mind
Is a sea of fears.
Therefore, your oneness-heart
Has become a flood of tears.

948.

His is the heart
That is as young
As a morning promise.
His is the life
That is as old
As an evening hope.

949.

I know where I stand.
I stand between
The nothingness-desert
Of my mind
And the fulness-sea
Of my heart.

950.

The beauty that feeds
The greedy eyes
Is no beauty at all.
The beauty that is hungry
For God's Eye
Is the only real beauty.

951.

The slow decline of his progress
Began the day he lost touch
With his heart's faith.

952.

Do you think
God's omniscient Eye
Cannot see
Your transient cry?
How can you expect
With this transient cry
To win God's ever-effervescent
   Smile?

953.

You cannot live in
Desire's bondage-cave
And aspiration's freedom-sky
At the same time.

954.

God never wants from you
Your mind's fearful prayers.
He wants from you
Only your heart's prayerful
   meditations.

955.

Your mind may be chained
To doubt,
But your heart is always hoisting
Faith's victory-banner.

956.

Although your life overslept,
You are not doomed
To utter disappointment.
Now that you are up,
Start walking and running
Along Eternity's Road
And begin to enjoy
Your endless journey.

957.

God's Heart
Is my lover within,
And God's Eye
Is my supplier without.

958.

When we live inside the body-room,
We see God the Stranger.
When we live inside the heart-room,
We see God the Lover.
When we live inside the soul-room,
We see God the Dreamer.

959.

The East is like a tree
Without branches, leaves,
Flowers or fruits.
The West is like a tree
Poorly nourished,
With dying roots.
Who can appreciate either tree?

960.

You are running forward,
Asking, "Where is the goal?"
I tell you,
If you have no sense of speed,
How can there ever
Be a goal for you?

961.

Not one but all my limbs
I broke
As I was speedily climbing down
Ingratitude-hill.

962.

A man of suspicion
Undoubtedly lives
A lonely insecurity-life.

963.

Every day you must aspire
If you want to remain
An active player
In God's life-transforming
Cosmic Game.

964.

The Guru is both vision and
   reality.
Through meditation we realise
The vision of the Guru.
Through dedication we manifest
The reality of the Guru.

965.

If you want to wage a successful
   war
Against despair,
Then once and for all fortify
Your aspiring heart
And searching life.

966.

If you feel that
To work for mankind
Is beneath your dignity,
Then you are, indeed,
An unfortunate God-seeker.

967.

If you care only for manifestation
And not for realisation,
There will be no true
Spirit of God-oneness
In your actions.

968.

Salvation-light:
This is the message of the West.
Liberation-height:
This is the message of the East.
Perfection-Delight:
This is the Message
Of my Beloved Supreme.

969.

Doctors call it
An emergency room.
I call it
God's Compassion-Exercise
   Room.

970.

Why do you want to remain
Always seated with folded hands?
Come out into the world.
Manifest God in a new way:
Through your life of self-giving.

971.

For centuries
I travelled alone in paradise
With my silence-eye.
Finally, whom did I see?
My Eternity's dear fellow-enjoyer,
My soul.

972.

Do you not see the difference
Between your past power-life
And your present light-life?
With power you became a hero-warrior.
With light you are earth's life-transformer.

973.

True, sleep covers all human doubts
And all human thoughts.
But since it does not transform
Doubt into faith and thought into will,
It is as useless
As a deplorably unmanifested man.

974.

The message of Heaven is brief
But most powerful:
God loves me unconditionally.
The message of earth is long, uncertain
And most painful:
Earth does not need me.

975.

O my mind,
Do not hide in
Your own darkness-night.
O my heart,
Wake up before
Ignorance-prince steps in.
O my soul,
Do spread your oneness-smile
Within and without my life.

976.

If you have an aspiration-heart,
Then allow it to enjoy
The soaring eagle-flight
Of your progress-smile.

977.

If you remain inside God's
　Consciousness,
You will see God
As your Father and Mother,
Your Sister and Brother,
Your Friend, Your All.

978.

My Lord Supreme,
I am tired of playing hide-and-
　seek
With You.
"My child, I am also tired
Of playing this ancient game.
Let us now start playing a new
　game,
A totally new game: oneness-
　fulness."

979.

Capacity is
His life's shrine.
Willingness is
His heart's deity.

980.

God the Sprinter feels sorry
For my body's incapacity.
God the Lover feels sorry
For my heart's incapacity.
God the Dreamer feels sorry
For my life's incapacity.

981.

My earth-born thought
Can never do the work of love.
My Heaven-born thought
Will do not only the work of love
But also the Work of God.

982.

No wonder you are a stranger
To your Heaven-shining skies.
You are not at all receptive
To Heaven's God-descending
　light.

983.

My heart's crying
Is my life's sacred hunger.
My soul's soaring
Is my Lord's secret Meal.

984.

You want to know where I live
Most of the time.
I live most of the time
In the silence-garden of my soul's
   music
Where no disharmony can ever
   eclipse
The sovereignty of my soul.

985.

His heart is studying
The technology of tears
So that his life can become
A factory of God-Smiles.

986.

How can God give you
A taste of His universal Delight
If you are not willing
To forget totally
The taste of your personal fears?

987.

Your life-plant is growing
Within the shadow of your
   suspicion-mind.
How then can you expect to see
The flowering of your oneness-
   smile?

988.

Every day you allow the
   temptation-bird
To sing inside your vital.
How can you then live
In Eternity's sunrise?

989.

Every morning my Beloved
   Supreme
Begs me to touch His Smiles.
Every evening my Lord Supreme
Commands me to wipe His Tears.

990.

If you want to become
A world-class seeker,
Then you must take a course
At God's Compassion-University.

991.

With his national mind
He began
His life's earthly journey.
With his international heart
He completed
His life's Heavenly journey.

992.

My Beloved Supreme
Leads my aspiration-heart,
And I follow His Vision-Eye.

993.

O my mind,
I do not mind if you are old,
But I do mind if you fail to tell me
A new, inspiring and illumining
   earth-story.

994.

God the Vision
Was in the beginning.
God the Satisfaction
Will be at the end.
God the Dedication
Is in between.

995.

A constant, prayerful, cheerful
And soulful obedience
Is unmistakably a record-breaking
Inner achievement-event.

996.

You want to know
Whether you should live or love.
If you love your body alone,
Then you should only live.
If you love your heart alone,
Then you should only love.
If you love God alone and nothing
   else,
Then you must at once live and
   love.

997.

There was a time when your mind
Won the world over
To division-night.
Now your heart
Is winning the world over
To oneness-day.

998.

A superlative God-lover
Is he who never loses his grip
On God's Compassion-Divinity.

999.

What you have done
May not have pleased God,
But what you have not done
Has certainly pleased God.
What have you not done?
You have not accepted
The daily invitation
From ignorance-prince.

1000.

I do not have to know
What the truth is.
All that I have to know
Is that God is the only Truth.

1001.

Dear to my Lord
Is my aspiration-heart.
Dearer to my Lord
Is my surrender-life.
Dearest to my Lord
Is my gratitude-breath.

1002.

If your mind climbs up the pride-ladder,
Your life before long
Will fade into obscurity
And your heart will not be rediscovered
By Heaven's Concern.

1003.

True, he cannot control his mind.
But his life has surrendered to his heart.
Therefore, his life is anchored
In the Golden Boat of the Lord Supreme.

1004.

His heart's ever-blossoming hope
Is holding both ends
Of the Infinity-Rope
Of God's Eternity.

1005.

He lives in ignorance-night
With only the echoing memories
Of his soul's long-lost promises.

1006.

My Lord, destroy me!
If You do not want to destroy me,
At least destroy my mind's hopelessness.
If you do not want to destroy
My mind's hopelessness,
Please, please destroy
My heart's helplessness.

1007.

Your soul is asking you
To sleep in your life's
   illumination-bed.
But what are you doing?
You are forcing your life
To lie beneath its annihilation-
   blanket.

1008.

Finally his heart's aspiration-life
Became so powerful
That it was able to totally paralyse
His mind's desire-life.

1009.

God will not be there to receive
   you
If you hurriedly reach
Your life's finish line.
He will not only receive you
But also garland you and embrace
   you
If you slowly, steadily and
   soulfully reach
Your life's finish line.

1010.

What is wrong with you, my
   mind!
Why can't you accept any defeat?
What is wrong with you, my
   heart!
Why are you afraid of winning
Continuous victories?

1011.

If your heart is ready
To sparkle with eagerness,
Then God will definitely come
And stand right in front of you
With His Infinity's Fulness.

1012.

What is he doing?
He is sleeping with his rainbow-
   dream
Inside his silence-heart.
What else is he doing?
He is making the final revision
Of his surrender-life-script.

1013.

You may not realise it,
But God is carrying you,
And you are quite heavy.
Perhaps it is beyond your
   imagination,
But God has also developed
Very serious back pain
Because of your weight.
Can you not lighten His Load and
   cure Him
With your obedience-surrender-
   medicine?
Try, you can!
You have simply no idea
How proud God will be of you
If you do.

1014.

My heart has undertaken
A very difficult task.
It wants to guide
My mind's irregular search for
   God.

1015.

My mind struggles for
   satisfaction.
My heart struggles for perfection.
My soul struggles for my life's
God-preparation.

1016.

Do you want to hear
What you say during your sleep?
You say that you love God alone
And need God alone, nobody else.

1017.

Your heart feels that God
Does not speak to it
Because it is imperfect.
Your mind thinks that God
Does not speak to it
Because it has already reached
Perfection-height.

1018.

An infant-cry is the soulful lover
Of self-transcendence,
God-discovery
And God-satisfaction.

1019.

Do you know God
Or do you just know about Him?
If you know God,
Then I shall immediately become
   yours.
But if you just know about God,
Then even if the entire world
   claims you,
I shall never become yours.

1020.

Today you are a God-dreamer.
Tomorrow you will become
A Heaven-sprinter.
The day after tomorrow you will
   become
Your soul's wonder-speed
And your Lord's Victory-Smile.

1021.

Something to give to my Lord
   Supreme:
My soul's promise-delight.
Something to give to humanity:
My heart's aspiration-might.

1022.

My child, I wish to have
A friendly competition with you.
You will run against Me
With your life's ignorance-sky,
And I shall run against you
With My Heart's Compassion-
   Sun.

1023.

His absurdity-philosophy:
True happiness can be found
Only in sorrow.
His stupidity-philosophy:
Happiness is sorrow
In disguise.

1024.

Truth is neither easy nor difficult.
Truth is spontaneous, self-
   revealing
And God-revealing all at once.

1025.

No satisfaction shines
Where division is king.
No imperfection abides
Where oneness is emperor.

1026.

History's exclamation mark:
Man's moon-adventure.
History's question mark:
Man's dissatisfaction-hunger.

1027.

My Lord Supreme,
Do give me the capacity
To need Your Heart.
My Lord Supreme,
Do give me the privilege
To love Your Life.

1028.

Since time will not wait for me,
I also shall not wait for time.
I shall go ahead of time
With my soul's silence-stillness-
   smile.

1029.

My mind tells me
That my prayer-life
Is something strange
Yet quite familiar.
My heart tells me
That my meditation-life
Is always familiar
And never strange.

1030.

My sweet child,
Early each morning
Instead of asking Me
Whether I love you,
Just ask yourself
Whether you need Me.

1031.

O my body and vital,
Be not afraid of my mind's
   greatness.
O my mind,
Be not afraid of my heart's
   goodness.
O my heart,
Be not afraid of my soul's oneness.
O my soul,
You are never afraid of my Lord's
   Fulness.

1032.

When a true God-lover
Cannot decide what to do
In his outer life,
God, out of His infinite Bounty,
Takes it as His bounden Duty
To help that person choose
The right thing to do.

1033.

Something is wrong,
But I do not know what.
Perhaps my heart does not
Love God intensely any more.
Something is right,
But I do not know what.
Perhaps my mind has sincerely
Started longing for God at last.

1034.

Where is my home?
My home is inside
My world's possession-cry.
Where is my Lord's Home?
My Lord's Home is inside
His Eternity's
Acceptance-Satisfaction-Smile.

1035.

Your heart's climbing cry
Is like a rope,
Longer than the longest,
Extending from earth to Heaven.
Once you start climbing that rope
Cheerfully and powerfully,
Who can prevent you from
    reaching
The highest perfection-
    satisfaction-height?

1036.

Your Inner Pilot is telling you
That you will, without fail,
Make progress.
You fool!
Why are you consciously and
    deliberately
Trying to prove Him wrong?

1037.

Pride and insecurity
Come from only one source:
    impurity.
He who is bloated with pride
And he who is insecurity incarnate
Are both absolutely useless.

1038.

Purity has the capacity
To immediately destroy
Insecurity and pride.
Purity has the capacity
To immediately create
Oneness with God's
Transcendental Will.

1039.

Whoever experiences
His life's surrender-smiles
As a permanent reality
Is undoubtedly the choicest
    instrument
Of his Beloved Supreme.

1040.

If you are loyal to God
And take Him as your only Friend,
How can you have any serious
    problems?
Impossible!
Even your mind-problems
Will be taken care of
By His Heart's Compassion-
    Concern-Sky.

1041.

If your consciousness
Remains deep inside your heart
And you are constantly
Thinking of God,
Then all your problems will be
    solved,
Even if you simply ignore them.
Needless to say,
This applies only to you,
Since you are a soulfully sincere
    seeker.

1042.

Three signs of progress:
To do something better
Than you have previously done it,
To maintain your standard,
To have a cheerful heart
Even if your standard goes down.

1043.

For years you have neglected
Your teeming weaknesses.
But now that you want
To conquer them,
What you need
Is an ever-climbing heart-cry.

1044.

Aspiration-fire is immediate
    purification.
It powerfully purifies
The sleeping body,
The strangling vital
And the doubting mind.

1045.

In your life of service to humanity
Confidence is supremely good,
But do not develop
Disproportionate self-confidence,
Not to speak of pride and
    haughtiness.

1046.

If you think that you are
Most graciously helping others,
You are badly mistaken.
You should feel that you are
    offering
Your service-smile
To the Supreme in others.

1047.

If your service-life
Is only increasing your ego-power,
Then rest assured
You are a stark failure
In the inner world.

1048.

Someday you will realise
That your Master is
The direct representative
Of the Supreme.
Someday you will realise
Your Master's Eternity's oneness
With the Supreme.

1049.

He started with utmost sincerity
Trying to please the Supreme
In the Supreme's own divine Way.
Alas, now he is shamelessly
Begging the Supreme to please him
In his own human way.

1050.

Either please God
In His own Way
Or go back to your old life
Where your desire-fires
Reigned supreme.

1051.

If you feel that God's Way
Is not the only way,
And you have a totally different way,
Then why should anybody
Care to prevent you
From following your own way?

1052.

True, nobody is indispensable.
But if you can please the Supreme
In His own Way,
Then He will definitely need you
Infinitely more than He needs
Anybody else.

1053.

My Lord Supreme,
May I sleeplessly remember You.
I mean, Your Compassion-Eye.
My Lord Supreme,
May I sleeplessly remember
Your Compassion-Eye.
I mean, Your Forgiveness-Heart.
My Lord Supreme,
May I sleeplessly remember
Your Forgiveness-Heart.
I mean, Your Oneness-Life.

1054.

My dreamer-eye,
My listener-heart,
My observer-soul,
My Liberator-God,
I enjoy your festival
Of Eternity's Satisfaction-Sun.

1055.

Purify your sound-breath,
Illumine your sound-life.
You will immediately feel
Ecstasy's silence-embrace.

1056.

They call it
My hermit-heart.
I call it
My divinity's tapestry of truth.

1057.

To make me happy
My Lord Supreme
Has kidnapped my heart.
To make me perfect
My Lord Supreme
Has granted me the
   Transformation-Flute
Of His Compassion-Light.

1058.

O secret and sacred
Bird of my heart,
You have given me
Your indomitable inner strength
And freed me from
The bondage of fate.

1059.

My impatient heart
Has become an incurable patient
Suffering inside
My aggressive vital-hospital.

1060.

My sound-activity
Has pleased neither Heaven nor
   earth.
My silence-receptivity
Has at once pleased
Both Heaven's eye and earth's
   heart.

1061.

You are aspiring to grow.
Indeed, this is a happy experience.
You are searching for truth.
Indeed, this is a happier experience.
You are surrendering your earth-existence
To the life of delight.
Indeed, this is the happiest experience.

1062.

Because of your purity-heart
Every day God is granting you
His Himalayan Smile.
Because of your surrender-life
Every day God is granting you
Your victory's crown.

1063.

The heart's inner purity
Helps us blossom
Out of the animal kingdom.
The soul's God-embracing beauty
Helps us blossom
Out of the human kingdom.

1064.

Yesterday your mind enjoyed
The gales of dark disbelief.
Today your entire life
Has become the burial ground
Of your shipwrecked mind.

1065.

When your mind starts enjoying
Complete union with God,
Your life, without fail, will become
The absolute manifestation of God.

1066.

The human activities
Of the divine soul
Do not confuse me.
They only increase
My genuine admiration
For its compassion-flooded reality.

1067.

His heart cannot race
Towards the unfathomable beauty
Of the unknown
Because he has allowed his mind
To become nothing but
A dry intellect-field.

1068.

God will be proud of you
If you can tell yourself
That there is no such thing
As failure.
God will love you infinitely more
If you can accept any so-called
    failures
As experiences He Himself is
    having
In you and through you.

1069.

He is a rank fool!
He no longer wants
To please his Master
Because he thinks that others
Who are not pleasing the Master
Are still very close to him.

1070.

To make the fastest progress,
Be an absolutely cheerful
Hero-warrior
And take both victory and failure
As parallel experience-rivers
Leading to the sea
Of progress-delight.

1071.

Those who want to please the
    Supreme
In His own Way
Will have Heaven's fastest
Satisfaction-speed.
Those who do not want
To please the Supreme in His own
    Way
Will have earth's slower than the
    slowest
Frustration-destruction-speed.

1072.

Your Master's outer smile
May at times confuse you.
Your Master's inner smile
Will not only illumine you
But also manifest the divine in
    you.

1073.

If we are real seekers,
Sincere seekers, genuine seekers,
God will definitely grant us
What He eternally is:
Infinity's Love immortal.

1074.

Alas, you have developed
Disproportionate pride.
Now it is you and nobody else
Who can and must take every day,
Every hour and every second
As a God-granted opportunity
To conquer your abysmal pride.

1075.

Some unfortunate seekers
Who are with a spiritual Master
Of the highest height
May jump out of his boat
Only to sink and fail.
But the Master himself
Can never ultimately fail,
For his is a God-ordained mission.

1076.

Impurity divides.
Purity unites.
Because God is pure,
He is One:
He is His Heart's Oneness-Song
In His Life's Fulness-Dance.

1077.

If it is possible
To create pride inside your mind,
Impurity will do it.
Alas, it has already
Done the damage.
If it is possible
To create insecurity inside your
  heart,
Impurity will do it.
Alas, it has already
Done the damage.

1078.

O my hesitation-mind,
Do you know
That there is something
Called illumination-eye?
O my illumination-eye,
I am sure you know
That there is something
Called God's constant
  Satisfaction-Heart.

1079.

The seeker's purity-heart-road
Is destined to join
The Highway of the Supreme.
When the hour strikes,
Both meet together and become
  one.

1080.

O my mind's confusion-bound
   intellect,
You are imperfect, to say the least!
Alas, even after you have covered
A very long distance
In the wrong direction,
You are not aware of what you are
   doing
Or where you are.
When will you learn
That satisfaction-smile abides
Only in intuition-core?

1081.

An insecurity-heart cannot run,
Walk or even crawl.
What is worse,
It sees right in front of it
At every moment
A tangled jungle-mind.

1082.

A purity-heart can live
Only in a beauty-life.
A beauty-life can live
Only in a surrender-breath.
A surrender-breath can live
Only in God's
Fulness-Satisfaction-Heart.

1083.

My hope-bird soars
Every morning and evening
In my soul's moon-embraced
And sun-blessed sky.

1084.

Your mind usually lives
Inside the forest of wild desires.
Can you not ask it
To live inside the garden
Of your soulful aspiration
Only for a day,
Just for a brief change?

1085.

If your life swims every day
In the river of insincerity-tears,
How can you ever reach
And become one with
The smiling Waves
Of God's Divinity-Ocean?

1086.

God is happy with you
Not because you are perfect,
But because every day you allow
   Him
To water your heart-garden
With His Infinity's Compassion-
   Light.

1087.

Doubt-clouds appear only
In the mind-sky.
They never appear
In the heart-sky,
Which is flooded with
The rainbow-beauty-life
Of the inner sun.

1088.

My sweet Lord,
When You give me something,
Do give me the capacity
To divide it.
My sweet Lord,
When I give You something,
Do give me the capacity
To multiply it.

1089.

A genuine God-lover
Is he who can easily differentiate
Renunciation-enjoyment
From possession-greed.

1090.

Every day cultivate adamantine will
In the depths of your heart
So that with no difficulty you can bestride
All your problems in the mental world.

1091.

Hope and doubt
Are two absolutely worst foes.
From time immemorial
They have been fighting,
Sometimes one winning
And sometimes the other.

1092.

He who is pleasing God
In God's own Way
Will find all earthly and Heavenly
Experiences in his life agreeable.

1093.

If you love God alone,
Then certainly you can easily articulate
Your aspiration in the inner world
And your dedication in the outer world.

1094.

Peace of mind
Cannot be obtained overnight.
To achieve peace of mind
We have to invest many silence-
    years
In spirituality.

1095.

Life's perfection-road
Is very long,
But the journey is richly
    rewarding.

1096.

Life is not competition.
Life is preparation —
Preparation for Heaven's and
    earth's
Transcendental Victory.

1097.

Once upon a time you were
Your soul's rainbow-dream.
Now you are
Your heart's golden reality.
In the near or distant future
You will become
Your life's splendid divinity.

1098.

Dreams make progress
And become reality.
Reality makes progress
And becomes divinity.
Again, divinity makes progress
When it becomes reality,
And reality makes progress
When it becomes
The ever-transcending Dream.

1099.

Now that he has uprooted
His life's expectation-tree,
God has unconditionally granted
    him
His own Heart-Home.

1100.

Long before you can bind God's
    Hands
With your mind's doubt-chains,
God will bind your life
With His Heart's Love-Oneness-
    Chain.

1101.

My Beloved Supreme,
My life is at Your disposal.
Do mould me, shape me and
   guide me
In Your own Way.
Do give me
Sincerity's determination-capacity
To come to You — You alone.

1102.

He is searching for his mind.
Where is it?
His mind is buried beneath
A heap of fallen memories.
He is searching for his heart.
Where is it?
His heart is on the topmost branch
Of his aspiration-tree.

1103.

In the morning I pray to my Lord
   Supreme
To deafen me to the clamour
Of the outer-world music.
In the evening I pray to my Lord
   Supreme
To awaken me to the nectar-
   delight
Of the inner-world music.

1104.

Your Himalayan-high
   detachment-eye
Has fathomed the birthless
And deathless sorrows
Of countless human hearts.

1105.

When my mind has pure
   thoughts,
It gets a part-time job
In Heaven.
When my mind becomes a
   surrender-will,
It gets a full-time job,
Full of radiant future promises,
In Heaven.

1106.

God does not want to know from
   you
What you want.
He just wants to know from you
What you want to become
And what kind of help
You need from Him.

1107.

If you are working only to become
A great autocrat,
Then you will eventually find
  yourself
On a doubt-frustration-journey.
But if you are working to become
A choice instrument of God,
To serve Him in His own Way
At His choice Hour,
Then God will definitely allow
  you to enjoy
His Eternity's Self-
  Transcendence-Journey.

1108.

Your progress-life has made you
Your heart's shadowless face.
Your meditation-life has made
  you
Your God's birthless and deathless
  Heart.

1109.

Love the divine in yourself
Infinitely more
Than you have been doing,
So you will not have to imitate
The human in others.

1110.

Your heart's murmuring
  meditation-river
Will pass through your life's
  desert
Because your mind is now
  enjoying
The absence of desire.

1111.

If you can put your ignorance-
  criminal
To death,
You will easily be able to look
Into the Heart of God's
Self-Transcendence-Reality.

1112.

His heart is fond
Of three special things:
The beauty of the sky,
The purity of the moon
And the power of the sun.

1113.

The omnipotence within me
And my Lord's Silence-Smile
Are one and the same thing.

1114.

Your oneness-heart
Does not have to say anything,
For it at once embodies
Both earth's ascending aspiration-hope
And Heaven's descending
Compassion-promise.

1115.

I must forget my "I-ness"
So that I can remember my oneness.
My oneness must be multiplied every day
So that my Lord and I can together enjoy
Our supreme fulness.

1116.

O my mind's sound-light,
O my heart's silence-delight,
O my soul's satisfaction-height,
When can I consciously claim you
As my own, very own?

1117.

His life's difficulties
Have now become beautiful and delightful
Because his mind's inspiration-bird
And his heart's aspiration-bird
Are together soaring high,
Very high.

1118.

When he looks at the beauty
Of the morning sky,
He thinks and feels
That God the Dream
Suits him best.
When he looks at the power
Of the midday sun,
He thinks and feels
That God the Sound
Suits him best.
When he looks at the purity
Of the evening moon,
He thinks and feels
That God the Silence
Suits him best.

1119.

I prayed to my Lord Supreme
For power.
My Supreme Lord has given me
   Love
Instead of power.
His Love has not only made
My heart powerful
But also is making
My life perfect.

1120.

If you do not turn from your
   ignorance-life,
Then who will do it for you?
If you do not want to enjoy
Nectar-delight in boundless
   measure,
Then who will do it for you?

1121.

His vital is untouched
By temptation.
Therefore, his life is embraced
By God the Satisfaction.

1122.

If you allow your desire-greed
To lead you,
Then you will be compelled
To allow your destruction-sorrow
To follow you.

1123.

Just do one thing:
Let your Beloved Supreme
Take the initiative
In what you say and do.
Lo, He is banishing the ignorance-
   thief
From the garden of your life.

1124.

Your heart-temple
Is empty of worshippers.
Why are you not inviting
Your body, vital and mind
To come and worship God there?

1125.

You want to possess God.
Indeed, He is worth possessing.
But who can ever possess God,
Who is at once the eternal
   Possessor
And the eternal Possession?

1126.

A dangerous and poisonous
Ignorance-snake
Has bitten you mercilessly.
Therefore, it is impossible for you
To witness the rebirth of your life's
Sweetness-fruitfulness-beauty.

1127.

A machine-like obedience-
   freedom
Turns man into a robot.
A childlike freedom-obedience
Turns man into a god.

1128.

Your life has broken through
Your mind's ego-barrier.
Therefore, your heart is able to
   stand
On the perfection-peak
Of God's creation.

1129.

Name God the Compassion.
Claim God the Liberation.
Become God the transcendental
   Silence.

1130.

Enthusiasm-beauty
Is the dawn of a seeker's mind.
Enthusiasm-power
Is the noon of a seeker's heart.
Enthusiasm-peace
Is the night of a seeker's life.

1131.

You are good,
But you want to be better.
You can be better
Only by having a gratitude-heart.
You are better,
But you want to be best.
You can be best
Only by becoming a surrender-
   life.

1132.

You are beautiful
Only when you praise
God the Creation.
You are powerful
Only when you praise
God the Manifestation.
You are fruitful
Only when you praise
God the Liberation.

1133.

In my case
My freedom is not worth having
Unless I can love my Lord
   Supreme
Only in His own Way.

1134.

My Lord Supreme,
I have taught myself
How to love You only
Even when You do not love me
Or care for me at all.

1135.

What do I want?
I want my animal life
To claim God the Forgiveness.
What do I want?
I want my human life
To claim God the Compassion.
What do I want?
I want my divine life
To claim God the Satisfaction.

1136.

Self-awareness and self-giving
Are two supreme gifts.
These two gifts
Are always their own God-
   winning rewards.

1137.

At last I have succeeded
In taming my mind
To want God, only God.
At last I have succeeded
In training my heart
To live for God, only God.

1138.

He loves his inner life.
Therefore he is beautiful.
He rules his outer life.
Therefore he is fruitful.

1139.

If you can imagine your future,
You are great.
If you can build your future,
You are good.
If you can surrender your future
   to God
For Him to use in His own Way,
You are perfect.

1140.

He thought his God-realisation
Was an easy task.
Therefore it became easy.
He thought his God-manifestation
Was a difficult task.
Therefore it has become most difficult.

1141.

The animal life needs instruction
From its teacher.
The human life needs correction
From its tutor.
The divine life needs
Perfection and satisfaction
From its Lover: God.

1142.

You may think that your mind
Is the architect
Of your life's progress-plan,
But it is not true.
God's Compassion is the Architect
Not only of your life's progress-plan
But also of your life's progress-play.

1143.

A life of surrender
To your Master's compassion-divinity
Is absolutely the safest way
To establish your conscious
And sleepless oneness-reality
With God.

1144.

When you feel
Your love for your Lord Supreme
Inside His Heart,
You give up your old life,
Which was undivine in every way.
When you feel
The Love of Your Inner Pilot for you
Inside your own heart,
You see a new life dawning
On your heart's horizon.

1145.

I take each failure as an opportunity
To increase my surrender
And destroy my frustration-life.
I take each success as an opportunity
To bring forward my gratitude-heart
And totally destroy my ego-life.

1146.

Your clever, tricky mind
Is torturing you daily.
When you need rest,
It tells you that you are lethargic,
Empty of energy-light,
And when you do not need rest
It deliberately wants to make you
Harmful lethargy-pleasure
By telling you that you need more
   rest.

1147.

If you give to your Beloved
   Supreme
What you have and what you are,
A frustration-pool,
Then you can become
What He has and what He is:
The Satisfaction-Ocean.

1148.

My only friend:
The satisfaction of my desire-life.
God's only friend:
The perfection of my aspiration-
   cry.

1149.

The divine forces are always ready
To act in and through you.
It is up to you to accept them
In a divine way.
If you do not accept them,
There will be no difference
Between your heart's excruciating
   suffering
And the suffering of a desire-
   imprisoned
Unaspiring human being.

1150.

Do not expect
What is beyond your capacity to
   receive.
Do not expect
What is beyond your capacity to
   achieve.
Otherwise, there will be a serious
   crash
Between your expectation-car
And your reality-train.

1151.

If you allow your sincerity-game
To go on and on —
Again and again confessing,
And then repeating the same
   mistakes
Without any determination-fire
To burn your insincerity-
   existence-life —
Then your progress on your
God-realisation-journey
Will be slower than the slowest.

1152.

Surrender means oneness-beauty.
On the strength of your surrender
You will become
The Oneness-Fulness-Reality
Of your Lord Supreme.

1153.

There is one divine quality
That can lead us the fastest
To our ever-transcending Goal,
And that is our unconditional
   surrender
To the Omniscience-
   Omnipotence-Will
Of our Inner Pilot.

1154.

When I am able to surrender
What I have and what I am
To my Eternity's Beloved
   Supreme,
I become inseparably one
With His Infinity's Delight.

1155.

When you surrender to your Inner
   Pilot,
You increase and multiply the
   strength
Of your oneness-bliss,
And oneness-bliss itself expands
To become the vastness
Of the universe-fulfilling Bliss.

1156.

If tomorrow I become a better
   person,
I must offer that better life of mine
To God.
If the next day I again become
   worse,
I must cheerfully offer that life,
   too,
To God.
In this way each day
I can go one step forward
Towards my ultimate
Oneness-perfection-delight
With my Beloved Supreme.

1157.

One day you may be spiritually lame,
And the next day you are the fastest sprinter.
True surrender is to offer
Both your slowness and your speed,
Whatever you have and whatever you are,
To your life's Absolute Supreme,
And to nobody else.

1158.

Inwardly send your soul's goodwill
To everybody and to every place
In God's creation.
Your goodwill will definitely
Be echoed and re-echoed
Everywhere in every heart,
And be received —
Of course, according to
The world's receptivity.

1159.

My Lord, I do not know
And I do not want to know
What Your Will is.
For if I know Your Will,
My mind may create only
Confusion and rebellion
And make me feel
That I am not doing the right thing
By obeying You.

1160.

My Lord Supreme,
You do not have to tell me
What Your Will is
Or what Your Intentions are.
Only allow me to cheerfully
Pray to You
For the fulfilment
Of Your Absolute Will Supreme.

1161.

My mind always likes
To take different sides.
My heart always takes
Only Your side, My Lord.
One day I shall compel my mind
To act like my heart.
O my Beloved Supreme,
I feel in the depths of my heart
That that day is fast approaching.

1162.

Be careful!
If you allow your vital
To make your heart impure,
Then your poor heart-vessel,
Like your mind,
Will be filled with doubt-poison.

1163.

If you see your enemy coming,
You can close the doors and
   windows
Of your life
To keep him out.
But if your enemy
Is already comfortably settled
Inside your heart-room,
It is not an easy task
To grab him and throw him out.
Therefore be extremely careful
Of your enemy within.

1164.

My human mind tells me
That you are lethargic
Because I get up long before you.
My divine heart tells me
That you have worked very hard,
Therefore your chosen hour
Is the right time for you to get up.

1165.

Each time he made progress,
He declared his previous standard
"The height of lethargy"
Because he had far surpassed
That height.

1166.

Speed and dynamism go together.
If you can convince your mind
That you are running very fast,
Then no matter what your actual
   speed is,
The pure dynamism
Of your imagination-deer
Will definitely enter into you.

1167.

An idea has entered into your
   mind:
"I am very bad, impure,
   undivine!"
You must replace it immediately
With another idea:
"I am God's child,
So how can I be impure and
   undivine?
Totally absurd!"

1168.

How to conquer the undivine
   forces
Inside your heart-room?
Either use your strength from
   within
To forcefully push them out
Or bring down light from Above
To powerfully pull them out.

1169.

When hostile forces attack you,
Have nothing to do with them.
Create a world of indifference
Within and around you.
Their own pride will compel them
To leave you.

1170.

Yesterday
My Master's silver advice
To me was:
Love all in God.
Today
My Master's golden advice
To me is:
Serve all for God.
Tomorrow
My Master's diamond advice
To me will be:
Become one with all in God.

1171.

Your vital has walked along
Frustration-road for a long time.
Now it is completely exhausted.
Your mind has walked along
Suspicion-road for a long time.
Now it is totally exhausted.
Your heart has walked along
Illumination-road for a long time,
Yet there is no sign of its being
   exhausted.
Your soul has been walking along
Eternity's Liberation-Satisfaction-
   Road
From time immemorial,
Yet it will never become
   exhausted.

1172.

O skyward eyes
Of purity-flooded beauty,
I know, I know,
You will not be satisfied
Until you have reached
The Liberator's Liberation-Feet.

1173.

You are telling me that you have tried
The conventional approach to realise God.
Alas, your austerity-approach
And your sacrifice-approach
Have not liberated your earth-bound life.
Such being the case,
I am advising you to try
A long-lost conventional approach
Inside your heart.
Indeed, this is your life's
Surrender-flower-approach.

1174.

Because your life was raised
On God's Compassion,
Your mind does not have to live
On doubt-poison.

1175.

Life was perfect then
When I soulfully whispered:
"I am only for my Beloved Supreme."
Life is totally imperfect now,
For I have boldly declared:
"God is and has to be for me,
For I have far surpassed others."

1176.

When I pray to my Lord Supreme,
I say, "My Lord, do keep my heart
In Your Compassion-Net."
When I meditate on my Beloved Supreme,
I say, "My Lord, do make my heart
And my entire being
Your Compassion-Net."

1177.

The world thinks
That something is seriously wrong
With my mind
Because my mind has forgotten
How to think.
My Lord Supreme tells me
That my mind has become
The boundless joy of perfection-receptivity.

1178.

True, God does not ignore anybody.
Therefore He does not ignore
Small-minded human beings.
But it is also equally true
That He never intends to use them
To serve Him in any way.

1179.

When the doubting mind
Accuses the heart of insecurity,
The loving heart does not
Accuse the mind of impurity.
When the mind accuses the heart,
It immediately creates a blemish
On the heart's beauty.
When the heart does not accuse
 the mind,
It immediately creates a golden
 opportunity
For the mind's self-transcendence.

1180.

When you are extremely soulful,
God sees you as a beautiful rose.
When you are not at all aspiring,
What does God see?
Only a few thorns.
God highly appreciates the rose,
But how can He appreciate
 thorns?

1181.

Try to reach your highest height
In the twinkling of an eye.
Your highest height may not be
Your Lord's highest Height,
But the very fact that you can
Raise your consciousness quickly
Gives Him tremendous Joy
And immense Satisfaction.

1182.

In your meditation
If you are desperately trying
To reach the acme of perfection
But you are failing,
Do not give up.
As one who does the long jump
Rests in between each attempt,
Wait and try again.
Who knows, in your next attempt
You may do extremely well.

1183.

There are many who do not want
 to try
To succeed in the spiritual life.
But you must be a hero-warrior
Who will try again and again
Until success-satisfaction is won.

1184.

Always he had more important
 things to do
Than to pay attention
To his spiritual life.
Indeed, even from a little
 meditation
He feared a spiritual overdose.

1185.

You may do the worst possible meditation,
But as long as you sincerely try,
God will one day shower
His bountiful Blessings upon you,
And you will be able to meditate
Extremely well.
Just try, wait and see.

1186.

Each genuine truth-seeker
Needs only one thing:
A sleepless inner hunger
For infinite Peace,
Light and Bliss.

1187.

If you see that you are being attacked
By undivine thoughts,
Or if sleep has entered
Into your entire being,
Do not fool yourself into believing
That you are doing your best meditation.

1188.

You are, indeed, a fool
If you think you have passed
Your inner examination
According to your own standard
And that for you
Aspiration is no longer a necessity.

1189.

Your Inner Pilot is the only judge
Who can tell you whether or not
You have successfully passed
Your spiritual examination.
It is up to you to have faith
In His infallible Judgement.

1190.

On the strength of your sincere practice
There shall come a time
When any time or any place —
Even in the hustle and bustle of life —
You will be able to enter
Your highest meditation
At your express command.
Then you will be a true hero-warrior
Of your Beloved Supreme.

1191.

My Beloved Supreme tells me
That there is nothing
I will not do for Him
Eventually,
And that there is nothing
He will not do for me
Sleeplessly.

1192.

Just as the Supreme
Has made your Master
His supremely chosen
　　instrument,
Even so, at His choice Hour
The Supreme will make you
His supremely chosen
　　instrument.
Just be obedient, be patient,
Inwardly and outwardly.

1193.

Your Lord Supreme
Is not standing in front of you
With an iron rod
Ready to strike you
The moment you make any
　　mistakes.
Far from it!
Through your obedience-light
One day you will realise
His Oneness-Delight with you.

1194.

Poor God can count
On His Fingertips
Those very, very few
Who are implicitly obedient to
　　Him,
Both in their inner aspiration-
　　lives
And in their outer dedication-
　　lives.

1195.

Today if you can fulfil
Your Lord Supreme
Cheerfully, devotedly and
　　soulfully,
Then there shall definitely come a
　　time
When you will please Him
Unreservedly and
　　unconditionally.

1196.

Progress comes from obedience.
Obedience comes from faith.
If you have faith in God
And faith in yourself,
Then automatically you will
 develop
The power of obedience.
If you obey God,
Then at every moment
You will make progress
Far, far beyond
The flight of your imagination.

1197.

Think not of the ferocious tiger
That your ignorance-life now
 embodies,
But of the beautiful white lamb
Or the swift-moving deer
That your aspiration-life
Hopes to become.

1198.

I am a tiny drop
Inside an infinite ocean of light.
I have only to expand slowly and
 steadily
To become the ocean itself,
And then I shall unmistakably
Be able to claim the entire ocean
As my own, very own.

1199.

As long as my heart can soulfully
 cry
To realise God,
I shall not mind in the least
Even if God deliberately delays
His choice Hour.

1200.

O my Inner Pilot,
I have not done anything.
It is You who have done
 everything
In and through me.
Now may I become only one thing
For the rest of my life:
A gratitude-heart within and
 without.

1201.

My Lord Supreme,
Your Rainbow-Smile is the source
Of my heart's freedom-life
And my soul's satisfaction-breath
Here on earth,
There in Heaven.

1202.

My prayer longs to reach
God's Feet.
My meditation longs to see
God's Eye.
I long to breathe
God's Heart.

1203.

How can you have
Translucent morning dreams
When you carry the heavy weight
Of ignorance-night
Inside your unaspiring heart?

1204.

Yours is the happiness-heart
That significantly helps God
In steering His Eternity's
Vision-Boat.

1205.

Each time he soulfully meditates,
On the strength of
His self-transcendence-mind
He sees that his life-tree
Is ascending and expanding.

1206.

If you are an excellent truth-
    seeker,
Then your Master's compassion-
    splendour
Will radiate
In your aspiring dream-eye.

1207.

Look at this stupid seeker!
His aspiration is reduced
To skin and bones,
Yet he thinks that God
Is still pleased with his mind,
Still fond of his heart
And still proud of his life.

1208.

Faith is what my heart has.
Doubt is what my mind knows.
Life is what my Lord places
Inside my heart.
Death is what I place
At the feet of my Lord.

1209.

My Lord Supreme,
Sometimes I wonder
If Your Heart-Dictionary
Houses all the words.
"My child,
My Dictionary houses all the
    words
That your dictionary houses
Save and except 'indifference'
And 'uselessness'."

1210.

Finally imperfection
Has left his mind.
Finally frustration
Has left his vital.
Finally hesitation
Has left his heart.
And now gloriously begins
His Heavenward life-journey.

1211.

I have three names.
My first name is
Aspiration-cry.
My middle name is
Dedication-smile.
My last name is
God-Satisfaction.

1212.

If you want to be inside
God's Silence-Delight-Heart,
Then you must completely forget
Your power-hungry past.

1213.

If you feel you have nothing
To discard in your life,
Then you are sadly mistaken.
You can at least discard
Your useless complaints
And deathless grievances.

1214.

My heart's pressing necessity
Is to shun the spiritual Masters
Who deliberately offer
Counterfeit realisations
To the world at large.

1215.

Previously he was his heart's
Silence-trance.
Now he is his life's
Transcendence-joy.
Soon he will be his God's
Perfection-Satisfaction-Song.

1216.

When silence sails his mind-boat,
God immediately sails
His Golden Boat ahead of him
And leads him to the Golden
   Shore.

1217.

Always treasure a powerful will
In the depths of your heart
So that you can avert
All ignorance-adventures on
   earth.

1218.

True, I have changed many things
In my life,
But I will not be completely
   satisfied
Unless and until I have fully
   transformed
The face of my heart.

1219.

To fathom the depths
Of my Lord's Compassion-Roots,
I must first become
A childlike surrender-blossom.

1220.

Cancel two things in your life
And you will be extremely happy.
Cancel your success-delaying
   ideas
And your progress-starving ideals.

1221.

His soul has made a solemn
   promise
To him
That it will not leave the body
Until all his divine dreams are
   fulfilled
Here on earth.

1222.

What you are is nothing
But an immense tide of desire.
Therefore, even your heart's silver
   dreams
Have become dull and tarnished.

1223.

Who will believe in time to come
That you seized a mountain-high
   greatness
Without earning it in the least?

1224.

God will grant you another chance
To rewrite your dull life-story
If you do not allow
Your body, vital and mind
To become immersed in
   attachment-wave.

1225.

I am now convinced
That two things will never leave
   me:
My heart's expectation-smile
And my life's frustration-cry.

1226.

When I suffer badly
From my mind's forgetfulness-
   disease,
My Lord Supreme appears before
   me
With His Compassion-flooded
Love-Medicine.

1227.

Unexpected troubles are knocking
At your door
Because you are surrendering
To your ceaseless desire-hunger-
   life.

1228.

Wherever he goes,
He creates a new Heaven.
Wherever he stays,
He destroys the dark despair of
   hell.

1229.

O superior human beings,
If you wear the shoes of contempt,
Do you know that your hours
Of deplorable folly
Will never meet with the Hour
Of God's infinite Wisdom-
   Delight?

1230.

No time for sorrow!
I shall become my heart's soul-
   bird.
I shall soar high, very high,
And drink deep the Fountain-
   Love
Of my Beloved Supreme.

1231.

At last he has defeated his ego
Mercilessly.
Now he loves and knows
Only one thing:
Oneness-song.

1232.

You are such a fool!
Why are you trying
To remember the pain
Of your lost illusion-mind?

1233.

If you do not have oneness-
   realisation,
Who knows what will happen to
   you?
You may be imprisoned
By world-jealousy and world-
   insecurity.

1234.

Definitely God has use for you.
At His choice Hour
He will reveal your inner
   capacities.
Be not afraid of Him!
He is not going to expose
Your past naked ignorance-
   breath.

1235.

The oneness-cry of my soul-bird
Is the only thing
That I shall love infinitely more
Than anything else.

1236.

"The perfection-satisfaction-
   smile
Of Heaven
Is just one step ahead."
This is what my obedience-mind
And my surrender-life
Are cheerfully telling me.

1237.

Yesterday I called it
A moment of self-indulgence.
But today I am calling that very
   thing
A year of destruction-death.

1238.

If you are a truly sincere soul,
Then God blessingfully does
Two things for you:
Secretly He buries
Your old ignorance-life.
Openly He hurries to you
And extols your new wisdom-
   flooded life.

1239.

Alas, he is extremely unhappy
Because he has
A mind that is too quick
To think wisely
And a heart that is too slow
To choose wisely.

1240.

Every day you walk along
The avenue of doubt.
At each step you have
Only one friend:
Frustration-dust.

1241.

My mind thinks
That it is really great.
My heart feels
That it can be really great
If so is the Will of God.
My soul knows
Only one thing:
My Inner Pilot is everything.

1242.

He bowed his head
To the humility-dust
Only to be pierced by the arrow
Of God's ever-increasing
And ever-transcending
 translucent Joy.

1243.

My Lord Supreme,
You are telling me
That I am another God,
Like Yourself.
Would You kindly cut another
 joke?
"My sweet child,
Another joke:
I wish to be a perfect student of
 yours,
Since you feel you have been
 failing
All along
To become a perfect student of
 Mine."

1244.

What has God's Compassion-Eye
Done for me?
God's Compassion-Eye has given
My body, vital, mind, heart and
 soul
Countless chances to prepare
 themselves
For a perfection-satisfaction-
 dance with Him.

1245.

My Supreme Lord,
What shall I do?
Do You want me to complain
Against the world,
Or should I explain to You
Why I am in
Such a deplorable situation?
"My sweet child,
I need no complaints from you.
I need no explanations from you.
I want you only to maintain your
　　soul's
Adamantine will-power-fire
To burn the ignorance-tree
That you see before you
And the ignorance-tree
That is inside you."

1246.

Each day dawns
With a Compassion-Smile
From my Beloved Supreme.
Yet my journey's goal
Is still a far cry.

1247.

Are you trying to teach me
　　something
Or are you trying to learn
　　something
From me?
If you are trying to teach me
　　something,
Then instead of teaching me,
I would like you to teach
My unruly, disobedient mind.
If you are trying to learn
　　something
From me,
Then instead of learning from me,
I would like you to learn every day
A purity-song from my heart.

1248.

My Lord Supreme laughed at me
For an hour
When He heard that I felt I have
Something exceptionally new to
　　offer
To the world at large.
My Lord Supreme cried for me
For an hour
When He heard that I have
　　declared
My life to be a total failure.

1249.

Alas, you are not schooled enough
To see purity
Inside earth's heart-garden.
Alas, you are not schooled enough
To see the Compassion-flooded
   Eye of God
Inside your soul's God-Hour.

1250.

Every day enlarge
Your aspiration-heart-room.
To your wide surprise,
You will see that one day
God Himself will come and remove
Your darkness-desire-corpse.

1251.

By no means does self-
   transcendence
Mean an impossible task,
And possibility can and must
   reach
Self-transcendence-shore.

1252.

You want to receive from God
His Satisfaction-Crown
In spite of the fact
That you have the appetite
Of a tiny bird
For your progress-life.

1253.

God does not need
Many things from me
To satisfy Him.
He needs only one thing –
Surrender –
And that, too, He does not need
In large quantity.
Even a morsel of my surrender-life
Can satisfy Him.

1254.

My Lord Supreme,
You have corrected my mind
With Your Concern.
You have perfected my heart
With Your Compassion.
You have fulfilled my life
With Your Forgiveness.

1255.

Try to establish
A conscious friendship with your
   soul.
Then you will see
That you are never too old
To transform your earth-bound
   life
Into a Heaven-free life.

1256.

Every day his Inner Pilot
Takes the pulse
Of his aspiration-heart
And grants him
A powerful Satisfaction-Smile.

1257.

You can never be a loser,
You can only be a winner
Every time
If you race
On a sincerity-progress-track.

1258.

For a long time
God the Justice has been giving
   me
His own Telescope
To see the Beyond.
Now God the Compassion has
   given me
His brand new Telescope
To see the Beyond
And has said to me
That I don't have to return it
But can keep it for my own use.

1259.

A silver dream-tree:
This is what my mind has.
A golden reality-fruit:
This is what my heart is.

1260.

Long ago we said farewell
To truth's inner instructions.
But now we have become hunters
Of that lost divinity-world.

1261.

Do not interrogate
Divinity's poise within you,
For inside it
What always looms large
Is God's Perfection-Choice.

1262.

If your mind is always tainted
With self-interest,
How can you ever have
A drop of divinity's oneness-
   delight?

1263.

A long chain of responsibility:
This is what the human life is.
A sleepless embrace of
   Immortality:
This is what the divine life is.

1264.

Disobedience means death.
How can you drink
The sunbeams from the Beyond
When disobedience reigns
   supreme
In both your inner life and outer
   life?

1265.

A doubting mind is nothing other
   than
An age-old corruption in man.
A trembling heart is nothing
   other than
An age-old frustration of God.

1266.

Because your inner heart is
Purity's self-revealing smile,
Your outer life is
Beauty's God-satisfying victory.

1267.

God usually does not interfere
In anybody's life.
But in my case He did interfere
When I felt absolutely sure
That I would never be able to
   become
A choice instrument of His.

1268.

No wrong can touch his life
Because every day his heart
Climbs up the ladder
That leads to Heaven's justice-
   delight.

1269.

Desires to which we did not yield
Have now become our illumined
   friends
And live in the dream-delight-
   river
Of our perfection-oneness.

1270.

Every day without fail
A sincere seeker-heart
Must have a new, strong
And stout bodyguard
To protect him from
Temptation's destruction-dance.

1271.

His mind-clock tells him
That he does not have to waste
His precious time
Waiting for God,
Since God's existence is quite
   uncertain.
His heart-clock tells him
To wait and watch,
For God will definitely come.
His soul-clock tells him
That God has already arrived
And asks him what he is doing
And why he is not taking care
Of the Supreme Guest.

1272.

Every day he makes teeming
   mistakes,
And every day God corrects his
   mistakes.
He deeply appreciates God's
   corrections.
Such being the case,
God wants to paint
A beautiful heart-portrait of him.

1273.

Do not allow your heart
To be afraid
Of earth's excruciating pangs.
Do not allow your mind
To be afraid
Of Heaven's stark indifference.
Go slowly and steadily.
Your aspiration-dedication-train
Will unmistakably reach
The goal of the Beyond.

1274.

You want to know
What God's Compassion-Breath
Is doing for me.
I want to tell you
That His Compassion-Breath
Is every day, every hour saving me
From my spiritual death.

1275.

God wants you to do Him a favour
Before He does you a favour.
He wants you to keep
Your heart-door open
For a few fleeting minutes,
And then, what He will do,
You know:
For hours and hours
He will walk on your life's shore.

1276.

From time immemorial
God has been doing
Your inner heart-house cleaning.
If you are pleased with Him,
How is it that you are not asking Him
To do your outer mind-house cleaning?
I assure you,
He will gladly do it.

1277.

My Lord is promising me
That He will gladly correct and transform
My past life-story
If I will be more careful in writing
My present life-story.

1278.

My inner life
Is beauty's progress-goal.
My outer life
Is insecurity's monotony-role.
Alas, how can I perfectly synthesise
These two lives of mine?

1279.

Every morning before I do anything
My Beloved Supreme gives my heart
A Compassion-Ride.
Every evening before I do anything
My Lord Supreme carries my mind
In His Forgiveness-Plane.

1280.

Every day your mind-thief
Leaves its fingerprints
On your life,
And you don't mind!
So tell me,
How can God grant you
His Heart-Room to live in?

1281.

God's Compassion-Heart-Apartment
Is for rent.
But He will allow you to rent it
Only if you can show Him every day
A new hunger inside your heart.

1282.

What is the matter with you?
Do you not see that every day
Your life's ignorance-cancer
Is spreading?
When are you going to ask God
To extinguish your life's
Burning passion-fires?

1283.

One encouragement-word
From the Lips of my Inner Pilot
Led me to become a hero-warrior.
Now another encouragement-
   word
From His Lips
Is leading me towards
His own Self-Transcendence-
   Height.

1284.

As if an impure mind is not
   enough,
Now he is suffering from
An impure breath.
Alas, how can his heart-flower
Ever blossom?

1285.

At long last my Lord Supreme
Has granted me a high
   promotion.
From now on
I do not have to fight
With my worst enemy, doubt,
More than five minutes a day,
Whereas in the past
I had to fight with brooding doubt
At least five hours a day.

1286.

There are five tollbooths
On the highway to Heaven.
The first one is
Surrender-plant-tollbooth.
The second one is
Gratitude-tree-tollbooth.
The third one is
Perfection-flower-tollbooth.
The fourth one is
Satisfaction-fruit-tollbooth.
The fifth one is
God's Oneness-Embrace-
   Tollbooth.

1287.

My soul's powerful smile
Touched my body's ignorance-smile
Only once.
Now my body is fully awakened,
Fully ready to accept
The Invitation from God.

1288.

God's Mind does not have
Undecided Time.
God's Heart does not have
Ungiven Love.
God's Life does not have
Unfulfilled Delight.

1289.

God does not demand
Any previous experience
From a cheerfully and sleeplessly
Surrendered seeker
To give him a high position
In His Heart-Palace.

1290.

O my insecurity-life,
I have a piece of advice for you.
Please, please allow only God,
And nobody else,
To have a free access to you.

1291.

I have asked my mind
To take care of me,
But my mind does not want
To take care of me
Because I am so stupid.
I have asked my heart
To take care of me,
But my heart does not want
To take care of me
Because I am so impure.
Finally, I have asked my Lord Supreme
To take care of me.
My Lord Supreme says,
"My child,
I shall definitely take care of you
Because your entire life
Is so sincere."

1292.

My Beloved Supreme
Has always wanted me
To have a tight security
From morn to dusk
And from dusk to morn
Around my heart-door.
Alas, what prevents me from accepting
His unconditional offer?

1293.

If you want to play with God
On His See-Saw,
Then you need three things
Before He will invite you
To play with Him:
A mind empty of criticism,
A heart empty of fear,
A life that is neither
Afraid of the world's criticism
Nor afraid of Heaven's
   indifference.

1294.

His stupidity has reached
Its highest height,
For he feels that his time on earth
Is more precious and valuable
Than even God's.

1295.

I came down from Heaven
To love your heart,
O earth.
Do you not know it?
I shall be taking
Our oneness-satisfaction
Back with me to Heaven,
O earth.
Do you never feel it?

1296.

Yesterday he gave up
The spiritual life totally.
He promised himself
That he would never think of God,
Or speak about God,
Or even look at God
If God appeared before him.
Today he hears from everyone
That God has made him
His choice instrument
To shatter the doubts
Of all human beings.
Now he says to himself,
"Alas, good news has come
At such a wrong time!"

1297.

The other day somebody asked me
If I could say a few nice things
About Krishna and Buddha.
I said, "Of course, of course.
They are my Eternity's friends.
Every day I see them.
Early in the morning every day
When I go from earth to Heaven,
Buddha places his wisdom-peace-bridge
Before me
For me to go up to Heaven.
Every evening
When I return from Heaven to earth,
Krishna places his love-delight-bridge
Before me
For me to come down to earth."

1298.

My Lord,
Quite often I speak ill of You;
Quite often I find fault with You.
I am sure these are
My unforgivable sins.
"My child,
They are not unforgivable;
They are easily forgivable.
But unfortunately you have committed
An unforgivable sin,
And that sin is
That you have totally given up
The idea of realising Me."

1299.

My Lord Supreme,
Please tell me why You have
An unlisted number.
"My child,
It is a top secret,
But anyhow I am telling you.
Both Heaven and earth bother me
Like anything.
I am totally sick of them.
Every day Heaven has to invite me
To participate in its birth anniversaries,
And every day earth has to invite me
To participate in its death anniversaries.
I am totally sick of them,
And therefore I don't allow them
To call me whenever they want to.
Whenever I want to call them
And bless them and illumine them,
I do call.
This is the only reason
Why I have an unlisted number."

1300.

If you want your heart
To walk along silence-road
To reach Infinity's peace-abode,
Then you must have
An excellent guide.
Needless to say,
Your own soul is by far
The best guide.

1301.

Every morning and evening
I am determined to sing and dance
On the highest peak
Of my sun-flooded aspiration-
   mountain.

1302.

If you are serious
In your surrender-life,
Then the precious panorama
Of perfection
Cannot remain a far cry.

1303.

My Lord,
How can I satisfy You
All the time?
"My child,
Just ask your mind
To walk forward
Slowly and steadily.
Just ask your heart
To dive inward
Speedily and unreservedly.
That is all.
This is the only way
You can please Me all the time."

1304.

I do not think of my mind.
I do not even allow my mind
To think of anything.
I just think of my Lord Supreme.
And what does He do?
He smilingly and lovingly
Takes care of me.

1305.

My Lord Supreme,
My love is love
Only in You.
Even my human love
Is immediately transformed
Into divine love.
And my human love
Is all for You.

1306.

Yesterday
You descended in your inner
    running.
But today
Again you are climbing up
Once more to give immense joy
To your Lord Supreme
And bring Him divine glory.
Therefore
Your Lord Supreme is extremely
    proud
Of your heart
And divinely grateful
To your soul.

1307.

When hope and he parted
    company,
He completely lost
His forward thinking mind
And his upward seeking heart
In life.

1308.

In my case,
Failure comes quite
    spontaneously
Before my success.
Therefore, when failure comes
    first,
I never pay any attention to it.

1309.

Realisation-fruit entirely depends
On our expectation-flowers.
Expectation-flowers entirely
    depend
On our patience-trees.

1310.

All your Lord's
Life-illumining Requests
Are written in letters of gold
On the golden tablet of your heart.
There He sees
Whether or not
You are truly obeying Him
And pleasing Him.

1311.

Unlit humanity
Thinks only of what it had,
Its past glories.
It does not think
Of today's aspiration-cry
And tomorrow's dedication-smile.
It is completely bound
To yesterday's stagnation-life-
    pool.

1312.

You may feel
That you are a hopeless seeker.
But you will be saved
By the sincere pangs of remorse
That torture your heart
The very moment
You do anything wrong.

1313.

Inwardly and outwardly
Our Beloved Supreme has proved
That He is right.
But you are deliberately,
Consciously, stupidly and
   unpardonably
Trying to prove
That our Beloved Supreme is
   wrong.

1314.

God will definitely prove His
   Worth
Before long.
You just ask your wiseacre mind
To accept God on a trial basis!

1315.

It takes only a fleeting moment
To faithfully remind yourself
   every day
Of your inner resolutions,
Which are nothing other than
Your soulful promises
To your Beloved Supreme.
And these promises
Are not only for today,
But for as long
As your aspiration remains
   unfulfilled.

1316.

If your Lord Supreme scolds you,
Your divine attitude will
   immediately say:
"I failed,
But please let me try again!
Please give me another chance
To please You,
To please You in Your own Way!"

1317.

If you send your heart-letter to
   God
With insufficient faith-postage,
How do you expect it
To reach God's Home?

1318.

His is the Inspiration-Light
That will help
The hearts of sincere seekers
No matter in whose boat
They are sailing
Towards the destined Goal.

1319.

Whoever can
Soulfully and powerfully
Smile the oneness-smile
Before the game,
During the game
And after the game
Is undoubtedly the real winner.

1320.

You want your Beloved Supreme
To write to you,
But how can His Letter reach you
When you have not given Him
Your proper address:
Your heart's
Love-devotion-surrender-home?

1321.

He perfectly knows
That each cent he gives
Gladly, cheerfully, soulfully,
Unreservedly and unconditionally
To mankind
Is his love-offering
To his Lord Supreme.

1322.

My Lord Supreme,
Your unconditional Grace
Has given me the Himalayan
   height
In the inner world.
Now can Your Grace not give me
The larger-than-the-largest heart
In the outer world?

1323.

My mind invited me
To come and stay a few days
In its guest house.
Alas, I accepted its invitation
Only to meet with utter
   frustration.
My frustration embarrassed my
   mind
And awakened it from ignorance-
   sleep.

1324.

God is an eternal Child
Playing with His friends
In the world-garden.
He has established His Oneness
With His creation
To such an extent
That He does not mind
If all His children
Are playing different games.
In fact, He enjoys it most
When His children play
The game of multiplicity
Inside the heart-home of unity.

1325.

Why did God aspire?
He aspired to transform His
   Vision
Into His Reality.
He was successful.
He aspired to transform His
   Revelation
Into His Manifestation.
He was again successful.

1326.

God can help you only twice:
Once when your heart's cry
Is sincere,
And once when your mind's smile
Is sincere.

1327.

God's Justice-Bank
May one day go bankrupt,
But His Compassion-Forgiveness-
   Bank
Will never go bankrupt.
This is the joint realisation
Of Heaven and earth.

1328.

God was with His creation
When it started,
He is with it now,
And throughout His endless
   Future
He will always remain –
Whether wanted or not –
A permanent Member of His
   creation.

1329.

Who makes progress?
A child.
He has hope, he has promise.
He looks forward and upward.
God is the eternal Child
Because His Vision is constantly
Transcending Itself.
God with His Vision is constantly
Moving forward, flying upward,
Diving inward.

1330.

You can underestimate
The capacity of any human being
On earth.
But don't ever underestimate
The aspiration of a God-seeker
And the dedication of a God-lover.

1331.

Countless people are wallowing
In the pleasures of ignorance,
And they are satisfied in their own
   way.
To them, ignorance itself
Is a kind of bliss.
But their happiness
Is no happiness at all
To the truth-seekers
Who are thinking of God calmly,
Praying to God soulfully
And meditating on God
   unconditionally.

1332.

Before you were aspiring,
You were happy with the world.
But you have to know
That that happiness
Is not the same happiness
You are now longing for.
That happiness
Was your temptation-fulness-
   happiness.
This happiness
Is the manifestation of God-
   Satisfaction
In and through you.

1333.

You say that
You can dare to deny God.
But, you fool,
Do you ever dare to imagine
That God can easily dare
To love you,
Illumine you and liberate you
From your self-styled clown act?

1334.

A true seeker has to remain
Always an eternal student.
It is through him
That the Beauty of God's Vision-
   Reality
Will be manifested and fulfilled.

1335.

An unaspiring man is so useless.
He does not want any higher
   wisdom,
Although there is so much to
   know,
So much to learn
And so much to become.
He wants to change the face and
   fate
Of the world
Before he even dreams
Of changing his own.

1336.

Why do I not want to see You, my
   Lord?
Is it because I shall disappoint You
Or is it because You will
   disappoint me?
"My child,
If your heart is not sincerely
   aspiring,
You will disappoint Me,
And if your mind is doubtful,
I shall disappoint you."

1337.

You can show your sweetest
   kindness
Even to those
Who are vehemently standing
In your way.
But under no circumstances
Must you surrender to their way.

1338.

When God saw His detachment-
   child,
He was so pleased
That He immediately granted His
   child
A long interview—
His first marathon interview with
   God.

1339.

You will always remain
   inexperienced
In the art of self-transcendence
If you allow the blinding fog of
   uncertainty
To invade your mind and heart.

1340.

You went to God
Only to pay a courtesy call,
To see Him as briefly as possible.
How then can you expect God
To treasure and cherish you?

1341.

O my doubting, earth-bound mind,
You may not feel it
But my aspiring heart
Definitely gets joy
From my Master's very presence.
It feels that his mere presence
Feeds my soul.

1342.

Because you are not sincere
And because you have forgotten
To write your return address,
God did not take the trouble
Of answering your prayer-letter.

1343.

There is no reason
Why we cannot hope
That one day our hope
Will be transformed into reality.
We will, without fail, be able
To see God's Vision-Eye,
Feel His Reality-Heart
And manifest His Oneness-Perfection
On earth.

1344.

Why are you resting indefinitely
On the bottom rung
Of the wisdom-ladder?
Do you not know that others
Have already started climbing
Up the ladder?
And even now they are seeing
That there are infinitely more rungs
To climb.

1345.

How do I dare
To measure up to God's Height?
I do so
Just by quenching every day
My hope-thirst.

1346.

"The race is to the swiftest."
This is one theory.
Again, in the inner world
The race can be to the one
Who has the utmost patience.

1347.

East and West
Are two wings of one blue-green
   bird.
This bird needs
Both the poise of the East
And the dynamism of the West
To fly in the firmament of the
   Beyond
And spread God's Light and
   Delight.

1348.

O my mind,
Keep silent for a few minutes!
Please let me do the talking!
O my heart,
When will you start talking
So that I can immediately
Start listening to you?

1349.

His life was to serve
The Supreme in his Master.
Every time
His Master needed something
To be done
For the divine manifestation,
He offered his services
   unreservedly
To his Master.

1350.

In every possible way
She is displeasing God.
But she is apt in making herself
   feel
That she is indeed
Pleasing Him.
What a deplorable seeker!

1351.

Play your role soulfully.
You will reach your goal
Unmistakably.
Something more:
God will beat your victory-drum
Thunderously.

1352.

My mind has disappointed me.
Therefore
I want to desert my mind.
My heart has pleased me.
Therefore
I want to treasure my heart.
My soul has embraced me.
Therefore
I want to manifest my soul's dream.
My Lord has blessed me.
Therefore
My entire earth-existence
Is all gratitude to Him.

1353.

If you are a true seeker,
You will feel that to be
With your Master,
Near your Master,
Beside your Master,
Is undoubtedly a true form
Of meditation.

1354.

We have only one goal
And that goal
Is transcendence-perfection.
It is not only your goal,
His goal and my goal,
But it is everybody's goal —
Including that of our Eternity's
Beloved Pilot Supreme.

1355.

You yourself must first become
Infinitely more spiritual,
Infinitely more self-giving
And infinitely more perfect
In your own way.
Then only you will get
The inner assurance
That you will be able to change
The world around you.

1356.

You are enjoying your rash whims.
God is enjoying His prolonged absence.
Only one member of your inner family
Is suffering sleeplessly:
Your poor little heart.

1357.

My Lord Supreme,
I am not listening to You,
He is not listening to You —
Nobody is listening to You.
Are You not by this time
Totally sick of Your creation?
"My child,
I am a perfect stranger to sickness.
But if you want to teach Me
How to fall sick,
Then do come and teach Me.
I am all ready."

1358.

My Lord Supreme,
I have displeased You.
How can I please You again?
"My child,
This question has been asked
By each and every seeker.
Again,
Each and every seeker
Has answered it.
Just try once more.
This time give Me
Your Eternity's surrender-life."

1359.

Even one single day
If I forget
To feed my heart's faith-flames,
Doubt-clouds not only appear
But also dance
On my mind's horizon.

1360.

Why do you exaggerate your
   mistakes?
I assure you,
Your offences are not as serious
Or as dangerous as you think.
Do not allow your stupidity-mind
To powerfully increase
Your baseless negative feelings
About yourself.

1361.

He is such a fool!
He thinks that he is
Either very good or very bad.
He finds it difficult to see
That his status is really
Somewhere in between.

1362.

That you remain in the spiritual
   life
Is undoubtedly a sign
Of your spiritual progress.
True, your life
Is nowhere near perfection-light.
But just because you have been
A truth-seeker and a God-lover
For such a long time,
You are definitely progressing—
Of course,
Maybe not to your satisfaction.

1363.

Step by step
Each genuine seeker
Is going forward.
If he is bad,
He will unmistakably become
   good.
And if he is already good,
He will become better
And then best.
For God will not allow
His Vision-Light to remain
Unmanifested through him.

1364.

If we have the capacity
To make mistakes,
Then our Beloved Supreme also
Has the capacity to forgive us.
He is in no way
Weaker than we are.
His Forgiveness-Light
Is infinitely stronger
Than our mistake-night.

1365.

I have some good news for you.
This news will save your life.
You are dying
Because you have got
What you wanted.
From now on, be wise!
Try to claim only
God's Aspiration-Sun
As your own.

1366.

You have committed so many
   blunders
That you now feel
You can no longer become perfect.
But that is absurd, absurd!
Your Beloved Supreme
Will never be satisfied
Unless and until you become
   perfect
To prove to Him that His Vision of
   you
Was absolutely perfect.

1367.

Life is God's Game
And He has invited you
To play with Him.
Right now you are not
Scoring properly,
But do not worry.
Again and again
God Himself will teach you
How to score successfully.

1368.

If you really want to think,
Then you must think
With a new inspiration.
If you really want to sing,
Then you must sing
With a new aspiration.
If you really want to dance,
Then you must dance
With a new liberation.

1369.

His twentieth-century realisation
Far, far surpasses
His realisation of the hoary past.
The human in him
Laughs and laughs
At his previous realisation-
    heights,
While the divine in him
Reveals a compassion-flooded
    Eye.

1370.

Who says he is
A hopeless and useless seeker?
He definitely has at least
One good quality.
Otherwise he would not be able
To follow any spiritual path.
Indeed it is his
Superb perseverance-quality
That keeps him alive
In the spiritual life.

1371.

Now that his life is estranged
From his Inner Pilot,
His heart is no longer fluent
In the soul's language.

1372.

When you read the ancient
    scriptures,
It is like appreciating
The beauty and the power
Of the ocean and the sky
At a great distance.
But if a spiritual Master
Comes to you
As the ocean and the sky,
It is your sole task
To fly into the sky
And dive into the ocean.

1373.

My sweet children,
You come to Me
Not only to receive from Me
What I have: Infinity's Love,
But also to give to Me
What you have:
Your nectar-surrender-tears.

1374.

Somewhere in the world
A supremely pure heart exists.
It definitely does.
It exists to please God
In God's own Way.
Right now we may not have
The same kind of pure heart,
But let us sincerely and sleeplessly
Strive for it.
We shall, without fail, succeed.

1375.

The outer dynamism of the
    Western soul
Is the Alpine message
That the East should treasure
At every moment.
The inner poise of the Eastern soul
Is the Himalayan message
That the West should treasure
At every moment.

1376.

Truth he does not dare to know.
Love he does not dare to feel.
Yet satisfaction is the only thing
That his mind wants to know
And his heart wants to feel.

1377.

To say
That he has studied the scriptures
Thoroughly
Is an understatement.
He has not only read them
Devotedly and soulfully
But also sleeplessly lives
In their Existence-Consciousness-
    Bliss.

1378.

Why do you need an outer career?
Only become a more dedicated
    instrument
Of your Beloved Pilot Supreme.
You will find
That your true inner career
Is the only career
That you actually wanted and
    needed
To satisfy yourself — the real in
    you —
Permanently.

1379.

Because you did not curb
Your desire-appetite,
God is sad.
Because you have betrayed God
Time and again,
God's Compassion-Eye
Looks miserable.

1380.

Realisation is everything.
Aspiration itself
Is a beautiful form of realisation.
Vision itself
Is a soulful form of realisation.
Revelation itself
Is a powerful form of realisation.
Manifestation itself
Is a fruitful form of realisation.

1381.

God the Eternal
Is birthless and deathless.
For Him there is no time limit.
The past, present and future
Are within His grasp.
He is eternally young
And supremely old.

1382.

In this world
There are some stupid people.
Again, there are some wise people.
Those who consciously wish to stay
Always with their Lord Supreme
And always are for Him alone
Are undoubtedly the wisest human souls.

1383.

God is playing all the time
Inside your heart-garden.
If you want to be His playmate,
You will definitely be His chosen child.
And what He will do, you know:
He will shape you and mould you
Into His very Image.

1384.

My Lord Supreme,
I am longing for infinite Peace,
Infinite Light and infinite Bliss.
I am longing to become
Your faithful, devoted
And conscious instrument.
Only if I can become
Your supremely chosen instrument
Will I be really happy.
For me, I assure You,
There is no other happiness.

1385.

My Lord Supreme
Is not on speaking terms
With me
Because my mind
Does not think of Him
Frequently
And my heart
Does not pray to Him
Fervently.

1386.

Just open your eyes
And see what has happened:
Your sorrowful sea of the past
Has completely surrendered
To your smiling sun of the
   present.
Did you ever think
That it was going to happen?

1387.

If you can cry like a child
For just five minutes,
You will win the Supreme's
   Forgiveness.
But let me tell you a secret:
Even one fleeting minute is
   enough,
For the Supreme is your heart's
Compassion-King
And your life's
Forgiveness-Emperor.

1388.

Three travellers —
My mind,
My mind's stupidity
And I —
Travel together all the time,
Looking for only one thing:
The dance hall
Where ignorance-king
And ignorance-queen
Each day perform.

1389.

My mind was looking for
A doubt-tree.
My heart was looking for
A faith-plant.
My life was looking for
A surrender-flower.
My soul was looking for
A perfection-fruit.

1390.

God
Is infinite and eternal.
His Forgiveness
Is infinite and eternal, too.
But do you really want God
To grant you His unconditional
   Forgiveness
Or do you want to continue
Swimming in ignorance-sea?
This is the question
Of paramount importance.

1391.

Because
Your heart cried soulfully,
God has lifted you out
Of the quicksand of failure.
Because
Your life surrendered
    unconditionally
To God's Vision-Eye,
He has carried you to the solid
    rock
Of continuous progress.

1392.

You do not have to study the
    Vedas,
The Upanishads, the
    Mahabharata
And the Ramayana
To dive into the secret
And sacred wisdom-light
Of those scriptures.
He who realises God
Not only embodies all the
    scriptures —
Their essence and quintessence —
But also goes far, far beyond
The knowledge-seas of the past.

1393.

In those days he did drink
Nectar-delight,
But at that time his capacity
Was limited.
Now his capacity is unlimited
And he is drinking the same
    thing —
Nectar-delight —
But in unlimited measure.

1394.

Unless you have renovated
Your mind-room
To God's complete Satisfaction,
God will not allow you to become
A member of His Relay-Team.

1395.

I am telling you
That you are doing something
Extremely serious
And extremely dangerous.
You are nibbling
Temptation-nuts.

1396.

God cannot expect
Satisfaction from everyone.
But when He sees that you,
His chosen child,
Have given Him satisfaction,
He will grant you
His Infinity's Satisfaction-Delight.

1397.

If your life is a life
Of gratitude-obedience,
Then God's Eye will always
    precede you
And God's Feet will always follow
    you.

1398.

My Lord Supreme does His Work:
He preaches constantly.
I do my work:
I practise what He preaches
Devotedly.

1399.

Where do I live?
I live with my Lord Supreme
In the tower of His Forgiveness.
What is the thing
That inspires me, illumines me
And fulfils me most?
The Breath of His universal
Breathless Life.

1400.

At long last
My heart is ready
To become Your Dream,
My Lord Supreme.
"Then, My child,
I am giving you back
Your completely forgotten
Oneness-realisation
With My transcendental Vision
And universal Mission."

1401.

Now that your heart-path
Is paved with hope-light,
God's Silence-Delight
Will beckon you
From God's Golden Shore.

1402.

I know, I know,
My heart's beauty-flames
Were born inside
My Lord's Responsibility-Fire.

1403.

Your believing heart-prayer
God immediately answers.
Your surrendering dedication-life
God proudly treasures.

1404.

Confidence
Is not a life of complacency.
A heart of confidence
Is God's perfection-blossoming
   Dream
In man and for man.

1405.

My heart-dreams are dancing
   today,
For from today on
My life will be able to study
In God's Satisfaction-School.

1406.

Alas, alas,
Just because I am
A little bit different
From my Lord Supreme,
I am compelled to carry
The heaviest load
Of worries and anxieties.

1407.

Unless your mind gives up
Its desire-hallucinations,
Your heart will never be able
To grant your mind
Its aspiration-dreams,
The dreams that you keep safe
In God's Bank.

1408.

Instead of bringing opportunity
To your doorstep,
You are chasing opportunity away
With your stupid, self-
   undermining
And self-criticising mind.

1409.

How can and why should God
Liberate you and your life
If you do not
Cheerfully and powerfully
 terminate
Your long-cherished,
Self-imposed isolation-life?

1410.

Now that you have jumped
The hurdles of doubt and
 suspicion,
God's final Decision
Is to make you
A choice representative of His
Here on earth.

1411.

Your mind-life
Has no faith in itself.
Therefore your aspiration-boat
Is sinking fast, very fast.

1412.

If your outer life is expert
At denying the purity-faith
Of your inner life,
Your inner life can also
Easily and satisfactorily deny
The very existence of the
 impurity-doubt
Of your outer life.

1413.

My brave mind
Came into the world to succeed.
My pure heart
Came into the world to proceed.
My compassionate soul
Came into the world to precede.
My unaspiring body
Came into the world only to
 concede.

1414.

You have all along been
An authority on the failure-life
Because you did not dare to send
Your resignation-letter
To your ignorance-master.

1415.

Unless and until
You make your heart-room
    spacious,
God will not grant you
His precious Key
To open His Heart-Door.

1416.

You want to know
Where my confidence-delight
    comes from.
It comes from
My sleepless and breathless hope-
    light.

1417.

This is not the only world
That my Lord has.
He has many, many worlds.
He listens to my soulful prayer
When I beg of Him
Not to show me the face
Of the life-lowering gossip-world.

1418.

What your mind has
Is only desire-dollar bills.
With these bills you can buy
Only stark frustration-goods.

1419.

My Lord is doing something
    special:
He is placing
The laurel wreath of surrender
Inside my aspiration-heart.

1420.

Just because I never untied
The knot that tied me taut
To my Lord Supreme,
God is now ready to write
Secretly and regularly
My earth-illumining speeches.

1421.

As my Lord has no time
To be tired,
Even so, I do not have time
To be disappointed,
Either in myself
Or in the world around me.

1422.

You are proud that your mind
Is stubbornly unchanging.
I tell you,
Soon your heart's invisible
    divinity
Will threaten, frighten and
    enlighten
Your mind.

1423.

You are fooling yourself twice:
Once when you say
That God has infinitely
More important things to do
Than to think of you,
And once when you say
That you do not need God's Help
To make you happy and keep you
  happy.

1424.

How can you ever mourn
The death of your doubting mind
If your heart has already become
Inseparably one with God
On the strength of its constant
Self-offering?

1425.

Do you know
What an intellectual pygmy
Does to me?
He just hates me
In season and out of season.
Do you know
What a spiritual giant
Does for me?
First he tells me what I should do
To please God all the time.
Then he himself does it for me.

1426.

An educated man
My mind respects.
A self-giving man
My heart loves.
A God-becoming man
My entire being needs.

1427.

If your heart loves God
In God's own Way,
If your life serves God
In God's own Way,
I cannot understand
How you can ever suffer from
An inner energy crisis.

1428.

My heart has been suffering
For a long time
From insecurity-flu.
My soul-doctor has tried
All kinds of medicine
With no satisfactory result.
Now for the first time
My soul-doctor is trying to cure
The insecurity-flu of my heart
With God's Oneness-Injection.
I am sure this time
Insecurity-flu will be transformed
Into security-rapture.

1429.

Now that you have discovered
Your heart's life-purifying tears,
Failure can no longer hover
In your mind's hesitation-sky.

1430.

Alas, he fails to notice
The bondage-chains
Binding his heart.
Alas, he fails to notice
God's Compassion-Beauty
Illumining his eyes.

1431.

Your life
Is your insincerity-serpent.
How can you ever dare
To lead the life of an angel
On earth?

1432.

No matter which new song I sing
To please my Lord,
It has always been available
In my God-Eternity's Songbook.

1433.

You keep your hopes hidden.
Naturally
Your hopes will remain unheeded
By God's Compassion-Light.

1434.

This world of ours
Is indeed a prayerless world
Of illusion and delusion.
Yet everybody expects
That God's Love-Light
Must reign supreme on earth.

1435.

My heart knows
What God-dependence is.
My life knows
What self-transcendence is.
And I know
What the Satisfaction-Smile
Of God's Descent is.

1436.

Although I suffered for years
From mind-analysis,
I did nothing to cure
My self-styled mind-patient.
Now to my extreme sorrow
I am stuck with
My heart-paralysis.

1437.

You want to know, after all,
What God's Compassion-Flood
Has done for you.
I want to tell you
That God's Compassion-Flood
Has totally knocked
Your ugly ego-life to the ground.
What more can you expect from
 God?

1438.

Enthusiasm:
This is what my mind
Unmistakably needs.
Aspiration:
This is what my heart
Sleeplessly needs.
Realisation:
This is what my life
Immediately needs.

1439.

Because his life's surrender-story
Was written
With his heart's purity-pen,
God's transcendental Satisfaction-
 Shore
Is beckoning him.

1440.

A faithless life
Is an endless death.
An endless death
Is governing the soulless mind
Of the modern earth-bound
 society.

1441.

Never, never tell a lie
To any human being!
If you tell a lie
To a human being,
He will ruthlessly insult you
And torture you,
And at the same time,
He will not forgive you.
But if you ever tell a lie to God—
Which you must not
And should not—
Then God will forgive you.

1442.

Since God calls
Both Heaven and earth
His Home,
He always keeps
A few things for Vision
In Heaven
And a few things for
 Manifestation
On earth.

1443.

Do not sleep
In front of the ocean of delight.
Jump into the ocean!
Throw your life's devouring
　　discontentment
Into the ocean!

1444.

O earth,
Do not worry.
God will take care of you, too.
How long can He live
Only in the Heaven-Light-Room,
Ignoring the earth-darkness-
　　room?

1445.

He has measurelessly increased
His familiarity
With his inner world's faith-
　　family.
Therefore God has granted him
His transcendental Satisfaction-
　　Crown.

1446.

One of God's great successes:
When one of His children
Can soulfully say,
"In me a new quality
Has come to the fore
Which previously I did not have
Or I did not use —
The heart-quality."

1447.

Every day God asks you to enjoy
The prosperity of your self-
　　confidence.
Instead of doing that, you enjoy
The prosperity of your self-
　　indulgence.

1448.

O my physical heart,
Without you I cannot continue
My earthly existence.
O my spiritual heart,
Without you I cannot even start
My Heavenward journey.

1449.

My outer strength
May or may not add
To my inner strength.
But my inner strength
Always adds
To my outer strength.

1450.

A God-seeker is he
Who first surrenders
And then becomes
And finally wins the race.
A God-lover is he
Who first becomes
And then surrenders
And finally wins the race.

1451.

His is the outer strength
That can either break or build.
Fortunately he is using
His outer strength
Only to build.

1452.

Yesterday you felt
Farther than the farthest from
  God,
But today
Your soulful meditation
Is making you feel
Closer than the closest to God.
Every day
A soulful meditation
Is the only thing
That God needs from you.

1453.

Although it is the most difficult
Choice to make —
God or me —
I have successfully solved
This most serious problem.
When I need something,
I shall say, "God, only God."
When I do not need anything,
I shall say, "Me! Who else can
  there be?"

1454.

Just as an outer runner
Daily practises and practises
To run his fastest race,
Even so, an inner runner
Must sleeplessly practise and
  practise
To reach his highest height.

1455.

His heart-door is wide open
To each and every human being,
Especially to those
Who are in the thought-crowded mind-fair.

1456.

The Supreme is not losing heart
Even though His Mission on earth
Right now is only a tiny plant.
For His inner Vision knows
That this tiny plant
Will ultimately become
A divine banyan tree.

1457.

You can easily upstage ignorance
With your heart's aspiration-cry
And your soul's illumination-smile.

1458.

One petal of a rose withers,
And the entire beauty of the rose
Is lost.
Even so, if one seeker does not offer
His aspiration-heart and dedication-life,
All his fellow travellers
Feel excruciating pangs.

1459.

To do new things gives him pure joy.
He was always inclined
Towards poetry and music,
But not art.
Therefore he got tremendous joy
From becoming an artist.

1460.

You want to be flooded
With God's Power.
I tell you,
There is only one way:
You have to overpower
Your ignorance-life
Ruthlessly.

1461.

There is no such thing
As a miracle.
It is only a hidden reality
That has been waiting and waiting
To blossom fully
At God's choice Hour.

1462.

I shall cast aside
My insecurity, jealousy and doubt.
All division in my nature
Must be transformed.
Unless this is accomplished,
I shall miserably remain
Earth-bound
In my unaspiring human life.

1463.

A mind-furnace:
This is what you have.
If you are dissatisfied with it,
Then nobody is preventing you
From having a heart-garden
Where your Beloved Supreme
Can sing, play and dance.

1464.

He mistakenly feels
That dynamism is only for those
Who live in the restless vital.
He is ready to spend his entire life
Praying and meditating
In one tiny corner.

1465.

My mind is no longer
A fault-finder.
My mind has become
A follower of faith,
Sailing its dream-boat
Towards the Perfection-Shore.

1466.

He always listens
To the Will of his Beloved
   Supreme
By not showing the world
Curiosity-increasing miracles.

1467.

God is extremely pleased with
   him
And proud of him
Because his life's newspaper
Is now featuring
His heart's ever-blossoming faith.

1468.

Your Lord Supreme knows
Both the encouraging things
And the discouraging things
That are happening
Inside your heart and mind.
Yet He remains silent.
His Role is only to grant
Endlessly and unconditionally
His inner Blessings and Guidance.

1469.

God will not offer you His Advice
Unless and until He sees
That you are ready to accept it
Cheerfully and wholeheartedly.

1470.

The mind's doubt-thieves
Are all caught.
The soul has now taken them
Into the heart-room
For their complete
    transformation.

1471.

He was such a fool!
His Lord's illumining Answer
Was not what he wanted to hear.
Therefore he was waiting
And hoping against hope
That his Lord would one day
Allow him to fulfil his desires
In his own way.

1472.

His poetry and his spirituality
Are like the obverse and reverse
Of the same coin.
He was born to be a poet,
He was born to be a God-lover.

1473.

Your mind's thoughts are
    produced
In a futility-factory.
How then can you ever dream
Of perfection-satisfaction
In your life?

1474.

While he was crying
For God-manifestation
And world-perfection,
The music-world and the art-world
Became enamoured
Of his poetry and his spirituality.
They wanted to become members
Of his inner family.
But it was his poetry and his
   spirituality
That together started
Their unprecedented God-
   manifestation
And world-transformation-
   journey
In and through him.

1475.

You are neglecting
Everything and everyone in your
   life.
I am telling you,
You are making a most deplorable
   mistake,
Especially when you are
   forgetting
To water your heart's
Surrender-gratitude-plants.

1476.

The messages of the Vedic seers
Not only illumined the receptive
   souls
Of that time
But also changed
The spiritual atmosphere of the
   world
For all time.

1477.

You are holding God
To His Perfection-Promise
In your life.
God also can hold you
To your surrender-promise
In His Life.

1478.

Because the world
Is all one family,
All the members of the family
Should powerfully smile at
And joyfully share in
The greatness-achievements
Of one member.

1479.

You are manifesting the Supreme
Through spiritual discipline.
He is manifesting the Supreme
Through human achievement.
Both forms of manifestation
Are needed
To fulfil the Supreme's Vision-
　Reality.

1480.

Every day your heart is learning
Patience-lessons.
Soon you will see,
You will get the perfection-
　certificate.

1481.

He who loves God
Devotedly and faithfully
Will not only feel
But also will offer
Something immortal
At the end of his life's journey.

1482.

Already doubt has stabbed your
　mind.
Now if you allow doubt
To stab your heart as well,
Then yours will be a world
Thoroughly drenched in tears.

1483.

For years and years
Your vital has been singing
The same old attachment-song.
When are you going to start
　dancing
Your soul's detachment-dance?

1484.

True, you have felt something
　divine
Inside your Master
At least for a fleeting second.
But to his extreme sorrow
You have not felt anything divine
Inside yourself.
Before you pass
Behind the curtain of Eternity,
Your Master wants you to feel
Something divine
Inside your own heart,
Even for a fleeting second.

1485.

Every morning and every evening
God smilingly and
　unconditionally
Allows him to deposit
All his teeming worries and
　anxieties
At God's own Doorstep.

1486.

When a seeker reads
Again and again
The spiritual poems
That give him tremendous joy,
He feels and knows
That this very joy
Is nothing other than
His own soulful meditation
And his own real inner
   awakening.

1487.

Why are you afraid of visiting
God's Silence-Fondness-Farm?
If you do not visit His Farm,
He is not going to come to your
   house
To give you your life's
Fulfilment-fruits.

1488.

He says that science
Has made life too easy.
Human beings have become
Lazy and lethargic.
I say that science
Is offering to humanity
More leisure time
To pray and meditate.
It is up to the individual
To avail himself
Of that golden opportunity.

1489.

God wants you to go to Him
With joy.
He does not want you
To torture your body
In order to prove that you love
   Him.
After all,
It is He who has given you
A useful body
So that you can walk, march and
   run
Towards Him.

1490.

You are wounded by a worry-dart,
But God the Doctor will call on
   you
Only if you are going to give Him
A sweet little smile
As His Fee to cure you.

1491.

Outwardly your Master
May not express his gratitude
For your tireless service,
But your aspiration-heart
Can easily make you feel
His blessingful gratitude-heart.

1492.

Unless you tackle temptation
With firm and solid tactics,
Your life will not be able to project
Perfection-light
Into your future day.

1493.

I am here, I am there,
I am everywhere.
You want to know
How I can do that.
I can do that
On the strength of my heart's
Scattered sorrows.

1494.

I know that the life
Of a true truth-seeker and God-
  lover
Is the only life for me.
There is and there can be
No other life for me.

1495.

True, nobody is perfect.
But in and through the leader
Of a country,
The soul of that country
Is trying to offer something
  unique
Not only to its people
But to the world at large.

1496.

God has already surprised you
With His unconditional Love for
  you.
Now it is your turn to please God
With your heart's climbing
  surrender-plants.

1497.

Since he is spiritually blind,
You can show him sympathy.
But do not forget
That the full inner vision,
Which is your own ultimate Goal,
Is still a far cry.

1498.

Invoke your Master powerfully.
His inner presence
Will permeate your consciousness
To such an extent
That others will see
His illumination-face
Upon your transformation-face.

1499.

Those who are great,
Those who are outstanding
In any field of life,
Must realise
That God is manifesting Himself
In and through them
To richly inspire His creation.

1500.

Do not lose
Your last drop of purity,
For it has the capacity
To bring you back
To your matchless oneness-
　heights
With your Beloved Supreme.

1501.

The sweet rain of truth
Unconditionally helped him fly
Into the highest Abode of Divinity
Where God was waiting for him
With His Immortality's Smile.

1502.

Do not be sad
To see your mind's sunset.
Behold the perfection-splendour
Of your heart's sunrise.

1503.

Every day my heart sings
A new song of gratitude,
And this new song
Increases
The joy of my perfection-delight.

1504.

God's Compassion-Eye
And
His Forgiveness-Heart
Are planning something for you:
Your desire-mind
Is soon going to surrender
To your aspiration-heart.

1505.

What the world needs from you
Is your heart's abiding faith
And not
Your mind's towering philosophy.

1506.

As long as we claim to be seekers
Of the infinite Truth,
As long as we claim to be
God-lovers,
There can be nothing
As important as obedience
In our inner life and our outer life.

1507.

Inner obedience
Is infinitely more difficult
Than outer obedience,
For to achieve inner obedience
One has the formidable task
Of fully conquering doubt.

1508.

Enslaved by words,
You immediately fall.
Emancipated by deeds,
You triumphantly rise.

1509.

In order to achieve
Transcendence-perfection
In your life of aspiration
And dedication,
Every day you must be ready
To brave inner and outer hurdles.

1510.

My Beloved Supreme,
I want to be a sincere, devoted,
Surrendered and perfect
   instrument
Of Yours.
I shall overcome all the hurdles—
Insincerity, insecurity, impurity,
Disobedience and
   ungratefulness—
That I may encounter along the
   way.

1511.

Great thoughts surround me
With God's breathtaking Heights.
Good thoughts reveal
God's infinite Beauty through me.

1512.

Your Master's name is inspiration.
Your Master's name is aspiration.
Your name is dedication.
Your name is manifestation.
His names and your names
   combined
Create a most significant gift
For mankind.

1513.

As soon as I see
Any of my inner barriers,
One by one
I shall break them
Into a million pieces
For my aspiration-life's
Self-transcendence.

1514.

A heart of purity
Sees that its life
Is at once
Inside mistrusting humanity
And frustrated humanity.

1515.

I am ready to touch the feet
Of hesitation and fear,
For they are protecting me
By delaying the fulfilment
Of my undesirable desire-bound
   life.

1516.

Postponement, I love you.
In my desire-life
You are preventing me
From touching the breath
Of the abysmal abyss.

1517.

If you really dislike
The dividing lines of your
   jealousy,
Then quite soon
They will reach their vanishing
   point.

1518.

If you are striving
To elevate your life,
Any obstacles you meet
Must be destroyed.
If you are going
To ruin your life,
Any obstacles you meet
Are your true saviours.

1519.

You are still
In your unmanifested perfection.
How then can God allow you
To enjoy companionship
With the Immortals?

1520.

Transcendence is perfection.
Perfection is transcendence.
When we transcend our capacities,
Immediately we get an inner joy,
An inner thrill,
Which is another name for
    perfection.
No perfection can ever be achieved
Without self-transcendence.

1521.

Your Master asked you
To sit in front of him —
Such an easy task!
And what did you do?
You allowed your unaspiring vital
And your doubting mind
To ascribe some motive
To his simple and blessingful
    request.

1522.

Fulfil your Lord's Requests
With a soulful cry
And
A fruitful smile
And say, "This is what He wants.
I am going to please Him
In His own Way."

1523.

Who has freed his life
From bondage-chains
By accepting falsehood
For his safety's sake?
None!

1524.

Just offer your Lord Supreme
Your inner obedience.
You will definitely be able to win
The Godward race.

1525.

Outer obedience and inner
    obedience
Must go together —
Two legs we need
To walk, march and run
Towards the ultimate Goal.

1526.

On your mark,
Get set,
Go!
In pin-drop silence
God's Eagerness-Heart
Is waiting for you
At the finish line.

1527.

He is cherishing the idea
That obedience is not necessary
   for him,
Since once upon a time
He served his Lord
And did Him a big favour.
What a deplorable mistake!

1528.

Are you blind?
Can you not see
That by fulfilling your Lord
   Supreme
You have increased
Your own inner and outer
   capacities?

1529.

If you mount
On the wings of meditation,
You will see no division-skies
And no destruction-clouds.

1530.

On the strength of your mutual
   oneness,
You and your Master
Together have pleased God.
Your Master gave you God's
   Message
And this Message was fulfilled
In and through you.

1531.

If you believe in your own
Ultimate perfection,
If you believe in the necessity
Of transcendence,
Then you have to have a
   permanent name
In the inner world
And in the outer world,
And that name is obedience.

1532.

Now that he has turned his back
On his unaspiring past,
He soulfully hears
The symphony
Of his heart's God-fulfilling
   dreams.

1533.

Be careful!
The disobedience-force that today
Does not allow you to listen
To your Master's
So-called 'insignificant' requests,
Tomorrow will have the capacity
To inwardly take you
Thousands of miles away from
  him.

1534.

My Lord Supreme,
Each time I do not obey You,
Each time I do not please You,
Each time I do not fulfil You,
I clearly see that I am feeding
A devouring tiger deep inside me.

1535.

You fool!
Do you think your aspiration-
  heart
Will be scared to death
If it sees
Your mind's thought-bullies?

1536.

He mistakenly thought
That he would escape,
That somebody else would fall
Into the vital-tiger's den.
Alas, soon he was found
Inside the cave of destruction
Which he himself had created
Through his disobedience.

1537.

No wonder I see you
As a picture of perfect self-
  deception.
I see you have gladly allowed
  yourself
To be caught in the currents of
  desire.

1538.

You will always remain
Unfamiliar to defeat
If you carry a smile
That touches every heart.

1539.

Overcome your weaknesses
On the strength of your sincerity
And obedience.
Your sincerity will save you,
Your obedience will illumine you.

1540.

Do you want to make progress
Or do you want to crawl
In your spiritual life?
If you feel the necessity
To walk, march and run,
Then obey your Inner Pilot
Every day, every hour, every minute.

1541.

My soul is the poet in me.
My heart is the poetry in me.
My Beloved Inner Pilot
Is the Reader in me.

1542.

I desired to become great
On the human level.
My desires killed me.
I aspire to become good
On the divine level.
My aspirations are illumining me
And fulfilling me.

1543.

An ungrateful heart
Is the darkness
Of man's life-torturing
Inner poverty.

1544.

You can plumb the depth
Of your inner light
Only if you come out
Consciously
From the abyss of your lifeless
Nothingness.

1545.

Every day ask yourself
Whether or not
You want to see your highest divinity.
If the answer is "Yes",
Then it is worth staying in the spiritual life
To realise God.

1546.

The chosen instruments
Of the Lord Supreme
Will always feel
That they are not indispensable.
The very moment
They feel that they are indispensable
Is the beginning
Of their spiritual downfall.

1547.

Can you imagine!
God has given up
His Infinity's Power
To play with me
Inside my insecurity-cave.

1548.

I am now enjoying
My supreme surrender-freedom.
Thousands of years have worked
　on me
For this most precious moment.

1549.

You can be a supreme authority
On divine victory
If your mind
Has a ceaseless thirst
And your heart
Has a sleepless hunger
For God.

1550.

A doubting mind
And
A sleeping body:
These are the two universal
　sicknesses
Of humanity.

1551.

In the inner world
Doubt is unmistakably
The most powerful enemy —
The enemy that makes us doubt
Our Lord Supreme
As well as our own capacities.

1552.

Unless you are totally freed
From the prison
Of your antic attitude
Towards God's
Compassion-Forgiveness-Flood,
How can you ever have
A heart of satisfaction-sun?

1553.

On my way to Heaven
Do you think I will ever forget
To carry
My Heaven-indifference-proof
　shield?

1554.

Every morning
My mind and I wander
Upon the shores of delusion.
Every evening
My heart and I sing hymns
At Heaven's Gate,
Yet we are not proud.

1555.

If you have not yet fulfilled
The Requests of your Beloved
   Supreme,
Then now is the time
For you to forget about the useless
   past.
Just voice forth:
"I will do it, I am doing it."

1556.

Today's difficulty-race
Is making your body, vital and
   mind cry.
Tomorrow's victory-crown
Will not only make those three
   happy,
But also will make three more
   members
Of your inner family happy:
Your heart, your soul and your
   God.

1557.

My Lord,
What You need, I also need.
"True, My child.
Unfortunately,
I am meeting with My Needs,
While you are not.
But do not worry.
I will definitely show you
How to do it."

1558.

Do you know what he has done
Quite recently?
He has sold his earth-cave to God
To buy God's Heaven-Home.

1559.

Now that he has escaped
The tempting chasm
Of insincerity,
He is hoisting the flag
Of his permanent victory.

1560.

When you are cheerfully
Able to offer
Your achievements to God,
You become a life of aspiration,
And the rest of the world
Will undoubtedly derive benefit
From your achievements.

1561.

Let us go back
Into the world of aspiration.
Let us aspire every day
To be worthy
Of our Lord's Compassion-Flood
And Forgiveness-Sea.

1562.

Yours will be the life
Of a continuous miracle-maker
Because
Your soul-vision is sprouting
Into your heart-reality.

1563.

What have inner disobedience
And outer disobedience
Done for him?
He has gone back to his old life,
Where he is once more wallowing
In the mire of ignorance.

1564.

How can God play His Cosmic
    Game,
His divine Lila,
If He is all the time
Finding fault with His human
    children?
Then there would be no Game.

1565.

O fear, doubt, anxiety and
    insecurity,
When are you going to learn
That you are
The unfortunate soldiers
Of ignorance-king?

1566.

Sincerity and obedience
Are the obverse and reverse
Of the same coin.
As a truth-seeker
You have to feel
That you are that golden coin.

1567.

At every moment
Be sincere
To your own inner longing.
Do you really want God?
If the answer is "Yes",
Then be sincere and remain
    sincere.
If you do not really want God,
Then for you there is no necessity
To remain sincere.

1568.

During my philosophical period
I thought
That God was God's own Head.
Now during my spiritual period
I know
That God is God's own Heart.

1569.

Each day observe
How many good thoughts you have
That inspire your life,
And how many discouraging,
Unaspiring and harmful thoughts
You allow to enter into your mind.
Then record them
In your inner notebook.

1570.

His complacent self-sufficiency
Makes him feel
That the progress he has made so far
Is more than enough for him.
He feels no necessity
To increase his inner hunger
Since at every moment
He is pleased with what he has
And what he is.
What an unfortunate seeker!

1571.

Yesterday I desired to achieve
So that I could become
Something or someone great
In the world.
Today my desire has been purified
And transformed into my aspiration
To serve the world.

1572.

He wanted to become great
Not by competing with others
Or with himself,
But by creating a new hunger
For God the Beloved Supreme.

1573.

I started my journey
With desire.
I am continuing my journey
With aspiration.
I shall complete my journey
With gratitude.

1574.

Selfless service is definitely
An act of rich creativity.
What have you created?
A feeling of fulfilling oneness
In your life.

1575.

Be good and remain good.
Be perfect and remain perfect.
If you are already good,
Then transcend your goodness.
If you are already perfect,
Then transcend your perfection.

1576.

Devoted and soulful service
Means a vast expansion
Of our conscious oneness
With God the Creation.

1577.

God took thousands of years
To make you realise Him.
Now it takes you
Only a fleeting second
To tell the world that you are
His supremely chosen
   instrument.

1578.

If others cannot appreciate
Your self-offering
And cannot offer their gratitude,
It is their loss,
For they are not making progress.
You just continue
Offering your services
Soulfully and devotedly
To your Beloved Supreme
And you will make
The fastest progress.

1579.

Try to run the fastest.
Aspire soulfully and devotedly.
There shall come a time
When there will be people on
   earth
To appreciate and value
Your aspiration-mountain.

1580.

If you allow
Your life-tree to be sprinkled
By small temptations,
How can it bear
Big illumination-fruits?

1581.

If you are convinced
That you are meant for the
   highest Reality,
Then go one step forward
And ask yourself
How you can reach the Highest.
To take you
To the top of the Himalayas
There is an inner elevator,
And this elevator is nothing other
   than
Your heart's unconditional
   obedience-light.

1582.

Obey your Inner Pilot,
Obey your Master,
Obey your soul's dictates.
You are bound to reach
And become
The Light of the Beyond.

1583.

He turns his life
Into his heart's purity-fragrance
To charm
His soul's God-Vision-Eye.

1584.

Do not try to advise the world
With your limited capacity
Or look down upon the world
    around you.
If you feel that you are better
Than those who are not aspiring,
You are playing with temptation-
    fire
Right in front of you.

1585.

Why are you trying to change
The outer world?
Why are you trying to make others
    feel
That their world is very bad
And yours is very good?
Why? Why?

1586.

When hope is gone,
I see one thing,
I feel one thing
And I become one thing:
The mud of ignorance.

1587.

God's first Message:
"My child,
I want you to please Me."
God's next Message:
"My child,
I am showing you
How you must please Me."

1588.

His writings represent
Both his inner world of realisation
And his outer world of dedication.
If you read his writings,
You will see inside you
An inner highway
On which you can drive your life-
    chariot
Faster than the fastest
To the destined Goal.

1589.

I like your heart.
I admire your soul.
I love your God.
But I vehemently dislike
The stone face
Of your stark solitude.

1590.

The philosophy of self-
    transcendence
Is the highest Message
That God has handed down to
    humanity.
Not only that,
He considers this Message
Equally applicable to Himself.

1591.

Anything that God is asking us to
    do
In our lives,
He Himself is also doing
In His own Life.
He is giving us the Assurance
That we can do the same thing
Provided our belief in Him
Is perfect
And our obedience to Him
Is unconditional.

1592.

God has given
A universe-sustaining heart
Only to those
Who have denied themselves
Completely.

1593.

Obedience embodies
The message of perfection-light.
Obedience embodies
The message of transcendence-
    delight.

1594.

Each time you obey
The Will of the Supreme,
Your body-consciousness becomes
   light,
Very light,
And you can easily fly
Into the highest Realm
Of His Infinity's Light
And His Immortality's Bliss.

1595.

Every day remind yourself:
Yours is not the mission that will
   fail.
Yours is the God-ordained
   mission
That is bound to succeed.

1596.

My Eternity's Beloved Pilot
   Supreme,
I know, I know,
I came into the world
For only one purpose:
To give You the utmost Joy
In Your own Way.

1597.

Although you may not be perfect,
You are supremely chosen,
For you have definitely
   established
A self-giving heart of oneness
With your Lord's Transcendental
   Will.

1598.

His life's morning stumblings:
Self-indulgence
And
Self-aggrandisement.
His life's evening stumblings:
An interference-mind
And
An indifference-heart.

1599.

My Lord,
You have made me
Your chosen instrument.
But I know that others
Can easily be made into
Your choice instruments
If You execute Your Compassion-
   Flood
In and through them.
Never will I say that I am
An indispensable instrument,
But I will always remain
Your grateful instrument.

1600.

I am a sea of gratitude
Within and without,
My Lord,
For You have chosen me
Out of Your infinite Bounty
To do something special for You
In Your Life of Manifestation.

1601.

My Lord Supreme,
What will happen
If I obey You unconditionally?
"My child
Your entire life will be flooded
With My Heart's sweetest
　　Intimacy."

1602.

With my praying hands
I go to see God.
With my meditating heart
I invoke God to come and see me.

1603.

You want to know
Where I live in the inner world.
In the inner world I live
Between my Lord's powerful
　　Smile-Ocean
And my heart's soulful
　　Tear-river.

1604.

You are telling me
That you have nothing to do
And therefore
You are not doing anything.
But I am clearly seeing
That you are doing something:
You are starving poor God to
　　death.

1605.

Now that you have put your
　　desire-life
On a perfect diet,
God is definitely going to invite
　　you
To His Nectar-Silence-Feast.

1606.

You tell me
That you are very brave.
Then show me your bravery
By fighting against your lower self
Constantly
And by loving your higher self
Unreservedly.

1607.

You are telling me
That you do not have any friend.
Nobody thinks of you,
Nobody likes you,
Nobody loves you,
Nobody treasures you.
Well, I clearly see that you have
An excellent friend.
Your ignorance-friend does think
   of you,
Does like you,
Does love you,
Does treasure you at every
   moment.

1608.

What else can you expect
Your confusion-mind-boat to do
But to carry you
To an alien destruction-shore?

1609.

The dawn of a permanent purity-
   day
Has made its permanent abode
Inside his heart.

1610.

God the Lover created this world,
And not man the doubter.
Since God the Lover
Created the world,
How can you trust or even ask
Man the doubter to take care of it?

1611.

The life that does not believe
In hope-power
Is nothing but a nightmare
To itself.

1612.

God does not think
That you are unworthy
Of realising Him.
But He knows
That you are unwilling
To realise Him.

1613.

You want to show the world
The smiling sweetness-moon
Of your eyes
Without having a oneness-life.
You simply cannot do that!

1614.

When are you going to come out
 of
Your self-pity-sea
And jump into
God's Satisfaction-Ocean?
When?

1615.

Alas, it was too late
For him to save himself,
For a false saviour
Had totally destroyed
His aspiration-heart.

1616.

I have two teachers:
God and ignorance.
I have so many questions.
God the Teacher
Does not answer my questions.
Ignorance the teacher
Is unable to answer my questions.
Alas, what am I going to do now?
I am totally lost.

1617.

It creates a tremendous
Encouraging excitement
In his vital and body
When his mind's doubt-thunder
 roars.
But his soul and heart
Laugh and laugh
At his mind's shameless stupidity.

1618.

You have been accepting
Temptation's invitation
For such a long time
And not accepting
God's Invitation.
Do you not think
That it would be nice of you
To accept God's Invitation
At least once?

1619.

My Lord,
Open my heart's new eye
So that I can prayerfully watch
 You
While You are flying towards me.

1620.

God asked me to sing one song:
The song of aspiration.
I sang that song for Him.
He liked my song so much
That He asked me to sing
A few more songs.
I was so delighted and excited
That I sang two more songs
One after another:
My life's surrender-song
And my heart's gratitude-song.

1621.

You are begging God
For a gift.
Has He not already given you
His best and highest Gift:
Compassion?

1622.

The roots of his happiness-life-
   tree
Are so strong
That the wild winds of despair
Will never be able to frighten him.

1623.

God's Life has already touched
My compassion-heart.
But alas, when shall my life touch
God's Compassion-Feet?

1624.

You call it
A dying temptation,
But I call it
A vanishing destruction.

1625.

A new aspiration-hope is rising
For him to reach
The highest height
Of his soul's promise-land.

1626.

Tell me, my friend,
Is it your dream
Or is it your mental hallucination?
Tell me, my friend,
Is it your vision
Or is it your perfection?
I do not see the difference
Between your dream and your
   hallucination.
Again, I do not see the difference
Between your vision and your
   perfection.

1627.

There was a time
When I used to live
On frustration-flames.
But now that I have a new life
Of aspiration-cry,
I am living inside the heart
Of the illumination-sun.

1628.

God was his Teacher.
The Teacher and His student
Were unable to please each other.
The student left the Teacher
And found a new teacher:
Ignorance.
God the Teacher is not sure
Whether it is worthwhile for Him
To look for a new student.

1629.

Before you
Is a powerful silence-sea.
Behind you
Is a powerful doubt-storm.
Do not delay, make the right
　choice!
Let the world be inspired
By your right choice.
Then it will also make the right
　choice
When the time comes
For it to make a choice.

1630.

If you do not want to forget
Your desire-language completely,
No harm,
But you must not use it.
God-Language is so soulful and
　powerful
And now that you have learnt it
Most satisfactorily,
Why do you have to use
Your vulgar desire-language?
Anyway,
In the new world that you are
　living in,
Nobody will understand
Your old desire-language.

1631.

This morning
My Lord Supreme said to me
That if I can show Him
That I have the capacity
To speak less,
Then He will give me the capacity
Not only to hear Him more
But also to fulfil myself
Infinitely more.

1632.

My Lord Supreme
Do tell me one thing:
Determination –
Is it something
That I do not have at all
Or is it something
That will remain indefinitely
   dormant
Inside my heart?

1633.

Do not pay any attention
To your unaspiring mind.
Just feed your hunger-heart
Even more than you have been
   feeding it
And let your unaspiring mind
Starve and die.

1634.

God is always ready
To grant me His two giant Wings
To lift me from my heavy despair.
But alas,
I have no confidence
In God's two Wings.

1635.

Unless you are ready to enjoy
The immediate collapse
Of your earth-bound mind,
How will you be able to enjoy
The infinite beauty and expansion
Of your heart's Heaven-free
   bridge?

1636.

In the outer world
When I run, I use new shoes
Once in a blue moon.
In the inner world,
God gives me a new pair of shoes
Every day.
He tells me
That a new pair of shoes every day
Will give me
A new inspiration, a new
   aspiration
And a new destination.

1637.

When I cry,
I cry only to see God's Face.
When I smile,
I smile only to feel God's Heart.

1638.

To see God's Face
You do not have to face
The mounting wave of doom.
To see God's Face
You have to love more and more
Your own mounting wave
Of inner bloom.

1639.

You are your life's
Selfish pleasure.
Yet you want God
To treasure you!
What can be more absurd?

1640.

You do one thing every day:
You admire your mind-elephant
To your satisfaction.
God also does one thing every day:
He loves your heart-deer
To His Satisfaction.

1641.

You are such a fool
That you cannot appreciate
The beauty and divinity of truth.
Yet you want
A monopoly on truth!

1642.

God's Illumination-Building
Does not believe
In having a conference room.

1643.

Do not go anywhere alone —
There is no safe place on earth.
You must always carry with you
Your soul's silence-smile.

1644.

His vital-bull and his mind-
    panther
Have at last decided
To sign a peace treaty.
Therefore
God in Heaven has invited
His heart and soul
To enjoy a supreme feast.

1645.

There is every possibility
That an unemployed God-lover
May eventually become
A true God-hater.

1646.

O my mind,
You are asking me why
I do not want to utilise you
The way I utilise my heart.
Every day my heart,
On its own,
Goes to the soul-laundry
To be laundered,
But you do not want to do that.
How do you then expect me
To use you every day
When you do not at all
Keep yourself clean?

1647.

You are telling me
That you do not know
What stupidity is.
I am telling you,
Stupidity is the thing
That tortures and ruins
Your God-given flower-heart.

1648.

O insecurity-weakness,
I never thought
That you could be
So unimaginably powerful!

1649.

When one soldier is out of step,
An army loses its strength.
Similarly, when one good thought
Either disappears from the mind
Or is out of employment,
It creates a serious problem
In one's inner life.

1650.

Your eyes are telling me
That you want to destroy
My teeming weaknesses.
Your heart is telling me
That you want me to transform
My weaknesses into strengths,
My imperfections into perfections
And my suffering into delight.

1651.

Now that your life
Is completely saturated
With surrender-nectar,
Your God-realisation-hour
Cannot remain a far cry.

1652.

You can borrow
Your heart's illumination-saw
To cut into pieces
Your confusion-treasuring mind.

1653.

In the morning
My Beloved Supreme
Keeps my soul filled
With promise-perfection,
And during the entire day
He keeps my heart filled
With hope-aspiration.

1654.

Do you want to know
What you can do
With your naughty mind?
You ask your mind
To look for and live for
The compassionate Heart of God.

1655.

Unless you deliberately set fire
To your mind's rubbish-store,
Your mind's fire-pure
   transformation
Will not take place.

1656.

O seeker,
Always be on the alert.
Your heart's blossoming faith
Can be devoured
By your mind's brooding doubts.

1657.

With your deception-life-boat
How can you ever reach
Perfection-shore
To see God's Satisfaction-Dance?

1658.

If you want to escape
From desire-fire,
Then ask your soul
To grant you every day
A new aspiration-flame.

1659.

God does not want to revise Your
   mind-book,
For there is nothing to revise.
It is all meaningless and useless.

God will be pleased to revise Your
   heart-book,
For it embodies profound
   wisdom-light.
There are a few minor mistakes
In the book,
But God will be more than pleased
To correct them
And make your heart-book
Absolutely perfect,
Illumining and fulfilling.

1660.

Your eyes want to tell me
That you have realised God.
Your heart tells me
That your God-realisation
Is still a far cry.
I am sorry,
I have to trust your heart
And not your eyes.

1661.

God expects
Each and every human being
To play at least one melody
Correctly and soulfully
Before his life-lease expires
On earth.

1662.

He always does unthinkable
   things.
We are dying to escape
From darkness to light.
And what has he done?
He has escaped from light
To ignorance
Consciously and deliberately.

1663.

Your soul kept its promise.
It did listen to God every day
And please God every day
In every way.
But your blind body, blind vital
And blind mind could not see it.

1664.

He is giving you
His affection-rainbow.
But if you do not value
His affection,
Do you think he will ever
Care to give you
His illumination-sun?

1665.

While he was sailing,
Both the illumination-shore
And the temptation-shore
Wanted him.
He did not want to satisfy
Only one of his hosts.
Therefore he offered
His mind to temptation
And his heart to illumination.

1666.

Not only on earth
But also in Heaven
There is a book that can never be
A best-seller.
Do you know what book this is?
God's Justice-Book.

1667.

O my doubtful mind,
Your life is ridiculous.
O my fearful heart,
Your life is ridiculous.
O my uncertain soul,
Your life is ridiculous.
O my sleeping body,
Your life is ridiculous.
O my strangling vital,
Your life is ridiculous.

1668.

Hammering and hammering
At your ignorance-rock,
Poor God has become extremely
   tired.
Do you not think
That it is high time for you
To start hammering
At your ignorance-rock
And give poor God a little rest,
Which He so rightly deserves?

1669.

Not only the doubt-tumour
In his heart
But also the heart itself
Has been surgically removed.
And now God the Compassion-
   Doctor
Has transplanted into him
A new heart of perfection-faith.

1670.

He has very strange theories about
   God.
He thinks that he can live
Without thinking about God,
Whereas God cannot live
Without thinking about him.
He also thinks that there are two
   Gods.
One God is a strict disciplinarian.
This disciplinarian God wants
   nothing
But perfection from the world.
The other God is God Himself
Who always remains Self-
   enamoured
And Self-satisfied.

1671.

God wanted me to show Him
My heart-garden.
Alas, I am able to show Him
Only my impurity-futility-weeds.

1672.

God wants you to be
His perfection-partner.
Instead of listening to Him,
You have become a partner
Of the temptation-world.

1673.

If you love the touch of the world
More than the Touch of God,
How can you expect
Eternity and Infinity
To claim you as their own?

1674.

His heart's life-boat has capsized
Because he did not care
To see the bloom
Of the aspiring consciousness-
   bud.

1675.

Your life will never be
A fallen leaf
If you every day worship
The Vision-Eye of God's Life-Tree.

1676.

When the hour strikes,
Every athlete-seeker
Will win his God-realisation-
   medal
In the heart-Olympics.

1677.

Consciously if you do not deepen
Your heart's love for God,
Unconsciously you will cheapen
Your life in God's world.

1678.

God will not let anyone else
Write your perfection-biography.
He has decided
To do it Himself.

1679.

You are your self-offering race,
God is His Self-Transcendence-
   Eye,
And I am my life-satisfaction-
   smile.

1680.

At last you have made God happy
By becoming
Your heart's rising aspiration-star.

1681.

Increase your aspiration-appetite
Every day.
You will not be daunted and
    haunted
By disappointment-dart.

1682.

The desire-storm of your vital
Has totally destroyed
Your heart's faith-flames
And even your life's aspiration-
    sun.

1683.

Who says that God does not need
Any favour from you?
He does need one favour:
Your heart's unconditional
Aspiration-cry.

1684.

If your heart is a faltering
Faith-flame,
How can you ever dance
Perfection-dance
In God's Immortality-Hall?

1685.

You do not have to offer
A gratitude-sea to God.
Even a dribble from your heart's
Gratitude-well
Can and will satisfy God.

1686.

O my mind,
You have overfed my ego,
And now what is happening?
You are suffering pangs
That are unimaginably
    excruciating.

1687.

Try to remain
On your life's dedication-diet.
You will soon be able to celebrate
The death of your desire-life.

1688.

You have asked your mind
To drive your life-car.
Quite often the car
Is out of control.
Why do you have to blame
God the Driver,
Whom you have not invited
To drive your life-car?

1689.

Luminosity is looming large
In your life
Because you have successfully
Commanded your mind
To be constantly in touch
With your soul.

1690.

Tranquillity comes from
The heart's diving.
Tranquillity comes from
The life's surrendering.

1691.

What does he do regularly?
He regularly dethrones his
　doubting mind
Early in the morning,
And then he enthrones his
　aspiration-heart
And keeps it
Inside his beautiful soul-room
For the entire day.

1692.

Alas, my heart's gratitude-drop
Is so fearful
That instead of entering into the
　sea
Of light and delight,
It is ready to be tortured
　constantly
By limitation, division and
　frustration.

1693.

Only your heart's
Detachment-injection
Can cure you of your life's
Attachment-failure-infection.

1694.

God has given His Realisation-Life
A specific job.
Every day
It goes out to install
Sweet oneness-will
Inside all human hearts.

1695.

Aspire to win
Your oneness-belt
In God's cosmic Fulness-Game.

1696.

Do you know
How God has become
The Possessor of infinite Wealth?
God has become
The Possessor of infinite Wealth
By investing countless Smiles
In His cosmic Vision-Stock.

1697.

Every day
You are mercilessly persecuted
By temptation dreams,
Yet you are not longing for
A perfection-reality-life.

1698.

Your deviation from oneness-goal
Has turned your entire life
Into meaningless and useless coal.

1699.

My Lord Supreme,
Do tell me if there is a way
To cure man of his chronic
    invention
Of destruction-weapons.

1700.

If you want to achieve
Perfection and satisfaction
Within and without,
Then enthrall your world
With nectar-spreading
    enthusiasm

1701.

My Lord,
How can I offer You enough
    gratitude?
"My child,
You and I are singing
The song of oneness.
This oneness-song goes beyond
The necessity of gratitude.
When oneness reigns supreme,
Who will be grateful to whom?"

1702.

You and your pride
Can live without God,
But God and God's Compassion
Cannot live without you.

1703.

If you are ready
To go with your Beloved Lord
Even to hell,
Then rest assured,
Your Lord will definitely turn hell
Into the highest Heaven.

1704.

I am not imitating him.
He has achieved something before
    me,
But now God's Hour
Has struck for me as well,
And I shall devotedly follow
In his footsteps.
What you call imitation,
I call oneness-sharing.

1705.

Man misunderstands
God's Justice-Light.
Man does not understand
God's Compassion-Height.

1706.

Let others call me a fanatic.
I will listen only
To my intuition-friend
Who tells me
When to run and sit
At my Lord's Compassion-Feet.

1707.

He who leads me to God
Is most precious,
For what else is he doing
If not playing the role
Of opportunity
For his faithful followers?

1708.

A seeker's winter of doubt
Is fleeting,
But his spring of faith
Can easily be lasting.

1709.

Frustration-night can veil
Your face
If you do not sail
Your life-boat
Towards the Illumination-Shore.

1710.

When your Master does anything
With serious and soulful
    concentration,
Do not miss the golden chance
To be with him.
Use every opportunity
To receive the utmost from him.

1711.

He wanted to go to hell
And see what it looked like.
Teeming doubts came to him
And said,
"You do not have to take the trouble
Of going to hell.
We have brought hell to you."

1712.

O ex-God-lover,
The stark ignorance-axe
Is fast descending
On your head.

1713.

God is older than anybody.
Again, what is God
If not an eternal Child
Playing in His infinite
Garden of Beauty?

1714.

What is selfless service?
Some call it humility-service,
Others call it humiliation-service,
But I shall always call it
Illumination-service.

1715.

Now that you have got
Freedom-confidence,
One by one, your forgotten hopes
Will reappear.

1716.

A true God-ambassador-messenger
Is he who delivers
Divinity's Smile
To humanity's crying door.

1717.

Be an eternal child.
Only an eternal child
Can appreciate
Divinity within and divinity without.
Only an eternal child
Can make inner and outer progress
To satisfy God in His own Way.

1718.

Whether it needs rest or not,
You must compel your wandering
  mind
To rest,
And ask your still heart's faith-
  flower
To blossom
Slowly, steadily and beautifully.

1719.

Do not cry.
I love you.
Do not cry.
The world needs you.
Do not cry.
God is still dreaming
Inside you and for you.

1720.

God should not have to
Plead with you.
Just do the right thing
Sooner than at once
And become His Eternity's
Choice and fond instrument.

1721.

Each truth-seeking cry
Will eventually become
A God-manifesting smile.

1722.

A servant of the transcendental
  Truth
Can never be lost
In the backwoods of ignorance-
  night.

1723.

Because of your
Disproportionate tongue-greed,
Your success-boat
Had to capsize and vanish.

1724.

In his inner and outer life
He was shining.
His Lord Supreme made him
A messenger boy on earth.
Why?
Only to teach him
How to shine in humility.

1725.

God's selfless Service is found
Here, there, everywhere.
Whatever good things
He has been doing for His
  creation,
He is now asking you to do.

1726.

Do not loiter
On your frustration-street!
God is inviting you
To come to His Street
And hoist His Satisfaction-
    Banner.

1727.

In top silence,
Patience-light
Broadcasts its indomitable power.

1728.

Through his selfless service-
    offering
He at once
Smashed his outer pride
And expedited his inner
    illumination.

1729.

You want to make a noble
    sacrifice,
But first ask if it is God's Will.
You must always go beyond
    morality
And allow Divinity
To make the decision for you.

1730.

Be grateful to morality,
For it has established
Some harmony on earth.
But remember,
You are a truth-seeker.
For you spirituality
Must always come first.

1731.

You are not only sitting
On the bondage-bench,
But you are enjoying
The boring sound of bragging.

1732.

God wants you
To come and play with Him
And acquire
Divine name and fame.
But you must first
Throw off the blame-blanket
That you have put on humanity.

1733.

If you serve
Faithfully, devotedly and
   punctually,
Although you have
Teeming problems and
   weaknesses,
Inwardly you will feel
Joy in boundless measure
From your selfless service-
   offering.

1734.

God's Vision-Island
Is waiting for you.
Can you not quickly embark
In your heart's swiftest progress-
   plane?

1735.

Keep swinging on
Your heart's gratitude-gate.
God will before long
Transform your earth-bound fate
Into a Heaven-free smile.

1736.

When your Master asks you
To obey the Divine in him,
You have to know
That he himself
Always obeys Someone —
His Eternity's Pilot Supreme.

1737.

What do I want?
I want to see my mind's
Falling desire-star.
What do I want?
I want to see my heart's
Rising aspiration-sun.

1738.

If you have made
Your ego-life a big eater,
How is it you cannot make
Your surrender-life a great God-
   dancer?

1739.

If you do not take
Your Lord Supreme's Gifts
With a gratitude-heart,
Who will be the real loser?

1740.

When he soulfully offered to
   others
What his Beloved Supreme had
   given him,
He immediately increased
His own devotion-delight.

1741.

God asks me to show Him
What I gave Him yesterday —
Proper enthusiasm.
If I can show proper enthusiasm
To Him today,
Then He will give me
What He truly is — Love.

1742.

If you do not perfect
Your determination-exercise,
God will not invite you to see
His Satisfaction-Dance.

1743.

The disciple offers the Master
His soulful receptivity.
The Master offers the disciple
His heart's sweetest gratitude
And his soul's highest blessings.

1744.

In the life of a true seeker
Receptivity is not a mere word
Found in the dictionary,
But a living reality
That touches the very Depth
Of God's Heart.

1745.

You are asking me,
What has God's Compassion-
   Smile
Done for me?
God's Compassion-Smile
Has demobilised my doubt-army
For good.

1746.

You are longing for
Your desires' death.
How can you kill your desires
Unless you are badly in need of
God's Breath?

1747.

Whenever you sincerely
And soulfully meditate —
No matter when, no matter
   where —
Your Master's inner sun
Will respond without fail.

1748.

When you are meditating
In your Master's absence,
Your imagination-power
Can either bring your Master
Right in front of your mental
    vision,
Or it can send
Your meditation-consciousness
To your Master.

1749.

You must defend
Your life's manifestation-power
With your heart's aspiration-
    tower.

1750.

Your faith-tree has dropped dead
And now what I still hear
Is a deafening sound.

1751.

The Lord Supreme
Needs only those
Who are eternally faithful,
Sleeplessly cheerful
And ready to follow Him
At all times.

1752.

You are perfectly surrendered
To your mind.
You have become
Your mind's best instrument.
You think that you know
    everything
Better than God.
Alas, what can poor God do for
    you?

1753.

God's Hour had struck for him.
But when he deliberately
Neglected his meditation,
The inner divine forces
Kicked him
Infinitely harder
Than he would ever have
    imagined.

1754.

When opportunity knocks at your
    door,
Pay attention!
If you ignore your opportunities,
The retribution will be
    unimaginable.

1755.

Unless you take your mind-
    student
To your heart's illumination-
    palace
Every day,
It will die to keep company
With confusion-crowd.

1756.

God has already given you
What He has for you—
His transcendental Smiles.
When are you going to give Him
What you have for Him—
Your heart's gratitude-tears?

1757.

The Hour has struck for you.
Proceed
According to your own capacity.
Why wait
For those who are not ready
To fly high, higher, highest?

1758.

What is transcendence,
If not a minor alteration
Of my earth-aspiration-cry?

1759.

Don't hide your doubt-drums.
Strike hard!
And let them burst into pieces
Immediately.

1760.

There should be no difference
Between your everyday heart-
    aspiration
And your life-newness.
There should be no difference
Between your everyday heart-
    soulfulness
And your life-fulness.

1761.

God is not interested
In the eagerness of your vital
To defeat others.
God is only interested
In the eagerness of your heart
To achieve perfection
In your own life.

1762.

Just think of
Your life's transformation.
God will then definitely love you
Infinitely more.

1763.

False light will tell you
What you can never do.
Real light will tell you
Not only what you can
   unmistakably do
But also
What you have perfectly done
   already
To please your Beloved Supreme.

1764.

To appreciate the beauty
Of a flower
Is not a difficult task.
But to become the flower itself
Is indeed a difficult task.

1765.

Cry and cry sleeplessly
If you want to change the world.
Love and love constantly
If you want to change yourself.

1766.

Self-deception:
This is what the human nature
   knows.
Self-perfection:
This is what the divine nature
   knows.
Self-transcendence:
This is what the supreme nature
   knows.

1767.

He mistakenly feels
That what others have to offer him
Is of no value.
In the name of self-sufficiency
He is just riding his own ego-
   horse.

1768.

If your Lord Supreme requests you
To do something,
Rest assured,
He has already given you the
   capacity—
Even more than necessary—
Long before you actually need it.

1769.

When I think of God,
I think of God's Quantity-Life.
When God thinks of me,
He only thinks of my quality-heart.

1770.

Mine is purity's
Attraction-heart.
Mine is impurity's
Repulsion-mind.
In between the two
I am totally lost.

1771.

When you walk
With your fellow travellers
Along Eternity's Road,
Like a magnet
You should try to draw
Inspiration and aspiration from
   them.

1772.

Just because God
Thinks of your enemy too,
Do you think
He loves you less?

1773.

Insincerity is dangerous.
Sincerity is adventurous.
Purity is prosperous.
Divinity is precious.

1774.

You do not have to
Give up anything.
Just value your spiritual life
And automatically you will feel
That this new life of yours
Comes first.

1775.

By accepting the spiritual life
You are telling me
That God comes first in your life.
Now do everything soulfully
To bring yourself closer to Him,
And also try to feel
That He, only He, is your
   Eternity's All.

1776.

Two things of yours
Always astonish me:
Your mind's confusion-forest
And your heart's perfection-garden.

1777.

Opinion:
This is what my mind wants.
Perfection:
This is what my heart wants.
Liberation:
This is what my life wants.
God-Satisfaction:
This is what I want.

1778.

During the day
Use your imagination-power
To remember your soulful and
   powerful
Morning meditation.
Imagination is a world of its own,
And this imagination-power
Can save you, illumine you and
   fulfil you.

1779.

Soulfully ask God
How to use the spiritual energy
You receive in your meditation.
Then it will never be wasted.

1780.

Indecision
Tells me two things perfectly:
What death looks like
And
Where death is.

1781.

God is not asking you
To desert your mind
Immediately.
He is only asking you
To illumine your mind
Completely.

1782.

God asks you to come Home.
He does not ask you
What you will do
When you come Home.

1783.

Yesterday
You allowed your mind
To be overcrowded with thoughts.
Today
You are allowing your mind
To be overcrowded with doubts.
Yet you want to have
A peaceful mind and a fruitful
   life!

1784.

Your heart's love-quality
Is quite poor.
How do you then expect
To awaken the sleeping human
    beings?
Your wishful thinking
Will eventually end
In a powerful frustration.

1785.

You want to be first in everything.
Now make up your mind
Once and for all
Whether you want to be first
In the world-illumination-race
Or in the world-possession-race.

1786.

Alas, you cannot explain
God the Great.
Alas, you cannot feel
God the Good.
Alas, you cannot imagine
God the Perfect.

1787.

What is your primary concern —
To love God
Or to serve God?
If you want to love God,
Pray for inner purity.
If you want to serve God,
Pray for inner certainty.

1788.

A talker may only
Talk on perfection,
But a listener can definitely
Grow into perfection.

1789.

God definitely wants you
To succeed in life.
But it is you
Who have to do always
The best thing.

1790.

The heart's silence-sunrise
Is the harbinger
Of the life's sound-joy.

1791.

You must implore
God's Compassion-Light
Before you dare to explore
The beauty and divinity
Of the inner world.

1792.

Be not afraid
Of revealing the truth.
Be only afraid
Of concealing falsehood.

1793.

Everything comes and goes,
But oneness-love remains,
And it remains so permanently.

1794.

Whether your mind
Is running after desire
Or desire is running after
Your mind
Is quite unimportant.
Both your mind and desire
Are quite harmful.
Therefore, watch out!

1795.

God has already built
A road for you.
Can you not at least
Walk on it
And see if it is satisfactory?

1796.

Ask your heart to give
The right kind of advice
To the world.
Ask your mind to receive
The right kind of advice
From the world.

1797.

God wants you to entertain Him.
Alas,
Instead of entertaining Him
   richly,
You have enchained Him
   mercilessly.

1798.

God has a question for you.
Answer it immediately:
Do you want Him
To save you from yourself
Or to save you from the world?

1799.

God does not mind
If your road is different
From His road.
But He will definitely mind
If both of you
Finally do not arrive
At the same destination.

1800.

Realisation is not
The end of the road.
It is only a challenge
On the way to God's
Perfect Manifestation on earth.

1801.

Each soulful thought
Enjoys a weightless flight
To its unparalleled destination:
God-Silence.

1802.

Indomitable will-power,
Universal oneness-love,
Sacrifice of peace, light and joy
In boundless measure for
   humanity:
These are his soul's qualities
That are being manifested
In and through his life on earth.

1803.

When your soul's qualities
Come forward and start
   manifesting,
Then not only your world
Of outer running
But also your world
Of inner running
Will acquire a very special
   significance.

1804.

In the outer consciousness
You have already established
Something immortal.
Now you must do the same
In the inner consciousness
With your heart's cry for mankind
And your life's love for mankind.

1805.

The loving and soothing zephyr
Of my Lord's Compassion-Sea
Has time and again saved my life
From its hidden destruction-
   imperfections.

TWENTY-SEVEN THOUSAND ASPIRATION-PLANTS

1806.

Everybody is appreciating,
Admiring and adoring
Your outer achievements.
But you have to know
That this outer glory
Lasts only for a fleeting moment.

1807.

When we think of the outer man,
We are fascinated
Because he has shown something great
To mankind.
But when we think of the inner man,
We are illumined
Because he has done something good
For God.

1808.

When the outer man does something,
The world immediately gets
Tremendous joy and ecstasy.
Then the outer achievement
Fades into oblivion.
But when the inner man does something,
It forever and forever lasts.

1809.

Why do you dwell
On the past?
The past does not determine
The future.
Only your prayer and meditation
Will determine your future.

1810.

Like your fellow seekers,
Can you not also try
To become good?
Just try.
You will undoubtedly succeed.

1811.

My Lord,
Do allow my present
To pay the penalty
For my undivine past.
I do hope in the future
I will have the capacity
To march along the road of sainthood.

1812.

Are you in life's prison cell?
Then can you not take God's Help?
He will purify and illumine your nature
So that you can enjoy
Your soul's freedom.

1813.

It may take the outer man
Many, many centuries,
But finally
At God's choice Hour
The outer man
Will definitely
Grow into the inner man.

1814.

The outer man
Collects the quintessence
Of countless experiences
During his earthly sojourn.
But the inner man
Already has the infinite wealth,
The inner wealth.
In fact,
The inner man eternally is
What the outer man
Is so desperately longing for.

1815.

Each time the mind
Goes beyond the confusion-
   barrier,
It sees immediately
The perpetual dawn of the heart's
   awakening.

1816.

Outwardly
He is the greatest champion
Of the world.
But inwardly
He is something
Infinitely more powerful
And infinitely more beautiful:
The supreme hero-warrior
To fight against humanity's
   ignorance.

1817.

He has proved
Something unprecedented:
The outer man
Of unparalleled name and fame
Can soulfully bow
To the inner man,
Who is eternally the ambassador
Of the Absolute Supreme on earth.

1818.

The outer man
Says to the inner man:
"What I have
Is all for you."
The inner man
Says to the outer man:
"What I am
Is and will forever be
All yours."

1819.

In his highest meditation
He became what his outer life
At times consciously,
At times unconsciously,
Had been searching for.

1820.

If you want to discover
Your inner life,
You have to walk along
The path of the heart,
Where there is
Universal Love, universal Peace
And universal Light and Delight.

1821.

Achieve something great
　outwardly.
Many on earth will admire you
And even adore you
For what you have done.
Achieve something good
　inwardly.
Countless people will get
A tremendous inner uplift
From your very presence on earth.

1822.

There are two roads:
The road of the mind
And the road of the heart.
By God's infinite Grace
Right from the start
You have chosen the correct road:
The road of the heart.

1823.

I am grateful to God,
For His world-family
Is quite happy
To receive my affection, concern,
Love and oneness.

1824.

Like the offering of a world
　Saviour,
The self-offering of the inner man
Elevates the consciousness
Of each individual on earth
And of each soul yet to come
Into the world.

1825.

Why do you need to search
For outer beauty?
The beauty of your soul's colour
Permeates the entire world.

1826.

When you become the inner man
You establish a constant
And sleepless reality
That lasts for Eternity.
You build something immortal
For the earth-consciousness,
Something for its permanent use.

1827.

Each human life will eventually
Be perfected and fulfilled
By a world of bitter and sweet
    dreams.

1828.

You are approaching the spiritual
    life.
Do you know what you want?
You want to be
The dearest, closest and most
    perfect
Instrument of God.

1829.

When are you going to believe
That God is using you
As a supreme instrument of His?
I can clearly see that in and
    through
Your outer existence
God is offering a new Vision
To the world.

1830.

Undoubtedly you are a good soul.
But in the heat of the moment
Even a good soul
Can do something very bad.
So, be careful!

1831.

Why do you feel
That you are very bad by nature?
Unless you feel
That you have come into the
    world
To do something good,
You may go from bad to worse,
And then finally
You will be washed away
Both in the inner world
And in the outer world.

1832.

There was a time
When you had many divine
    qualities.
But now what has happened?
The undivine forces have caught
    you
And made you their instrument.
You have yourself become
Nothing other than
An undivine force.

1833.

If you want to make
Illumining and fulfilling progress
Constantly,
Then do not cherish yesterday's
    dreams.

1834.

Even if you have done something
Very wrong,
Do not give up hope.
Your inner divinity
Can once again come to the fore.
Just consciously become
A student of God.
You and God will cheerfully
Be able to claim each other.

1835.

Inside me there is Someone
Eternal, infinite and immortal.
Who is that Person?
God, and nobody else.
Now you want to know
Who my God is.
My God is my own
Transcendental Self.

1836.

Dreams never to be born:
I love God more than He loves me,
God needs me more than I need
    Him.

1837.

Joy and oneness
Are inseparable.
Fragrance is beauty's joy.
Flower is purity's oneness.

1838.

Where is our Eternity's joy?
Inside our oneness-perfection.
Where is our oneness-perfection?
Inside our sleepless
Soul-determination.

1839.

Concentration gives us victory,
But we need meditation
To maintain our victory-joy
When fear and doubt
Threaten to take it away.

1840.

Some seekers do not yet have
Any inner wealth.
They have just started
Acquiring it.
But you have a great advantage,
For inwardly you already have
Something very special:
Your selfless oneness-heart with
 God.
Now you only have to become
Fully aware of it.

1841.

The beautiful life of detachment
Has powerfully and gloriously
 given him
A heart of enlightenment.

1842.

Concentration
Is the midday sun-power.
As soon as you see this sun,
Your entire being is flooded with
 strength.
Meditation
Is the moonlit peace.
As soon as you see this moon,
You can feel peace within
And peace without.

1843.

His mind was not accustomed
To the Eastern meditation-
 philosophy.
But his beautiful and soulful heart
Of love, goodwill, fondness and
 oneness
Was fully prepared
To follow the already familiar
Meditation-path.

1844.

Why are you waiting for your
 mind?
Your mind will take years and
 years
To discover
What your heart already has
In boundless measure.

1845.

Sing a song
With words having tremendous
Prophetic power.
Lo, you have become
Part and parcel
Of the universal harmony.

1846.

My Lord,
Inside Your Songs
I feel my happiness,
And this happiness of mine
Has at once
Your Power and Your Love.

1847.

My heart is all gratitude
To music,
For it keeps me all the time
In tune with my Universal Self.

1848.

God has told me
That He grants me special
    Blessings
When I compose soulful songs.
He has also told me
That He then stays beside me,
Not ninety-nine per cent
For me
But absolutely one hundred per
    cent
For me, for me.

1849.

If you want to have a full-time job
In God's Palace,
You must give up staying inside
Your unlit jealousy-mind.

1850.

You are hiding from God
Because you are afraid
Of failing in His Life-
    Examination.
Those who at least stand
Before the Examiner
And want to pass His
    Examination
Are far better than your useless
    self!

1851.

If you can accept
Soulfully and cheerfully
The inner Decision of your Lord
   Supreme,
Then you are absolutely
The best seeker.

1852.

Accept cheerfully
What life is offering you,
And you will see,
There is no such thing
As humiliation.

1853.

Yours is a vast, translucent
   wisdom-light
Because your heart is completely
   impervious
To the world's insecurity-
   invasion.

1854.

The slave was turned
Into a master
By a miracle.
Now he is criticising
His very saviour.
Is this not the height
Of his ingratitude?

1855.

Where is your sympathetic
And devoted attitude?
In the name of perfection
You are criticising others
Mercilessly.
Do you not see
That what is coming forward
Is not your sense of perfection
But your unconscious,
Unwanted self-imposition
And self-glorification?

1856.

A man of the mind will say,
"Here is an ugly dry log."
A man of the heart will say,
"Even now how beautiful
Is this sapless tree before me."

1857.

Each beautiful
And illumined thought
Is a God
In another world.

1858.

The ordinary human eye
Sees the world's outer barrenness.
A spiritual heart
Sees the flowers and fruits
Of the world's inner source.

1859.

What God wants from you
Is devoted oneness
With His Vision.
Your mind may not grasp
His Message immediately,
But your oneness-heart
Will definitely realise God
In His own Way.

1860.

My compassionate Father,
As soon as You tell me
That You wish me to have something,
It is well understood
That your Affection-Heart
Will grant me that very thing.

1861.

You are really something!
If God's most soulful Request
Has no value for you,
I have simply no idea
What you will value in life.

1862.

If you do not have the inner urge
To please your Supreme Pilot,
Then why do you stay in His Boat?
You are only forcing Him
To carry the weight
Of a dead elephant.

1863.

Your mind is now
A whirlpool of confusion.
Your heart is now
A shattered wheel of destruction.
Alas, how can you ever be happy?

1864.

If you tell God a lie,
How can you escape any
    retribution?
The inner world
Is always wide awake
So do not try to fool God,
And do not fool yourself.

1865.

There was a time
When meditation was a difficult
    subject
For a Western seeker.
But now his heart
Has become an excellent student
Of meditation-studies.

1866.

You want to be
Closer to God.
Then do only two things:
Pray to God to receive you,
Meditate on God to receive Him.

1867.

Yes, someday God will definitely
Grant you an interview
For your total transformation.

1868.

My Lord, let me be
In constant communication with
    You.
When I want to say something,
I shall pray.
And when I want to learn
    something,
I shall meditate.

1869.

Let me climb up the Heavenly
    ladder
To sit at the Feet
Of my Lord Supreme.
When I reach a certain height
Of consciousness,
There I will see my Beloved
    Supreme.

1870.

I shall become calm and quiet
So that my Lord Supreme
Can climb down the Heavenly
    ladder
And descend into my heart.

1871.

During his first interview with
    God,
God took away his attachment-
    arrow
And gave him His own
    Detachment-Shield.

1872.

To your mind-jungle
Meditation may seem strange.
But to your heart-garden
Meditation will never seem
    strange—
Never!

1873.

In the morning
Meditate on the waves and surges
Of the ocean.
You will find dynamic life-energy.
In the evening
Meditate on the deep vastness
Of the ocean.
You will feel Infinity's peace.

1874.

By using your inner
Rocket-concentration
When you win the outer race,
You win it not only for yourself,
But for all mankind.

1875.

Just make tremendous progress
And tremendous improvement
In your own life.
Others will definitely be inspired
By the result.

1876.

When he saw his Master
For the very first time,
It took him only
A few fleeting moments
To bring his inner existence
To the fore.
He is indeed a chosen seeker,
For there are many, many on earth
Who simply will not be able
To do what he has so easily
And so spontaneously done.

1877.

Tremendous power of
 concentration
You do have
To run the fastest
And reach the Destination of
 Newness.
Now you need
The power of meditation
To enter into the Goal of Fulness.

1878.

When you soulfully meditate,
The first thing you get
Is peace,
And this peace
Marks the beginning
Of your heart's journey
Along the path of perfection.

1879.

When we sing,
We embody and become
The power of music.
This power has free access
To the Universal Heart.

1880.

Once you acquire
The power of perfection
In your meditation,
Doubt the intruder
Will no longer be able
To disturb your heart's
Inner poise.

1881.

You have simply no idea
How good you are.
The beauty and fragrance
Of your inner flower
At once remain
Inside your heart
And spread
Throughout the world.

1882.

Only on the human level
Do we see that there is something
Called sacrifice.
On the divine level
There is no such thing
As sacrifice.
It is all oneness —
Oneness-perfection
And oneness-satisfaction.

1883.

Once you have achieved
Oneness-delight
Through your meditation-light,
You become the breath and the body
Of the universe.

1884.

Even a great champion,
If he is not spiritual,
May greatly suffer
From a baseless future-fear.
He says to himself:
"Who knows,
Tomorrow I may not be able
To perform as well as today.
The day after tomorrow
Somebody will surpass me
And take away my glory."

1885.

From the human life
We are trying to reach
The divine life.
So let us at least give up
Our animal qualities.
Let our hearts be sympathetic
To our fellow travellers.
Let us allow God to fulfil
At least one Dream of His
In and through us.

1886.

My mind will tell me
Only what others have taught it:
"A flower is beautiful."
But my heart feels and sees
   everything
As a new experience.
It may even discover tremendous
   power
Inside a tiny flower.
Then how can we say
That the heart is mistaken
When it tells us,
"A flower is powerful."

1887.

I always try to stay
Inside the nest
Of my heart's pure tears.
I always hate to live
Inside the house
Of my mind's wild laughter.

1888.

Just repeat the words
Spoken by a Son of God
And watch:
Something will immediately
   happen
Inside your heart.

1889.

O Lord,
You have given me
The power-aspect of life
To please me.
Now do give me also
The peace-aspect of life
To please You.

1890.

He was a man
Of tremendous determination,
But one day a dangerous wrong
   force
Attacked him.
Because of one moment's
   surrender,
His whole life-career ended.

1891.

Through concentration
You have reached your goal.
But if you want to take
Countless people towards the goal
That you have already reached,
Then you need meditation.

1892.

Have some sympathy for others!
Do not get malicious pleasure
From hearing
About their deplorable fate.
Today you have escaped,
But tomorrow
Humiliation may be your name.

1893.

If you want
Outer success and inner progress,
You need something more
Than the capacities of the body,
Vital, mind and heart.
You have to bring to the fore
Your inner divinity,
The capacity of the soul.

1894.

Let my vision dive
Deep within
So that I can see the world
With the beauty
Of a poet's heart.

1895.

A poet is not a grammarian.
His poetic ear
And his soulful heart
Take him to a realm
Far beyond human logic.

1896.

When you pray,
You are talking
To your Heavenly Father,
And He has to listen to you.
When you meditate,
Your Heavenly Father
Is talking to you,
And you have to obey Him.

1897.

My Lord,
I beg of You
In all my heart's sincerity,
Just give me Your Message
    supreme
And I shall without fail
Execute it.

1898.

Be like a deer
That wants to run fast, very fast
With the Lord Supreme
And give Him joy.
Your Lord Supreme will always be
With you and for you.

1899.

He wanted his impure desires
To soar,
But the higher worlds caught them
And put them into prison.

1900.

You are experienced
In the art of self-transcendence.
Therefore
God the Lover needs you
And God the Beloved utilises you
In a very special way.

1901.

The Golden Age will blossom
In those
Who live in God's Compassion-Sea
And invoke God's Satisfaction-Sun.

1902.

The Golden Age will rapidly blossom
In the hearts of those
Who most devotedly love God
And at the same time
Shall not remain detached
From His earth-family.

1903.

The unanimous opinion
Of God-lovers:
God has unconditionally done
Everything for them.
God is unconditionally doing
Everything for them.
God will unconditionally do
Everything for them.

1904.

Yesterday
Your life was a squadron
Of countless fears and deaths.
Today
Your life is an inexorably
Deathward journey.

1905.

No matter where you cast your glance
To escape,
You see nothing but a blinding fog
Of uncertainty.

1906.

My Lord Supreme,
Whom in this world
Should I obey?
"My sweet child,
Obey only the one who shows you
All kindness, all compassion
And all forgiveness.
Only he deserves
Your constant obedience."

1907.

Doubt is confusion.
Confusion
Is the beginning of destruction.
Destruction
Is the unpardonable negation
Of God the Delight.

1908.

No darkness can ever stop
My progress.
It is my unwillingness to
    transform
Darkness into light
That has stopped my progress.

1909.

Now that sincerity
Is your real name,
Your heart's inner cry
Shall be able to answer
All your life's questions.

1910.

Self-giving is transcendental,
But you have to make it
Universal too.
Something more,
You have to make it
Absolutely practical.

1911.

My inner quality tells me
Whom to believe and love.
My inner capacity shows me
How to believe and love.

1912.

You ask,
How can God the Compassion
Be so inconsiderate?
No, it is you who have to be
Infinitely more desperate
To realise Him.

1913.

God does not want to fulfil
Your desire-life.
Instead He wants you
To enter into the aspiration-life,
Your real life, your only life.

1914.

If you are fast asleep,
How can you hear God sing?
But if you wake up,
God will not only sing for you
His most favourite Song,
Nature's transformation,
He will also teach you how to sing it.

1915.

Why does everyone need a project?
Everyone does not need a project,
But if anyone wants to make
Very fast progress
In his spiritual life,
Then he definitely needs a project.
When he has a project,
God cheerfully and powerfully gives him
Three injections:
Inspiration-injection,
Consecration-injection
And perfection-injection.

1916.

You want to know
What is the worst waste of time.
The worst waste of time
Is when you think
That God does not care for you at all
And that you will never be able
To become a choice instrument of His.

1917.

What promise to me
Will God always keep?
The transformation
Of my earth-bound sorrow
Into His Heaven-free Joy.

1918.

My Lord Supreme,
What is the best way to give You joy?
"My child,
Do not expect anything good
From your lower nature.
Do not expect anything bad
From your higher nature.
And always keep
Your inner determination burning
To give Me cheerfully
Everything that you have and that you are."

1919.

O seeker-artist,
How do you get ideas
For your paintings?
"I do not get any ideas
For my paintings.
I just get an inspiration-message
From within,
And then I begin to paint."

1920.

Great minds may think
That they are lonely,
But good hearts never feel lonely,
For they have established
Their universal oneness-delight
Everywhere.

1921.

I have forgiven all my sins
Except one unforgivable sin
And that sin is,
I do not love
My Beloved Supreme only.

1922.

He tells me
That he keeps very tight security
Around his mind.
How is it possible then
For teeming doubts
To enter into his mind
Every day?

1923.

For you it is nothing
To give God counterfeit coins
Since you have plenty.
But a true God-seeker
Has only one true coin,
And that coin is his God-coin.
He gives it to you free of charge.

1924.

Do not be afraid
Of the passion-flames of your
    vital.
Your soul's volcano-will-power
Can and will easily drown them.

TWENTY-SEVEN THOUSAND ASPIRATION-PLANTS

1925.

For a clear mind,
Try prayer.
For a pure heart,
Try meditation.
For a bright life,
Try aspiration-dedication.
For a perfect life,
Try surrender,
Surrender to God's Will.

1926.

You are telling me
That a swarm of unwanted
   thoughts
Is buzzing inside your mind.
I tell you,
It is entirely your mind's fault
That it wanted to be the host.

1927.

Even if there is no room vacant
Inside your heart-hotel,
God will immediately
Make a new room,
For God does not believe in
A "No vacancy" sign.

1928.

If you think
That you can easily drown
In ignorance-sea,
I tell you,
God's Compassion can smilingly
And, of course, unconditionally
Save you.

1929.

Listen,
I have good news for you:
God has unconditionally decided
That He will not allow you any
   more
To be surrounded
By self-imposed sorrows.

1930.

Be an unconditional
Truth-seeker and God-lover.
Rest assured,
All earthly superlatives
Will fade into oblivion.

1931.

I was devastated
By the news from the inner world
That I have all along
Been multiplying and glorifying
My untold earthly sufferings.

1932.

There is only one departure gate
For your journey home,
And that departure gate
Has been beautifully decorated
With your gratitude-heart
And surrender-life.

1933.

Indeed, this is a world of pretence.
Here you do not know anything.
You do not even have to learn
   anything.
Yet you can become a solid
   member
Of the world conference
For a better world.

1934.

My Lord,
If a soulful cry
Competes with a fruitful smile,
Who will win the race?
"My child,
Always the fruitful smile will win.
A soulful cry
Comes from a human heart,
But the fruitful Smile
Comes from God Himself."

1935.

My desire-life
Surrenders to my aspiration-heart
Only when I see my soul
Speedily driving my body-chariot.

1936.

My expectation-cliff,
Did you not find any better place
To put me
Than in a frustration-chasm?

1937.

You know perfectly well
That you cannot govern your life
Even for a single day.
Then why do you not vote for
      God?
Once He becomes the Ruler
Of your life,
You will see that He can easily
And unconditionally
Govern your life.

1938.

You fool,
Why did you allow
Ignorance-snake to bite you?
Can you not see
That you have totally lost
Your beauty-flooded vision-eye?

1939.

Do not be doomed to
    disappointment.
Your life will not remain forever
    fettered
By an iron fate.
Time's waters will wash away your
    fetters
And you will be granted
By the Lord Supreme
A new opportunity
To long for the perfection-life.

1940.

Now that your heart
Is on the silver summit of
    aspiration,
Your life is bound to grow
Into a sea of satisfaction-delight.

1941.

If you are sleeplessly pure,
Then you will never be found
On the shipwreck of your
    unfulfilled hopes
Yours will be a life of perfect
    fulfilment.

1942.

My Lord,
What have I seriously done wrong
That you do not allow me to
    remain
Inside the nest of Your Protection-
    Eye?
Do tell me.
I am all ready to change my life
Once and for all
To please You in Your own Way.

1943.

O my stupid mind,
How is it
That you do not want to enjoy
A short holiday
From your mad and wild
Doubts and suspicions?

1944.

Do not expect others,
Who are in so many ways
As weak as you are,
If not worse,
To stop you from doing
The wrong thing.
It is only your prayer to God
That can eventually help you
Overcome your weaknesses.

1945.

O my mind,
Be not afraid of God's Greatness.
O my heart,
Be not afraid of God's Goodness.
This time, when God invites you,
You must accept His Invitation.
His Invitation is all Sweetness,
All Fondness and all Fulness.

1946.

As the matchless weapon of the
    strong
Is non-violence,
Even so, the unparalleled weapon
    of the pure
Is surrender.

1947.

One problem I cannot leave alone:
My ungrateful disobedience
To God's unconditional
    Compassion-Eye.

1948.

What have I been longing for
All along?
Purity's cheerful sound-light
And divinity's soulful silence-
    delight.

1949.

Alas,
A stupid little desire
Has the capacity
To keep me from accomplishing
A big, wise aspiration.

1950.

Now that once again
You are on speaking terms
With God,
Do not forget to ask Him
To grant you
A life of grateful obedience.

1951.

When you go out,
Be sure
God the Compassion goes with
    you.
And also be sure
To be a perfect instrument
Of God the Satisfaction
On the way.

1952.

Previously you prayed
Frequently.
Now you are praying
Frequently and fervently.
Soon you will start praying
Frequently, fervently
And unconditionally.
Then the Golden Shore of the
　Beyond
Cannot and will not remain a far
　cry.

1953.

Look beyond
Your compassion-face.
God's Satisfaction-Heart
Is claiming you
As Its very own.

1954.

He deliberately crashed
His heart-plane
Into God's Compassion-Sea
To receive a new life
Of aspiration, dedication and
　perfection.
Lo and behold,
He was more than successful.

1955.

There was a time
When I died
For the perfection of man.
Now I am living only
For the Manifestation of God.

1956.

You have turned your ignorance-
　life
Upside down
And you are now far beyond the
　reach
Of temptation-snare.

1957.

Because I was raised
On God's Compassion,
I can easily and inseparably
Become one
With humanity's imperfection
And inspire humanity
To look upward, to dive inward
And not to lose hope.

1958.

It was you who wanted
The greed-hare to lead you.
Therefore
It is you who will have to allow
The sorrow-tortoise to follow you.

1959.

Oneness is the perfect expansion
Of our inner reality.
Let our heart's oneness only
   increase
To make us feel
That we belong to a universal
   world-family,
And this world-family
Is a fulfilled Dream of God.

1960.

If you deliberately try to cloud
The happiness of humanity,
God will never come to you
As His Satisfaction-Giver.

1961.

Your heart has been walking
For a long time
Along enthusiasm-road.
Can you not ask your mind
To walk even for a day
On enthusiasm-road?
How can you be truly happy
When your mind fails
To do the right thing?

1962.

Your mind is full of busy
   thoughts.
Poor God,
The Giver of Silence-Delight,
Has been standing at your mind's
   door
For a very long time.

1963.

What kind of disciple are you
If you do not think
That self-discipline is the only
   hallmark
Of your aspiration-dedication-
   life?

1964.

What is my faith
If not my heart's
Spontaneous calmness
And my life's
Beautiful and powerful
   fruitfulness?

1965.

There was a serious clash
Between my heart's sincerity
And my mind's superfluity.
God immediately declared
That it was all my mind's fault,
That my mind was the real culprit.

1966.

God does not want you
To put your ignorance-criminal to death.
He wants you to inspire the criminal
For his fire-pure transformation.

1967.

Nothing
Is as utterly disheartening
As my weak dream-plants
That will not grow into
Reality-trees.

1968.

You have always been responsible
For the satisfaction of your life.
Alas,
Satisfaction is still a far cry.
Can you not once give God a chance
To take the initiative
In granting you
A life of abiding satisfaction?
Let Him try.
I am sure He will bring about
Satisfaction for you.

1969.

As the desire-life
Is a very bad investment,
Even so, the aspiration-life
Is a perfect investment.
Here, one day you will grow into
God's Omnipresence
And God's Omnipotence.

1970.

I have been watching and wondering at
How fortunate I am
To have a faith-flooded heart
And a silence-fulfilled life.

1971.

It is true
That no one worth possessing
Can ever be possessed.
But every rule
Admits of exception.
My Beloved Supreme is not only
Worth possessing,
But I can possess Him quite easily
On the strength of
My absolutely surrendered life.

1972.

You want to know
What I am doing now.
I am sleeping
With my heart's silver dreams.
I am also doing something else:
I am inviting you
To come and enjoy with me
My unprecedented experience-
  ecstasy.

1973.

No earthly word
Can ever come to my aid
When I try to tell the world
That what I have
Is God's Compassion-Sea
And what I am going to become
Is God's Satisfaction-Flood.

1974.

I had a world-class dream:
A freedom-flooded life.
Lo and behold,
My heart of silence is enjoying
The manifestation of that dream
Into reality.

1975.

There is one thing
That can never become outdated,
And that is the satisfaction
Of your heart's surrender-delight.

1976.

My life's
Unconditional surrender
Means God's final Revision
And perfect Edition
Of my life's script.

1977.

When our life is spontaneous,
Our experience is real,
And this reality
Is our own divinity's perfection-
  delight.

1978.

Watch!
Can you not see the old God
With His new Footsteps
Entering into your heart-room?

1979.

If you have sincerity
In your determination
And determination
In your sincerity,
Then Divinity's Goal
Cannot remain a far cry.

1980.

How can you maintain purity
Throughout the day?
Just keep a flower with you
And look at it with a soulful smile
As soon as impurity
Tries to assail your mind.

1981.

A rich person can definitely
Realise God.
Lord Buddha was a prince.
Sri Ramachandra was a prince.
Janaka was a king.
Like that, there were
Quite a few rich people on earth
Who did realise God.
Again, there are some people
Now living on earth
Who are both materially and
  spiritually rich.

1982.

How can you feel
The living Presence of God
All the time?
Cry for a sincerity-mind.
Cry for a purity-heart.
Cry for a divinity-life.

1983.

Do not forget
To take your silence-medicine
Every day
If you want to keep away
From sound-disease.

1984.

Why do you think
That the body is inferior to the
  vital,
Inferior to the mind
And inferior to the heart?
No, God wants your body
To be a divine instrument of His
Exactly the same way
As He wants your vital, mind and
  heart
To be His divine instruments.

1985.

Early in the morning
Every day
My Lord's supreme Blessing
  invites me
To walk along the beach of my
  soul.
I obey Him
And try to remember my sweetest
  oneness
With my Beloved Supreme.

1986.

God definitely
Does not come to a seeker
To see his heart's
Empty refrigerator.

1987.

The blessing of aspiration
Is an enlightening heart-garden
Where inspiration-dedication
  seeds
Grow quite rapidly.

1988.

Ignorance leaves him
With only a desire-train
To try to reach his soul's
Divinity's Reality-Shore.

1989.

Life is not meant to be
A wasteful amusement park.
Life is meant to be
A soul-enlightenment-shrine.

1990.

Peace and dynamism
Must go together.
To His children of the East,
God has given peace
In boundless measure.
To His children of the West,
He has given dynamism
In boundless measure.
The combination of the two
Will make a perfect world-family.

1991.

You are a world-class aspirant.
Therefore
In your case it is quite possible
That you are running
Faster than the fastest
To God.

1992.

The present excitement
And
The future excitement:
I have seen the Face
Of a living God.
God will make me
An exact prototype
Of His divine Reality.

1993.

As hurdles are for jumping,
Even so,
Inspiration is for singing,
Aspiration is for transcending.

1994.

If you play
The flute of creation,
You can easily enjoy a brisk pace
Towards God's Freedom-Light.

1995.

If your mind really wants
To serve God,
Then you should immediately
Try working
At a world-service-plaza.

1996.

At last knowing what to do,
He is now racing the long run
To reach the Vision-Eye
Of his Beloved Supreme.

1997.

The mind's certainty
And the heart's intensity
Can see the perfection-descent
Of God's Satisfaction-Smile
From Above.

1998.

A Gift from the Supreme
May come at any time, any place,
And it always far surpasses
Human dreams.

1999.

Your life's only necessity
Is divine authority.
How can you and why should you
Be afraid of that authority
Which is nothing other than
God's Compassion-Sea?

2000.

I am so fortunate
That my life has now grown
Into a golden dream
That is sailing
On an endless smile-river.

2001.

My Beloved Supreme,
I am totally lost
Without the Smile of Your Eyes.
"My child,
I am immediately lost
Without the love of your heart."

2002.

God does scold the weak souls
That fail to manifest Him
Successfully on earth.
This is a direct report
A seeker has received
From the soul's country.

2003.

God has dismissed my vital
For its restlessness.
God has dismissed my mind
For its carelessness.
God has dismissed my heart
For its helplessness.
But God has not dismissed me
For I am still all soulfulness.

2004.

The story of a former God-seeker
  is this:
God does not need him any more
And earth ridicules him evermore.

2005.

If you lose your grip
On the obedience-rope,
You are bound to find yourself
Inside the abysmal abyss
Of destruction.

2006.

God is ready to invent
A new way every day
For you to please Him.
Now the question is,
Are you going to accept it?
Are you? Ever?

2007.

Your life may be a slow
Aspiration-train,
But you will reach
Your God-ordained destination
Unmistakably.

2008.

O my mind,
I am now all ready
To clip
Your shameless jealousy-wings
With my soul's oneness-light.

2009.

God will grant you
His Victory-Speed
If you are willing to sit
At His Compassion-Feet
With your heart's surrender-smile.

2010.

I see my helpless soul
Between my Lord's
Blessingful Messages
And my mind's
Deaf ear.

2011.

My Beloved Supreme
Has lovingly and carefully shaped
My aspiration-statue
From ignorance-clay.

2012.

If you love God only,
Then God will sleeplessly protect you
From doubt's giant embrace.

2013.

Every day my aspiration-heart
Takes a number of exercises.
Otherwise my life will suffer
From my desire-burden's excessive weight.

2014.

He who loves God
In the aspiration-world
Has no responsibility of his own.
The Compassion of God
Does everything for him.
He who loves ignorance
In the desire-world
Has also no responsibility of his own.
The temptation of ignorance
Does everything for him.

2015.

The tentacles of attachment
Have crippled
His unlit earthly years.

2016.

Why do you not claim
The ever-claimable God
Instead of claiming
Ignorance-rogue?

2017.

While crying,
If you get satisfaction,
Then God is unmistakably
   coming to you
For your liberation-smile.

2018.

I whistle
My universal oneness-song
In the sweet arms
Of my golden dreams.

2019.

Where am I?
I am in between
My heart's newness
And my Lord's Fulness.

2020.

The only time you can be beaten
By the world
Is when your mind becomes
   bound
By the chain of your fat pride!

2021.

In the outer world
Sincerity-children
Are in great demand.
In the inner world
Purity-saints
Are in great demand.

2022.

My self-chosen ignorance-life
I started to forget
The day I chose to treasure
My Lord's Silence-Smile.

2023.

If you are consistently receptive
To God's blessingful Smile,
Then your liberation
Will not remain a far cry.

2024.

Because of your heart's
Inner revelation
Today we are able to see the lustre
Of your outer illumination.

2025.

Now that I am
My heart's silence-light,
My Lord has become
His own Ecstasy-Height.

2026.

A pioneer-soul
Is he who has
Two beautiful and powerful
God-serving wings.

2027.

Mine is the mind
That is hopeless helplessness.
Therefore, mine is the life
That is forced to be
An eternal ache.

2028.

His mind is embarrassed to pray
Because its little inferior brother,
The vital,
Saw it praying to God the
    Destroyer
And not to God the Liberator.

2029.

You are a fool
If you think
That it is not necessary
To keep your heart-rooms
Filled with shrines.

2030.

The worst culprit is he
Who does not want to pray
To tomorrow's God
And meditate on tomorrow's God.
Who is tomorrow's God?
The Peace-Dance of Oneness-
    Delight.

2031.

O my soul's hunter-seeker,
You can easily kill
My life's ignorance-tiger.
Just try!
You are bound to succeed,
You are bound to succeed!

2032.

Yesterday my mind
Was walking up a steep hill.
Today my heart
Is a beacon light
On that steep hill.

2033.

I worship
God's Compassion-Flood.
God energises
My life-blood.

2034.

O desire-man,
Your heart's door
Has a very strong lock.
No man-made key can open it.
Therefore, I am praying
To God's Vision-Eye
Not only to open your heart
But also to help me enter
Into your heart
And play with you there
God's Satisfaction-Game.

2035.

God's Compassion-Heart
Is always for sale,
But God's Justice-Eye
Is never for sale.

2036.

My prayer is my heart's
Hidden power.
My meditation is my soul's
Revealed light.

2037.

A soulful seeker will never allow
The wild hunger
Of his untamed vital-tiger
To be deathless.

2038.

Do not allow your hope to fade!
It is never too late
To become a perfect instrument
Of God.

2039.

His life's crucifixion
Is the daily giver
Of human aspiration.

2040.

If you desperately need God,
God will grant you
A full moon in your hope-sky.

2041.

Yesterday my desire-life
Desired to bind God
From the Sole of His Foot
To the Crown of His Head.
Today my aspiration-life
Is begging my Lord Supreme
To liberate me.

2042.

Two are the incurable
And unending diseases in my life:
My mind knows everything,
My life does not learn anything.

2043.

My serving life
Belongs to him alone
Who needs my loving heart.

2044.

How can I be your friend,
My mind,
When you are disproportionately
   infatuated
With your little self?

2045.

A church-goer is supposed to be
A God-believer.
But, alas!
A God-believer is supposed to be
A God-lover.
But, alas!

2046.

If you want to neglect anything,
Then neglect your old
Unaspiring life.
Let it totally die
Of neglect!

2047.

How and why should God
Open His Heart-Gate to you
If you secretly enjoy
The storm of hate?

2048.

Your soul's God-love will outlast
Your heart's inner frustration
And your mind's outer
   destruction.

2049.

Alas, why have I allowed
My deception-mind
To hijack my heart's
Aspiration-airplane?
Why?

2050.

Your mind may be
In jealousy's prison,
But your heart is definitely
In the delight-waves
Of oneness-sea.

2051.

I prayed to God
For a doubt-free mind.
Therefore, His Protection-
   Umbrella
Is shielding my head.

2052.

I have two beloved Guests:
God the visible Cry
And God the invisible Smile.

2053.

If you are a true truth-seeker,
How can you fear
Investigation?
If you are a true God-lover,
How can you not fear
Procrastination?

2054.

A heart of silence
Is the perfect answer
To my mind's volley of questions.

2055.

What are you doing?
Can you not hear
That your soul
Is summoning you?
Can you not see
That real happiness-petals
Are blossoming within you?

2056.

Because your mind is searching
For hope,
Your soul will free your life
From ignorance.

2057.

Although yours
Is a self-chosen pain,
The physician within you
Has decided to cure you
Completely.

2058.

Every day my Beloved Supreme
Affectionately and blessingfully
Trains my devoted heart
On my soul's beautiful track.

2059.

The Compassion-Eye of my sweet
   Lord
Is always ready to lead,
But is my insecurity-heart
Willing to follow?

2060.

I have a cute monkey-mind
To entertain my outer life.
I have a soulful flute-heart
To enlighten my inner life.

2061.

My Beloved Supreme,
Do give me only one boon:
That I shall not make
Even a single mistake
In my next lifetime.

2062.

Every morning I ask myself
Only two questions:
Why am I not loving my Beloved
   Supreme
More, infinitely more?
Is God pleased with me,
Really pleased with me?

2063.

Alas, my Beloved Supreme and I
Do not see eye-to-eye with each
   other.
This morning I was so excited
In telling my Lord Supreme
That I have become, at last,
The purity-glow of my soul.
My Beloved Supreme
Immediately corrected me:
"My child,
It is not the purity of your soul
That you have become.
You have become the pretence-
   show
Of your vital!"

2064.

During your meditation
God appears and reappears
Many, many times before you,
But your blind despair-life
Prevents you from recognising
    God.

2065.

My Beloved Supreme tiptoed
Through my golden dreams
And left behind on my bed
His Compassion-Eye
And His Forgiveness-Heart.

2066.

Until I have unmistakably realised
That my desire-life is a dead-end
    street,
How can my Lord Supreme show
    me
And lead me along
His free Highway?

2067.

How can you have
A free parking permit
In God's Self-Transcendence-
    World
When you have not prayed to God
To give you one of His
Earth-transcending
And Heaven-transcending
Vision-Cars?

2068.

At long last
My mind has become divine!
This morning
My mind gave a standing ovation
To my heart
For its free access to my soul.

2069.

My heart is every day
Carefully nurturing the aspiration
Of its infant brother, mind.

2070.

Aspiration-medicine cures
Both the mind's foolishness
And the heart's barrenness.

2071.

Oh, I need help,
I need everybody's help!
My life is chained
To my mind's despair-night.

2072.

You may at most
Touch another's mind,
But never, never
His mind's doubts.

2073.

Only a heart of implicit faith
Is chosen to be
On Heaven's Board of Directors.

2074.

Do not be a fool!
God has already lowered
The God-realisation-price
Considerably.
He is not going to lower it
Any more.

2075.

Self-pity,
Are you not the worst foe
Of my God-given
Satisfaction-capacity?

2076.

Behold!
God has given you
A front-row seat
To watch His Satisfaction-Dance.

2077.

A common experience:
A doubting mind
Eventually becomes
A betraying mind.

2078.

Unless you have a mind
Of equanimity,
How can you live
Inside the Satisfaction-Home
Of God's Heart?

2079.

Because I am spanning
The summits of the mind,
My life is able to live
In the house
Of tomorrow's perfection-smile.

2080.

My heart touched God's
Dream-Boat
Only to become
A reality-passenger.

2081.

My Lord Supreme,
Only one prayer I have:
Do give me a gratitude-heart
Of birthless origin
And deathless end.

2082.

God has broken my mind
So that my heart can claim
His Life as its very own.

2083.

You doubt me.
That means you do not see
God's Vision-Beauty
In me and through me.

2084.

My heart's mountain-moving
　faith
And my Lord's Compassion-
　descending Eye
Shall eternally remain
Two excellent friends.

2085.

My mind is never ready
To choose anything.
My heart is always ready
To choose silence.

2086.

God always wants
A purity-heart
To be His Satisfaction-Standard-
　Bearer.

2087.

As a doubting mind
Deserves an immediate death,
Even so, a faithful heart
Deserves an eternal life.

2088.

My Lord, alas,
My heart-bridge is broken.
"My child,
Do not worry.
Give your soul a chance.
It will be able to repair it
Easily and perfectly."

2089.

Your mind's brilliance
Will lose all its charm
Long before your heart
Is ready to wake up fully.

2090.

Your inner life needs
A constant reminder
Of purity's beauty.
Your outer life needs
A constant reminder
Of sincerity's certainty.

2091.

Your mind's ignorance
Will examine you.
But your soul's wisdom
Must examine you first
If you want to become
A perfect God-lover.

2092.

Alas, my heart's surrender-plant
Does not grow,
And my life's gratitude-fruit
Never ripens.

2093.

Beg your conscience
To examine you.
It will help you to become a good
    student
At God's Perfection-School.

2094.

My Lord,
Yesterday You were something to
    me.
Today You have become
    everything
In my life.

2095.

Heaven gave him
An all-seeing soul.
He is giving Heaven
An all-loving heart.

2096.

Desire-life
Burns his body.
Aspiration-heart
Not only illumines him,
But also satisfies God.

2097.

God's most favourite Dance
Is my nature's
Fire-pure transformation.

2098.

Why do you have to wait
For time to carry you to God?
Can you not carry
Your little human body
To God immediately?

2099.

His mind's aspiration-plant
Is saving him
From frustration within
And frustration without.

2100.

All that is needed
Is aspiration
To realise God.
All that is needed
Is surrender
To become another God.

2101.

My gratitude-heart tells me
What I can ultimately become.
My surrender-life tells me
What I eternally am.
What can I ultimately become?
God's Vision-Eye.
What am I eternally?
God's Self-Transcendence-Song.

2102.

Since you have become the ugly face
Of your jealousy-mind,
How can your heart-wings
Carry you through space?

2103.

Do not interfere with God.
Let Him become a regular Visitor
To your heart-temple.

2104.

I am God's.
This is what God
Secretly and compassionately tells
    me.
God is mine, only mine.
This is what I openly and proudly
Tell the whole world.

2105.

Happiness-moon is rising.
I am adoring its beauty.
Perfection-sun is rising.
I am becoming its delight.

2106.

Who else can be
The mischief-creator
If not my mind,
The usual ringleader!

2107.

Lend a hand to your fellow seeker
Now, right now,
And before long you will see
Your aspiration-bud
Blossoming into
A realisation-flower.

2108.

My mind is an attachment-jungle.
My life is full
Of entanglement-thorns.
Oh, how can I satisfy
My Beloved Supreme,
How can I?

2109.

A life of spirituality
Is God's Certainty.
This life can never be
Uncertainty's confusion-jungle.

2110.

My heart's faith-boat was built
By God's Vision-Eye.
Therefore, it can weather any
    storm
In any sea, at any time.

2111.

Alas, alas,
His soul came into the world
To tell the most authentic
Life-story
To a sleeping humanity!

2112.

When I live in the desire-world
And do not pray and meditate,
I clearly see that my mind's ego
Is my life's tallest tree.
When I live in the aspiration-
    world
And pray and meditate,
I see that my heart's oneness
Is undoubtedly my life's tallest
    tree.

2113.

When I surrender my desire-life
And my aspiration-life
Soulfully and unconditionally
To my Beloved Supreme,
I say to Him,
"My Lord, to You I give
What I had before — my desire
    life —
And what I am now — my
    aspiration-life.
Both at the same time
I place at Your Feet."
My Lord Supreme grants me
His own Satisfaction-Tree,
Which is infinitely taller
Than my desire-life-tree
And my aspiration-life-tree
Put together.

2114.

O my Lord Supreme,
I shall give You what I had —
    desire —
What I am — aspiration —
And what I shall become —
    satisfaction.
I shall offer You
My desire-life of the past,
My aspiration-life of the present
And my satisfaction-life of the
    future,
All three together,
To make You happy all the time
In Your own Way.

2115.

My mind is such a fool!
Every day it is satisfied
With imagination-trophies
Without running a race
Either in the inner world
Or in the outer world.

2116.

I wish I were another God.
I really and truly want to advise
The present God
To be more strict with His creation
So that perfect Perfection-Life on
    earth
Before long can blossom.

2117.

The Eye of Heaven
Has started visiting him every day,
For it has observed
A miraculous change in his mind.

2118.

O my dream-worlds,
How I wish I could remain
Always inside you.
Quite often I reject you,
Yet I survive.
But I am absolutely certain
That if ever you reject me,
I shall not be able to live on earth.
O my dream-worlds,
You are my Lord's Vision-
   Perfection;
You are my Lord's Realisation-
   Satisfaction.

2119.

The mind meets with obstacles
Because it secretly treasures
Confusion-night.
The heart meets with no obstacles
Because it knows
There is nothing but
   illumination.

2120.

Every morning my Lord comes to
   me
And gives me
His Compassion-Umbrella,
His Protection-Shoes,
His Perfection-Pen.

2121.

Two unexpected dreams
Have turned into realities.
God's beautiful Face
Is glowing on earth,
Man's soulful heart
Is playing in Heaven.

2122.

How can you be so cruel!
How can you be so stupid!
How can you desert
The lonely sea of humanity!

2123.

I do not mind failing,
As long as
I do not stop trying
Altogether.

2124.

When I say it is all my fault,
Openly
My Beloved Supreme starts
    crying.
When I say it is all God's fault,
Secretly
My Beloved Supreme starts
    smiling.
When I say it is neither
God's fault nor my fault,
Immediately
My Beloved Supreme starts
    dreaming
A new Dream.

2125.

The day before yesterday, by
    mistake
I kept my mind's frustration-
    window open.
Yesterday, by mistake
I kept my vital's destruction-door
    open.
Today I am forced to see
That the flame of my aspiration-
    heart
Is completely extinguished.

2126.

Thirteen self-giving minutes a day
Can please God the man on earth
And transform man the God in
    Heaven
Far beyond anybody's
    imagination.

2127.

In the depths of my heart
A blue bird is constantly singing.
Although I am now chained
To earth-bound time,
My blue bird is telling me
That if I listen to it
While it sings soulfully,
It will free me from earth-bound
    time
And carry me
Into God's Vision-Sky to fly.

2128.

Yesterday you enjoyed
An arsenal of doubt.
No wonder today
All your heart's aspiration-flames
Are totally extinguished.

2129.

You are a mind-juggler.
You are not a heart-voyager.
How then can Heaven allow you
To walk along its splendour-road?

2130.

Only when my heart becomes the host
Does humanity have a constant free access
To my God-pleasing life.

2131.

Who am I?
A beautiful love-beam
From God's Heaven.
What shall I become?
A perfection-dream
For the world's soul.

2132.

An ordinary soul is afraid
Of the door of birth.
An ordinary man is afraid
Of the door of death.

2133.

Do not tell the world
That your aspiration
Has deserted you.
But tell the world
The absolute truth:
That you have deserted the man
Who is in the process
Of becoming God in you.

2134.

It is undoubtedly a fruitless search
Whenever you want to see and feel
Even an iota of Peace, Light and Bliss
In your mind-closet.

2135.

Who says mourning is not good!
When I mourn the disappearance
Of my devotion-heart
I get added strength
To revive my old aspiration-life.

2136.

Not knowing what to do,
Quite unexpectedly
He spoke ill of God
And quite unexpectedly
He spoke well of man.

2137.

Never think
That you are the puppet
Of your heart's fading faith.
Do you know who you are?
You are the ever-rising sun
Of God's infinite Vision-Smile.

2138.

Both God and I are waiting.
God is waiting
For my life's surrender to arrive,
And I am waiting
For God's Love to arrive.

2139.

My fears and God's Tears
Follow me wherever I go
Both in the inner world
And in the outer world.

2140.

Every day I go
To my Lord's Compassion-Library
To read only one book,
And the name of that book is
"God's Forgiveness-Smile".

2141.

The day is fast approaching
When the hope-caravan of the
    seekers
Shall successfully and gloriously
Pass through the frustration-
    desert.

2142.

Falling, crying and smiling
Are three
Oneness-brother-friends.

2143.

In vain I knocked
At your mind's door
For admittance.
In vain God knocked
At my heart's door
For admittance.
Oh, open your mind's door soon
And teach me
How I can open my heart's door
To God.

2144.

Where is the difference
Between my heart's forgetfulness
And my life's ungratefulness?

2145.

Can you not see
That your heart becomes
   damaged in transit
While travelling home
From the vital and mental worlds?

2146.

When I sleep in Heaven,
Everybody there tells me
I look beautiful
And should come down
And show my beauty
To earth.
When I sleep on earth,
Everybody there says I look ugly
And must never think of
Visiting Heaven.

2147.

I prayed to God
To grant me His infinite Peace,
Light and Bliss.
My Lord said to me,
"My child, before I do that,
I have to announce
To the world at large
Your ego's unconditional death."

2148.

For many, many years,
My Lord Supreme,
I have been praying to You
For many, many things.
But from today on
I shall pray for only one thing:
Do make me
A well-tuned heart-instrument
Of Yours.

2149.

My soul was the beautiful
   beginning
Of God's Vision-Eye.
My heart is the fruitful fulfilment
Of God's Promise-Reality.

2150.

God accompanies you everywhere.
Can you not accompany Him
Only to one place:
His sleepless Satisfaction-Home?

2151.

Every day you have to energise
   yourself
With your superhuman dreams.
Otherwise, you are bound to
   stagger
Along the road of self-doubt.

2152.

My Lord Supreme,
You have given me
Two weak hands.
"But My child,
I have given you also
My own powerful Heart."
My Lord Supreme,
You have given me
Two blind eyes.
"But My child,
I have given you also
My own Immortality's Vision-
   Life."

2153.

Do not cling
To what is not your own
And what can never be your own:
Your ignorance-life.

2154.

You are an imprisoned
Darkness-dancer.
How can you also be the
   distributor
Of your soul's ecstasy?

2155.

Yesterday my desire-life
Desired to bind God.
Today my aspiration-life
Is begging God to liberate me.

2156.

Life's two longest-lasting diseases:
"I know everything!"
"I know nothing!"

2157.

Your idleness-mind
Has conquered
Your willingness-heart.
Therefore your life is doomed
To utter disappointment.

2158.

God has lowered
His transcendental Height
Considerably.
Now I must raise
My universal height a little.
Try I must, try I must,
So that my ascent and my Lord's
   Descent
Will meet together.

2159.

When I soulfully pray
For His Compassion,
My Beloved Supreme tells me
That I am as beautiful as He is.
When I powerfully meditate
On His Forgiveness,
My Beloved Supreme tells me
That I am as perfect as He is.

2160.

My heart's gratitude-nest
Is the new Home
Of my Beloved Supreme.

2161.

Every day my Beloved Supreme
Breaks His old Record
And establishes a new Record
In my outer life
With His Compassion-
   Acceptance.
Every day my Beloved Supreme
Breaks His old Record
And establishes a new Record
In my inner life
With His Forgiveness-Delight.

2162.

Will you believe, can you believe,
That my Beloved Supreme
Loves the blue-gold flames
Of my heart-temple
Infinitely more
Than He loves anything else
In His entire creation?

2163.

Do you know that you have
A pure heart?
And do you know that you also
   have
Two impure eyes?
On the strength of your pure heart
You have covered half the
   distance.
Now try to have two pure eyes!
Then you will be able to cover
The full distance.
Finally you will be able to sit
Right in front of the Throne
Of your Beloved Supreme
Permanently.

2164.

Only a pure surrender-life
And a sweet gratitude-heart
Can have every night
God's dream-flooded sleep.

2165.

There is so much in me
That needs to die.
There is so much in me
That wants to live.
My Lord Supreme tells me that
At present
There is nothing inside me
That I should keep;
There is nothing inside me
That I should even imagine
    treasuring.

2166.

Yesterday I did not pray
And I did not meditate.
Therefore, my Lord Supreme
    remained
His unfulfilled Promise.
Today again I have not prayed
And I have not meditated.
Therefore, my life is now
My own abandoned hope.

2167.

To liberate my life
From humanity's insane
And inhuman voice,
I have no other choice
Than to become another God.

2168.

God's first Invention is:
I am.
Man's first discovery is:
I do not know.

2169.

My human life
Is neither an animal-hunger
Nor an angel-dance.
My human life
Is a Perfection-Dream of God.

2170.

My Lord Supreme has cancelled
    His Visit
Not because He is irresponsible,
Not because my heart is
    ungrateful,
But because my mind
Will not cheerfully accept
His supreme Oneness-Authority.

2171.

The inner world
Does not want to tell you
What it has and what it is.
The outer world
Does not want to know
Who you are and what you have.

2172.

My Lord Supreme told me
This morning
That my gratitude-heart
Has nullified the distance
Between my earth and His
   Heaven.

2173.

I want my mind
To be a twenty-four-hour truth-
   seeker.
I want my heart
To be a twenty-four-hour God-
   lover.
I want my life
To be a twenty-four-hour God-
   dreamer.

2174.

He is seeking the impossible.
He wants his soul's Heaven-phone
To ring
Inside his mind of impurity.

2175.

My sweet Lord,
I am sure You know
Perfectly well
That You hurt me deeply
When You say I do not love You
The way I used to love.
My fellow human beings,
You deeply hurt me
When you try to convince me
That I do not care for you
The way I used to care.

2176.

Again and again
I fail my Beloved Supreme
In my life's examination.
Yet again and again
He asks me to sail with Him
In his Eternity's Vision-Boat
To His Infinity's Self-
   Transcendence-Shore.

2177.

His mind's open smile
Cures humanity's headache.
His heart's secret tears
Cure humanity's heartache.

2178.

The golden faith-flames
Of your heart's aspiration
Can and shall melt
Your mind's doubt-suspicion-
    shame.

2179.

Claim God's Heart
And receive God's Hands.
Lo, death is bowing low!

2180.

The more you try to hide
Your inner insecurity,
The more you expose
Your outer embarrassment.

2181.

After years of making
Deplorable mistakes,
He is now smiling
The perfection-smile
In his aspiration-life.

2182.

Divinity's oneness-plateau
Is the supreme summit
Of humanity's sleepless hunger.

2183.

O bright newness of the day,
I adore you.
O deep stillness of the night,
I love you.

2184.

Your life is divinity's beauty
Because God has made your heart
Sweet with sleepless hunger.

2185.

If you are longing
To unfurl the sail
Of your dream-boat,
God will definitely shelter
Your pure longing.

2186.

My heart's
Indomitability-seed
Is my life's
Certainty-tree.

2187.

Unless you own
Tears of overwhelming gratitude,
How can you profusely drink
God's Silence-Delight?

2188.

When God goes out shopping
In His universal Market,
He starts loving unreservedly
His Vision-made human dolls.

2189.

When my life became
Purity's humility-sand,
God came to me
And stood before me
On His Divinity's Compassion-
   Feet.

2190.

My Lord's invisible Smile
Becomes visible
Only when I make
My heart's mounting cry
Invincible.

2191.

When I become
My life's surrender-shuttle
Between earth's aspiration-station
And Heaven's illumination-
   station,
God dances
His absolute Satisfaction-Dance.

2192.

To dare to love God
Is not my mind's audacity
But my heart's sleepless necessity.

2193.

The seeker in me knows
Why to love God.
The lover in me knows
How to please God.

2194.

Nothing is unclaimable by me —
No, not even my Beloved Lord's
Ever-transcending Vision-
   Delight.

2195.

God the Supreme Bidder
Shall easily and unmistakably win
At your heart-auction.

2196.

What a useless mind you have!
It cannot even hatch
A tiny oneness-bird.

2197.

God always keeps your heart-wealth
Inside the protection-pocket
Of His Satisfaction-Smile.

2198.

Alas,
My mind's restless twists
Are afraid of meeting with God
Even in silver dreams.

2199.

If you do not humble yourself,
How can you either
See God's Face
Or hide from yourself?

2200.

I went to God with all my credentials.
God laughed and laughed and laughed.
He said to me,
"Come back in a few years' time
With your new achievements."
I went back to God for the second time,
This time with an empty heart.
As soon as my Lord Supreme
Saw my empty heart,
He became excited and delighted.
He said to me,
"Ah, that is Mine!
Where did you get it?
Who gave it to you?
Your empty heart is absolutely
My own Wealth.
My child, I am so grateful to you
And so proud of you
Because you have returned to Me
My own Possession, My own Wealth,
My own Achievement."

2201.

My Lord,
Do break my doubting mind
With Your Thunder-Feet.
My Lord,
Do remake my aspiring heart
With Your Splendour-Eye.

2202.

Every day
Mine is the life that gasps
For the breathless Breath
Of God's Forgiveness-Smile.

2203.

Yesterday my Lord granted me
A receptivity-heart
So that today He can speak
A private word to it.

2204.

If you want to be relieved
Of your heartache,
Then you must fracture
Your ego-mind
Ruthlessly.

2205.

Your Heaven-passport is ready.
Are you ready
With your silence-life-fee?

2206.

Your mind is confined
In confusion-cage
Because it does not believe
In the heart's illumination-palace.

2207.

Every morning
I sing my mind to sleep
And then immediately
I inspire my heart to fly.

2208.

My mind, may I offer you
A simple suggestion?
Since you want to be really good,
You must be a stranger
To your own greatness.

2209.

Surrender unconditional
Will be the next scene
In his life's
God-pleasing drama.

2210.

As your insecure eyes
Are quite familiar
With a mob of fears,
Even so, your unsurrendered
    heart
Is quite familiar
With the sob of tears.

2211.

If you play with doubt-clouds,
Your heart's faith-parachute
Will never open.

2212.

I shall not underestimate
God's Compassion-Ocean.
I shall not underestimate
Man's surrender-life.

2213.

There is only one thing
Easy to earn,
And that thing is
God's Compassion-Salary.

2214.

Today I am commemorating
The death-anniversary
Of my doubting mind.

2215.

Every day his heart's newspaper
Covers stories
About God's Perfection-Vision
And God's Satisfaction-
　Manifestation.

2216.

You can hide
Anything you want to.
But never hide
Your faith-key.

2217.

Someday your aspiration-journey
Will definitely bring you
To the shore of Realisation-Sea.

2218.

You only know
The poverty of my faith.
But you do not know
The infinity of my Lord's
Compassion for me.

2219.

Who needs to enjoy the guidance
Of his insecurity-boss?
Yet who revolts against it?
Not you, not he;
No, not even me!

2220.

When doubt-drought destroyed
His heart's faith-plant,
His spirituality's life-clouds
Immediately gathered.

2221.

God will grant you
His unconditional Satisfaction-
 Certificate.
You just have to go to Him
And receive it from Him.

2222.

God the Inventor proposes
His Infinity's Peace.
Man the discoverer chooses
His eternity's war.

2223.

Just try to have
At least one powerful meditation
Every day.
Your temptation-tire
Will automatically blow out.

2224.

Your self-transcendence-
 marathon
Has shattered the summitless
 pride
Of your ruthless life-devouring
 dragon.

2225.

You will miss
The Heaven-bound flight
If you do not dismiss
Your mind's uncomely thoughts.

2226.

Mine is the gratitude-heart
That originates the powerful
 waves
Of my surrender-life.

2227.

You do not have to cook,
You do not have to serve,
You just have to eat daily
Your meditation-meal.

2228.

Your heart's surrender-flower
Is bound to outlast
All your previous blunders.

2229.

There is not a single map
That can show you
The road to God.
Therefore, you need not read
Even one map
Before you embark
On your God-voyage.

2230.

He left his heart of hope
As a great legacy
To aspiring mankind.

2231.

The latest news from Heaven:
God will not mind
If I do not cry for Him,
But He will definitely mind
If I do not smile at Him
And with Him.

2232.

Do not misunderstand God,
Your Eternity's Boss,
If He asks you every day
To come to Him
And collect His Blessing-Bonus.

2233.

Because you love to live
In your mind's cluttered room,
Your life has become
A totally shattered home.

2234.

What can you buy
Either in Heaven or on earth
With reluctance –
Your counterfeit mind-coin?

2235.

My Lord Supreme does not mind
When my account with Him
Is overdrawn.
But He does mind
When I stop withdrawing
Out of sheer embarrassment.

2236.

Each dark corner of my life
Not only pains
My Lord Supreme
But also takes away
My God-hunger
Indefinitely.

2237.

Transformation without frustration
Is quite possible
If I forbid my aspiration-dedication-life
To play with doubt.

2238.

You have only one right place
To keep your victory-trophy,
And that place is
Your heart's gratitude-room.

2239.

If your heart-checks to God
Are bouncing every day,
Then God will disconnect
His Telephone Line to you.

2240.

Is it not beneath your dignity
To become a second-class disciple?
Is it not beneath the dignity
Of your divine soul?
Do you not think
You will torture your soul
Most ruthlessly
If you settle for being
A second-class disciple?

2241.

My mind always runs away
When it sees my soul
Coming to inject joy into it,
Through its frustration-veil.

2242.

The seeker in him finally realised
That the world-university
Had given him
Its most powerful ignorance-diploma.

2243.

Alas,
I thought the circus of ignorance
Was all inside my little universe.
Now I see that the circus of ignorance
Is everywhere.

2244.

Since everything must be transformed
Eventually,
Why not let us start
With our life's ego-horse,
Which has to be transformed
Into God's fondest lamb.

2245.

Before it gets too late
You must return,
You must go back
To your heart's gratitude-garden!

2246.

No earth-possessing life
Can ever be enlightened.
No Heaven-longing life
Can remain unillumined.

2247.

If love speaks
Through your heart,
That means
Perfection has already started
    speaking
Through your life.

2248.

I completely forgot
That God is old.
I could have learnt
So much from Him.
I totally forgot
That God is young.
I should have invited Him
To come into my heart-garden
And play with me.

2249.

Do you not recognise
Your soul's old friend: God?
Do you not recognise
Your heart's new friend: man?

2250.

Unless you powerfully announce
The end of self-doubt,
You will never hear
The love-beat
Of God's Divinity-Heart.

2251.

God's Eternal NOW Radio Station
Every day broadcasts
The same most significant news:
God-lovers have chartered a plane
To God's Satisfaction-Kingdom.

2252.

There are many prisons in life,
But the destructive confusion-
    prison
Of man's mind
Shatters man's entire being.

2253.

If you are acquainted with
Inner commitments,
Then your life can never
Be a stranger
To sublime achievements.

2254.

One solitary voice
Continues to call me.
It says
My heart shall succeed
And my life shall proceed
Forever and forever.

2255.

The beauty
Of his sacrifice-life
And the purity
Of his surrender-heart
Every day play
With God's Vision-Eye
And God's Satisfaction-Heart.

2256.

Beyond the walls of self-
   imprisonment
God stands
And grants the true God-lover
And truth-seeker
His Immortality's
   Enlightenment.

2257.

The kindness-heart
Of oneness
Liberates two slaves:
Doubtfulness and fearfulness.

2258.

Fly out of your insecurity-nest!
Angels, with Heaven's delight,
Are eagerly waiting for you.

2259.

Destiny sits at his feet
Because his God-surrendered
   head
Is too small
For destiny to sit upon.

2260.

His heart's oneness-purity-smile
Far outweighs
His mind's division-impurity-
   frown.

2261.

Only a boundless purity-heart
Can pass through
The fogbound ignorance-future.

2262.

Don the garment of optimism!
You will immediately be able
To free yourself
From your mind's faded hopes.

2263.

Within he feasts
On the fragrance of silence-light.
Without he feasts
On the strokes of sound-drums.

2264.

Your mind's stubborn stupidity
Will never be able
To see God-Beauty's
Earth-transforming morn.

2265.

You have at least one
Good quality:
You do not consider
Your restful slumber
As your peaceful trance.

2266.

The more I try
To hide my weaknesses
From God,
The sooner God's
Compassion-Forgiveness-Radar
Finds me.

2267.

Purity's gratitude-heart
Is the main receptionist
In God's humanity-transforming
Head Office.

2268.

You are not
Your life's faded hopes.
You are
Your soul's promise-sun.

2269.

A life of volcano-ego
Is nothing but
A self-addressed life.

2270.

Although my mind
Is in the confusion-clouds,
I am still a hope-bird
Of my Lord Supreme.

2271.

Develop a voracious
Aspiration-appetite!
You will meet God
Halfway to Heaven.

2272.

My soul laughs and laughs
At my mind's persistent efforts
To devalue my heart's divinity.

2273.

The malady of your life
Is ruining
The melody of your soul.

2274.

Purify your mind soulfully.
Otherwise, you and your mind
Will be totally lost
In the labyrinths of obscurity.

2275.

Commit your sincerity-breath
To God's Compassion.
He will teach you summit-prayers.

2276.

Praise is something
That we may
On very rare occasions need.
But justice-light is something
That we always need.

2277.

To distrust your heart's
Good qualities
Is to increase your mind's
Bad qualities
Ten times
Immediately!

2278.

Alas,
Every day I ask God
The same stupid question:
"My Lord,
Do You really love me
More than I love You?"

2279.

Two dreams are running
   together:
The transformation-dream
Of man's life
And the Satisfaction-Dream
Of God's Heart.

2280.

Your eyes have captured
God the Inspiration.
Your heart has captured
God the Illumination.
Your life has captured
God the Perfection.
And finally
You are going to capture
God the Satisfaction.

2281.

Unless your life becomes
The humility-dust
Of God's Compassion-Feet,
How can you ever draw
Every detail of God's Face?

2282.

I am so happy
That my mind has at last
Resigned its chairmanship
Of the doubt-committee.

2283.

Take a close look
At your inner life!
Are you not ashamed
Of your continuous
Insecurity-illness?

2284.

God may consider the world-mind
As His finished product,
But He considers each human heart
As His unfinished product.

2285.

No matter what kind of seeker
You are,
No matter how developed
You are
In your spiritual life,
You have to be careful
Of your mind's impurity-pickpocket!

2286.

God's turn came.
He showed you
How to realise Him.
Your turn is coming.
You have to show Him
How you are going
To manifest Him.

2287.

Every morning
I sing my prayer-song
At my Lord's Feet.
Every evening
I dance my meditation-dance
Inside the Heart-Garden
Of my Lord Supreme.

2288.

When the God-Hour strikes,
The Absolute Supreme will
Without fail
Grant you His Confidence-Power
So you can become
His transcendental Tower.

2289.

The arch-enemy of your soul
Is not your impure mind,
Not your insecure heart,
But your unwilling life.

2290.

No wonder you have lost
Your security-wallet!
You forgot to put
A picture of God's Satisfaction-
    Face
Inside it.

2291.

Alas, what shall I do
And what can I do?
Heaven is already disgusted
With my imperfections,
And hell is already overcrowded.

2292.

A man may be
Ordinary
But his dreams can be
Extraordinary.

2293.

A man's desire-life
May torture him
But his aspiration-life
Can illumine the world.

2294.

If you are unwilling to learn
At your own heart-university,
Yours will be a life
Of paralysing grief.

2295.

If you encircle your ego
With a victory-fence,
Then you remain a stranger
To perfection-achievement.

2296.

Because you are lost
In a crowd of unruly emotions,
Heaven does not want
To accept you
And earth does not want
To recognise you.

2297.

No matter how thick
Your mind's doubt-fog is,
The Hope-Light of God's Heart
Can easily shine through it.

2298.

There was a time
When I knew nothing
Except my mind's business hours.
But now I know two things:
My heart's aspiration-hours
And
My life's dedication-hours.

2299.

As God's Eye can tell
Where the seeker's heart is,
Even so, the seeker's heart
Can tell where God's Eye is.

2300.

If God is pleased with you,
Deliberately He may not fulfil
All your desires.
If He is extremely pleased with
   you,
Then He may fulfil
Some of your innocent desires.
But if He is completely pleased
   with you,
Then He is not going to satisfy
Even one earthbound desire of
   yours,
For He wants you to be a co-sharer
Of His Infinity's free Delight.

2301.

I can neglect all my wealth
Except my inner wealth:
My surrender, my constant
   surrender,
To the Will of my Beloved
   Supreme.

2302.

No matter who houses a bad
   thought—
A desire-man or an aspiration-
   man—
A bad thought is a dire challenge
To humanity's progress-life.

2303.

The faith-tutor
Of your aspiration-heart
Can easily teach you
How to spurn doubt-spies.

2304.

Early in the morning
When I pray and meditate,
I see the compassion-blossomed
  Eye
Of my Compassion-Lord
  Supreme.

2305.

I have not calculated
My loss and gain.
Therefore, my Lord Supreme
Has made me the manager
Of His own spiritual Shopping
  Centre.

2306.

The human in me dies
When it stops progressing.
The divine in me permanently
  lives
The moment it begins its journey.

2307.

To possess God
Is to claim God.
To claim God
Is to love God only.
To love God only
Is to remain far beyond
The domain of expectation.

2308.

Unless you exercise your divine
  right
To your inner conviction,
You will not be able to breathe
God's Satisfaction-Air.

2309.

Self-transcendence
Is the inner wealth
That pleases the Inner Pilot
More than anything else.

2310.

I long for a sweet Smile
Every day from my Lord Supreme.
He tells me
That He will grant me a sweet
  Smile
If every day I am ready
To go beyond the bleak
  boundaries
Of my mind's doubt-desert.

2311.

Each God-lover and God-
    distributor
Is a sonorous gong
That announces God's new
    Awakening.

2312.

With his soul's self-offering-paint,
He has been painting
Humanity's weak face
And strong heart.

2313.

Once you have accepted
The slow-withering demise
Of your selfless dedication,
You are nothing but
A stagnant pond of teeming
    imperfections.

2314.

To inject joy
Into the sadness-vein
Of this world,
Sweep out humanity's doubts
With your soul's
Indomitable bravery-broom!

2315.

Unless you truly mourn
The disappearance of your
Devotion-life,
You will not get back
The Sweetness and Fondness
Of your Beloved Supreme.

2316.

What can poor God do?
You never listen to Him!
Therefore,
God has deliberately moved
Out of your neighbourhood.

2317.

In our inner life
We want victory in everything
To make us happy.
In our outer life
We want our ego's failure
To make us happy.

2318.

Although both your nature
And my nature
Have to be changed,
I can conquer only my own nature
And see the Oneness-Smile
Of my Inner Pilot.

2319.

When I gave God my life
For safekeeping,
He immediately showed me
His self-transforming Secrets.

2320.

God is ready to illumine your mind.
But will you ever be ready
Either to invite Him
Or to accept His Invitation
For the illumination of your unlit mind?

2321.

O my mind,
I shall love you with all my heart
If you can just say
That you are hopelessly stupid
And that God is infinitely wiser
Than you.

2322.

Surrender-medicine
You have to take every day
If you want to keep
Your body, vital, mind and heart
Absolutely free from inner illness.

2323.

The stupid statements of your mind
Torture your heart.
Therefore your soul,
Out of its infinite compassion
For your heart,
Is challenging your mind's
Unfounded statements.

2324.

When are you going to realise
That your insecurity-life
Has destroyed your purity-heart?

2325.

If you obey
Your heart's silence command,
Your life will enjoy
Free flights to Heaven.

2326.

The vanity of the vital
Is a fatal disease
That can kill an aspiration-heart.

2327.

Heaven's foreign policy is:
Heaven will give what it has,
Beauty's smile,
And earth will give what it is,
Purity's cry.

2328.

An old, sad story:
Heaven ignores earth,
Earth defies Heaven.

2329.

Before I start loving God,
I must conquer
My mind's animal hunger.

2330.

He is God's roommate
Who unmistakably thinks and
   feels
That he is tomorrow's new God.

2331.

Will God ever be pleased
With a seeker
If he does not empty
His mind's headaches
And his life's heartaches
The moment God summons him?

2332.

An aspiration-heart
And a hesitation-mind
Always prefer
To remain strangers.

2333.

Each undivine thought
Has strong connections
With invisible chains.

2334.

God is not going to reprimand you
If you do not listen to His
   Command.
But He is under no obligation
To give you another chance.

2335.

God simply does not want
His sweet children
To eat anything other
Than what He eats:
Nectar-Delight.

2336.

Be generous to God
With your heart's aspiration-cry.
Be generous to man
With your life's dedication-smile.
Be generous to yourself
With your soul's perfection-dance.

2337.

My life has become a victim
To yesterday's doubtful life
And tomorrow's fearful heart.

2338.

The thought-machines break
   down
The moment they are put to use
For God-service.

2339.

When I stand before humanity,
I never know what to say.
When I stand before divinity,
I never know what to offer.

2340.

My Lord Supreme,
Why are You not giving me
Some advice today?
"My child,
You would not listen
To My yesterday's advice.
Unless and until you listen
To My old advice,
I am not going to give you new
   advice.
Each day I am ready to bless you
With new advice.
But every day I want you to listen
To My advice
And please Me in My own Way.
Otherwise, for you there will be
   no advice
Either in the inner world
Or in the outer world
From Me."

2341.

While I am on earth
I think only of
My Heavenly duty.
While I am in Heaven
I think only of
My earthly responsibility.

2342.

If it is too difficult for you
To open your mind's
Willingness-window,
Then you must try at least
To open your heart's
Willingness-door.

2343.

God's blessingful Oneness
With him
And man's soulful oneness
With him
Will end his mind's illusion-era.

2344.

Now that your life has become
A lightless lethargy-land,
How can you run
On God's Satisfaction-Sidewalk?

2345.

Your soul's most convincing
    conviction
Has every right to command your
    life
And make it into
God's Satisfaction-Delight.

2346.

A self-offering-surgeon
Is always successful
In operating on
The sickness of the world.

2347.

Man's gratitude-bridge
Is shorter than the shortest.
Yet on the other side of the bridge,
Who waits?
God, our Beloved Supreme!

2348.

Every day you enjoy interviews
With your impatience-life.
How then do you think
That you will be able to live
Without the blows of defeat?

2349.

There is only one sentence
In God's entire Autobiography:
"The galaxy of stars
And the darkest night
Are inseparably one."

2350.

My Lord Supreme,
Who has a real claim on You?
"My child,
He who does not expect anything,
Either from Heaven or from
   earth."

2351.

I dare not even imagine
That there is something on earth
That can and will shatter
My heart's fragile poise.

2352.

There was a time
When I admired
The flame of your aspiration.
Now I am adoring
The sun of your realisation.

2353.

I am completely lost
When I read my life's want-list.
Again, I am completely lost
When I read my soul's need-list.

2354.

When I am in the mind
I see
That a man of purity
Is rare.
When I am in the heart
I see
That a man of certainty
Is rare.

2355.

Your eyes want to know
When I am going to realise God.
Your heart is telling me
That I have already realised God.

2356.

Yesterday
My heart and I
Scaled a mountain.
Today we see
That it was not a mountain
But an anthill!

2357.

Prayer
Is the Beauty of God
In me.
Meditation
Is the Prosperity of God
In me.

2358.

The damage has already been
   done!
His doubting mind has uprooted
His heart's faith-plant.

2359.

If you consistently make
The wrong choice,
How can God grant you
His tomorrow's earth-guiding
   Voice?

2360.

Awake to the hymn
Of the blue bird within you.
Your past failure-life
Will then be able to sit
At the Compassion-Satisfaction-
   Feet
Of your Beloved Supreme.

2361.

Do not hide your heart
Inside your mind.
Keep your heart always
Before your soul,
For this is the only way
You can see the truth
At its summit
And play with God
Inside His own Heart-Garden.

2362.

God does not expose
My mind's ignorance-life.
He only proposes
My heart's divinity-life.

2363.

My soul has been telling me
For the past few years,
"My child,
Unlearn and unlearn and unlearn
Everything you have learnt
At the university of life!"

2364.

Profit or progress?
If I want profit,
I may not make any progress.
If I make progress,
Then automatically I profit.

2365.

If your life and heart
Can become visible tears,
Then the invisible God
Will become a visible embrace.

2366.

God, your Inner Pilot,
Will never demote you
For losing faith in Him.
He will give you chance after chance
To regain your faith.
Just climb up
Your consciousness-ladder!

2367.

O my mind,
Do you not know
Who you are?
You are an endless speech
Of utter stupidity-parrot.

2368.

Each time I meditate
Soulfully and unconditionally,
My Beloved Supreme invites me
To come to His Backyard
And enjoy the precious panorama
Of His Vision-Light.

2369.

If you cannot educate your mind
To practise silence,
You will not be able
To evict peace-thief
From your heart-room.

2370.

Nobody else,
Only a lover of mankind,
Can be the true winner of God.

2371.

Every day my Beloved Supreme
Enjoys the choice memories
Of my self-giving heart
And my light-manifesting soul.

2372.

It is you alone who have to decide
Whether you are going to hanker
After humanity's call
Or become
God's unconditional football.

2373.

The moment I offered
The gratitude-garland
Of my heart
To my Beloved Supreme,
He granted me
The Infinity of His Vision-Eye
And the Immortality
Of His Satisfaction-Life.

2374.

He is devoted only to himself.
Therefore
His mind has no ego-limit.
He is devoted only to God.
Therefore
His heart has no oneness-limit.

2375.

Not a difficult task,
To be ruined by failure.
Not an impossible task,
To remain unspoiled by success.

2376.

O seekers of the past,
O seekers of the present,
O seekers of the future,
You have only one thing
To accomplish:
Please, please do not allow doubts
To invade
This beautiful earth of ours!

2377.

The moment I offered my ego-life
To my Lord Supreme,
He granted me immediately
His Soul's Golden Boat
And His Life's Golden Shore.

2378.

A new beginning
Is beckoning his aspiration-heart.
If he lives
Inside his aspiration-heart,
He will enjoy consciously
God's perennial Life.

2379.

Two secrets of mine
Are crying aloud:
I have not fed God the man.
I have not lifted man the God.

2380.

Heaven's tears are falling.
Yet the world's
Staggering problems
Remain unsolved.

2381.

His world is having a holiday
Because his self-giving life
Is making
Its Heavenward journey home.

2382.

Two silent miracles:
God cries
More than I cry.
God needs me
More than I need Him.

2383.

His aspiration-heart
Has won God's Vision.
His transcendence-life
Has become the bridge
Between God the Known
And God the Unknowable.

2384.

O mind,
Why do you allow doubt
To make you old?
O heart,
Why do you allow insecurity
To stab you?

2385.

The beauty of imagination
Heaven gave to earth.
The divinity of aspiration
Earth will give to Heaven.

2386.

Is there any human being
Who has not passed through
The gloomy tunnels
Of impurity's disturbance-mine?

2387.

The road map of human life
Is constantly changing.
While changing
It is leading humanity
Either to its destined illumination
Or to its unwanted destruction.

2388.

Can you not give your Master
Your aspiration-snack
Since he is going to give you
His full realisation-meal?

2389.

If you do not begin your spiritual life
With a soulful hope,
Nobody will be able to erase
The sad record of your past life.

2390.

The compromising messiah
Cannot and will not succeed.
It is the uncompromising messiah
Who will transform earth's face
   and fate
For God to appreciate and utilise
In His new creation.

2391.

A life of unconditional surrender
Is the most beautiful signpost
Of the perfection-flowering
   Beyond.

2392.

The wisest fool on earth
Is he who knows perfectly well
That God exists,
But feels that he does not need
   Him.

2393.

One more insult for God:
"I am such a useless human being
That even God will not be able
To change my nature!"

2394.

I give God what I have:
My heart's gratitude-seeds.
God gives me what He is:
His Infinity's
Horizon-spanning Satisfaction-
   Heart.

2395.

This morning my Lord gave me
His transcendental Smile:
A long-awaited miracle.
Alas, once again I am dining
With ignorance-prince:
A long-forbidden action.

2396.

An old joy has returned:
God is clasping my eyes
With His invisible Hands.
A new joy shall begin:
I shall not hide from God
My pangs of spiritual poverty.

2397.

How can you expect God
To be your Progress-Partner
If you do not allow Him to enter
Into your mind's dark doubt-
   room?

2398.

The art of knowing
Is a fruitful subject.
I ask my heart to study it
Seriously.
The art of not knowing
Is a useful subject.
I ask my mind to study it
Faithfully.

2399.

Heaven's tears are bountifully
    falling
Not because I blamed the world
For my failure-life,
But because I did not acclaim God
For my success-life.

2400.

Touch, O touch my aching heart,
My Lord Supreme!
You have not fed me
For a long time
With Your Blessing-Smile-Food.

2401.

Your heart's cheerful willingness
Is always
Your life's absolutely perfect
    choice.

2402.

Desire does not know
What true satisfaction is,
And God does not want
Desire to know.
Aspiration knows
What true satisfaction is
Because God wants
Aspiration to know.

2403.

Heaven offers hospitality
Only to those
Who feel that Heaven
Is their only necessity
Before they can sleeplessly play
With God.

2404.

God's Compassion-Height
Changes your realisation-
    timetable
Which was previously set
By God's Justice-Light.

2405.

The soul that challenges
The oblivion of its God-
    manifestation
Upon earth
Is indeed a most powerful soul.

2406.

A life of unconditional surrender
Is undoubtedly the best
   extinguisher
Of desire-fire.

2407.

Every day I play
On my gratitude-flute
And I beg only one Person
To listen to my playing,
And that Person is
My Inner Pilot.

2408.

As long as God knows
Everything about me
And will do
Everything for me,
I do not have to worry
About anything.
This is the shortest road
To constant satisfaction.

2409.

If you are an aspiration-sprinter,
God the Justice will show you
His Heart's Diamond-Track
And God the Compassion will ask
   you
To run on the Track.

2410.

My body wants so many things
From my soul,
But my soul wants only one thing
From my body: obedience.

2411.

God's Compassion-Giftshop
Has many, many beautiful gifts.
Seekers buy many, many things
From the Shop,
But they seldom buy one
   particular gift:
Gratitude.

2412.

Each aspiration-breath
Has the capacity
And is the capacity
To destroy the blind power
Of death.

2413.

Every day God writes
Forgiveness-Letters
To those who have failed
And given up,
And Compassion-Letters
To those who are willing
To sit for the examination once
   again.

2414.

Until you deliberately throw away
    the key
To your doubting mind's door,
You will not be given the key
To your aspiring heart's door.

2415.

God's Justice-Scoldings
Have at once
Awakened his sleeping body
And illumined his doubting
    mind.

2416.

You have to cut the cord
That has bound you to the world
Mercilessly
Before you can expect God to
    grant you
His Cord to bind Him
Eternally.

2417.

Outwardly what you have
Is a chattering monkey-mind.
Inwardly what you are
Is a roaring lion-soul.

2418.

How can you be happy
If you keep God's Name
Only on your clever lips
And not inside your wise heart?

2419.

If you want to own
Eternity's Ecstasy,
Then you have to disown
The fantasies
Of your undisciplined
And desiring mind.

2420.

Self-giving
Is the paradise of perfection
In a seeker's aspiration-heart.

2421.

You fool!
You are looking for
Death-currency
To exchange for
Your life-coin.

2422.

Let my mind live
Where it wants to live.
My heart and I
Would like to live
Only in God's Oneness-Vision.

2423.

An aspiration-seeker carries God
Inside his heart
And carries the world
In his hands.
This is what God wants him
To do.

2424.

Do not open your mind-door!
Doubt will grab you
And compel you to live with it.

2425.

The human mind
Knows only one road,
And that road
Is its own eternally unlit
Confusion-road.

2426.

Do not remain
In the grip of ingratitude
If you want to see
Your heart grow
Into a life of beatitude.

2427.

You cannot enjoy the Fragrance
Of God's Smile
If you are enjoying the foul smell
Of your desire-life.

2428.

Even God cries
When you tell the world
That you will have absolutely
  nothing
To do with it.

2429.

Your mind-tree
Will always disappoint you.
Your heart-flower
Will not only please you
But also claim you
As its very own.

2430.

Every day make friends
Only with certainty,
And do not gamble
With possibility.

2431.

Each soul is a smile.
Each smile
Is an ecstasy-experience
In God's Perfection-Garden.

2432.

The beauty of life's purity
Always increases
The oneness of God's creation.

2433.

One life of self-control
Can and will save
Millions of other lives.

2434.

His mind experiences
God's Indifference-Frown.
His heart experiences
God's Compassion-Beauty.

2435.

Your heart is already
Under the surveillance
Of God's Will,
And it is so happy.
Can you not ask your mind
To be also under the surveillance
Of God's Will?

2436.

He is his life's
Stupidity-smile.
God in his heart
Is a futility-cry.

2437.

If you sit near God,
You will be able to escape
The ruthless torture
Of earthly rumours.

2438.

Obedience is self-giving.
Self-giving is the fulfilment
Of God's Vision-Reality
In man.

2439.

Since you will not be able
To escape God's Radar,
Why not start climbing up
Your aspiration-ladder?

2440.

Ego-elephant wants to live
Happily and proudly.
But what actually happens?
It lives lonely
And dies miserably.

2441.

God is waiting
In His timeless Temple
To welcome you
And your heart-flames.

2442.

A guiding soul
And a loving heart
Are God's favourite ambassadors
Here on earth.

2443.

His life of sleepless self-giving
Alternates between
God's Vision-Eye
And God's Satisfaction-Heart.

2444.

My wise soul and my pure heart
Patronise only one
Divine enterprise,
And that enterprise
Is God's Satisfaction-Enterprise.

2445.

Tell me,
My fellow seeker,
How could you allow
Your aspiration-heart
To give up?

2446.

God chose you to be
A very special person.
Your mind chose you to be
A friend of its frustration-life.

2447.

If you take aspiration-vitamins,
Your heart will reach sooner
God's Satisfaction-Home.

2448.

Now that you have resumed
Your aspiration-career,
God's Satisfaction-Trophy
Will not remain a far cry.

2449.

If God is
Your number-one candidate,
Then nobody will ever dare
To intimidate you.

2450.

Cherish not the miseries
Of your past disobedience-life.
Cherish only the fragrance
Of your present obedience-life.

2451.

What your mind knows
And treasures
Is a torrential downpour
Of doubt.

2452.

God has cheerfully and proudly
Placed your heart-tapestry
On His Victory-Platform.

2453.

A watchful mind
And a wakeful heart
Expedite the Godward journey.

2454.

Your heart has scaled
The Himalayan heights.
Yet it is not happy,
For it every day wants to sing
The song of self-transcendence.
Your mind has scaled
Only pygmy-heights.
Yet its happiness knows no
    bounds.

2455.

There was a time
When I used to only think of God.
Now God is asking me
Also to fight for Him.

2456.

God has made him the owner
Of God-pleasing cries
And man-pleasing smiles.

2457.

Each heart
Is God's Hope-Plant.
Each life
Is God's Promise-Tree.

2458.

If your mind is mourning
The death of your old life,
Ask your mind
Why is it not buying a coffin
For its own death.

2459.

If God can love
Even your useless life,
Can you not love
God's useful Heart?

2460.

In the spiritual life
To hunger for a high rank wilfully
Is indeed a useless effort.

2461.

Life is nothing but an illusion
When you have a downhill
   experience
In your aspiration-journey.

2462.

A life of perfection
Never stops.
It only moves forward,
Upward and inward.

2463.

There are very few seekers
Who are cheerfully willing
To take exercise
In God's Gymnasium.

2464.

Someday the world
Will appreciate my heart –
Perhaps once my mind
Starts appreciating my heart.

2465.

In the spiritual life
The worst misfortune
Is the seeker's
Hesitation-journey.

2466.

God will be happy to answer
Every day
If you write Him
A tearful aspiration-letter.

2467.

A life
Of surrender-perfection
Is a daily
Full-time job.

2468.

His aspiration-breath
And God's Satisfaction-Heart
Are always to be found together.

2469.

God knows how to speak
Only His Silence-Language.
Therefore, if you want
To understand Him,
Then you must learn
His Silence-Language.

2470.

If you can preserve purity,
You will be able to deserve
Everything—
Even God's highest Height.

2471.

Your life's full moon
Will rise
If you can sing
Every evening
Soulfully
A surrender-song.

2472.

A crown of doubt
And the throne of faith
Are always reluctant
To be seen together.

2473.

If your life has become
A life of surrender,
Then God will gradually replace
Your fleeting time
With His eternal Time.

2474.

Unless you make
A point-blank assault
On your self-doubt,
God will not grant you
His own God-Confidence

2475.

If you come into the world
Armed with your realisation-
   light,
Earth will definitely surrender
Its ignorance-night to you.

2476.

There is only one thing to do,
And that thing is
To conquer the noise
Of your outer life
With the silence
Of your inner life.

2477.

My simplification-life expedites
My God-journey.
My aspiration-life eventually
   becomes
My God-destination.

2478.

Since God gave you your life,
Can you not be good enough
To allow Him
To live in your life?

2479.

I do not need world-recognition.
Therefore
I keep my humility-mind
And my purity-heart
To protect me
From desiring world-recognition.

2480.

Since you do not need
This life of yours,
Why not offer it to God
As soon as possible
And see if He can use it
In a new way?

2481.

God does not allow anybody
To sponsor His aspiration-
   athletes.
He always wants to remain the
   Sponsor
Of His aspiration-athletes,
For these aspiration-athletes
Are His Eternity's Pride.

2482.

Realisation dawns
When the illusion
Of self-importance
Is totally gone.

2483.

If you are a genuine seeker,
Then you cannot allow self-doubt
To slow down
God's Vision-Plan.

2484.

Every soul carries
The Banner of God's Faith
In mankind.

2485.

If your life is encircled
By the fence of fear,
Then your heart will be encircled
By the Fence of God's Tears.

2486.

I call it
My secret soulfulness.
God calls it
His sacred Fulness.

2487.

His daily rebirth
In the spiritual life
Is not his mental delusion
But his psychic realisation.

2488.

A true God-lover
Does not know
What self-service is.
He knows
Only selfless service.

2489.

The mind's intelligence-lamp
Eventually has to surrender
To the heart's wisdom-sun.

2490.

How do you expect
Your God-given faith-heart
To sail your mind-boat
With its heavy doubt-load?

2491.

Because you do not care
For His Compassion-Heart,
God's Justice-Voice
Will soon thunder.

2492.

An obedience-seed
Is the most powerful source
Of the confidence-tree.

2493.

A doubting mind
Will ultimately lose its wager
With a flaming heart.

2494.

The game of world-comparison
Ends on the road
Of self-perfection.

2495.

Today's
Aspiration-life of yours
And tomorrow's
Realisation-life of yours
Are unmistakably
Very close relatives.

2496.

The world knows
Your open acceptance of God.
But God knows
Your secret denial of Him.

2497.

God tells him
That he can talk to God
Only if
He walks with man.

2498.

Your aspiration will be known
Both as your hunger-cry
And as God's Feast-Smile.

2499.

You may disguise
The ugliness of your mind,
But you can never disguise
The poison in your doubt.

2500.

Infinite inspiration-flowers
God carries from Heaven to earth
Every day.
Infinite aspiration-plants
God carries from earth to Heaven
Every day.

2501.

Since I started seeing
With my heart,
I see there is nothing
Beyond my life's soulful reach.

2502.

You can have access to God
By longing for your heart's
Perfection-song.

2503.

To establish oneness
With the world within
And the world without
Is the best way for those
Who want to realise God
And satisfy God in His own Way.

2504.

Before temptation knocks
At your door,
Fence your life around
With purity's divine smile.

2505.

God will not show you
His Heart's Treasury
If you fail to show Him
Your own heart's oneness-coin.

2506.

A Tear from God's Eye
Is humanity's beautiful
   aspiration.
A Smile from God's Eye
Is humanity's powerful
   realisation.

2507.

If self-offering
Does not apply to you,
How can God-becoming
Ever apply to you?

2508.

The secrets of the inner heights
Dwell far beyond
The territories of the mind.

2509.

If you are really wise,
Then you will solve
Not only today's fleeting problems
But also tomorrow's teeming
   problems.

2510.

Your mind's flattery-gift
God will never accept.
He will accept only
Your heart's ecstasy-gift.

2511.

In exchange for
Your heart's purity-gift
God will grant you
His Soul's Divinity-Crown.

2512.

My soul's adamantine will
Can easily shake
The impossibility-tree
At any time.

2513.

The modern world thinks,
"God has to be demonstrated."
The ancient world thought,
"God has to be realised."

2514.

God tells me
That there is nothing
I cannot repay Him for
With my heart's unconditional
   surrender.

2515.

If you are waiting
For the mental clouds to part,
Then even Eternity's patience
Will laugh at your stupidity.

2516.

You have desecrated
Many soulful and valuable things
In your life,
But do not desecrate
The purity-breath
Of your heart-shrine.

2517.

If your Master's words
Go unheeded,
Then your heart's happiness-
   flower
Will never blossom.

2518.

Even God does not believe
That the human mind
Will acquire receptivity from God
To receive His Compassion-Light
And Satisfaction-Delight.

2519.

You invite
Attention.
Frustration comes
Uninvited.

2520.

You lived your life
Intensely.
That does not mean
That God loved your heart
Immensely.

2521.

The best defence
Against doubt-danger:
Your heart's silence-meditation.

2522.

As your mind cries
For the outer world,
Even so, your heart can easily cry
For the inner world
Which is constantly favoured
By those who make a comparison
Between the two worlds.

2523.

For the human mind to think
That it is as powerful as God
Is not an uncommon experience.

2524.

God definitely wants
The human fraternity
To last for Eternity.

2525.

A life of patience
Is for a stoic soul.
A life of forgiveness
Is for a liberated soul.

2526.

A sleep-talking mind
And a life-fulfilling heart
Cannot live in the same boat.

2527.

You will hear the God-songs
Of the hoary past
If you pray to God
To appear in your dreams
Every night.

2528.

Now that you have given up
Your self-imposed illusion-life,
Your heart will be able to enjoy
The sunburst of God's Day.

2529.

Live in the heart.
The sea-secrets and the mountain-secrets
Of God's Life
Will reveal themselves to you.

2530.

There is no such thing
As a thankless task.
It is all beautiful Blessings
From our Beloved Supreme.

2531.

I want everything in my life
To be changeable
Except my love of God.
I want my love of God
To remain totally unchangeable.

2532.

On earth
Humanity's incurable cry
Is my home.
In Heaven
Divinity's imponderable joy
Is my home.

2533.

At the beginning
God never expects
Unconditional attention,
But He does expect
Undivided attention.

2534.

Alas, why have I chosen
A blind mind and a wild vital?
Why, why,
In this short span of life?

2535.

The scientists
Are secretly admiring
The seekers
But openly ridiculing
The seekers.

2536.

Yesterday
I was God's faithful dog.
Today
I am His beautiful lamb.
Tomorrow
I shall be His powerful lion.

2537.

I do not have the courage
To tell earth
That its life is all impurity.
I do not have the courage
To tell Heaven
That its soul is all indifference.

2538.

As your mind's intellectual life
Has narrowed your vision,
Even so, your soul's intuitive light
Has widened your heart.

2539.

No great soul
Is allowed to go off duty
Once it enters into the world-
   arena
For God-manifestation.

2540.

To a desire-bound life
A few tiny flames
Of aspiration-free breath
Are more than enough.

2541.

Your Heaven-world-preparation
Is destroying
Your yesterday's frustration
And creating
Your tomorrow's illumination.

2542.

Heart-mountain-happiness
Is the chosen instrument of God
For His constant manifestation
On earth.

2543.

Never allow despair
To hover over
Your heart and soul.

2544.

God is ready to wait for you
Indefinitely.
But the question is
If you will ever go
To see Him
In His Palace.

2545.

If you are before God,
Pray to Him to grant you
His Eternity's quenchless
Aspiration-thirst.

2546.

If you change your life,
God will allow you
To arrange a meeting
Between Him and humanity.

2547.

Now that I am no longer
In my aspiration-heart,
My life has become
A rudderless boat.

2548.

The Beauty-Eye of Heaven
Holds Eternity's
Perfection-Truth.

2549.

Each human being can become perfect
Provided he thinks
That his heart's kingdom
Is not just imagination.

2550.

You are your own incurable illusion.
Therefore
Who is going to save you
From the abyss of self-oblivion?

2551.

You and your heart must attend
Your ego's funeral
So that God will allow you
To return to your soul's
Original homeland.

2552.

If you want to resemble God,
Then do not remain
Inside your ignorance-fettered
Mind-cave.

2553.

A seeker does not know
What luxury is.
He only knows one thing:
His necessity for God.

2554.

If man accepts
What God proposes,
Then God will give him
His Heart's celestial Treatment.

2555.

If your sincerity-song
Has no end,
Then God's Satisfaction-Smile
   also
Will never come to an end.

2556.

My Lord, unless You force me
To be good,
You will see no satisfaction
Either in my life
Or around my life.

2557.

Pray to God the Time
To grant you a friendship
That will give you
An inspiration-sky,
An aspiration-moon
And a realisation-sun.

2558.

A God-server needs
No other qualification.
His God-service pleases
Not only God the Compassion
But also God the Justice
Equally.

2559.

The soul is a treasure
That we have not yet seen.
The heart is a treasure
That we have seen but lost.

2560.

The unknowable future
You must shut out
If you want to give God a chance
To perfect you
And satisfy you.

2561.

An impurity-force
Has pulled you down.
A purity-force
Can easily pull you up.
A divinity-force
Every day can teach you
A new self-transcendence-song.

2562.

The mind's impurity-cave
Is the only place
Where divinity-light
Does not want to shine.

2563.

A serenity-mind
And a purity-heart
Are God's private detectives
In the seeker's inner world.

2564.

Who possesses the Possessor?
He who thinks that the Possessor
Is the Liberator
And he who knows that the
   Possessor
Is the Self-giver.

2565.

Mine is an empty heart-cage
That every day longs for
Its soul-bird
To fly into it.

2566.

Silence consoles
The suffering human in us.
Silence extols
The smiling divine in us.

2567.

Do not keep
Your fear-door open.
Destruction-missiles
Are right in front of the door.

2568.

A seeker of peace
And a lover of God
Are every day blessed and
   garlanded
By the Supreme Himself
In His supreme Palace.

2569.

I call it
My heart's obedience-plant.
God calls it
His Life's Satisfaction-Tree.

2570.

If you soulfully try
To imitate God,
Then God will bountifully make you
A most intimate instrument of His.

2571.

O world of sound,
Do not try to fool me.
I definitely know the Sound
Of my Lord's Footsteps.

2572.

This morning my Lord told me
That if I can tame my wild life,
He will give me a free ride
To Heaven.

2573.

Always cloudy:
Man's possession-sky.
Always sunny:
Man's renunciation-sky.

2574.

My Lord does not mind
If I grow slowly
In my spiritual life.
But He will definitely mind
If I do not become
Spiritually strong
And completely perfect.

2575.

Unless you get from God
Your heart's permanent possession,
Love,
How will you measure
Your own life's divinity?

2576.

If you have sleepless aspiration,
Then eventually you will be able
To meet the gods
That are standing
Behind Heaven's closed doors.

2577.

Never fear!
Never surrender!
Your heart's faith
Will persevere and succeed.

2578.

Each morning prayer
Should be a sweet, whispering
  breath
From God's Fulness-Vision.

2579.

He is now rising
From his mind's oblivion-sleep.
Therefore, he is quite close
To God's Compassion-Signal.

2580.

How can your dedication-life
Surrender to your temptation-
  vital?
I can't believe it,
And I don't want to believe it.

2581.

There is no such thing
As an innocent desire.
Therefore
You cannot safely indulge
Any desire.

2582.

His life-maker
Is his love of God.
His heart-breaker
Is his doubt of man.

2583.

God faithfully watches
His gratitude-son
And His surrender-daughter
Playing the game
Of His Satisfaction-Dream.

2584.

I am waiting
For God's Satisfaction-Sun
And God is waiting
For my heart's dawn.

2585.

As long as I have a closed mind
And a closed heart,
God thinks it is useless
To keep close watch
Over my life.

2586.

The remembrance of happy days
Can easily help you escape
From today's frustration-night.

2587.

A desire-bound impurity-breath
Is nothing other
Than slow suicide.

2588.

Your lazy mind will tell you
That it is not worth seeing God.
Your lazy life will tell you
That God will definitely
Wait for you.

2589.

To be one of the lucky few
Is to cure yourself
From the contagious doubt-
   disease.

2590.

What I have done to God
Is something I would like
To forget every day.

2591.

If you have a heart,
That means
You have faith-bullets, too.
Fire immediately
Your faith-bullets
At your ignorance-night!

2592.

Ignorance-weight-loss
Can be guaranteed
Only when the soul's wisdom-
   light
Illumines the mind-night.

2593.

A tiny temptation-flame
Has burnt
His life's aspiration-shrine.

2594.

A new faith-flower
Is blossoming
Beautifully and charmingly
From his heart-flames.

2595.

It is always dangerous
To drive on the desire-highway.
But it is never, never dangerous
To drive on the aspiration-
   highway,
For God is a sacred Inspirer
And secret Driver there.

2596.

It is up to you
To become an aspiration-plant
Or not.
But never invoke the hostile forces
To destroy
The tender aspiration-plants
That are growing so beautifully
Around you.

2597.

His soulful heart
Has marvellously qualified
As an excellent student
In self-giving school.

2598.

A deep breath of determination
Is the precursor
Of a new realisation
And a new perfection
In life.

2599.

Transfer your life
From your desire-impermanence-train
To your aspiration-transcendence-train.

2600.

The beauty of my silence-soul
Has now become
The divinity of my gratitude-heart.

2601.

Show God your receptivity-hunger.
Immediately He will give you
A Satisfaction-Feast.

2602.

The seekers who make constant progress
Never go to eat
At suspicion-restaurant
In their mental world.

2603.

My concentration-life shows me
God's Protection-Fence.
My meditation-life actually sees
God's Protection-Fence around me
Protecting me.

2604.

If you do not feed
Your heart's gratitude-flames
Every day
With your soulful love,
Your life-racquet
Will have all broken strings.

2605.

At times
Seclusion you definitely need
For your soul to strengthen
Its Himalayan promise
To your Beloved Supreme.

2606.

My soul every day patronises
God's Vision-Store.
Therefore
My soul is well-liked
By God the Owner.

2607.

Now that once more
You have started
Your life's cheerfulness-career,
Your inner progress and outer progress
Will surprise you unimaginably.

2608.

Every day God expects
A new heart-flower from you,
For this is the only way
The ever-transcending God
Can carry you with Him.

2609.

Your soul has instructed your heart
How to go
To God's Satisfaction-Land.
Your heart is about to embark
On this unprecedented journey.
You just follow your heart!

2610.

God does not like to give anything
To an empty eye
Or an empty hand.
He gives everything
To an empty heart.
An empty eye
Is visionless.
An empty hand
Is giftless.
But an empty heart
Is guileless.
Therefore, in an empty heart
He can abide
And also give to it
What He wants to give.

2611.

When your aspiration-fire
Goes out,
God the Guest
Also goes out.

2612.

His soul's aspiration-life-story
Has been edited by God Himself.
Therefore
It is absolutely flawless.

2613.

A sky-blazing message:
Humanity's helpless cry
And divinity's powerful smile
Shall eternally live together.

2614.

In his inner life
A seeker wins the race
By virtue of his faith.
In his outer life
A seeker wins the race
By virtue of his surrender.

2615.

His untouchable thoughts
Have caused his premature death
In the spiritual life.

2616.

What can equal God's Ecstasy?
Man's bold promise to Him
To become another God.

2617.

Only an unconditional God-lover
God gladly allows
To wear the Silence-Smile
Of His transcendental Self.

2618.

God is ready to give you
Instant realisation.
Will you be able to receive it
With your constant aspiration?

2619.

God does not know
A better way for me
Since I have deliberately stooped
To suspicion-night.

2620.

Since you are a part-time seeker,
God does not want you and Him
To be mutual admirers.

2621.

If you are a true truth-seeker
And a true God-lover,
Then you can never allow your life
To become a faded promise-
   flower.

2622.

My ability has neither
Sincerity nor purity.
My ability is only
A dance of my doubting mind.

2623.

God's Control-Tower
Is only for those
Whose lives have become
Endless surrender-hours.

2624.

What you desperately need
Is a heart-retreat
From your mind's busy
And meaningless life.

2625.

I belong
To God's Vision-Beauty.
God belongs
To my dedication-duty.

2626.

Invention is worse than useless
If there is no good intention
Behind the invention.

2627.

Perfection is attained
Only when
There is nothing more
To gain
And nothing more
To lose.

2628.

Simplicity is at once
God's natural Blessing
And man's sleepless promise.

2629.

His mind's aspiration-flame
Is like a flicker
In a very distant universe.

2630.

Try ancient aspiration
If you want to save
The modern world
From its ultra-modern desires.

2631.

Unknown
Is his dedication-life.
Unknowable
Is his aspiration-heart.

2632.

Since the animal in you
Does not relax,
Why do you allow the human in
　you
To relax
And the divine in you
To sleep?

2633.

Alas,
His life-breath stopped
With a sad and brief
Spiritual story.

2634.

Each happy life-car
Needs
An encouragement-engine.

2635.

The Heaven-Hotel
Of the Absolute Supreme
Enjoys vacancies
Almost every day of the year.

2636.

Man's unhappiness
Is apt to snap
God's golden Compassion-
　Thread.

2637.

Your life
Is the question of the past.
My life
Is the answer to the future.

2638.

It is absolutely time for you
To find a new direction
In your life's Godward journey.

2639.

A seeker's shopping list
Has only two items:
God's Compassion-Eye
And
God's Forgiveness-Heart.

2640.

I thought I had the answer,
But now I see
That my life is not only
A colossal question
But also
An unending question.

2641.

God's Compassion-Flood
Has enabled him to declare
That his mind's unwillingness-capacity
Is a mere word.

2642.

If your heart
Deliberately amplifies your sorrow,
I tell you,
You will never find
Any illumining and fulfilling
Inner resource.

2643.

There is only one perfect gift
That I can offer
To my Lord Supreme:
My life's sleepless dedication-flower.

2644.

Why are you shopping
Inside the mind-cave?
The heart-department store
Is right in front of you!

2645.

My Lord Supreme quickly taught me
How to be good
Because He saw
That I was all ready
To turn His creation bad.

2646.

If you are insecure,
Then every day
You will be forced to learn
Illusion-lessons
From the world-atmosphere.

2647.

Your heart's homeland
Is where your consciousness
Sings and dances
Only for God.

2648.

God's constant Forgiveness
Is a supreme necessity
And not an unwanted superfluity.

2649.

Do not live inside
Your dark mind-cave.
It is quite unsafe.
At any moment
Suspicion-snake may hiss at you.

2650.

If God asks you
To send Him a picture of you,
It means that God's Blessings
And your life
Are about to become
Inseparable.

2651.

If you do not step
On your divinity-ladder,
Futility-ladder
Will bring you down
And throw you
Into the abysmal abyss.

2652.

How do you dare to think
That on the strength
Of your obsolete aspiration
You can win the realisation
Of tomorrow's brightest dawn?

2653.

When God forgives you,
He promises to you
That He will also forgive
Your associates in the inner life.

2654.

Purity's oneness-heart
Will never suffer
From the bite of insecurity.

2655.

It is an amazing fact
That a fleeting second of peace
Can inundate a seeker's life
With the soul's satisfaction-
    delight.

2656.

Aspiration is the beginning
Of perfection.
Perfection is the beginning
Of satisfaction.
Satisfaction is the beginning
Of nothingness nullified
And fulness multiplied.

2657.

In this crowded world
What I need is a Smile
From God's Protection-Eye.

2658.

God does not mind giving you
His Compassion-Credit Card,
But will your proud mind
Allow you to use it?

2659.

You must never allow
Your mind-lawyer
To cross-examine
Your life's oneness-heart.

2660.

You are such a fool!
Your whole life has now become
The repetition
Of a broken record.

2661.

It is your sordid vital
That has imprisoned
Your aspiration-life,
Which was meant only
For God's use.

2662.

Doubt-frost can kill everything
In a seeker's life.
Therefore, keep your heart of faith
Always soulful and powerful.

2663.

Death's shadow
You can see on your face,
But never upon your soul's
Divinity-eye.

2664.

You have every reason
To be happy
Because your determination
Remains unchallenged
And your aspiration
Remains unexamined.

2665.

An impossible friendship:
Between my mind's
Blighting unwillingness
And my heart's
Cheerful willingness.

2666.

Temptation-food
Is always full of calories.
Aspiration-food
Has no calories.
Therefore, O God-seeker,
Eat aspiration-food
As much as you want to!

2667.

Start to believe once more
In your future promise.
God will grant you
The springboard of His Vision-
   Eye.

2668.

Even the unlit human in him
Wants nothing
But God's Satisfaction
In God's own Way.

2669.

I laugh at your outer success,
I laugh.
I admire your inner progress
More than you can ever imagine.

2670.

Panic-stricken prayers
Are not for God's Satisfaction
Or His Manifestation on earth.

2671.

Your soul will not allow you
To enter into your heart-temple
With your muddy mind-thoughts.

2672.

Only a ready-made disciple
Can derive
Blessingful and fruitful spiritual
   wealth
From each and every wise piece of
   advice
From the Master.

2673.

The modern mind has made
The longest distance-record
Not only in criticising
God the Compassion
But also in running away from
God the Forgiveness.

2674.

The Ambassador of Heaven
Gives only one message to earth:
"O God-lover,
Your life must grow into
An eternal Now."

2675.

In the inner world
My Inner Pilot cares for me.
In the outer world
He dares for me.
Therefore, I always see
A happy and blessingful oneness
Between my inner world
And my outer world.

2676.

There is such a short span
Between birth and death.
Therefore
It is not possible to see
A fully grown happiness-flower
On earth.

2677.

You have already done
Many bad things.
Do not do the last bad thing!
Do not desecrate your heart-
   shrine!
For if you do that,
That will be the end
Of your aspiration-life.

2678.

Unless you renew
Your aspiration-permit on time,
Your close connection
With your Inner Pilot
Will cease.

2679.

I wrote a confidential letter
To my Lord Supreme this
   morning.
Therefore
He has made a Compassion-Call
   to me
On the inner plane.

2680.

God has made me a member
Of His intimate Family,
Not because I have done
    something,
Not because I have become
    something,
But because God wants to prove
To the world at large
That even the worst creation of
    His
Can become a member
Of His intimate Family
If He so desires.

2681.

Unless God can make me worthy
Of His transcendental Height,
His Vision will not succeed.
Therefore
He will definitely take me
To His own highest Height
Of self-transcendence.

2682.

Your mind is looking
For a messiah.
Alas, it fails to see
That it already has a messiah:
Confusion-prince.

2683.

My heart longs for God.
My soul communes with God.
My life works for God.

2684.

Be brave!
The future of your choice
Will definitely expedite
Your God-journey.

2685.

Aspiration-garden
Will become dry
If there is no
Enthusiasm-gardener.

2686.

Since your enemies
Will not relax willingly,
You must not allow
Your heart's adamantine will
To relax.

2687.

You are a fool!
You are expecting everything
From a pointless
And fruitless life.

2688.

Pessimistic predictions
Must be ignored
Like feeble and useless ants.

2689.

If your mind-lawyer
Cross-examines you,
Do not be afraid,
For your soul will come to your aid
With its effulgence-light.

2690.

Since he does not mind
If he loses
In the battlefield of life,
He feels that
He does not have to choose
Between fleeting time and
  Eternity.

2691.

Man's longest marathon
Is from a frustration-life
To an illumination-soul.

2692.

His life is lost
Between his mind's ugliness-wall
And his heart's willingness-door.

2693.

God wants me to write
A very simple and soulful book
So that every day
He can read and appreciate it
And inspire and teach me to write
A better and simpler book.

2694.

Help your life
To proceed every morning
With ant-perseverance.

2695.

If you have the willingness
To offer your gratitude-life,
Then God definitely has the Heart
To give you absolutely the best
Exchange rate.

2696.

There is no free parking
On earth,
Even if you are
A direct God-messenger.

2697.

I am happy
Because I still need God.
God is happy
Because I still love Him.

2698.

Borrow anything from God,
As long as you are grateful
To yourself
For having the wisdom
To borrow from God
And not from anybody else.

2699.

To be illumined
By God's Compassion-Eye,
My outer name
Should be surrender
And my inner name
Should be gratitude.

2700.

At long last
God is making my surrender-life
Worthy of His Compassion-Eye.

2701.

For me there is only one path
To Heaven,
And that path
Is my heart-purity's self-giving
And self-ascending path.

2702.

Unless you cherish
Your soul's warrior-dream,
How will you be able to defend
Your freedom-life on earth?

2703.

His soulful life lay prostrate
At God's Feet
To have a vision
That does not carry yesterdays.

2704.

He is totally lost
Between the lion-appetite
Of his mind
And the mouse-capacity
Of his heart.

2705.

Fulness-fountain is flowing
Inside your heart.
When will you start glowing
Brilliantly and triumphantly?

2706.

If you have retired from
The spiritual life,
Either you have decreased
Or increased
God's Headache.

2707.

If confusion is your mind,
What else can be your life,
If not all delusion?

2708.

He has no particular desire
Either to live or to die.
His unconditional surrender
To God's Will,
God is definitely going
To treasure.

2709.

If it is God's Pen,
It will never run out
Of Compassion-Ink.

2710.

What is the meaning
Of self-giving?
Self-giving means
Life's energising
Satisfaction-sunshine.

2711.

The final destination
Of ego
Is the abysmal abyss
Of utter loneliness.

2712.

He has recorded
God's Compassion-Message
And God's Perfection-Message
On the tape recorder
Of his aspiration-heart.

2713.

Do not mislead yourself
Any more.
If your heart is not fit
For the perfection-life,
How can you expect your mind,
Vital and body
To be fit for the perfection-life?
No! The heart has to be ready first.
Then only the mind, vital and
   body
Will follow it.

2714.

Alas,
When will you get up
And not just remain lying down
Shamelessly and indefinitely
On lethargy-bed?

2715.

O world,
I may accept
What you have to say,
But I really do not
Agree with you.

2716.

When my heart's silence
Knocks at God's Door,
God immediately reveals
His Infinity's Satisfaction-Smile.

2717.

Whenever he is tired,
Due to heavy pressure of work
Inner and outer,
God comes and gives him
His Heart's Affection-Massage.

2718.

God cries only once:
When I tell Him
That I do not deserve Him.

2719.

He gave his all to God
To become God's
God-Satisfaction-Doll.

2720.

The Silence-Smile
Of God's Eye
Always serves as a microphone
To my heart.

2721.

When are you going to realise
That your doubting, impure mind
Is a meaningless and worthless
Nuisance
In your life?

2722.

The heart's
Aspiration-preference
And the soul's
Perfection-preference
Must be found
In a seeker's Heavenward journey.

2723.

If you become
A devoted instrument
Of my Beloved Supreme,
I shall make you
His Victory-announcer.

2724.

If you want to be
A trouble-shooter,
You must first be
A divine warrior
In the battlefield
Of your own aspiration-life.

2725.

A life of excellence-song
Can never wrong anybody,
For its excellence satisfies
The inner world
And the outer world
Alike.

2726.

Why do you have to
Wait in line?
Since God is waiting for you,
Go immediately to God!

2727.

Do not be afraid of reality!
If you are afraid of reality,
You will be caught
In the confusion-vortex.

2728.

God's Tears
Are flowing down my face
Because I am afraid
Of being carried by God's Arms.

2729.

What you need
Is a heart of purity
That will act as a buffer-zone
Between your doubting mind
And your strangling vital.

2730.

Your heart's aspiration-rocket
Will blast off
If you can take
Your meditation-exercise
Seven times a day.

2731.

You want to know
How to forget your worries.
Just establish your soul's
Guiding supremacy
In your outer life!

2732.

If you are serving
Your desire-life,
How can you have
A crying heart
For God?

2733.

God burst into applause
When He saw earth
Desperately trying to steal
His Sweetness-Smile.

2734.

Where else can be
Your life's satisfaction-fruits
If not inside the orchard
Of your aspiration-heart?

2735.

The oneness-ascendancy
Of the inner world
Must stay the division-supremacy
Of the outer world.

2736.

Who told you
That the mind does not
Acknowledge
The existence of truth?
The mind does acknowledge
The existence of truth
But it cleverly ignores
The necessity of truth.

2737.

You fool!
Will there be no time
In your life
When you will discover
That your hallowed heart
Is always being massacred
By your suspicion-mind?

2738.

No matter how high
Your opinion is
Of your mind,
I tell you,
Your mind can never be a match
For your sincerity-heart
In the inner world.

2739.

Earth's sad cry:
God is not approachable.
Heaven's sad cry:
God is concerned more about earth.

2740.

His heart has never told a lie.
Therefore
God has granted him
His Fulness-Fountain-Love.

2741.

Who is there to depreciate
The taste of faith-food?
Who is there to digest
Doubt-food?
Do you want to try?
Then try!

2742.

Your heart prays and meditates
Every day.
Your mind never prays
And never meditates.
It only enjoys vacation.
How then does your mind expect
To climb up the realisation-tree
Like your heart?

2743.

He is a real fool
Who thinks a meditation-warm-up
Is enough every day
And a dedication-workout
Is redundant.

2744.

Be careful!
Be careful with your aspiration-heart
And dedication-life!
Even angels, high in Heaven,
Go astray.

2745.

Your heart's faith-world
Is too strong to be destroyed
By the desire-hurricane
Of your vital.

2746.

If you want to win
In God's Satisfaction-Contest,
Then do not allow yourself
To be caught
By the trappings of success.

2747.

If you consciously
Do not drop the curtain
Upon the past,
You will be paralysed
By the destructive presence
Of ignorance-titan.

2748.

When your life-car
Is on the soul's highway,
You will discover
That there are no speed limits.

2749.

I want to be caught
By the net of my Lord's Love.
I want to catch my Lord
With my self-giving breath.

2750.

The past is dust.
Unless you have realised
This infallible truth,
God will not give you
A boarding pass
To enter into
His immortal Love-Airplane.

2751.

God's Bodyguard will not allow you
To enter into God's
Sacred and secret Courtyard of Silence
Because you are on friendly terms
With earth's destruction-sound.

2752.

My heart's sleepless cry
Is begging for my soul's
All-liberating illumination-home.

2753.

One day if you miss
Your morning aspiration,
Then try to feel
That you have torn deliberately
A petal from your heart's
Perfection-lotus.

2754.

O my doubting mind,
Your unwelcome arrival
At my heart's door
Has disturbed my heart
Far beyond your imagination.

2755.

Your mind's ravenous appetite
For power
Has damaged your heart
And shocked your soul.

2756.

Only an aspiration-heart
And a dedication-life
Can ultimately conquer
The nightmare of the mind's
Perilous fantasies.

2757.

Do you know why and how
You are making the fastest
    progress?
You are making the fastest
    progress
Because you have unconditionally
    disowned
Your life's ignorance-tree.

2758.

If you are a true heart-lover,
Then you will never be able
To abide by the dictates
Of your dictator-mind.

2759.

Do you know
What I want to be?
I want to be the rising sun
Of tomorrow's hope.

2760.

God's Compassion-Letter
And His Forgiveness-Message
Are saving my human life
From my animal life
And asking my divine life
To elevate my human life.

2761.

If you want to bask
In God's perpetual Gaze,
Then remove from your shoulder
Your self-imposed bondage-load.

2762.

I play with God
Many games.
When I play with Him
My surrender-game
And when He plays with me
His Compassion-Game,
I feel that 'earth' is another name
For Heaven.

2763.

As a beggar
When I knock at God's Door,
He tells me to wait
And He keeps me waiting
Indefinitely.
As a seeker
When I knock at God's Door,
He immediately opens the Door,
Lets me in
And asks me why I am so late.

2764.

Every day I sing
My two favourite songs:
I love God the Beautiful,
I need God the Bountiful.

2765.

If you do not consciously ignore
Your insecurity's complaints,
God is not going to send you
His personal security-guards.

2766.

You always ask yourself
If there is anyone to save you
And illumine you.
I tell you, deep inside you
There are God-intoxicated
Love-messengers
Who will not only save you
And illumine you
But also fulfil you in God's own
    Way.

2767.

You may not give serious thought
To God and God's creation,
But God the Creation-Lover
Will always give serious thought
Not only
To your Heaven-free longings
But also
To your earth-bound desires.

2768.

Every morning
If you do not sign your name
When God leaves His Vision-
   Register
In front of you,
You will not be accepted
As a member of His immediate
   Family.

2769.

Temptation is the world's
Oldest disease.
Aspiration is at once
The world's most ancient
And most modern medicine.

2770.

If you want God to be
All the time inside your heart,
Then be purity's breath.
If you want God all the time
To be beside you,
Then be humility's life.

2771.

The moment I think of you,
I see your face covered by
A used and soiled
Blanket of insecurity.

2772.

My heart's patience
Makes my life longer
And the calendar year shorter.

2773.

Unless you banish the notion
Of reward
Whenever you do something
For God,
God will not allow you to become
A member of His inner Family.

2774.

If you have the audacity
To play with the temptation-
   world,
How will you escape
Destruction-fire?

2775.

Doubt is slow death.
This slow death
Is bound to drain
Secretly and unmistakably
Your aspiration-heart.

2776.

You fool!
How do you dare
To split the universe
When you cannot split
Your own doubting mind
And searching mind?

2777.

If you do not put an end
To your self-doubt-dance,
Then you will soon become a victim
To your own voracious vital.

2778.

A seeker's heart knows
That its surrender-song
Is at once beginningless
And endless.

2779.

God is ready to give you
Some free space
In His Parking Lot
In Heaven,
But where is your life's
Aspiration-car?
Where?

2780.

To cure your mind's
Jealousy-malaria,
What you need is not
The earth-produced quinine
But the Heaven-produced
Nectar-delight.

2781.

In the morning he reads
His heart's love-magazine.
In the evening he reads
His soul's delight-magazine.
This is how he has made his life
Increasingly happy.

2782.

Your mind-room has no door.
Therefore
You cannot come out
Of your room
And God cannot come in.

2783.

He who speaks
Always in favour of God
Can never have an alliance
With ignorance-prince.

2784.

If you champion
Your soul's determination,
You will be the blue-gold colour
Of God's Satisfaction-Delight.

2785.

God wants each life
To be His Vision's Doll,
Flooded with
Beauty, purity and surrender.

2786.

Every day
His first task in life
Is to send a prayer-letter
To his Beloved Supreme
In Heaven.

2787.

You always want God
To make the first move
In your life.
God can do that,
But because of your deep-rooted
Doubt-injuries,
You will not trust God
No matter what He does or says.

2788.

Sever your frustration-friendship
If you want to enjoy
Your satisfaction-partnership
With God.

2789.

My mind will eventually learn
The art of freezing.
My vital will know
The destruction-message
Of boiling.
My heart will know
The message of melting-oneness.

2790.

Do not think
Of your suffering days.
Just think
Of God's Rays
Which will illumine you
And liberate you.

2791.

My life's self-pity-songs
Have not only puzzled
My soul
But also astonished
The cosmic gods.

2792.

Obedience has to be
Your first choice.
For that you do not need
A needle-sharp mind.
For that you need only
A purity-sanctified heart.

2793.

The body is born helpless,
But not the soul.
The mind suffers from impurity,
But not the heart.

2794.

My Lord,
I know You will never
Abandon me.
Therefore, I never give up
My hope for perfection-life.

2795.

The heart needs
Purity-exercise every day.
Otherwise, the heart will become
As impure as the vital,
And poor God will feel extremely
    miserable
For His stupendous loss.

2796.

Yesterday my interest was
In God-loving.
Today my interest is
In God-serving.
Tomorrow my interest will be
In God-becoming.

2797.

The mind enjoys
Its opinion.
The heart enjoys
Only God's Dominion.

2798.

His love-life, devotion-life
And surrender-life —
Everything in him
And everything of him —
Will be a fiasco
Because of his devastating
    insincerity.

2799.

Dethrone your mind-dictator
If you want God
To build a love-monument for
    you.

2800.

My mind belongs to those
Who want to know and dominate
The world.
My heart belongs to those
Who want to love and serve
The world.
I belong to those
Who think and feel
That they are of God's
   Compassion-Eye
And for God's Satisfaction-Heart.

2801.

Your heart's silver silence
Must ever remain wakeful
To watch God's Compassion-
   Dance.

2802.

If you are the owner
Of sterling faith,
Then God will definitely
Shorten your journey.

2803.

My life's sincerity-determination
Has always been
My only alarm clock.

2804.

A purity-heart has always been
A pillar
Of man's inner society.

2805.

Your turn is coming!
You have to prove
That you are definitely worthy
Of God's Compassion-Blessing-
   Sky.

2806.

No matter when he speaks,
No matter what he says,
He always quotes
From God's Forgiveness-Lectures.

2807.

Unless you can turn your life
Into happiness-curry,
You will never get the ingredients
For realisation-meal.

2808.

Every morning without fail
He uses his aspiration-alarm
To awaken not only himself
But also everybody else
From ignorance-sleep.

2809.

Do not be a fool!
There cannot be any hiding place
For your ignorance
In your inner life of aspiration.

2810.

He has covered half the way
To God-realisation.
This experience his mind takes
As encouraging
And his heart takes
As discouraging.

2811.

Silence your mind totally
If you want to see
The illumination-sun
Inside your heart.

2812.

My heart-carpenter
Has promised to build for me
A beautiful shrine
Where I can worship
My Eternity's Lord Supreme.

2813.

I may not know where
Your hiding place is,
But definitely I know
That you are not doing
The right thing by hiding.

2814.

God is always ready
To shepherd you home.
But will you ever care
For His Help?

2815.

My Lord,
Where were You
When I needed You?
"My child,
What did you do
When you had Me?"

2816.

One extraordinary deed
Made his life worthwhile,
And that deed
Was establishing his heart's
Sleepless oneness.

2817.

My heart is always ready
To be with God,
No matter where He is,
Even when He is in
His Amusement Park
And not in
His Enlightenment Garden.

2818.

A bountiful smile:
This is the eternal gift
Of the Master
To his disciple.

2819.

Every day
You must renew
Your heart's aspiration-visa.

2820.

Reclaim
Your soulfulness-life.
Reclaim
Your eagerness-heart.
Reclaim
Your perfection soul.

2821.

Our mountain of possessions
May satisfy the beggar in us
But not the God-lover in us,
Who has already got God
For his own.

2822.

The delight-plant is very delicate.
Be careful when you touch it
And be prayerful when you water it
With your heart's devotion-cry.

2823.

You are not ready to buy
God's Lottery Ticket,
For you are afraid of the power
Of man-possessed wealth.

2824.

If you are waiting for your heart
To strengthen itself,
If you are waiting for your mind
To straighten itself,
If you are waiting for your life
To enlighten itself,
Then, alas, I don't think you will have
One moment of true happiness.

2825.

If you do not attend
Your aspiration-class every day,
Who will revive
Your soul's lofty mission
On earth?

2826.

God's eternal Toy
Is man's fulfilling heart
Of gratitude.

2827.

There are very few
Human beings on earth
Who can play satisfactorily
On their life's gratitude-piano.

2828.

To eat every day
A sweet hope-orange
Is not a difficult task.

2829.

Even an iota of aspiration-light
Will strengthen you to ignore
The dark world-criticism.

2830.

If you think you are unique,
Then show me that you are
Not willingly standing
On the world's ignorance-shore.

2831.

There is a sign
On God's Front Gate.
It says only to come in
And not to go out.

2832.

You have proved to me
That God is approachable.
I have proved to you
That God is lovable.
You have proved to me
That God's Sound-Life
Is for everybody.
I have proved to you
That God's Silence-Life
Is only for a select few.

2833.

How can full satisfaction
Claim you
Unless you disown
Your insecurity-property?

2834.

Every day my heart sails
In the golden boat
Of imagination-delight.

2835.

Nothing can be
As beautiful and fruitful
As divinity's God-illumination-
   souvenirs.

2836.

Secretly he receives from God
God's Compassion-Letters.
Openly he reads to God
Man's ingratitude-letters.

2837.

The sorrows
Of his heart
Steer the boat
Of his progress-life.

2838.

I see God's Purity-Face
Inside flowers.
I see God's Beauty-Face
Inside children.

2839.

I have given up
All my mind's fantasies.
Therefore, God has given me
His Heart-Dreams of intimacy.

2840.

If you want to climb
The God-Satisfaction-Tree,
Then brave the buffets
Of your insecurity-thoughts.

2841.

God's Compassion-Smile
Is for everyone.
But alas,
Very few human beings
Value it.

2842.

Tell me Your Will, my Lord.
Am I supposed to be
Ahead of Your Satisfaction-Heart,
Or am I supposed to be
Behind Your Compassion-Eye?

2843.

How to feed the inner cry?
Just try to claim
A higher life
As your own.

2844.

Heaven's immigration officers
Rejected him
Because his aspiration-passport
Had expired long ago.

2845.

Here in this very body
I shall not only see
The Heart of God
But also reveal
The Life of God.

2846.

At every moment
What I need
Is an injection of divine energy
To climb up
My life's aspiration-tree.

2847.

No matter how impure
A human heart is,
God does not withdraw
His Promise-Manifestation
In and through it.

2848.

You are afraid of appearing
At the aspiration-examination,
But you are longing
For the realisation-results.

2849.

Earth entertains Heaven
With its purity-cries.
Heaven enlightens earth
With its beauty-smiles.

2850.

The mind's luxury
And the heart's poverty
Are quite often available
Inside the same body.

2851.

Enthusiasm and self-transcendence
Are two great
Complementary realities.

2852.

He who cheerfully enjoys
His responsibility's weight
Is a chosen instrument
Of God-Eternity.

2853.

Hill-climbing aspiration
Is always necessary
For the fastest progress
In life.

2854.

His mind's roommate
Is a jealousy-criminal.
His heart's roommate
Is an ecstasy's self-transcendence-rival.

2855.

In my heart's home,
Everybody will be invited
To come
And nobody will be asked
To go.

2856.

My mind,
I do not want you
To be an offensive thinker,
But an expansion-lover.

2857.

My Lord, You tell me
If I am tired.
If I am tired,
Do take care of me
While I am resting!

2858.

What happens
When the inspiration-cage
Is smashed?
The aspiration-bird inside
Dies.

2859.

Your unwillingness
Is not predestined.
Your oneness-heart
With God's Will
Is predestined.

2860.

May each life become
A hope-fountain
So that each heart will become
Beauty's joy.

2861.

Your soulful smile
Represents
God's Satisfaction-Mirror
In you.

2862.

Why do you allow your
   aspiration-life
To be hampered
By indulgence-flow?

2863.

Every day God asks me
If I enjoy His Affection-Touch
On my shoulder.

2864.

Surrender-perfume
Permeates
His entire being
Every day.

2865.

God has come to you
To see your soulful heart
Of aspiration,
Not your hurtful face
Of frustration.

2866.

I am happy
When I am not the owner,
But God is the Owner,
Of my heart's obedience-light.

2867.

Do not surrender
To your reluctance-body.
Be one with your heart
And fight against it!

2868.

You are a do-it-yourself seeker.
Therefore, God's Compassion
Does not want to interfere
In your life.

2869.

It is high time
For you to free yourself
From your unbelievably powerful
Ignorance-instigated deeds.

2870.

You are telling me
That you are tired
Of the amusement-life.
Then why are you not mixing
With the enlightenment-heart?

2871.

You are afraid of discarding
Your desire-knife.
But you can at least blunt the edge
Of your desire-knife.

2872.

Aspire soulfully and sleeplessly.
You will see that
The death-dealing hand of time
Will be transformed into
The life-flowing heart of time.

2873.

It is an easy task
For your heart
To smell the sweet fragrance
Of your soul.

2874.

God's Compassion-Smile
Is the matchless salary
Of a God-employee.

2875.

His vital is happy
That at long last
It is able to enjoy vacation
From its aggression-destruction-
    life.

2876.

At every moment
God's Heart-Boat
Offers new room
To new passengers.

2877.

God's Eye
And
My heart
Met together
Only to shed ceaseless tears.

2878.

His heart's paradise-sun shines
Wherever and whenever
His Master compassionately
Writes his name.

2879.

If you do not nourish your heart
With love,
You will not be able to go
Even a step farther
In the inner world.

2880.

The sweetest fruit
Of Heaven
Is man's unconditional
Surrender.

2881.

I always thought
I was special,
But now I see
That I have been fooling myself
Inside my mind's
Illusion and delusion-forest.

2882.

The year
Is ending today.
My earth-fear
Is also ending today.
And my Lord's displeasure with me
Is also ending today.

2883.

At last I am now able
To discard my jealousy-dammed
Mind-machine.

2884.

In the inner world
Each man is blessed
With the opportunity
To recreate his outer life.

2885.

If you have the capacity-key,
Then the opportunity-door
Cannot remain forever locked.

2886.

Unless you discard
Your mind's dictionary of excuses,
God will not grant you
His Dictionary of Love and Peace.

2887.

Take a deep dive
In your consciousness-pond.
You will be totally transformed
And perfectly ready for God.

2888.

You must never allow your mind
To be callous
To your heart's God-needs.

2889.

Every day
God wants me to show Him
My life's determination-jaw.

2890.

My Lord,
If You do not want
To give me freely,
At least allow me to borrow
A pair of ignorance-cutting
  scissors.

2891.

If you are not pure
At every moment,
You will not be able
To stay permanently inside
Your heart's hope-blossoming
  garden.

2892.

The soul is God's lawyer.
Be careful when you are dealing
With God's lawyer:
The lawyer is always
On God's side.

2893.

Invite God
With your heart's aspiration-
  silence.
He will definitely come.

2894.

Temptation has retarded your
  progress;
Therefore, you are sad.
But I tell you,
This is a universal experience!

2895.

My Lord,
How long am I supposed to
  remain
With man
In his extremely cold
Unwillingness-climate?

2896.

No desire knows
What it actually wants.
It only unconsciously expedites
The express arrival
Of death.

2897.

There is nothing wrong
When you laugh
At a doubt-orphan.
Truth to tell,
A doubt-orphan
Deserves to be ridiculed!

2898.

O my sweet Master,
Do help me to remember
Every day
That I came to you to be
Your absolutely perfect disciple.

2899.

O my sweet Master,
Do help me to remember
Every day
That your indifference-eye
Is my life's immediate death.

2900.

O my sweet Master,
Do help me to remember
Every day
That it is not I
Who am dedicated to you
But it is you
Who are dedicated to me.
I am just watching
Your heart's constant dedication-
    life.

2901.

God has granted you
His uncharted Vision-Will
Because your life has become
Your heart's oneness-thrill.

2902.

The surrender-heart
Of a sleepless God-lover
Finally becomes
The most precious sweetness
Of God's Compassion-Dewdrops.

2903.

My life was born
With God's Beauty.
My heart will live
With God's Immortality.

2904.

Vital joy without purity
Is a sign of inner poverty.
Purity without self-giving
Is an impossible reality.

2905.

Can fear ever save me?
Yes, it can!
Fear can save me
Only if I am soulfully afraid
Of my Beloved Supreme
When I am about to do something
To dissatisfy Him.

2906.

The inner world is open
To the heart-voyager.
The inner world is closed
To the truth-doubter.

2907.

O my heart,
Do not think
That God does not care for you
Just because my soul
Is swifter than you.
My Lord does care for you
With His blessingful
　Appreciation.

2908.

Every morning he practises
His life's surrender-act,
And every evening he practises
His life's gratitude-act.

2909.

God felt miserable
When He saw
The funeral-flames
Of my aspiration-deceased
Temple-heart.

2910.

His parents
Should have informed God,
The unparalleled Doctor,
About the incurable disease
He was born with:
Ignorance.

2911.

Heaven will not allow you
To come in
Unless you buy
A round-trip ticket
From earth.

2912.

Heaven wanted him
To end his life-journey
So Heaven could get from him
Most authentic news about earth.

2913.

You will be given
A free ticket to Heaven
If your heart is strong enough
And your life is pure enough
To knock on the world's
Aspiration-door.

2914.

Before you check into God's Hotel,
Be sure that you have
Carried with you
Your heart's unconditional
Surrender-passport,
And that you have totally
   discarded
Your hesitation-mind.

2915.

One pure second
Of your heart-life
Can embody the power
Of ten God-manifesting
Roaring hours.

2916.

Each moment shall become
A fruitless eternity
If the calculating mind
Does not surrender
To the endless silence
Of the heart.

2917.

Little lives are not false;
They are weak.
They, too, can be turned into
Radiant images of the soul.

2918.

Even if you fail
In your inner examination,
Do not allow your mind
To become a surge of revolt,
For you will be given
Another chance.

2919.

My mind,
Will you keep a secret?
My Lord has decided
To sing the song of illumination
Inside you.

2920.

He who wants to treasure
Only the future
Is sailing the boat
That will definitely sink
On the way.

2921.

Someday meditation
Will not only give you joy
But also increase
God's Satisfaction-Power in you.

2922.

Mental scholars are afraid
Of approaching the truth,
Unlike truth-seekers
And God-lovers.

2923.

You do not have to remain a
  candle flame
All your life,
For God will definitely grant you
One day
One of His Wisdom-Suns.

2924.

Who can expect a dramatic change
In his life?
Either he who has surrendered
To his own ignorance-night,
Or he who has surrendered
To God's Vision-Light.

2925.

Unless you renounce your pride
In knowing the world
And in not knowing the world,
You can be neither safe nor
  perfect.

2926.

The common problem is:
Man wants the uncommon
  solution.
The uncommon solution is:
Man satisfies himself
By getting the things
That he does not have.

2927.

Doubt comes to tell you
Not only how far away you are
From God
But also how close you are
To your death.

2928.

Even his earth-bound time
Flows to God's
Infinite Shores.

2929.

Your faith is dying!
Be prepared to face
Untold inner pangs.

2930.

Two most precious lifelong
   experiences
Are engraved on my heart:
I am not indispensable
And
My Lord Supreme is
   unconditional.

2931.

You will be totally lost
In your life's quagmire
If you do not try
A new approach —
I mean an unconditional
Surrender-approach
To God's Will.

2932.

I have seen many
Indifferent minds,
But not even one
Indifferent heart.
I have felt many
Insecure hearts,
But never
An insecure soul.

2933.

If you love to dream,
You will have endless light.
If you love endless light,
You will become God's Power-
   Hand.

2934.

Every morning
You must keep a new prayer
In your aspiring heart's
Dedication-pocket.

2935.

From God's Hospital
I have received the latest report:
My doubtful mind is on the road
To its complete recovery.

2936.

My aspiration-heart has
   consumed
The fear-spreading vocabulary
Of my doubting mind.

2937.

Mine is the faith-dictionary
That has never been challenged
By doubt's limited vocabulary.

2938.

There is no difference between
A God-appointed Ambassador
And a God-personified Lover.

2939.

My prayer-life
Wanted to bind God
Unconsciously.
My meditation-life
Rectified it
Miraculously.

2940.

Your life's tape recorder
Is only to record
God's Victory-Messages,
And not
Your life's past failures.

2941.

Since your frustration-vital
Does not want to commit suicide,
Ask your illumination-soul
To be strict with the wild life
Of your vital.

2942.

O my faith,
I shall count on your full support
When I go to my new Employer,
God,
To ask for a job.

2943.

How can you allow
Your mind's ugly doubts
To sneer at earth's
Blazing aspiration-flames?

2944.

In the battlefield of life
The human mind
May pass the examination,
But it will never be able
To surpass the heart.

2945.

Every accident
Can be prevented
Either by
God's powerful Smile
Or by
Man's soulful cry.

2946.

The fine for disobedience
Is so exorbitant
That finally his mind
Has had to resort
To an obedience-life.

2947.

Even a brick wall
Has more receptivity
Than a desire-bound
Ingratitude-heart.

2948.

God's Compassion-Net catches all,
Only to liberate them
In His Infinity's Satisfaction-Delight.

2949.

A proud man wants to lead the world,
But he fails.
A humble man wants to follow the world,
But when he is about to follow the world
God appears
And starts leading him.

2950.

If you see
With the eye of your soul,
You will never be able
To tell the world
That God is His Negligence-Eye.

2951.

What your life now is,
Is a visible sincerity.
What God is going to give your life
Before long
Is an invincible purity.

2952.

When my conscience advises me
And I listen to it,
My life becomes the cornerstone
Of my Lord's inner creation.

2953.

In my inner world of aspiration
And in my outer world of dedication
One thing reigns supreme,
And that is the Silence-Ecstasy
Of my Beloved Supreme.

2954.

The face of Heaven
Is more beautiful than powerful.
The heart of man
Is more fearful than cheerful.

2955.

His mind is clothed in silence.
Therefore
Today his heart is able to sing
Divinity's hymn
For the heart of humanity.

2956.

Two are the companions
Of my sleepless soul:
Man the preparation
And
God the Satisfaction.

2957.

If you do not want
God's Compassion
To open your mind's
Closed shutters,
Then God's Justice,
With no hesitation,
Will do the needful.

2958.

Prayerful
Are the eyes of a dreamer.
Beautiful
Is the heart of a lover.
Fruitful
Is the life of a server.

2959.

What has obliterated
His hope-life?
Not his doubtful mind,
Not his insecure heart,
But the unwillingness
Of his ego-born life.

2960.

I have discovered
A new road to peace:
"My mind does not know anything."

2961.

My Lord Supreme,
You can neglect anything
In my life
Except my poor and fragile heart.

2962.

Three deadly weapons:
An ingratitude-heart,
An all-knowing mind,
An ego-granted realisation.

2963.

If you are devoted
To your own self-glory,
How will you ever dare
To demolish your life's inner
   barriers?

2964.

He dreams God's Dream
Every day
In his purity-sanctified heart.

2965.

There is only one
Secret and sacred chain
That links man and God,
And that chain is
Man's cheerfulness-heart.

2966.

Do you want to hear
The heartbeat of oneness?
Then start climbing the hills
That separate your mind
From your heart.

2967.

There can be a safe
And sunny world for you,
But have you played your role?
Have you put your body, vital,
Mind, heart and soul
In perfect order?

2968.

God fills my heart
With His own Heart's
Silence-Smiles
Every day.

2969.

Can receptivity be learnt?
Yes!
Your soul's luminosity
And your life's spontaneity
Can teach your heart
How to be receptive.

2970.

If you are ready
To walk bravely
Along life's despair-road,
God will grant you
His Beauty's Vision-Crown.

2971.

Can a snow-white purity-mind
    exist
Like a snow-white purity-heart?
Yes, it can!
Ask your soul.
It will help you unconditionally
To get a snow-white purity-mind.

2972.

Your mechanical mind
Will always be afraid
Of heading Heavenward
For abiding peace.

2973.

God loves me; I need Him.
May this experience-story
Remain deathless,
Even when my mind
Is doubtful and obstinate.

2974.

You grope in the darkness
Of your mind
Because you have not prepared
A garden-shrine
Inside your heart.

2975.

If you want to dine
In God's Satisfaction-Restaurant,
Never enjoy vacation —
Not to speak of temptation —
In the inner world!

2976.

It is not that every day
Doubt does not invade his mind.
But the moment
Doubt invades his mind,
He destroys it!

2977.

If your inner house
Is not supported
By hope-pillars,
How will your outer life succeed
And how will your inner life
    proceed?

2978.

If you do not include
God's Compassion
In your daily life,
You will, without fail,
Meet with the red danger sign.

2979.

If your mind is afraid
Of climbing higher,
Then how will your life
Travel into Infinity?

2980.

Now that he is all love
For his aspiration-game,
His desire-game
Has totally left him.

2981.

On the threshold of a new year
May our minds have
A new determination-dictionary
And may our hearts have
A new dedication-dictionary.

2982.

If you are not inspired
To improve your spiritual
    vocabulary,
Your life's dreams
Will never be transformed
Into reality.

2983.

My heart's
Two secret and sacred longings:
I shall please God
In God's own Way.
I shall no longer carry
My past failure-life.

2984.

My body, vital and mind
Are now unanimous
In their decision:
They will study at the heart-
    school,
And the only teacher
Will be the soul.

2985.

What is my spiritual wealth?
My love of God.
What is God's spiritual Wealth?
My heart's oneness-smile.

2986.

Unless you point-blank deny
The animal in you,
The human in you
Will not love you
And the divine in you
Will not utilise you.

2987.

A seeker and a quitter
Have absolutely nothing in
  common.
They follow their own ways
Right from the beginning to the
  end.

2988.

God wants each and every human
  being
To hoist His Victory-Banner.
But who is ready?
Not you!
Who is ready?
Not he!
Who is ready?
Not I!
God is helplessly looking
For the hero-instrument
Who will hoist His Victory-
  Banner.

2989.

Transformation is a slow process.
But once it is achieved,
It is treasured by both
Humanity's heart-cry
And divinity's soul-smile.

2990.

Unless you correct yourself,
Your imperfect life
Not only will torture you
But also will lower the standard
Of the world.

2991.

A God-lover
Does not know how to hide.
He does not know
How to expose himself, either.
He only knows
How to reveal His Beloved
  Supreme.

2992.

With love
I see the world.
With devotion
I feel the world.
With surrender
I become the world.

2993.

The mind talks and talks
So that it does not have to listen.
The heart remains silent
So that it can all the time listen.

2994.

One day
Spirituality will become
Not only comprehensible
But also acceptable
And adorable.

2995.

Do not allow doubt-storm
To destroy your heart's
Beautiful light and delight-camp.

2996.

Do not play with untamed
   thoughts
From the mind-jungle.
They are extremely dangerous!

2997.

Alas,
When God telephoned me,
I was playing hide-and-seek
With my doubting mind
And my insecure heart.
Therefore
I could not answer the call.

2998.

You can make your mind
Claim God
The way your heart
Has claimed God.
First beg your mind.
If you do not succeed,
Then force your mind!

2999.

In my life
There is nothing to say
And there is nothing to
   understand.
There is only one thing,
And that is
Constant self-revelation.

3000.

I give credit to my gratitude-heart
For everything I know.
I give credit to my surrender-life
For everything I have become.

3001.

Now that you have surrendered
Your life to God,
You have at least one Person
Who will listen to you,
And that Person is God Himself.

3002.

Are you a thief
That you have to enter
Into God's Heart-Room
On tiptoe?

3003.

Always carry your soul-map
With you
If you really want
To reach Heaven.

3004.

Nobody wants to know
Your mind's expert opinion.
Everyone wants to have
Your heart's perfect union.

3005.

You are afraid
That God does not speak
Your language.
But God does speak
Your heart-language.

3006.

Something in my heart tells me
That I shall not only realise God
In this lifetime
But also manifest God on earth
Far beyond my expectation.

3007.

His wisdom-life
And his ignorance-death
Are fighting all the time
Inside his heart.

3008.

God's Fountain-Love
Is not above
My division-head
But deep inside
My oneness-heart.

3009.

You may not know,
Perhaps you will never know,
That you are not only
Humanity's hope
But you are humanity's only hope.

3010.

Enthusiasm is energy.
Energy defeats
Failure-life.

3011.

There may not be
Any place for God
Inside you,
But inside God's Heart
I am sure there is always
A place for you.

3012.

Your vital attachment
Has totally destroyed
The heart-plant
Of your inner beauty.

3013.

If you are
God's chosen instrument
On earth,
Then do not take anything
For granted.

3014.

If you surround yourself
With purity,
Heaven's divinity will
At every moment
Shake hands with you.

3015.

It is not
His fear of death
But his fear of life
That has separated him
From human society.

3016.

It happens all the time
That when God sends for me
I am unavailable.

3017.

One song
I shall never forget:
My Lord's
Daily Forgiveness-Song.

3018.

I want to complete
The last page of my life's book
Only with my heart's gratitude-
    tears
And my life's surrender-cheers.

3019.

If you blow
Your ego-trumpet,
How do you expect God
To keep you
Inside His Compassion-Net?

3020.

Your confidence-light
You must feel
At this very moment
And not leave
To the distant future.

3021.

To speak to you
About your heart's surrender-life
Is more useless
Than talking to a brick wall!

3022.

Do not try
To imitate perfection.
Your very attempt
Will end in a sad fiasco.

3023.

Each individual
In his own clever way
Thinks he can easily have
A cloud-free aspiration-cry
If he wants to.

3024.

So much I owe
To God the man!
I really do not even dare
To think of it.

3025.

If you want to repeat
Anything in your life,
You can do so,
Except for one thing:
Do not repeat
Your life's repeated defeats.

3026.

Your heart's purity-bird
Has flown away
Because your mind
Has totally destroyed
Your life's beauty-nest.

3027.

If you have a soul,
Which you have,
Then you must ask your soul
To show its victory-light
Inside your body-room.

3028.

God's only question
To humanity:
"Children,
When will you start
The victory-voyage
Of life?"

3029.

Only a purity-pilgrim
Has the right
To walk on the soul's
Perfection-road.

3030.

You are not the only one
Who suffers from
The infectious doubt-disease.
Doubt-disease has covered
The length and breadth
Of the world.

3031.

It is now high time
For you
To gather together
All your heart's
Immortal treasures:
Affection, purity, love
And oneness.

3032.

God the Justice
May not wait
At the end of every road.
But God the Compassion
Will definitely wait
At the end of each and every road.

3033.

Even his eyes
Do not have
Any trace of desire,
Not to speak of
His heart.

3034.

The outer world
Does not want to claim him
Because the inner world
Does not trust him.

3035.

If your mind knows
How to confine your life,
Then your heart knows
How to pine for liberation
And also
How to dine with God-
   Satisfaction.

3036.

God does not want you to have
A hermit-heart.
He wants you to have
His own Emperor-Heart.

3037.

His mind enjoys
Only one thing:
Constant confrontation
With God's Compassion.

3038.

Your heart's cheerful willingness
To obey God
Will wash away
Your mind's ignorance
Of millennia.

3039.

I sing my God-songs
Only for God
The Listener.

3040.

Poor God
Has no time for Himself.
He uses all His time
To listen to humanity's
   complaints
Against Him.

3041.

You may be helpless,
But never, never think
That you are hopeless,
Absolutely hopeless.

3042.

You can boast
Of your desire-fire
Only until
God the Fireman arrives.

3043.

His heart was surprised to see
That his mind
Had totally collapsed
Owing to its unwillingness
To obey the soul.

3044.

His lack of enthusiasm
Has helped him
To build his own
Failure-prison.

3045.

Tell God your troubles.
If you do not tell Him,
He will spend all His time
Listening to others' troubles,
And you and your troubles
Will remain inseparable.

3046.

God does not command you.
It is you
Who command your life
To be disobedient
To God's Will.

3047.

Your body, vital, mind and heart
All want to play with God.
But God plays only
With your heart
And its purity.

3048.

God did not want you
To give up.
He just wanted you
To give in
To His Immortality's Will.

3049.

If you see
A sincerity-landmark,
That means
That secretly an angel-heart
Is leading you
On the right path.

3050.

Now that you have stepped down
From your ego-pedestal,
God is not just walking,
But running
Towards you.

3051.

Your body
You cannot expand.
Your mind
You cannot expand.
But your heart
You can definitely expand.
What for?
To embrace God's universe.

3052.

Nothing can change him.
No, not even the threat
Of imminent death!

3053.

Are you walking
Beyond the borders
Of an unbounded time?
Then you are bound to have
A new Companion:
God.

3054.

What do you want?
Do you want
God's two strong Arms
Or
His one Silence-Heart?

3055.

His mind forgets
That he has not made
Many attempts.
It only remembers one thing:
No success.

3056.

I do not want to be
A tennis ball,
But I really want my life
To be as perfect
As the surrender
Of a tennis ball.

3057.

They say
Man is evolving
And progressing.
Alas, what do I see?
Barbarian behaviour
Is the order of the day!

3058.

Why does God refuse
Man's desires?
Is it because He is
Incapable?
Or is it because He is still
Compassionate to mankind?
Aspiration-lovers and desire-lovers
Have different answers.

3059.

Every day
When I pray soulfully
And meditate peacefully,
God provides me
With a new heart-room
To work on my life's ideals.

3060.

God's Compassion plays
With the broken hearts.
God's Satisfaction chats
With the chosen lives.

3061.

A willing God-servant
Always loves mankind
Not only unreservedly
But also unconditionally.

3062.

There is always
A terrible fight
Between false hope
And real success.

3063.

A self-giving moment
Has the giant capacity
To move a chain
Of ignorance-mountains.

3064.

In the morning
I pray to my Beloved Supreme
To shut my mind-gate
Against uncomely thoughts.
In the morning
I meditate on my Beloved
  Supreme
To grant me the capacity
To come out of the deep cave
Of blind darkness.

3065.

The death
Of your devotion-life
I cannot believe—
I cannot even imagine!

3066.

If you want to run a race
Every day,
Then I advise you to run only
Your life's cheerfulness-race.

3067.

Humanity's unfulfilled
Desire-sorrow
Is no match for
Humanity's fulfilled
Desire-joy.

3068.

Alas,
His heart is totally defenceless
Against his mind's
Unexpected doubt-invasion.

3069.

Did you ever imagine
That you would be so pure
That you could see God's Eye
And be at God's Feet?

3070.

You have taken upon yourself
An impossibility-task:
To forge God's
Blessing-Signature.

3071.

Everything that you have
Is undivine.
Even inside your humility
What looms large
Is your pride.

3072.

An impurity-heart
Is a loveless heart.
A loveless heart
Is a God-Visionless heart.

3073.

One good decision
Leads to another:
"I shall realise God….
I shall become perfect."

3074.

I will fail God:
This is a secret
That I do not want
Under any circumstances
To be divulged.

3075.

A mind of suspicion
Needs a heart of purity
For its newness-illumination
And vastness-perfection.

3076.

You want to know
Who will be the keeper
Of my heart-castle.
God the Lover
Has graciously agreed
To do the job
Unconditionally.

3077.

His hope-tree
Was shattered
The day his mind's doubts
Replaced his heart's faith.

3078.

Each life must cultivate
Every day
A green newness-field
To collect a bumper crop
Of aspiration.

3079.

Your ceaseless thirst
For purity in God's world
Will someday
Definitely be quenched.

3080.

My mind enjoys
Isolation,
My heart enjoys
Consolation
And I enjoy
My Lord's Compassion.

3081.

Make up your mind!
Do you want God to please you,
Or do you want God's infinite
    Blessings
To please God?

3082.

Do you want to serve God?
Then you need more
Heavenly credentials
And you need no
Earthly experience.

3083.

God is your
Open Admirer.
Can you not
At least try
To be His secret admirer?

3084.

Your heart's gratitude-bird
Flies away
Quicker than your mind's
Imagination-bird.

3085.

The gratitude-heart
Of your meditation-life
Earns God's most powerful
Silence-Smile.

3086.

God does call
Your heart's aspiration-name
All the time.

3087.

When you talk to God about me,
It is not just
Between you and God.
I must also know
All about it.

3088.

Your heart has to be
Always
A patient pilgrim
On your inner path.

3089.

Insecurity is a contagious disease
That one sufferer receives
From another deplorable sufferer.

3090.

I always wanted
To be tall in the inner world.
I always wanted
To be strong in the outer world.

3091.

Do not miss a moment
If you do not want to leave
Any room for regret
In your aspiration-life.

3092.

Destruction-mountain
Lies right on top
Of depression-land.

3093.

One peaceful word of Yours
Has awakened my heart.
One powerful word of Yours
Has illumined my heart.

3094.

Who can appreciate stupidity?
Not even the man
Who possesses stupidity
In abundance!

3095.

You will not be able
To recognise God
Unless you admire
God's selfless Dedication-Army.

3096.

You are yearning
For an extra-special love.
What you actually need
Is an extra-fruitful awareness.

3097.

What you need
Is not desire-deprivation.
What you need
Is desire-illumination.

3098.

My body revolts
Against my heart
Every day.
My heart does not know
And does not want to know
How to revolt
Against my body.

3099.

He who indulges in cynicism
Thinks that there is nothing good
On earth.
But the Absolute Supreme
Knows that there is nothing not
    good
Either on earth or in Heaven.

3100.

My Lord,
This heart is Yours.
Even if You do not forgive me,
I shall not forget
The Compassion-Beauty of Your
    Heart.

3101.

There shall come a time
When each soulful prayer-tree
Will reach Heaven's perfection-
   height.

3102.

Where were you
When God came to your door
To deliver
His Infinity's Immortality-
   Delight?

3103.

His very compassion-smile
Can make heavy hearts
Immediately and immeasurably
   light.

3104.

I strive
Because I am alive.
I am alive,
Therefore I must reach
God's Heavenly Throne.

3105.

My Lord is not discouraged,
Although I have failed many
   times.
On the contrary,
He is begging me to continue.

3106.

Your heart's ultimate awakening
Will definitely bring to you
God's transcendental Crown.

3107.

Let everybody look upon
Your outer life.
Only God will look upon
Your inner life.

3108.

He wants his pride in himself
And God's Pride in him
To be equal.
Is there anybody
Whose stupidity
Can equal his?

3109.

You can change your life
In a twinkling
Even with a feeble effort
Provided you love only God,
Your Supreme Beloved,
In your wakeful hours
And in your sleeping hours.

3110.

Your purity-heart
And God's Satisfaction-Smile
Will together guard
Your soul-castle on earth.

3111.

There is not a single day
When I do not see
Wave-doubts
On my mind-shore.

3112.

A silence-mind
In silence appreciates
God's Lecture.
A purity-heart
With devotion receives much
From God's Lecture.

3113.

He is so brave
Within and without
That ignorance-teacher
Had to expel him
From ignorance-school.

3114.

God for God's sake only:
This is the supreme reality
That each seeker must understand
When he enters into the spiritual
   life.

3115.

You are chanting God's Name
Sleeplessly.
Definitely you can expect
God's sure Descent
From Heaven.

3116.

A soulful sincerity-cry
And a powerful purity-smile
Are fast-fading flowers
Of my life-tree.

3117.

All outer entanglements
Are avoidable
If you love and feed
Your inner shrine.

3118.

Only an unconditional
God-lover
Is allowed to fly
God's Love-Kite.

3119.

Ignorance-feast has ruined
Not only his inner life
But also his outer body.

3120.

He was attacked mercilessly
By teeming doubts.
Therefore, he was desperately
   carried
To Heaven's emergency room.

3121.

Your extra attachment-pounds
Have considerably slowed down
Your inner progress-speed.

3122.

The heart that loves God
Only for God's sake
Has a road map
To God's secret and sacred City.

3123.

If you pray to God
And meditate on God
Along with a thousand outside
   interests,
Do you think God
Will ever satisfy you?

3124.

God's Justice-Light
Wanted to illumine him.
Alas,
Instead of illumining him,
It has frightened him.

3125.

No previous qualification
Is needed
When you want to study
In God's inner School.

3126.

You may desire everything
From God,
But ask yourself
If you deserve anything.

3127.

If you are not deeply absorbed
In your inner life,
You will remain a stranger
To God-Satisfaction-Country.

3128.

A mind of silence
Is the best preface
To the meditation-book.

3129.

God's Compassion
Has a very special love
For the seeker's listening ears.

3130.

Work with what you have.
Then God will give you
Not only what He has
But also what He is.

3131.

Your heart-tears
Definitely have the capacity
To tear down
Your mind's impossibility-
 barriers.

3132.

Because you are reluctant
To leave your familiar
Ignorance-home,
You are delaying indefinitely
God's Satisfaction-Smile
On your face.

3133.

God will call you
To be near Him
Only if you have not squandered
Your hope-wealth.

3134.

There is no insincerity involved
When I say
That my daring aspiration
Will be responsible
For your illumining realisation.

3135.

My Lord,
Where have You been
For so long?
"My child,
I have been looking
For a place
Of silence and happiness
For your heart
To permanently live."

3136.

Your unlimited aspiration
Will be available
Only if you are ready
To free yourself
From fame-prison.

3137.

If you want endurance
In your life,
Then you must cultivate purity
In your heart
First.

3138.

Each unaspiring,
Unrevealed
And unmanifested soul
Is like a caged lion
In man's life-circus.

3139.

First become
A deathless longing for God.
Then your life will automatically become
A deathless seed
In the Heart of God the Creator
And a deathless flower
In the heart of God the creation.

3140.

When my heart feeds
My humility-feet,
I walk along purity-road
And reach my satisfaction-destination.

3141.

Your business
Is to be conscious
Of your faults.
God's Business
Is to make you conscious
Of your unmanifested divinity.

3142.

Although ignorance-night
Tempts him,
He has kept his heart
Far, far away
From its temptation.
His heart is at the Feet
Of his Beloved Supreme.

3143.

Openly you must criticise
Your lower nature.
Secretly you must treasure
Your higher nature.

3144.

When my silence-soul speaks
To my heart,
My reasoning mind ridicules
My soul and my heart.
Therefore, I am fully prepared
To discard my mind.

3145.

You have entered
Into life's battlefield
On earth.
Therefore, impurity-army
Has vehemently attacked you.

3146.

Your devotion-arrows
Are missing!
What can your love-bow alone do?

3147.

Once you allow
Any aimless thought-birds
To fly in your life,
They will tirelessly fly
And ruin your peace of mind.

3148.

I always want to study
Your soul-history,
But alas,
You have not kept
Even a simple diary
Of your soul's life.

3149.

If you are truly
An unconditional truth-seeker,
That means you have become
A living testament
To God's Compassion-Firmament.

3150.

If you are feeding your desire-life
Every day,
Then definitely you will take
A false start
In your Heavenward race.

3151.

I have endured
A volley of insults
From this ungrateful world.
But its final insult,
That I do not love God in man,
Is impossible for me to endure.

3152.

Alas,
I really feel sorry for you,
For you have locked your mind
In a bitterness-cave.

3153.

Your soul is smiling
Through your heart's tears.
Therefore
God is addressing you
As His Eternity's Fondness-child.

3154.

The love-bond
Between man's emptiness
And God's Fulness
Is something
That God sleeplessly treasures
And man unconsciously forgets.

3155.

As long as determination-mind
And aspiration-heart
March ahead of me,
I am definitely going to win
In the battlefield of life.

3156.

You are not a child
Of the fearful past.
You are a son
Of the fruitful future.

3157.

God's Silence-Smile
Is a messenger
Between my aspiration-heart
And God's Satisfaction-Eye.

3158.

He has sheltered his life
Under a canopy of ignorance-
    sleep.
Therefore
The delight-wings of his heart-
    bird
Are ruthlessly clipped.

3159.

You live in the valley
Of forgetfulness.
There your demanding vital
Demands
God's measureless Fondness.

3160.

God will not accept
Fragments of my broken heart.
He only accepts
My purity's oneness-heart.

3161.

In the morning
Love feeds his heart.
At noon
Hope leads his life.
In the evening
He and hope together swim
In satisfaction-sea.

3162.

Can you believe
That God Himself
Wants to preside over
My self-transcendence-play?

3163.

During his meditation
God whispers immortal Messages
In the ears
Of his silence-heart.

3164.

God has not closed
His Fondness-Door
Against you.
It is you who have closed
Your acceptance-door
Consciously and deliberately.

3165.

You live in dark
Ignorance-cave,
Yet you want to hear the whispers
From Immortality's heights.

3166.

I do not want to know
How long I have been sleeping
In the cradle of ignorance.
But I do want to know
When I will be able to free myself
From the cradle of ignorance.

3167.

Always sail
In the blue-white hope-boat.
You are bound to reach
The Golden Shore of the Beyond.

3168.

There is no such thing
As the wrong place
When you sincerely
Look for God.

3169.

If you are more than satisfied
With your purity-flames,
God is not going to give you
His Divinity-Sun.

3170.

Every day he plows
The barren mind-soil.
Yet he hopes to collect
A bumper crop of realisation.

3171.

God took a glimpse
Through His Vision-Eye
And found that my case
Is not as hopeless
As I thought.

3172.

Because you did not
Obey God today,
You are sentenced
To a lifelong ignorance-torture.

3173.

At long last
I have started playing
Soulfully and untiringly
My heart's gratitude-game.

3174.

The constant rivalry
Between my mind and my vital
Is utterly stupid and fruitless.

3175.

If you pay attention
To God's Compassion-Talks,
Your life will grow into
A marvellous creation of God's.

3176.

If our hearts could sing
Instead of our minds talk,
We would not have any
Unfortunate misunderstandings.

3177.

Take shelter
In your aspiration-life!
Otherwise
You will soon be forced
To live in the graveyard
Of your unfulfilled desires.

3178.

You think
You can desert your soul.
I tell you,
You are attempting
An impossible task.

3179.

Only at God's choice Hour
God reveals to man
The Power
Of His all-knowing
Vision-Eye.

3180.

His heart's cry
And his soul's smile
Together
Will plant and cultivate
A divine life on earth.

3181.

What you need is
Not the fulfilment
Of your desire-life,
But to have a life
That will grow
Into the steady flow
Of faith-river.

3182.

Since you have plunged
Into the aspiration-ocean,
Your triumph over your past life
God Himself will announce.

3183.

Alas,
God's Satisfaction-Smile
Has never dawned
In his life.

3184.

Self-transformation
Is not possible
For the seeker
Who is secretly in love
With insecurity.

3185.

Despite his outer knowledge,
He is worse than useless
In the inner world.

3186.

You are not ready
Even for the aspiration-walk
And you want to win
The realisation-race?

3187.

The soul does not need
A big audience
To reveal
Its immortal divinity.

3188.

Sincerity-hotel,
Humility-hotel
And purity-hotel:
These hotels have quite often
Many vacancies.

3189.

How will it be possible
For you to see
Your heart's illumination-sun
If you enjoy
Your mind's depression-storm?

3190.

How can a fool
Take the final step
When he is afraid of taking
Even the initial step?

3191.

Unless you are brutally sincere
With yourself,
You will not be able
To cross ignorance-sea
At a single leap.

3192.

You are gasping
For God's Breath.
Therefore
Strangling death
Is bound to disappear.

3193.

Your mind is shrouded
In confusion-fog.
Therefore, your life's worries
Will never disappear,
Even if Heaven's light
Appears to you.

3194.

If meditation cannot give you
Your needed satisfaction,
Then try surrender.
It will work!

3195.

I know one day
I shall thank you profusely
For scolding me.
But today
I am inwardly cursing you
For scolding me.

3196.

He is totally lost
Between
His unscrupulous past
And his superfluous present.

3197.

His soul's goodwill
Bathes
The purity of the saints
And the impurity of the sinners
Alike.

3198.

He offers his gratitude-life
Every day
To God the Lover.
He offers his surrender-life
Every day
To God the Transformer.

3199.

God will grant you
His Attention
If you are sure
That His Companionship
Will give you
Perpetual satisfaction.

3200.

Every day God wants to hear
The surrender-story
Of the aspiration-hero
Who lives only to please God
In God's own Way.

3201.

Two real messages of my heart:
Gratitude is beautiful,
Obedience is fruitful.

3202.

You think you can thwart
The Will of God!
Just show me if you can end
The whims of your mind.

3203.

If you see God's Face
But you do not see
The revelation of His Grace
On His Face,
That means you have not seen
God's real Face.

3204.

The racing motor
Of humanity's mind
Is not going to see
Divinity's Immortality-Life.

3205.

God created my life for me
Out of Compassion.
I have built a cage for myself
Out of attachment.

3206.

He knows how to do
Only one thing.
Every day he enlarges
His mind's imaginary
   catastrophes.

3207.

When my heart thinks of God,
It sees a reservoir
Of Nectar-Delight.
When my mind thinks of God,
It sees nothing but God's
Supreme Indifference.

3208.

If you want to remain
The servant of your desire,
God will definitely wait
Until you desire to be
His Infinity's partner.

3209.

Although the mind-bird
Is always inside the cage,
It thinks that it is always
Outside the cage
And freely flies all-where.

3210.

God will not give you the capacity
To look up to Him,
Because you have taught your
  mind
To look down upon man.

3211.

At last he has freed himself
From his old compelling desire.
He will no longer try
To lord it over the world.

3212.

His life's greatness-achievements
He gave to mankind.
His life's surrender-achievement
He gave to God.

3213.

You must start your life's journey
As a persistent traveller.
Then only God will make you
His enlightened traveller.

3214.

God's Compassion-Eye
Shows him concern constantly.
God's Forgiveness-Heart
Illumines him daily.

3215.

Activity will show you
Its blazing fire.
Inactivity will show you
Its useless ashes.

3216.

His life is playing hide-and-seek
Between
His heart's setting sun
And his mind's thickening night.

3217.

Others rule your mind
Because you and your heart
Do not live inside each other.

3218.

God does not need
A handful of thanks from you.
He needs only
A heart-melting cry.

3219.

Simplicity, sincerity and
    humility—
These are the three purity-guards
Of your heart-temple.

3220.

Because of your two powerful
Determination-arms
And two aspiration-eyes,
You are bound to be victorious
In your life's battlefield.

3221.

Your heart-runner
Will be able to run most speedily
Without suffering
From doubt-cramps.

3222.

Next door
To your silver heart
Is your soul's
God-manifesting Golden Shore.

3223.

To destroy your mind's
Confusion-jungle,
You have to be always
In the valley of aspiration
And not relaxation.

3224.

God wants an iota
Of pure love from you
To satisfy Him,
But never, never
Your leftover love!

3225.

If you are playing
The cosmic game,
You must expect
Only one thing
As your supreme reward:
Perfection.

3226.

Your past desire-life
Is born again.
Therefore, God is hiding
His Satisfaction-Face
Once more.

3227.

Alas,
Unfounded doubts are governing
The beauty and purity
Of God's entire creation.

3228.

Again and again you are abusing
Your privileged position.
Therefore, you are becoming
Not only a deplorable
But also an unforgettable
Failure.

3229.

You are not meditating
On God the Eternal Time,
But you are meditating
On the man-made hands
Of a fleeting clock.

3230.

The divine in you touches the Feet
Of God's Will.
The human in you foolishly tries
To bend God's Will.

3231.

Success wants to solve
Humanity's problems,
But it badly fails.
Progress solves humanity's
    problems.
Do you know how?
God Himself does it
For progress.

3232.

A non-seeker is he
Who has a futility-heart
Inside his stupidity-mind.

3233.

If you do not love the world
In spite of its obvious
    imperfections,
God is not going to grant you
His extra-special, precious Love.

3234.

If you can show God
Your uncorrupted heart,
Then God will not only show you
But will also give you
His uninterrupted Happiness-
   Heart.

3235.

Your rich heart begs
At your poor mind's door.
It begs your mind to accept
Its ecstasy-sea.

3236.

You asked for too little.
Something more,
You asked too late.
How can you then satisfy God?

3237.

Since you are ruthless
With your imperfections,
Your life can never
Be hopeless.

3238.

He has an infinite appetite
For God's Appreciation
Without having any aspiration
To satisfy God
Even on rare occasions.

3239.

No matter which incarnation
I think of,
I just think of one thing:
The winding road
Of my mind's confusion.

3240.

Play the soul-stirring flute
To awaken humanity
From its age-long ignorance-
   sleep.

3241.

You are not at all prepared
For your inner examination.
How do you then expect
Abiding satisfaction
In your outer life?

3242.

Once his life was famed
For aspiration.
Now his life is famed
For dedication.

3243.

You need not practise
To win God's Compassion-Eye,
For His Compassion-Eye
Is unconditional.
But you have to practise
To win God's Satisfaction-Heart,
For His Satisfaction-Heart
May be conditional.

3244.

Your doubtful mind
Is teaching you how to walk
   backward.
Where is your faithful heart
To help you march and run
   forward?

3245.

You have lost
Your life's hope-seeds.
Alas, your soul's promise-trees
Will never come into existence.

3246.

You are your disobedience-sky.
How will you have
Beauty's moon and divinity's sun
In your sky?

3247.

I really cannot understand
How you can be seized
With desire-pangs
And aspiration-happiness
At the same time!

3248.

Throw your devotion-javelin!
You are definitely going to pierce
The veil of ignorance-life.

3249.

God has promised to visit
My silence-heart
With His blessingful Eye
And fruitful Feet
At least once a day.

3250.

You know how
To argue with God,
But God does not know how
To love you less.

3251.

The soul's flight of delight
Is never delayed.
It always flies
At God's choice Hour.

3252.

Your universal negligence
Indicates that soon
God will lose all confidence
In you.

3253.

When did God tell you
That you are indispensable?
He only told you
That you are useful
And you can remain useful.

3254.

How do you like your new life
Where God comes first
In everything you say
And everything you do?

3255.

One unguarded moment
Destroyed the satisfaction
Of his entire day.

3256.

What shall I do with my life?
Since I have no need for it,
Either I can destroy it,
Or I can offer it to God
In case He can use it.

3257.

If you are afraid
Of mounting inner stairways,
The solutions to your life's
   problems
Will never be found.

3258.

Unless you realise
That ignorance is the hardest
   pillow,
You will not look for wisdom-
   light,
Which is really the softest pillow.

3259.

To stop your desire-fire,
You have to bathe in the ocean
Of God's Forgiveness-Light.

3260.

A secret war is going on
In my spiritual life
Between my heart's patience
And my mind's impatience.

3261.

Not only his mind
But also his entire body
Is infected
With measureless pride.

3262.

If you refuse to surrender
To ignorance,
Then God will definitely allow
  you
To live inside
His Compassion-Harbour.

3263.

You need
Indescribable satisfaction
To conquer
Your irresistible temptation.

3264.

He has two medicines
To cure all his diseases:
Time and silence.

3265.

He is playing hide-and-seek
With his doubting mind.
Needless to say,
This is a forbidden game.

3266.

What you are doing
Is just nourishing my fantasies.
What I want
Is my long-lost heart-ecstasy.

3267.

What saved his life?
Not his life's outer capacity
But his heart's inner sincerity.

3268.

If you see
Through the eye of the heart,
You will be ready to receive
The delight of perfection.

3269.

Always put the accent
On God's Compassion
And not
On man's promise-mountain.

3270.

I am of God,
I am for God.
Indeed, this experience
Is the springboard
Of my God-commissioned life.

3271.

If you are a non-seeker,
That means you have become
The unconscious possessor
Of a barren life.

3272.

At long last
He is enjoying a little rest
From his dark doubt-dreams.

3273.

If you disobey your Master,
You can rest assured
That you will have a different
   name:
Failure.

3274.

Since you do not know
When your life ascends
And descends,
You are definitely very far away
From perfection-delight.

3275.

I have seen and I have heard,
But I want to see more
And I want to hear more
Of God's Compassion-Blessing.

3276.

Out of sheer curiosity
If you accept the spiritual life,
How can you expect
Divine thoughts to nurse you?

3277.

A wordless prayer of silence
Has surmounted
All his previous resistance-
   barriers.

3278.

You have to discard
Quite a few things
From your life.
Start by discarding
Your uncomely thoughts.

3279.

No matter how powerfully
You think,
Your ego-castle is bound to
   crumble
Before long.

3280.

When your spirituality becomes
Your unhappy duty,
Futility becomes
Your unwanted companion.

3281.

If you can show God
Your heart's tenacity-capacity,
God will definitely come
And stand before you
And also crown you
With His Heart's Satisfaction-
   Crown.

3282.

Alas, he did not know
That he was going to be struck
So mercilessly
By unseen inferiority-blows.

3283.

The ferocious vital-tiger
Can easily destroy
The auspicious breath of a seeker
If he is not all the time
Cautious and conscious.

3284.

Picture yourself
In your heart's satisfaction-
   garden,
For it is there
That you actually belong.

3285.

You have spoken to God
A great many times.
How is it that you have not asked
   Him
Even once
What He wants from your life?

3286.

It is high time
For you to wake up,
You fool!
Your conscious life
Is unable to please God.
How do you think
That your unconscious sleep
Is going to satisfy God?

3287.

If God can initiate everything
In your life,
Can you not at least imitate Him
And prove that someday
You will be His worthy heir?

3288.

If you doubt your own inner life,
God the Justice will someday
Definitely shout at you.

3289.

God has already sent you
His urgent Love-Message,
But alas,
You are nowhere to be found!

3290.

If you hold nothing back from
   God,
God will keep you immune
To ignorance-disease
Always.

3291.

He has been bitten
By the doubt-cobra.
Alas, faith-antidote is not
   available
Either here or there or anywhere.

3292.

His heart's surrender-song
Was cut short
By his mind's thunderstorm.

3293.

Ask your false, flattering friends
If they can flatter God
And bring Him to you!

3294.

He who does not aspire
Has either consciously
Or unconsciously
Blinded himself
And become a blind instrument
Of fate.

3295.

Each time he enters
Into his tranquillity-trance,
God grants him two boons:
A silver dream-boat
And a golden reality-shore.

3296.

You can at least
Delay your departure
If you really have to enter
Into the ignorance-country
And dine with the prince of
   gloom.

3297.

God never counts the cost
Of His Love for you.
Can you not do the same
When you are loving God's
   creation?

3298.

Alas,
When is my heart
Going to blindfold
My earthly critic-eyes?

3299.

Now that my mind
Rests in silence-light,
Doubt-gravity no longer
Pulls my life down.

3300.

When God carries me
In His Heart-Pocket,
He tells me that I have to share
My God-realised breath
With humanity's ceaseless tears.

3301.

A constant gratitude-heart
Is a way of loving God
In God's own Way.

3302.

God visits me twice
Every day.
He visits my mind-room
Only to say how unsatisfied
And dissatisfied He is.
When God visits my heart-room,
He tells me
My heart's perfection
And His Life's Satisfaction
Will play their oneness-game
For all Eternity.

3303.

In the morning
God gave me
A lesson in His Beauty.
In the evening
God gave me
A lesson in His Silence.

3304.

The heart that sleeplessly cries
For God's Compassion-Light
Is made of God's special
Fondness-Vision-Delight.

3305.

The supreme Height of God's
   Compassion
Can forgive humanity
But will never illumine humanity.
For the illumination of humanity,
The Supreme needs
Humanity's conscious
   willingness.

3306.

No matter how sublime my life is,
I will not be able to transform
Humanity's confusion-clime.
But I will maintain my hope
That someday, somehow
My Lord Supreme will transform
Humanity's mind-confusion-
   clime
Into Divinity's Illumination-
   Kingdom.

3307.

Two masters live in the same
   house:
The ignorance-prince
With his master, doubt,
And the wisdom-emperor
With his master, faith.

3308.

There are two
Heart-illumining songs:
My purity's obedience-heart,
My humility's satisfaction-life.

3309.

You want God to see you
Only through your heart-door,
But God wants to look at you
Through your narrow mind-door
    as well.

3310.

His aspiration-campaign ended
In total failure
Because the members
Of his outer family
Did not support him at all.

3311.

On the strength of his devotion,
His folded hands
Not only decreased
The animal strength in him
But also increased
The divine power in him.

3312.

This life has only one project,
And that is
To inspire the outer world
And aspire for the inner world.

3313.

Do not drag
Your despair-heart
And your doubt-mind!
Let them fall easily
Into the chasm of oblivion.

3314.

If you believe
In the higher worlds
And do not help this world,
Then your confidence-life
Is nothing short of
A stupidity-mind.

3315.

When the cosmic gods
Are on their way to church,
Christ comes to them
Running,
And asks them
To show him their temples
First.

3316.

A surrender-life
Is a God-satisfied heart
In God's perfection-dreaming
　　creation.

3317.

He desired all his thoughts
To be docked
In God's Heart-Harbour,
And God has fulfilled
His snow-white desire.

3318.

God refuses to ignore
Either my ignorance-mind
Or my unwillingness-life.

3319.

Your mind hesitated.
Therefore
You missed the boat.
Your heart is hesitating.
Therefore
You will miss the Boatman.

3320.

He has sent
A surrender-letter to God.
In return,
God has sent him
His Heart's Satisfaction-Telegram.

3321.

God has no pride;
Therefore
He can enter into your heart
Uninvited.
But once He has entered
Into your heart,
Will you be ready
To offer Him His due Throne?

3322.

In silence
He shoots my inner troubles.
In silence
He announces my outer victory.

3323.

His mind constantly lives
Between
Blind desire and dark hate.

3324.

I do not want to live
On renewed hope.
I want to live
On the summit
Of my new aspiration-mountain.

3325.

Who deserves
What God has given?
He who has made his life
Into an unconditional heart-
　flower.

3326.

The song of excellence
Can be sung
Only by a seeker's
Earth-illumining soul.

3327.

If you really need God,
Then you do not have to
Wait in line.
You can go to God
Immediately.

3328.

He wanted to earn
A doctorate in perfection.
God said to him:
"My child,
Be perfect in your devotion-life
First.
Then I shall grant you
A doctorate in perfection."

3329.

God values
Your surrender-life
Infinitely more than
Your aspiration-heart.

3330.

You want God
To come to you first.
But I tell you,
If you go to God first,
Your heart's ecstasy-experience
You will feel infinitely more.

3331.

He is a divine disciplinarian.
Therefore
All those who are around him
Are receiving from him
Satisfaction-delight.

3332.

There is always a better way
To offer one's gratitude-heart
To God,
And that way is to feel
That God's Compassion-Eye
Is available at every moment
For man's heart to use.

3333.

A mind of doubt
Is humanity's old headache.
A life of self-offering
Is humanity's old
And most effective medicine.

3334.

If you want to visit Heaven,
Then learn God's familiar
    song first —
The song of your heart's
Perfection-surrender.

3335.

If you want God
To sit beside you
At every moment,
Then immediately join
The God-loving army.

3336.

He is a scoundrel.
He wants to be a saint.
What he needs every day
Is the reassurance
Of his love for God.

3337.

If you are going to be
A perfect instrument of God,
Then you cannot afford
The doubt-risk in your life
At any time.

3338.

His mind enjoys
Collision with truth.
His heart enjoys
Collision with doubt.
His soul does not enjoy
Any collision.
It only wants to be
With God-believers
And God-lovers.

3339.

You fool!
Your earthly credentials
Will not change
Heaven's opinion of you.
For Heaven to appreciate
And admire you,
You need only one
Heavenly credential,
And that is your sleepless
Self-offering.

3340.

If you want to build
A better tomorrow,
Then invite humanity's cry
And divinity's smile
To help you together
In your project.

3341.

When he gave serious thought
To God,
God in secret taught him
His Vision's Silence-Song.

3342.

If you do not obey God promptly,
Your heart's sincerity-remorse
Will mercilessly torture you.

3343.

My heart's purity
Is my life-illumining song.
My soul's divinity
Is my Lord's God-revealing Dance.

3344.

How can the heart of oneness-love
Be satisfied
When the unsatisfied vital
And the unsatisfied mind
Ruthlessly and shamelessly argue?

3345.

The higher worlds forgot to tell
  me
Two things:
God loves me infinitely more
Than I love Him,
God treasures my heart's
Companionship.

3346.

A heart of selfless self-giving
Is the brightest part
Of my inner being.

3347.

The God-hungry heart
Is the only heart
That can be inwardly genuine
And outwardly generous.

3348.

The best news today!
God has found a vacancy
For my heart to fill.

3349.

Run after opportunity
If opportunity does not run
After you,
For opportunity is the beginning
Of your God-blossoming divinity.

3350.

He speaks of nothing,
Not because he has nothing,
But because the power
Of nothingness
Silences him.

3351.

God's Hour will come back
Again and again.
But will your God-receiving hour
Meet with God's
Earth-illumining Hour?

3352.

Your heart-alarm
Rings and rings.
But alas, your ignorance-mind
Continues to sleep.

3353.

A heart of sleepless cry
Is the highway
To the transcendence
Of the Beyond.

3354.

God does not sell expensive things
In His Love-Store.
He only sells expansive things.

3355.

The higher world
Thinks that it does not need
   humanity.
The lower world
Ridicules humanity.
Only God's World
Understands and values
   humanity.

3356.

What God wants immediately
From you
Is a soulful cry
For humanity's progress-height.

3357.

I admire him
Not because he is great,
Not because he is good,
But because God has confidence
In him.

3358.

Every morning God comes to him
And affectionately tells him:
"My child,
Renew your meditation-permit."

3359.

His soul carries inspiration-
   messages
From Heaven to earth
And his heart carries aspiration-
   messages
From earth to Heaven.
Therefore, God blesses his
   beauty's soul
And God blesses his purity's heart.

3360.

When insecurity-insect bites you,
You have to know
That God has left you
To enjoy His Vacation
Elsewhere.

3361.

If you are planning
To go to God,
Then God is asking you
To go to Him
With your dancing heart,
Not with your trembling life,
And certainly not
With your doubting mind.

3362.

There is only one stupid question
On earth:
When shall I realise God?

3363.

At night
He dreams only God-dreams,
And during the day
His life becomes a sleepless wave
Of gratitude.

3364.

When temptation invites you,
You can accept this invitation
As destruction
Or as another opportunity
To strengthen your mind's power
And increase your heart's cry.

3365.

If you do not laugh
At your own stupidity,
God will not open for you
Your closed divinity-door.

3366.

If you can look
Beyond today's torture,
Then tomorrow's satisfaction-
 splendour
Will make you its choice friend.

3367.

Since God has given you
His Oneness-Heart,
Can you not give Him
Your life's newness-eye?

3368.

Because of your self-deception
You are still a human being.
Because of your God-deception
God thinks you are a strange
 being.

3369.

I could not live with God,
Not because
He really did not care for me,
But because
I wanted to replace Him.

3370.

Even the slowest
And the smallest
Aspiration-steps
Will unmistakably take you
To the highest floor
Of God's Mansion.

3371.

He has lost his old world
Only to find his own new world,
The world that God Himself
Chose for him
For His Manifestation.

3372.

O my Lord Supreme,
What I have for You
Is only a tiny heart of gratitude.
Therefore
Do not expect much from me.
If You expect more from me,
I shall certainly fail You,
And I know You do not deserve
   that.

3373.

If you want to see
The garden of my heart's delight,
Then you must make friends
With my Eternity's only Friend,
God the unconditional Lover.

3374.

God never manufactures
   hardships
To help us reach Him.
It is we who unconsciously or
   consciously
Fracture our limbs
In order to draw His compassion.

3375.

Unless I sleeplessly increase
My love-light for God,
He will not grant me
His Infinity's Nectar-Delight.

3376.

A true seeker
Stands between humanity's
Utter dissatisfaction
And divinity's
Shadowless satisfaction.

3377.

If you are afraid
Of the billows of your mind-sea,
God will not grant you
The pillars of His transcendental
   Palace.

3378.

A true God-lover,
In the beginning of his life,
Realises that what God is
Is Vision.
And then,
When his journey is far advanced,
He realises that what God is
Is Illumination.

3379.

A careless mind
And a fearless heart,
Although immediate neighbours,
Never see eye-to-eye
With each other
On any subject.

3380.

My Lord, do give me
Purity's moon-heart.
My Lord, do give me
Divinity's sun-life.

3381.

A prayerful seeker,
A hopeful seeker
And a God-fulfiller
Sail always in the same boat.

3382.

Unless and until
The sovereignty of humanity's
   head
Touches the dust
Of divinity's protection-feet,
Humanity's pride will remain
As destructive
As a mad, wild elephant.

3383.

The day I realised God's
   Compassion
I also realised something else:
My perfection-light
Will never remain a far cry.

3384.

When I concentrate,
God gives me His Power.
When I meditate,
God gives me His Light.
When I contemplate,
God gives me His Oneness-
   Delight.

3385.

Unless man discovers
The stupidity of his mind,
God is not going to invent
A new illumination-mind for him.

3386.

Your desire-life tells you
What you can do for yourself.
Your aspiration-life tells you
What God is always going to do
   for you.

3387.

If your soul is endowed
With God's Vision-Light,
Then your life's mission
Cannot forever lag behind.

3388.

Ignorance-wildfire surrenders
Only when God unconditionally
   threatens
The ignorance-fire
Of man's bygone centuries.

3389.

Since God is utterly sick
Of your old mind,
Can you not show God
The other thing that you have:
A new heart?

3390.

My heart's satisfaction
Is founded upon
God's Compassion-Eye.
God's Compassion-Eye
Is founded upon
The knowable God's Love
For the unknowable God.

3391.

He who has become
His heart's obedience-life
Has become the choicest
   instrument
Of His Beloved Supreme.

3392.

A seeker's heart
May be helpless today.
But tomorrow
His heart will not only be
   powerful
But also shadowless.

3393.

Discrimination, discrimination –
This is absolutely necessary
For the evolution
Of the morality-bound life.
But acceptance of everything
In God's Life
And transformation of everything
In God's own Way
Is the transcendental Message
Of God's Absolute Vision.

3394.

His doubting mind
Was wonderstruck
When it saw his heart's
Devotion-elevator
Reaching the highest height.

3395.

If you are devoted
Only to yourself,
You will definitely become
The champion
Of ignorance-discovery.

3396.

I show my Lord
My face,
And
My Lord shows me
His Tears
On my face.

3397.

The day you allowed
Your gratitude-heart
To be destroyed
Was the day when Heaven
Shed a few silence-tears.

3398.

Success
Does not solve
Any human problem.
Progress
Always does it.

3399.

O my mind,
It is you who overfed my ego.
Why do you not accept the
    complaints
Against my poor ego?

3400.

In my letter to God
I sent only one short message:
"My Lord, I love You only."
God immediately sent me
An express telegram:
"I am coming. I need you badly."

3401.

Those who love
God alone
Will be needed
By God alone.

3402.

You fool,
Why do you love impatience?
Do you not realise
That your life of impatience
Means a shorter time
To achieve something great?

3403.

I feel sorry for you
Because every day you are bitten
By a mad desire-dog.

3404.

Unless you become a perfect
    stranger
To self-indulgence,
Your soul's effulgence-delight
You will never be able to claim.

3405.

I cannot imagine how you can
    allow
So many teeming ego-thoughts
To enter into your life
Every day.

3406.

Let God take care
Of your hesitation-mind
From now on.

3407.

Ignorance does not
Surrender to anyone
On its own.
You have to forcefully
Conquer ignorance.

3408.

God never keeps
His Compassion-Eye
And His Forgiveness-Heart
Empty.

3409.

Today he is celebrating
The death
Of his mind's deception-night.

3410.

Only a fool like you
Can think that self-torture
Is another name
For self-improvement.

3411.

Next to a oneness-heart,
A purity-mind
Is the best protection.

3412.

You may not be thinking of God
For His Satisfaction-Heart,
But God is thinking of you
For your perfection-life.

3413.

He who misses obedience-
    opportunity
Will never be given the chance
To sing God's supreme Glory.

3414.

God will never
Reserve a seat for you
In Heaven
Because
You have never
Reserved a seat for Him
Inside your heart
On earth.

3415.

He lives between
The living image
Of his heart's gratitude
And the living image
Of his life's surrender.

3416.

God will hear
The tale of your tears
Only if you agree
To surrender your life's
Fascinating falsehood.

3417.

God sings the ultimate Vision-
    Song
Only inside the heart
That has grown into
An unconditional surrender-light.

3418.

The noise of the world
Is determined to give God
Two deaf Ears,
A doubting Mind
And a tearful Heart.

3419.

God will not allow you
To exclude your mind
From your heart's
Oneness-dream-boat.

3420.

I am not irritated,
I am not exasperated,
But I am extremely humiliated
When I see that my mind
Does not aspire every day
For its perfection-life.

3421.

Silence is the emergency exit
To escape the world's
Ruthless torture.

3422.

The strength of an elephant
Bows to my patience-heart.
The speed of a deer
Bows to my surrender-life.

3423.

The Infinity-increasing Delight
Of the Transcendental
    Consciousness
Was founded upon
The Eternity-spreading Light
Of the Universal Consciousness.

3424.

Two pieces
Of sad and unexpected news:
I have failed God,
And God will not give me
Another chance.

3425.

Your mind, the impurity-outcast,
Must be illumined.
This is the only way
Your mind can become
A choice instrument of God.

3426.

If you do not keep your heart
Under heavy protection-guard,
Your heart may be ruthlessly
  conquered
By your aggression-vital.

3427.

Alas,
My life's inner vacuum
Can only be felt
And never described.

3428.

The heart's attachment-thickness
Is always founded upon
The mind's ego-sickness.

3429.

It is a difficult
But not an impossible task
To successfully lose
The heart's sadness-weight.

3430.

Unless you take surrender-
  nutrition
Every day,
You cannot make fast progress
In your inner life.

3431.

Every day I watch
God's inner Television
Only to adore
His Compassion-Eye
And worship
His Forgiveness-Heart.

3432.

God does feel sorry
When your heart
Is not on speaking terms
With Him.

3433.

Your life's hungry ignorance-
  dragon
Forecasts the message
Of your life's destruction-night.

3434.

You are always trying to score
An easy success-goal.
Therefore
The supreme Heights of the
   Beyond
Will always remain unknown to
   you.

3435.

Your oneness-soul feels miserable
When your mind enjoys
Rumours and counter-rumours.

3436.

What can I expect
From your shallow mind?
And what can I not expect
From your deep heart?

3437.

His heart's inspired utterance:
"God does love me dearly
In spite of my mind."

3438.

First feel
That truth is lovable.
Then only will you feel
That truth is invincible.

3439.

My God-identification card
God wants me to show
To ignorance-night
In inconscience-world.

3440.

Unless your heart is stirred
By God's sleepless Breath,
How can God's Peace
Be your life's property?

3441.

The heart's voiceless message:
God-realisation is not
An excitement-race
But it is
An enlightenment-goal.

3442.

The turbulent weather
Of your mind
Is keeping you unprepared
All the time
For God's Compassion-Arrival.

3443.

Before God-realisation
Nobody is exempt
And nobody will be exempt
From the punishment
Of ignorance-tax.

3444.

Alas,
I never thought
That my mind-thief
Would run away
With my heart's purity-funds.

3445.

Your vital knows how to export
Excitement-fire.
Your heart knows how to import
Enlightenment-flames.

3446.

His heart's
Aspiration-fire brigade
Is no match
For his life's desire-fires.

3447.

Even if you are fast asleep
In your heart-heaven's waiting
    room,
Your life is definitely
Going to make some progress.

3448.

I admire your hero-
    determination!
You do not want to be caught
Any more
In your mind's confusion-
    quandary.

3449.

If your life
Soulfully lies prostrate
At God's Protection-Feet,
Your life's perfection-dream
Will not remain a far cry.

3450.

If you are a real God-lover,
Then you will not carry with you
Your yesterday's frustration-life.

3451.

When I enter into his heart,
I immediately enjoy watching
The delight-flow
Of his heart's fulness-fountain.

3452.

I admire your lion-hunger,
But how can I admire
Your mouse-capacity?

3453.

Ecstasy-intoxication,
Unlike other intoxications,
Is always appreciated and admired
In all times and climes.

3454.

Who says that it is
An impossible task
For you to extricate your life
From your hopeless futility-fate?

3455.

Your mind has to do
Only whatever you allow it
To do,
And nothing more!

3456.

My worst enemy on earth
Is my fear
Of God's universal
And transcendental
Infinity.

3457.

As you have a heart
Claimed by purity,
Even so, try to have a mind
Claimed by clarity.

3458.

Sometimes you forget
To please God.
Therefore
You must not be surprised
If God forgets to think of you.

3459.

Transformation is not
    destruction.
It is the fire-pure change
Of a human life
Into a divine breath.

3460.

You are a champion
In progress-promise,
But not in progress-jump!

3461.

You wanted to climb up
The desire-stairs,
But unfortunately the desire-
   stairs
Have brought you down
Into the abysmal abyss.

3462.

His mind of desire
And his heart of aspiration
Every day play tug-of-war,
But the final results are not yet
   out.

3463.

You must not be disheartened
By your imperfection-night.
You should only be brave
By having a sleepless perfection-
   cry.

3464.

When you develop
A celestial and natural
Need for God,
God-realisation will not remain
A far cry.

3465.

Frustration is man's
Absolutely worst creation
In God's beautiful world.

3466.

Once you allow
Your desire-train to run
Speedily,
You will never be able
To stop it.

3467.

You must realise
That even God's Indifference
Can be His real Blessing
In disguise.

3468.

From now on
My heart is going to treasure
Only one thing:
Celestial pleasure.

3469.

God has not rejected you.
It is you who have rejected
   yourself
By rejecting your life.

3470.

If you are in doubt,
Why do you not ask God
Immediately?

3471.

Faith
Is the only instrument
That can easily discover
Truth.

3472.

Your hunger for perfection
And God's Satisfaction-Smile
Will definitely meet together
When God's God-Hour arrives.

3473.

His Silence-Eye
Cuts my ignorance-rope
Faster than my eyes
Can see.

3474.

Why do you allow your stupid
   mind
To create insecurity
Between you and God's
   Compassion?

3475.

God devours
What your life has:
Sincerity.
God devours
What your heart is:
Purity.

3476.

Human life is either
To conquer or surrender.
In between
There is nothing.

3477.

The velocity of Love divine
My earth-life has to acquire.
The velocity of Compassion
   supreme
My Heaven-life has to acquire.

3478.

He could not believe his eyes
When he saw this morning
On his body's lethargy-head
A venomous mask
Left by his uninspired mind.

3479.

My faith in God
Has taken up the challenge.
It will definitely transform
My confused mind's confusion-room
Into God's Illumination-Palace.

3480.

Since you have thoroughly studied
The ignorance-history of man's life,
Will you not start reading
The Compassion-History of God's Love?

3481.

Every day I am watching
A most soulful and powerful game.
It is a game that is played
By my heart's consciousness-flames
And my Lord's Consciousness-Sun.

3482.

A poor seeker's life
Goes up and down,
Topsy and turvy,
On the consciousness-trampoline.

3483.

His days pass by
With futility's
Helpless dreams
In the midst of God's
Compassion-Rain.

3484.

You are a real fool!
That is why you have purchased
A round-trip aspiration-ticket
Which will take you to Heaven
And return you to earth.

3485.

When God rings your doorbell,
Go to answer the door
Immediately,
Carrying with you
Your mind's hell.

3486.

The impurity-mind
Of the outer world
And the insecurity-heart
Of the inner world
Are immediate neighbours.

3487.

A life-division-hunger
Is nothing but a weakening
And crippling disease.

3488.

What is an intellectual mind?
An intellectual mind
Is a mind that expedites
The arrival of futility.

3489.

Look in your heart's
Lost-and-found.
The unhorizoned Smile
Of God's Vision-Eye
Is blossoming there.

3490.

Who can demand
Your heart's freedom-life
If you relinquish
Your aspiration-hunger?

3491.

He has no particular eagerness
To live.
He has no particular eagerness
To die.
He has only one eagerness:
To see always
God's Satisfaction.

3492.

His life
And his life's service-joy
Always remain inseparable.

3493.

Every morning my Beloved
 Supreme
Teaches me a heart-melody
From His Compassion-Song.

3494.

Why is your mind so critical?
Is it because your mind
Is empty of inner beauty
Or because your mind
Is full of outer ugliness?

3495.

My Lord,
I have enough trouble
Of my own.
I really do not know
How I can solve others' problems
While my own problems
Remain completely unsolved.

3496.

This soulful world of ours
Desires constantly
Our prayerful efforts
To reveal our Inner Pilot.

3497.

God has asked you
Not to worry.
He has not told you
To remain complacent.

3498.

I always hear
A mountain-silence-song
Inside my soul's heart-garden.

3499.

Forgiveness and oneness
Are the two
Really satisfactory roads
That lead to peace-palace.

3500.

I can be as beautiful
And as perfect as God.
This is a sweet God-secret
That God has revealed to me.

3501.

Give God a chance
To empty your mind.
Give God a chance
To fill your heart.

3502.

The road to perfection-delight
Passes through
Dedication-village.

3503.

Because you have closed
Your mind's ignorance-shutters,
God is growing
His own Faith-Plants
Inside your heart.

3504.

You cannot see
The face of oneness-world
Do you know why?
Because self-importance
Is ruling your life.

3505.

Nothing is permanent here on earth
Except one thing:
The immortal hope of my soul-bird
For full God-manifestation
On earth.

3506.

Your mind is caught
By self-righteousness.
Your heart is caught
By indolence.
Therefore, your life
Can never remain wide awake
To God's Vision-Call.

3507.

God does not want to fail.
Therefore
He will not allow humanity
To disappoint Him.

3508.

A seeker of the absolute Truth
Will every day be blessed
With a whisper-breath
From Heaven's Fulness-Delight.

3509.

If you allow
Your aspiration to sleep,
Your life will die
Even before you dream
Of its death.

3510.

The only way
To amputate imperfection
  successfully
Is the sleepless surrender
Of your entire being
To God's omniscient Will.

3511.

Do not doubt Truth.
Truth loves you.
Do not fear Truth.
Truth will liberate you.

3512.

You are indulging in temptation.
That means you are inviting
Destruction-sword.
Be careful!

3513.

Only a soul
Liberated from
The meshes of ignorance
Can have a heart
Of God-Ecstasy.

3514.

God's Tennis Court
Is meant only for those
Who like to play all the time
Surrender-game.

3515.

Audit your aspiration
With your life's self-giving
Vision-light.

3516.

My soul is extremely fond
Of the silence
In a seeker's hermit-heart.

3517.

You do not want to become
God's Toy.
Therefore
Why should God
Employ you?

3518.

He thinks
That he cannot become
Another God.
Therefore
He vilifies God,
He even denies God!

3519.

My inner faith-doctor
Easily cures
My outer doubt-disease.

3520.

My Beloved Supreme,
Your Eye told me
What to do,
And Your Heart
Is teaching me
How to do it.

3521.

How can your inner life prosper
When you are out of tune
With your Master?

3522.

Two seeker-hearts
May not look alike,
But they have
The selfsame goal.

3523.

If you want to find yourself,
Then you definitely need
A Heavenward-soaring
Aspiration-heart.

3524.

As the soul
Makes a non-stop journey
From God to man,
Even so,
The heart is needed
To make a non-stop journey
From man to God.

3525.

God does not need your love,
Since your love for yourself
Is as important
As your love for God.

3526.

Because you are determined
To hide,
Do not think that God
Is also determined
To search for you.

3527.

If you take a detour
Around your mind,
God will lead you
Into His universal Heart-Home.

3528.

God's Compassion-Eye
Is always in command.
Therefore
My life is a happiness-song.

3529.

What separates me
From God?
My self-styled unwillingness.

3530.

I cannot believe
God's Compassion-Eye
Is asking my surrender-life
To compete with It!

3531.

I am not asking you
To run.
I am asking you
Just to walk,
Since you are a beginner.

3532.

If you are discouraged
And disheartened,
Then God will definitely
Feel miserable.

3533.

What a delight to know
That once upon a time
I was God's conscious partner!

3534.

Do not forget
That an iota of self-giving
Is still self-giving.

3535.

Purity
Is a subject.
Doubt
Does not study
That subject.

3536.

If you have a secret love
For your past failure,
How can you have any love
For your present success?

3537.

Years from now
You will be happy
That I cared
For your heart's cry
And that you cared
For my soul's smile.

3538.

Doubt
Doubts my belief,
But belief
Illumines my doubt.

3539.

Lord,
You were so far away!
Therefore
I had to take shelter
In my mind's austerity-cave.

3540.

My ignorance-master
Has forbidden me
To possess liberation-wealth.

3541.

Desire-wind
Powerfully blows
Only to put you
To death-sleep.

3542.

The sweetness
Of his silence-prayer
Keeps him powerfully alive.

3543.

My soul
Has made it a point
To come always
To my heart's aid.

3544.

He who cheerfully gives
Is a flowing river.
He who ungratefully receives
Is a stagnant pond.

3545.

Alas,
What am I seeing?
I am seeing
Your setting divinity-sun!

3546.

If you want to regret,
Then regret.
If you want to forget,
Then forget.
Only you must not remain
Imperfect.

3547.

A twentieth-century seeker
Needs independence
Both inner and outer
To become
A perfect instrument of God.

3548.

A heart of love
And
A soul of promise:
Definitely
A winning combination.

3549.

God's Compassion-Eye
Is all you need.
Everything else is useless,
Therefore unwanted.

3550.

A turbulent trip
But not a dangerous crash
Marked his heart's journey
In his aspiration-plane.

3551.

Even if you take a slow start,
There shall come a time
When you will be able to achieve
The rocket-speed
On your way to the destination.

3552.

An iota of insecurity
Has the power of ten elephants,
Not only to destroy your life
But also to destroy
All your inner potentialities
And outer possibilities.

3553.

I fold my devotion-hands
So that God's Compassion-Eye
Can play the role
Of the strongest magnet.

3554.

If you are an unhappy seeker,
And if you are in the habit
Of grumbling,
You will soon be forced
To live a counterfeit life
Of spirituality.

3555.

If you live
In the land of desires,
Your mind is bound
To be helpless
And your heart is bound
To be homeless.

3556.

He has absconded
From the city of imperfection.
Therefore
He is now befriended
By satisfaction.

3557.

Do not live
In the vital-village any more.
It is high time for you to live
In your soul's universal country.

3558.

One doubtful mind
Has instigated another doubtful mind.
This is why the world
Is on the verge of destruction.

3559.

Frustration-floor
Has to be washed every day
So that perfection-beauty
Can blossom
In our aspiration-life.

3560.

An insecure seeker
Cannot be a great sprinter
In the aspiration-world.

3561.

O my poor soul,
To me you are nothing
But a shipwrecked navigator.

3562.

You have lost
Your aspiration-heart.
That means
I shall not see
Your dedication-life
Any more.

3563.

Brighten your heart's
Aspiration-flames.
God will enlighten
Your God-approaching life.

3564.

An illumination-heart:
This is what you are.
A confusion-mind:
This is what you have.

3565.

God has given man's faith
The capacity to shorten
God's Justice-Hour.

3566.

Where is the difference
Between your hesitation-heart
And your confusion-mind?
Where?

3567.

What makes you think
You are a total failure?
I tell you,
In God's Eye,
You have never failed
And you never will.

3568.

The soul compassionately
Waits and waits
For the mind to be ready
To receive God
And His infinite Compassion-Light.

3569.

Every day
Sincerity and humility
Go to God to see
If they can do something
For Him.

3570.

God's Compassion-Sun
And my aspiration-flame
Have decided on a merger.

3571.

To reach
The dream-flooded heights,
I need a soulful cry
And not
A hurtful despair.

3572.

Do not be exasperated
With yourself.
Go and present yourself
At God's special Heart-Room.
He is all ready to receive you.

3573.

He likes to keep his life
Always
Under the special Heart-Canopy
Of God.

3574.

Your determination
And God's Compassion
Enjoy seeing your life
Under perpetual construction.

3575.

Somehow God and I
Have become two compatriots
And derive much satisfaction
From each other.

3576.

Where were you
When God looked for you
So desperately
Inside your heart-room?

3577.

Excellence-edifice
Cannot be founded on
The stale achievements
Of the past.

3578.

Humanity
And its overcrowded worry-rooms
Surprisingly remain together.

3579.

By singing his life's
Surrender-songs
He has remarkably improved
The beauty of his heart's
Aspiration-cry.

3580.

My heart is teaching me
How to be pure.
My soul is teaching me
How to be happy.

3581.

Your impurity-mind
Proves
Your unillumined life.

3582.

It is a painful task
For me
To befriend stark fools.
It is an impossible task
For me
To be of any real help to them.

3583.

Humility-host
Has the rare capacity
To richly enjoy the company
Of any guest.

3584.

His ambiguous mind's freedom
From doubt-hallucination
Did not last long.

3585.

His over-fed ego
Cannot believe
That he has
An equality-heart.

3586.

His mind has retired.
Unfortunately
It is now reduced
To inactivity-ashes.

3587.

Whenever you are ready,
God will examine you.
There is no deadline.

3588.

He does not believe
Even in a temporary
Discipline-life.
He only believes
In his luxury-life.

3589.

At any time
You can visit God.
He has a twenty-four-hour
Receiving service.

3590.

He is so undivine
That even the hostile forces
Do not mind
If he remains untouched.

3591.

My love of God
And God's Love of me
Enjoy giving mutual shelter.

3592.

Unwanted third-class seekers
Are everywhere available.
But you are not expected
To be one of those.

3593.

Since your heart
Is a fast starter,
Your life can be
A fast finisher.

3594.

Dissatisfaction-tiger
Is devouring you
Because you have crossed
The disobedience-border.

3595.

Because you are
Your lukewarm aspiration,
Heaven is
Its cool indifference.

3596.

He is all ready
To burn
His unhappy heart-boat.

3597.

His soulful heart
And his powerful eyes
Together
Take God-manifesting exercises
Every day.

3598.

Each life
Is a love-lit lamp
To illumine
Humanity's sorrows.

3599.

When the seeker disobeys
His Master,
It is the beginning
Of his spiritual death.
When the Master withdraws
From the seeker,
It is the completion
Of his spiritual death.

3600.

My life came
Out of God's Eye
And is now returning
Into God's Heart.

3601.

Each life has to become
A surrender-river
Before it can give what it has
And what it is
To the satisfaction-sea.

3602.

If you want to become
A first-class member
Of surrender-society,
Then pray to God
To grant you
His blessingful Gift:
Wisdom-Flames.

3603.

If you do not carry
All the time
Faith-key inside your heart,
The Supreme will not allow you
To become a member
Of His Heart-Transformation-
   Team.

3604.

Who wants to possess a secret?
No, not God!
Who wants to reveal a secret?
Who else, if not man!

3605.

Your life is a mountain
Of mere words
And not a fountain
Of self-giving deeds.

3606.

In the inner world
If you are not prepared
To meet resistance,
That means you are not taking
The inner world seriously.

3607.

God's loyal servants
Are the perfection-cry
Of man's heart
And the satisfaction-smile
Of man's soul.

3608.

I wanted to shake hands
With a responsible mind.
Alas, a stupid mind
Came up to me instead
To shake hands.

3609.

Burn, burn
Your desire-comfort-pillow
So that you do not
Have to wallow
In the pleasures of ignorance-
    mire.

3610.

His arrival on earth
Was beautiful.
His return from earth
Was fruitful.

3611.

What does God do
On His day off?
He sorrowfully watches
The fragile friendship
Between man and the cosmic
    gods.

3612.

If you want to stop
The strong bite
Of insecurity-insect,
Then immediately turn your life
Prayerfully and consciously
Into confidence-lion.

3613.

You have not lost
Your God-realisation-timepiece.
You have just misplaced it.

3614.

Is there any place on earth
With no problems?
Yes, there is a place on earth
With no problems,
And that place is not
A man-discovered place,
But a God-invented place.

3615.

God equally treasures
My success-life
And my failure-life.
This is the very beginning
Of my God-realisation.

3616.

Your clever mind does not want
    doubt
Because doubt is too expensive.
Your wise heart does not want
    doubt
Because doubt is too explosive.

3617.

The heart with no certainty,
The mind with no purity,
The life with no divinity
Will never be allowed
To claim God.

3618.

Start your aspiration-life
Immediately
If you ultimately want to become
A God-hungry man,
Sleeplessly and unconditionally.

3619.

I was born to serve
In God's outer world.
I was born not only to love
But also to become
In God's inner world.

3620.

Your mountain-problems
Will always remain
Because you treasure your mind's
Himalayan doubts.

3621.

I was always waiting,
I am always waiting,
I shall be always waiting
Only for one thing:
God's complete Satisfaction
In me.

3622.

To leap over life's hurdles
You must discard all the pieces
Of your mind's puzzle.

3623.

I do admire your patience-heart,
But your speed-life
Is altogether a deplorable story.

3624.

Unless you reclaim
Your eagerness-heart
And intensity-life,
How do you expect
God's consistent Concern?

3625.

He has no friend,
Not even
His ever-approachable
Loneliness.

3626.

The strength of your folded hands
Can only be appreciated
By your aspiration-heart
And not by
Your suspicion-mind.

3627.

Your mind-hat is so heavy.
Your mind-hat is so ugly.
Nevertheless, you are so fond
Of your mind-hat.

3628.

There is only one
Failure-life
And that failure-life
Is when I feel God loves someone else
More than He loves me.

3629.

If you subscribe
To inspiration-magazine,
God will before long grant you
The enjoyment of Heaven-adventure.

3630.

Your life has fallen
Into a well of self-oblivion.
Therefore
Your soul's illumination
Is unable to offer you
Its God-oneness-ecstasy.

3631.

The only place to discard
Your wild emotion-flames
Is in God's Forgiveness-Heart.

3632.

Away with my desire-mind!
Away with my bondage-life!
I have now become
My upward-marching quest.

3633.

God's motto is,
"Wake up!"
Man's motto is,
"Lord, do not give me up!"

3634.

The misdeeds
Of man's mind
Gave birth
To God's Headache.

3635.

If you are confined
To the useless thought-room,
How can God's Fondness
Reach you?

3636.

He houses at once
In his own heart
Earth's soulful dreams
And
Heaven's powerful vision.

3637.

Be devoted
To your prayer-life
And be not attached
To the success-results
Of your efforts.

3638.

If you do not have
Cheerfulness-escalator
To use,
Then definitely sadness
Will heavily weigh on you.

3639.

You call it
Your self-confidence.
I call it
God's Compassion-Satisfaction.

3640.

Who does not know
That ignorance-life
Is not only an old story
But also an ever-told story?

3641.

Soulfulness is undoubtedly
The beginning
Of a beautiful success
And a fruitful progress.

3642.

God's Compassion-Eye
Is always ready
To come to your immediate
    rescue.

3643.

You will receive
The will-power-trophy
Only for your sleepless self-
    offering.

3644.

To make you exceptionally
Great and good,
God is first granting you
The receptivity-award.

3645.

Every day study faith-lesson.
It will help sustain you,
Even through your life's
Darkest disasters.

3646.

Your mind at once
Makes and receives
An endless chain of complaints
Every day.

3647.

Only faith-soldiers
Can fight against
Endless doubt-enemies
And be ultimately victorious.

3648.

God's Ultimatum:
Either God for God's sake
Or man for man's destruction-
   choice.

3649.

If you cannot afford
To renew each day
Your meditation-permit,
God will not grant you admittance
To His Satisfaction-Heart-Room.

3650.

How can you make anybody
   happy,
How can you yourself be happy
When you are totally lost
On the island of indifference?

3651.

Do not catch a falling star,
But catch the rising sun
And put it inside
Your aspiration-heart.

3652.

Either you swim in the sea
Of soulful delight,
Or you will be caught in the grip
Of destruction-depression.

3653.

The life that does not aspire
For God-realisation
Is not worth even
An empty eggshell.

3654.

When you pray soulfully
And meditate powerfully,
You come to realise
That each heart
Is a beautiful bird of paradise.

3655.

Surrender suffers no loss.
Surrender suffers no failure.
Surrender suffers no
   unworthiness.

3656.

The mind's main disease
Is that
It does not want to unlearn
Anything bad.

3657.

Unless you have
A taste of aspiration-flames,
How will you value
God's supreme Presence?

3658.

Your sweetest dreams
Are founded upon
Purity's oneness-heart.

3659.

He enjoys
Only one thing:
The tide of his mind's
Indifference-sea.

3660.

Ignore your mind's
Depression-cloud.
Dare to expect your heart's
Cloudless satisfaction-smile.

3661.

Aspiration is
A consciously widening
   opportunity
For golden possibilities.

3662.

The death of division
And the breath of oneness
Mark the glorious beginning
Of liberation.

3663.

Attachment-sickness-strings
Are extremely difficult
To break.

3664.

Science secretly
Salutes nature
Without being seen.

3665.

Believe it or not,
Insecurity is a sleepless
　hummingbird
In each unaspiring life.

3666.

You chose death over life,
And now you enquire
Why life is not loving you
And why life is not
At your express command.

3667.

Confidence is at once
A soulfully evolutionary force
In the inner world
And a powerfully revolutionary
　force
In the outer world.

3668.

Truth-tree
Is not only unreachable
But also unbelievable
For the desire-bound mind.

3669.

Never allow your mind
To misdirect
Your heart's winged hopes.

3670.

He started his spiritual journey
To be blessed
By illumination-shore.
But instead, alas,
He was embraced
By hesitation-shore.

3671.

God places
His Heart's Nectar-Crown
Upon the seeker's
Selfless service-head.

3672.

Your division-sickness
Has pained
Your inner life
And stained
Your outer life.

3673.

Your fuzzy conceptions
Of God
Live next door
To your mind's unruly deceptions.

3674.

A heart of aspiration
And a mind of determination
Receive special Fondness-
    Blessings
From God.

3675.

If you do not love God
Unconditionally,
There shall come a time
When you will have to surrender
To the brutal tyranny
Of ignorance-world.

3676.

Love is
A universal tide
For a transcendental ascent.

3677.

Every morning and evening
He runs
In the perfection-possibility-
    meadow.

3678.

The world may forgive
Your crimes,
But the world will never forget
Your stupidity.

3679.

Why are you threatening
Your life
Instead of illumining
Your heart?
Why?

3680.

He lives in between
His changeable mind
And his unchangeable heart.

3681.

He is ready to enjoy
Monarchy,
Even if it is the monarchy
Of misunderstanding.

3682.

God allows only
The prayerful seekers
And soulful lovers
To eat free of charge
Every day
In His Consciousness-Bliss-
    Restaurant.

3683.

God is begging you
To fill your mind-suitcase
With His supremely royal
    Garments.
And what are you doing?
You are just secretly hiding
Your teeming doubts
Inside your mind-suitcase.

3684.

At last I am awakened,
Only to see my desire-life
Groaning in utter despair.

3685.

He does not allow anybody
To accompany him
Except one permanent
    companion of his:
His heart's inner poise.

3686.

If you have a mind,
Then keep it always ready
To receive from God.
If you have a heart,
Then keep it always ready
To hold God.

3687.

You may see yourself alone
When you are at the foot
Of the aspiration-mountain.
But you will definitely
Feel yourself alone
When you are on the highest peak
Of the mountain.

3688.

You are looking for the place
Where hope is.
Do you know where it is?
It is inside the fire
Of your determination-eye.

3689.

You can always do more.
This is what my Beloved Supreme
Tells me
Before I do,
While I am doing,
And after I have finished.

3690.

In the four corners
Of my heart-garden
Whom did I see?
I saw God the Dreamer
And nobody else.

3691.

Do not ignore him!
He has come from the Supreme's
Golden Shore
To allow you to become a student
In his illumination-class.

3692.

I really do not know
How I can believe God
When He tells me
That my mind has
The same capacity as my heart
In cultivating
Purity and divinity.

3693.

Because you order
From ignorance-menu,
The satisfaction-eye of the Master
Remains utterly unavailable.

3694.

Do not drag
Your doubt and despair
Into your aspiration-life
If you ever want to become
God's sacred ambassador
On earth.

3695.

You have triumphantly passed
Your life-examination
Because you have not ignored
Your poverty-stricken heart
Or your voracious vital-appetite.

3696.

Along the heart-path
No hesitation-walker
Is permitted to walk.

3697.

One of the many things
That the higher worlds
   deliberately
Do not show us:
Their indifference to the mortal
   world.

3698.

What did you give God today?
I am sure you have given Him
Your heart's insecurity-insect.

3699.

God's favourite meal
Consists of my heart's
Gratitude-tears
And my life's
Satisfaction-smile.

3700.

God Himself will broadcast
Your inner progress
And outer success
If you just claim God
To be your only
Surrender-breath.

3701.

I have told God
My only secret and sacred truth:
"My Lord, I love You only."

3702.

The stars in the sky
Are desperately trying to hide
From the stars in his heart.

3703.

In honour of God's Birthday
I am definitely going to multiply
My heart-love
By my life-devotion.

3704.

The random use
Of the reasoning mind
Has turned his life
Into a deplorable failure.

3705.

God does not think of you:
Indeed, this idea
Is your mind's
Visible absurdity.

3706.

Prayer
Is for the salvation
Of truth-seekers.
Meditation
Is for the liberation
Of God-lovers.

3707.

Do not allow
Your mind's fear
To persecute
Your heart's poise.

3708.

His aspiration-heart
Is at last happy,
Because the ego-elephant
Of his vital
Is very severely wounded.

3709.

Your helpless pretension
Will soon turn your life
Into a hopeless perdition.

3710.

Because your mind
Is laughing too loudly,
Your heart
Is crying too pitifully.

3711.

To have faith in others
Is to multiply
One's own inner strength.

3712.

An unconditional surrender-head
Wears the crown
Of God-Delight.

3713.

The heart of purity
Is powerful.
The face of sincerity
Is beautiful.

3714.

You do not have to appreciate
God's Heart.
Just imitate
God's Eye.

3715.

A truth-seeker
Does not misunderstand.
A God-lover
Does not misrepresent.

3716.

You love
Your powerful insecurity-heart.
God loves
His blessingful Compassion-Eye.

3717.

God does want to be caught
While walking
Inside your heart-garden.

3718.

Alas,
His soul's determination
Is challenged
By his mind's hesitation.

3719.

The best protection
Against self-doubt
Is man's conscious cry
For perfection-hunger.

3720.

I can become
Another God.
This is the only Message-Light
That God gives me
Every day.

3721.

Long before true happiness
Could approach you,
Your impure self-indulgence
Has killed you.

3722.

Do you not know
What your insecurity is?
It is your old and incurable
Heartache.

3723.

When death calls him,
His soul helps him
Remain unavailable.

3724.

Be a champion
In self-discovery
Instead of man-flattery.

3725.

He becomes his meditation-heart.
This is his special way
Of thanking God.

3726.

Because you love
God's Compassion-Eye,
God also loves
Your gratitude-heart.

3727.

Willingly He descended
To save the world.
Wilfully His Compassion-Eye
Is challenged
By the mind of the world.

3728.

Your desire-life is not fulfilled.
Therefore
You are not on speaking terms
With God.
But God really wants you
To speak to Him.
Therefore
He is unconditionally blessing
   you
With an aspiration-heart.

3729.

How do I occupy my time?
I teach my heart
How to write surrender-letters
With love-pen
To my Beloved Supreme.

3730.

Nothingness
Alarms my mind.
Nothingness
Awakens my life.
Nothingness
Prepares my heart.

3731.

When I say I have nothing,
It gladdens humanity's
Division-unreality.
When I say I am nothing,
It pains divinity's
Oneness-reality.

3732.

Leave your inner life
And outer life
Only at God's Heart-Door
And nowhere else.

3733.

A spiritual seeker
Does not have to travel
On many roads.
He only has to run
On one road:
The road of surrender.

3734.

God's bountiful Smile
Always runs infinitely faster
Than man's fearful cry.
Therefore man is able to remain
Standing on the safety-shore.

3735.

Soon to be announced:
My vital has cheerfully
And unconditionally surrendered
To God's all-loving Heart
And all-illumining Eye.

3736.

Satisfaction-pension
Will always be there
For those who have offered
Their aspiration-services
Soulfully and unreservedly
To God,
Their beloved Employer.

3737.

My mind wants to investigate
Even God's Heart-Room.
My heart wants only to adore
God's Forgiveness-Feet.

3738.

More and more you resemble God.
Do you know why?
Because
You expect nothing from yourself
For yourself,
But
You expect everything from
    yourself
For God.

3739.

His heart is happy
Because his mind does not contain
Superficial thoughts
And artificial ideas.

3740.

Every day I launch
My hope-ship.
I am sure one day I shall reach
My heart's satisfaction-shore.

3741.

God is not a fool like you.
He always takes notes
On what you say to Him
In silence-secrecy.

3742.

I call it
My meditation,
But my Lord calls it
The flowering of His Compassion-
   Eye.

3743.

My loving heart
Has a message for me:
God is always for me.
My serving life
Has a message for me:
I am always for God.

3744.

My life is now
Dead to weakness
And born to God's
Confidence-Delight.

3745.

God is now setting
Not only new
But also high standards
For those who want to love Him
And serve Him
In His own Way.

3746.

I am ready
To be the last seeker
To reach God,
Provided God Himself
Does not mind.

3747.

Do not lose your aspiration-heart!
If you lose your aspiration-heart,
Your frustration-mind
Will become larger than the
   largest.

3748.

If you hurl jealousy-arrows
At the world,
The world may eventually forgive
   you.
But your universal oneness-soul
Will never forgive you.

3749.

You simply cannot imagine
How beautiful you will look
If you just once
Remove your ego-mask.

3750.

Your smart mind knows nothing,
Yet it does not want to learn
Anything more.
Your expert heart knows
   everything,
Yet it wants to learn every day
Something more.

3751.

O earth,
Do give me one more chance.
I shall definitely be able
To prove to you
That I can be a compassion-sky.
O Heaven,
Do give me one more chance.
I shall unmistakably
Prove to you
That I can become a perfection-
   sun.

3752.

His life stands between
His mind's fantasy-stories
And his heart's ecstasy-songs.

3753.

My inspiration-bird wants to sing
Only at one place:
Inside my dreaming heart-garden.

3754.

Please wait a minute!
My Lord Supreme has just arrived
To teach me how to love you,
How to illumine you
And how to please you.

3755.

Every day
Before he prays,
God teaches him
A new purity-song.
Every day
After he is done
With his prayer,
God teaches him
A new divinity-dance.

3756.

Negativity-chain
Is pulling your mind.
Do you know why?
Because
Positivity-train
Your heart has missed.

3757.

Do not keep anything
Between your life's new dawn
And your soul's ancient promise.

3758.

Do only the thing
That makes God happy
And at the same time
Keeps you busy.

3759.

Why do you suffer?
God has given you ample
   opportunity
And enough capacity
To climb over the mountain of
   sorrows.

3760.

While dancing the dance
Of oneness-life,
The smile of sacrifice
Is nothing but an illusion.

3761.

God has already coloured
Your aspiration-heart
With soulfulness.
Can you not colour
Your inspiration-mind
With newness?

3762.

Every night
Lethargy-thief comes
To steal away your life-energy
Completely,
And it is successful
To a degree.
Can you not be wakeful and
   watchful,
And catch the lethargy-thief
Red-handed?

3763.

I have forgiven all your crimes
Except one,
And that crime is your incessant
World-criticism-cry.

3764.

God loves and treasures
The crying heart of every soul
More than He loves and treasures
Anything else
Either on earth or in Heaven.

3765.

I wish to get an invitation
From your soul's dream-boat,
And not an express command
From your demanding vital.

3766.

You came to me
To learn a little about meditation.
I am all ready to teach you.
Alas, why are you then playing
Your life's self-deception-game
Instead of your life's illumination-
   game?

3767.

Aspiration,
Liberation
And satisfaction
Are not at a remote place.
They are just around
The heart-corner.

3768.

When doubt came
To shake hands with his mind,
To its wide surprise
It saw that faith
Had already embraced his heart.

3769.

Man is unhappy
When he sees that what he has
   inside
Is all nothingness.
God is happy
For He knows that He is nothing
But Nothingness itself.

3770.

Do not enter
Into your mind's stupidity-market
To buy futility-goods.

3771.

You do not have to broadcast
The beauty and purity of your
   heart.
Your face can and will
Do it for you.

3772.

To choose a division-mind
Over a union-heart
Is to choose immediate death
Over a beautiful life.

3773.

My heart's hunger-cry
And my Lord's Feast-Smile
Are soon going to meet.
This meeting is ordained
By Heaven's flower-beauty.

3774.

If you really want
To make your desire-story short,
Then start singing immediately
A long aspiration-song.

3775.

Earth's ignorance-sea
Every day devours
Its own lifeguards:
Beauty and purity.

3776.

Today both Heaven and earth
Are celebrating your greatest
  victory.
How is it
That you are not aware of it?
Can you not see
The total disappearance
Of your emperor-ego?

3777.

Why do you dig in your mind-
  desert?
There is nothing
And there can be nothing
Beautiful and fruitful there.
It is a useless task.

3778.

God's Compassion-Fund
Is always ready
To accept your teeming doubts
And darkening worries.
But will you ever be ready
To give God
What you so deplorably have?

3779.

You have been thinking
Of others,
But you never think
Of their satisfaction-lives.
How then can you expect them
To give you
Their smiling oneness-hearts?

3780.

When the beggar in me says
That he has nothing,
I suspect him.
When the emperor in me says
That he is nothing,
I know that he is telling
The absolute truth.

3781.

A self-giving heart-soldier
Is gladly recruited
By God's Satisfaction-Heart
For God's Army.

3782.

My heart of tears
Safely steers my life-boat
To my soul's illumination-shore.

3783.

If your carelessness
Has the capacity to kill you,
Then God's unconditional
   Fondness
For you
Feels the necessity to revive you.

3784.

My mind
Has a lot to unlearn.
My heart
Has a lot to learn.
My soul
Has a lot to contribute.

3785.

To look
Into your Master's eye
Is to enter
Into your own unexplored
   universe.

3786.

Your life of rumour
Is responsible for the tumour
In your aspiration-heart.

3787.

A climbing prayer-heart
And a drowning seeker-life
Never meet together.

3788.

If He is a real God,
Then He will definitely
Leave His Calling Card
Everywhere.

3789.

God may delay
In examining your mind's
Success-reports,
But He will never delay
In examining your heart's
Progress-reports.

3790.

Think of each minute
As either the choice minute
Or the last minute
To realise God.

3791.

My perfection-life
And my satisfaction-heart
Are the two glorious Dreams
Of the Supreme.

3792.

Dear God,
Do give me the time
To prepare myself
So that I do not fail You
When You invite me
To dine with You
In Heaven.

3793.

Within I worship
My insecurity.
Without I worship
My sincerity.

3794.

My heart
Does not have to stay alone.
Do you know why?
Because it cheerfully follows
God's Timetable.

3795.

If you can take
Large doses of faith,
You will soon see
Beautiful satisfaction-roses
Inside your heart-garden.

3796.

Before God-realisation,
Each human being
May be attacked mercilessly
By ferocious human tigers.

3797.

God does not understand
Why any human being ever suffers
From the strong winds
Of insecurity-hurricane.

3798.

The mind's dark
Doubt-adventure
Never ends.
The heart's pure
Faith-pilgrimage
Never ends.

3799.

Because of his
Divinity-flooded life,
For him to nurse
A mind-grievance
Is an unthinkable crime.

3800.

At the end of each earthly
    pilgrimage
The obedient God-lovers,
The obedient truth-fighters
And the obedient peace-
    distributors
Will be garlanded and crowned
By the Absolute Supreme Himself
In His own transcendental Palace
Of Love and Satisfaction.

3801.

Try to claim
God's Smiles
The way He claims
Your tears.

3802.

Something is definitely wrong
With this world.
It does not even recognise
That every day
It suffers from the sharp pinch
Of imperfection.

3803.

Your vital knows
The curse of temptation.
Now you have to know
The height of liberation.

3804.

God does not mind
That He has to raise my blighted
    mind
As long as I cheerfully offer Him
My mind.

3805.

Never allow
Your depression-vital
To clip your heart's
Enthusiasm-wings.

3806.

His mind was brave enough
To free his life
From obscurity's fatal grip.

3807.

If you do not have
Enough aspiration-postage,
Your letters to God
Will always remain undelivered.

3808.

You must defy
Confidently and persistently
The tenebrous suspicion-nights.

3809.

If you have to run,
Which you must,
Then you should run
With God's earth-inspiring
Perfection-Banner.

3810.

God's Affection-Light
Every day
Blessingfully and powerfully
    waters
His heart's aspiration-plants.

3811.

Drive forward, drive forward!
Your life-car does not need
Reverse gear.

3812.

God triumphantly thrives
On man's beautifully happy
Smiles.

3813.

If you do not have
A cheerful heart
In your spiritual life,
You will never see
Your soul's
Birthless and deathless dawn.

3814.

Unload your expectation-
 elephant
If you want to fly
With your soul's
Transcendental silence-heights.

3815.

Alas,
Every day I see
A tough tug-of-war
Between my deplorable fate
And God's immeasurable Grace.

3816.

God really did not want
The human life
To be divided into
Half joy and half sorrow.

3817.

To be perfect
And to be fulfilled,
You must touch God's Feet
With your hope-heart.

3818.

Wherever he goes,
His heart carries for him
A thousand prayer-flowers.

3819.

Because you love God only,
God is coming
To teach you how to dance
To His Self-transcending Tune.

3820.

You have become
Your life's lost lustre
Because you are no longer
 avoiding
Your temptation-thoughts.

3821.

Good can come from bad.
This is a universal experience.
Bad can come from good.
This is an unknowable experience.

3822.

Why is your stupid mind
Afraid to follow?
And why is your wise heart
Afraid to lead?

3823.

The waterfall
Of his aspiration
Has made his life
Into satisfaction-delight
Undreamt of.

3824.

You are stupid!
Therefore
You alone can foolishly try
To force your way
Into God's Heart.

3825.

The summit
Of his soul
Came down to shake hands
With the climbing heart
Of his life.

3826.

Your self-giving heart
Is God's
Treasured Experience-Delight.

3827.

Now that he is
A choice instrument of God,
He devotedly hears
When God tiptoes
Across his heart.

3828.

His spiritual heart-machine
Broke down
Even before it was put into
    operation.

3829.

It is your fault
And not God's
That your life-flute
Is totally mute.

3830.

Alas,
He started with a dubious mind,
And now, what is worse,
He has become a mischievous
    mind!

3831.

When God comes into your life,
He brings His Compassion-
    Chimes
To ring inside
Your aspiration-heart.

3832.

You have all along known
What a vapid mind is.
Now try to know
What a rapid life is.

3833.

O my stupid mind,
When are you going to end
Your stupid conspiracy
Against God's Compassion-Light?

3834.

By virtue of his aspiration
He has become
His heart's stupendous
Swiftness-flight.

3835.

On either side of aspiration-road
There are surrender-shops
Where you can purchase
Celestial souvenirs.

3836.

Since God has not fulfilled
Your desires,
Your life has limitless
God-realisation possibilities.

3837.

If you sincerely dig
Deep within,
Your heart's aspiration-spring
Will not be able to hide
Any more.

3838.

Because of the universality
Of his oneness-heart,
Peace follows him
Wherever he goes.

3839.

You are deserting your heart
To please your mind.
But I tell you,
Your mind will desert you
Before long
And your heart will permanently
And unconditionally
Stay with you.

3840.

You may give up
Your faith-life,
But God will not withdraw
His Concern-Heart.

3841.

You fool!
Why do you want to revive
Your long-dead
Worst doubt-adversaries?

3842.

In secrecy
God has told him
To maintain
His perfection-hunger
All the time.

3843.

You are afraid of dreaming
God's Dream-Life.
Therefore, God's Reality-Life
Has no confidence in you.

3844.

Your life is confined
To weakness-wheelchair
Because your mind
Has unconditionally surrendered
To inner world and outer world
Fears.

3845.

Now that you have lost
Your heart's aspiration-pocket,
Where will you keep
Your soul's satisfaction-coins?

3846.

God's Compassion-Fund
Gladly accepts
Anything I want to give,
Including
My heart's teeming worries
And my mind's confusing doubts.

3847.

An aspiration-melody
Definitely grows
Into a beautiful realisation-song.

3848.

My happiness-heart proves
That God the Creator
Has real Compassion
For God the creation.

3849.

Before I was born,
God the Vision
Played the Kettledrum
Of Delight.
And now I am playing
The kettledrum
Of self-oblivion.

3850.

There is no such thing
As a sunrise
Of satisfaction-surprise.
There is only a sunrise
Of satisfaction-universality.

3851.

One thing
Unmistakably I have realised:
My gratitude-heart
Is my Eternity's silence-surrender.

3852.

His hope-life
Loves prayer.
His promise-life
Loves realisation.

3853.

You have received
The realisation-diploma
From God
Not because you have done
Something great for God,
But because God wants to do
Something good for Himself
In and through you.

3854.

He knows that one day
He will see God
Without fail
Because he is
An island of hope.

3855.

Your mind's secret motives
Are soiling
Your heart's sacred deeds.

3856.

You have taken God's side:
You have done the right thing.
You have left the rest:
You have once again done
The right thing.

3857.

To me
World-blame and world-acclaim
Do not have the same meaning,
But have the same value.

3858.

What I constantly need
Is a liberated heart
So that I can be caught
By the transcendental Beauty
Of God.

3859.

Poor fellow,
What can he do?
He does not know
Why and how
His body-shell
Is so tough
And his heart-core
Is softness incarnate.

3860.

I am not sorry,
O my sleeping mind,
That I woke you up,
Never!

3861.

My Lord is ready
To give me another chance
To change my life,
But I do not know
When I am going to accept it.
I really don't want
To fail any more.

3862.

You lead a life of compromise,
Yet you want God to feed you.
Is it not the height
Of your stupidity?

3863.

Do not hide
Your heart's inner cry
Behind a false humility-curtain.

3864.

If you beg
Your soul-beauty-Provider,
You will be granted
An abbreviated God-realisation-
   journey.

3865.

As the purity of the evening
Puts the day's turmoil to rest,
Even so, the divinity of your soul
Will put your impurity-mind
To eternal sleep.

3866.

If you are
A real human being,
Then you will have
Only one answer to God:
A cheerful YES!

3867.

Three undeniable facts:
Heart devotedly follows faith.
Mind unmistakably follows
   doubt.
Man helplessly follows death.

3868.

Do you think that God
Does not mind
When you delay your meeting
With Him?

3869.

The only reason
Why he succeeds
Is because he begs
His Inner Pilot to proceed
Ahead of him.

3870.

My realisation-bird smiles
While watching
My inspiration-bird sing
And my aspiration-bird fly.

3871.

If you worship the wrong god,
Why do you expect the right God
To guide your eyes
And lead your life?

3872.

Since God has decided
Not to be deafened
By your insistent demands,
Can you not be wise
Once and for all?
Plead with God
To fulfil your prayers!

3873.

If God gives you
Your merit-medals,
You will be simply shocked
To find
That you merit nothing.
Therefore,
Pray to God to give you
His Credit-Miracles.

3874.

I have asked myself
Many times
What true joy is.
I have now the answer:
True joy
Is my life's forgotten story.

3875.

Do not say
That you have realised God,
But say
That God is experiencing you
Every day
In an ever-new way.

3876.

Behold,
Your heart of illumination
Is inviting your ailment-life
To take its rescue-remedy!

3877.

My Beloved Lord Supreme
Is leaving His blue-gold
    Footprints
Inside my aspiration-heart-room.
Therefore, my life of chaos
Will immediately end.

3878.

A life of flattery
Will miserably fail
When it tries to reach
The real heights
Of human life.

3879.

My mind brings me into
A tunnel to darkness.
My heart becomes
A bridge to light.

3880.

As your heart
Is meant for deeper things,
Even so, your mind
Was meant for higher things.

3881.

You can sing
Your life's liberation-song
If you can keep yourself happy
In the heart
Of your aspiration-cry.

3882.

Your mind is uncluttered.
Therefore
Constantly you feel
That God has
A very special Concern
For your life.

3883.

If you are already
An unwilling prisoner
Of your mind,
Who can force you to be
A willing prisoner?

3884.

Each new day beckons you
To walk on the road
Of self-transcendence.

3885.

A single-minded search
For God
Will liberate you
From your age-long ignorance-
     dream.

3886.

Secret sins
Eventually become
Open crimes.

3887.

Your life
Must capture time
In time
To live for God alone.

3888.

When his insecurity-insect bites
It bites everyone
With no preference.

3889.

Each day
My Beloved Supreme weeps
Inside my dark and dingy
Mind-cave.

3890.

A scholar is satisfied
Because of everything he knows.
A God-lover is satisfied
Because God knows everything.

3891.

Your heart's aspiration
Must not wait
For the doubting mind-guard
To fall asleep.

3892.

All my complaints
Turned into gratitude-tears
When my Lord Supreme
  approached me
With His Smile-flooded Face.

3893.

Nobody admires
Your doubt-rockets.
Everybody not only admires
But also adores
Your heart-boat.

3894.

His suspicion-mind
Has compelled him
To walk along the dark
And dry road
Of misunderstanding.

3895.

My heart creates soulful tears
Only when
I hear my Lord singing
His Self-transcendence-Songs.

3896.

The day I spoke about myself
And not about my Lord Supreme
I became an alien
From Heaven.

3897.

My aspiration-barrenness
Is due to
My conscious entrance
Into frustration-night.

3898.

God secretly won me back.
Now I openly treasure
My oneness-love with God.

3899.

By God's Grace
Everything is possible.
Insecurity-plants can be
    transformed
Into powerful security-banyan
    trees.

3900.

With one Eye open,
God asks the world
To be perfect.
With another Eye open,
God tells the world
That He Himself will do
The work of perfection
For the world.

3901.

My soul's promise to my Lord
    Supreme
Is the longest and strongest bridge
Over my life's abyss.

3902.

My Beloved Supreme tells me
That my smiling dreams
Have to be transformed
Into my dancing realities.
Then only will I be able
To please Him
In His own Way.

3903.

O my heart of aspiration,
Stay with me.
My soul of delight is coming
To take you and me
To Heaven's Ecstasy-Palace.

3904.

I shall not use any more
My common sense,
For my common sense
Is a common thing
Which everybody has.
From now on I shall use
Only one sense:
My surrender-sense,
Which lives only in God
And only for God.

3905.

A useless seeker
Knows how to give
Constant advice.
A first-class seeker
Knows only how to abide by
God's self-giving Advice.

3906.

All my friends
Have come and gone.
Only one friend is left:
My hope-friend.
This hope-friend of mine
Will stay with me forever,
Since its Creator,
God the Dream,
Will always remain inside me
To grow into
God the Reality.

3907.

Nothing remains
Save and except one thing:
My conscious need for God.

3908.

Humanity's dream is not a question
That has to be answered.
It is a reality
That wants to be manifested
In God's Heart-Garden.

3909.

You can meet with
Ordinary people
And enjoy their company.
But never forget
That you have to give
Something special to them.

3910.

O doubter-mind,
Can you not stop doubting
Only once?
Can you not stop thinking
Only once?
Can you not start loving
And becoming a oneness-heart
Even for a fleeting hour?

3911.

You are oblivious
To your soul's compassion-light.
But your soul's self-giving
Is always quite obvious
To God's Vision-Light.

3912.

Equanimity-balance within me
Is gone
Because I have asked my mind
To steer my life-boat.

3913.

I ask God,
Is there any special reason
Why He tortures me?
God asks me,
Is there any special reason
Why I do not please Him
Cheerfully and unconditionally
All the time?
Is there any special reason?

3914.

Frustration-clouds veil your face
Because your heart's aspiration-
   flames
Do not desire to reach
Your soul's illumination-sun.

3915.

His hunger for possession
Never ends.
His thirst for renunciation
Never begins.
Therefore, God does not know
When to come and visit him.

3916.

At long last
God is extremely proud of you
Because the disobedience
Of your vital-bull
Has completely surrendered
To the obedience
Of your heart-lamb.

3917.

Do not cry, do not cry!
God lives also
In the heart of tomorrow.
I assure you,
Tomorrow's heart
Of satisfaction-delight
Will be all yours.

3918.

Before doubt strikes your mind,
Can you not grow faith-plant
Cheerfully and carefully
Inside your heart-garden?

3919.

Do not ignore any warning!
Each warning is as fatal
As the final warning.

3920.

When he joined the spiritual path,
He had a brief period
Of inner torture.
Now it is all over.
His heart is all confidence-light.

3921.

There is only one thing on earth
That can justify life,
And that thing is
Man's satisfaction-love,
Which grows inside man's heart
And glows inside God's heart.

3922.

I tell you
With absolute certainty
That there is no special reward
For your self-styled struggles.

3923.

The crying voice
Of every heart
Fulfils man's
Heavenward choice.

3924.

You need not long for anything
   else
As long as your heart has the
   capacity
To attract God's Compassion-
   Attention.

3925.

O my mind,
You think your deplorable
   misdeeds
Are quite adorable.
Is it not the height
Of your stupidity?

3926.

Before Heaven accepts you,
Heaven sends one of its
   messengers
To go through your references.

3927.

A strange twist of fate
Has compelled him to descend
From his aspiration-peak
Into his frustration-abyss.

3928.

You want to board
The realisation-plane.
Show me first
Your aspiration-ticket!

3929.

If you throw jealousy-stones
At this world,
The world of ecstasy
Will never welcome you.

3930.

If you are ready to dream,
Then only will God the Supreme
Stand before you
As God the Satisfaction-Reality.

3931.

God gave me one more chance
To transform my information-
　mind
Into an inspiration and
　aspiration-heart.

3932.

When a seeker fails
In his aspiration-life,
It must be taken as a great lesson
For all the other seekers.

3933.

My life's ecstasy-melody
I hear
When I do not cherish
My weakness-wheelchair.

3934.

Please wait for me one more
　moment,
O my Lord Supreme.
Your Compassion-Telegram
I was afraid to open
For fear that I would not be ready
To follow You speedily
In Your own Way.

3935.

I have consulted my expert heart.
It tells me that my mind-tiger
Will eventually turn into
My heart-lion,
The lion that roars for divine
　victory.

3936.

You call it
Your inner silence-delight.
I call it
Your heart's life-deafening sound.

3937.

The heart is so compassionate
That it does not want the mind
To lag behind
In any walk of life.

3938.

An unexpected visitor
Entered into his heart
To tell him that the Heavenly God
Does not mind if he fails
So long as he wants to try
Again and again.

3939.

Doubt is undoubtedly a god,
But it is a false god.
Why do you have to obey
A false god?
Obey the real God:
Faith.

3940.

You have tried.
You have not succeeded.
That does not mean
That you will not try any more.
Try once more!
You will not only succeed
In the life that becomes
But also proceed
In the life that eternally is.

3941.

Do not be a fool!
You are supposed to pray and
  meditate
Right on the battlefield of life.
The Himalayan caves
Are totally out of date.

3942.

The soul's mother tongue
Is God-Beauty's
Satisfaction-nourishing Heart.

3943.

Do not allow yourself
To be devoured by past mistakes,
For God is expecting from your
  life
A profound inner transformation.

3944.

Two visible hands
Have imprisoned you.
One invisible Hand
Is liberating you.

3945.

The luxuries of your outer life
Are impoverishing
The beauty and purity
Of your inner life.

3946.

You live in your mind's
Stupidity-cave.
Therefore, you deny your soul's
Divinity-palace.

3947.

What counted
Was God's Compassion.
What counts
Is God's Forgiveness.
What will count
Is my gratitude.

3948.

Do not settle for anything less
Than the complete
    transformation
Of your earth-bound ignorance-
    cry.

3949.

Like his soul,
His heart also wants to become
A professional
In God's Cosmic Game.

3950.

He has been campaigning
For God the Justice,
But God the Compassion always
    wins
In his life.

3951.

Do not be surprised
To discover a ray of delight
Inside your heart.
There shall come a time
When your heart will be
    inundated
With God's Self-transcending
    Delight.

3952.

If you deliberately ignore
Your heart of faith,
Then you are unmistakably
Opening your life
To accept the invitation
Of a terrible disaster.

3953.

If you keep
Your sweet and illumining dream
Alive,
Then fulfilling realities
Cannot remain a far cry.

3954.

There is no borderline
Between
The stupidity of the mind
And the impurity of the vital.

3955.

If your mind has complaints,
Then those complaints
Your mind must discard.
Do not bring
Your mind's complaints to God,
For He has
Infinitely more important things
To deal with.

3956.

Each life has a few false starts.
But eventually each life
Will not only finish the race
But also win the race.

3957.

If you do not offer
Your love-blossoms,
Then you will soon see
Hatred-thorns before you.

3958.

To have a heart
Of selfless dedication
That is not supported
By a heart of aspiration
Is a stupidly unconventional way
To walk along God's Road.

3959.

You think
Truth is too painful.
But I assure you,
Truth will one day prove to you
That it is only bountiful.

3960.

A mind of hesitation
And a vital of frustration
Are the two short circuits
In your aspiration-current.

3961.

Those who do not know
How to share
Have to know
That God also does not know
How to care for them.

3962.

It is simply not yet your turn
To realise God
And to play God's Role
On earth.

3963.

Do not chase anything.
But if you have to chase,
Then only chase away
Your temptation-tiger.

3964.

You have made God so happy
By leaping over
Your high ego-hurdles.

3965.

The mind has to become
   accustomed
To running side by side
With the heart and the soul.

3966.

God wants man to discover
His Heavenly bloom.
Instead of doing that,
Man invents his own earthly
   doom.

3967.

If you walk
Only on hope-clouds,
You will miss
Reality's satisfaction-feast.

3968.

He is totally lost
Between his mind's
Brooding doubts
And his heart's
Increasing faith.

3969.

Do come to me
To learn a little meditation.
Do come to me
To give me a little
Of your dedication.

3970.

He talks
Of only one thing:
His heart's deathless sorrows.

3971.

He does not want God,
He does not need God.
He is swelling
With his own self-importance.

3972.

Sadness weighs upon your heart
Because you have not
Freed your mind
From its suspicion-madness.

3973.

You have to carry
Your deplorable fate
Since your heart is not willing
To accept God's Will
As your only Saviour.

3974.

God does not want
To catch your consciousness
Off guard.
He wants you
Only to keep your consciousness
Always high.

3975.

Consciously
You may think you need life
And not death.
But
Unconsciously
You choose ignorance-death
Over life.

3976.

You cannot get along
Even with God's Compassion-
    Heart.
How can you ever hope
To get along
With man's deception-mind?

3977.

Every day
God gives you
A faith-transfusion.
But even then every day
You take doubt-poison!

3978.

A true and sincere God-lover
Does not and cannot live
On a meagre aspiration-income.

3979.

Simplify your life,
Purify your heart,
Multiply your God-love.
Lo, God is claiming you
As His very own.

3980.

You do not have the patience
To wait for God's Hour,
But you think that the world
Has time to wait with patience
For your transformation-hour.

3981.

You do not have the patience
To wait for God's Hour.
How do you then expect God
To grant you His Eternity's
Satisfaction-Tower?

3982.

Do not think
That it is an impossible task
For you to liberate your mind
From suspicion-swing.

3983.

If you want to spend all your life
Observing others,
God is not going to prevent you.
God will just start observing those
Who have no one else to observe
But Him.

3984.

A heart of fear
And a mind of doubt
Are the two great extinguishers
Of my inner life.

3985.

God wants to keep
His Love-Length and His
    Divinity-Depth
Always unmeasured,
And I want them to be
Sleeplessly treasured
By my aspiration-heart.

3986.

Even when his inner road
Becomes dangerous,
He does not surrender
To the comfort-loving
And comfort-spreading
Outer road.

3987.

Whom do I love most?
I love most
God the Dreamer.
Why?
Because God the Dreamer
Never fails me.

3988.

If you try a little harder,
I assure you,
You will be able to liberate
   yourself
From your dingy mind-slum.

3989.

If you allow your ego to pretend,
Your ego will not only bend
Your life-tree
But also uproot
The whole tree.

3990.

There is a continuous battle
Between my earthly greed
And my Heavenly need.
Needless to say,
My earthly greed always wins,
Only to lose miserably.

3991.

The human vital knows how to
   resist.
The human mind knows how to
   insist.
Alas, there is nothing divine in me
That will teach me how to desist
From doing the wrong things.

3992.

The Inner Pilot tells him
That he excels in everything
Because he is of His Ancient
   Source.

3993.

Do not try to escape
From His all-seeing Eye.
His all-seeing Eye
Is not going to torture you.
Its very purpose is
To illumine you.

3994.

If you wait for the approval
Of your friends
In everything that you do,
You are not going to succeed
At all
In this lifetime
In anything.

3995.

Earthly ears are useless.
Only with your Heavenly ears
Will you be able to hear sleeplessly
God's Silence-Cheers.

3996.

I am not going to be tortured
Any more
By my long-lost forgotten hopes.
I am going to revive them and
    fulfil them
Once and for all.

3997.

He sails his life's
Failure-boat
Endlessly
In the frustration-sea.

3998.

At last my life-boat
Is returning
To its Golden Shore,
Sailing away from
A thick and blinding mist.

3999.

All he believes
Is his doubtful mind.
All he needs
Is his destruction-vital.

4000.

Blame not the stars,
Blame not the sky,
Blame not the sun.
Blame only yourself
For not being willing
To accept God's Will as your own
When He asks you to become
As beautiful as the stars,
As vast as the sky
And as powerful as the sun.

4001.

Secretly I placed my old life
At God's Feet.
Openly, cheerfully and
    unconditionally
God handed me His own Life.

4002.

God's Compassion-Heart
Makes His Eternity's long Story
Short,
And this Story He narrates
Only to those
Who are eager to become
Part and parcel
Of His Immortality's Smile.

4003.

The distance between
God and the God-lover
Is always measured
In the heart of oneness-time.

4004.

God's Forgiveness-Heart
Touched the very core
Of your remorseful tears
Long before you became conscious
Of your tears.

4005.

My aspiration-heart
Is always a cheerful giver.
My suspicion-mind
Is not even a willing taker.

4006.

For the first time in his life
He thinks and feels
That God is planning
His aspiration-training schedule.

4007.

If you are beginning
To believe in God,
You will be able to see yourself
Coming out of expectation-ambush
And entering into satisfaction-garden.

4008.

In the morning he becomes
A towering meditation-mountain.
In the evening he becomes
A flowering satisfaction-sky.

4009.

O my mind,
You want many things,
But what you actually need
Is a long silence-sleep.

4010.

Do you long to listen
To God?
If you are longing,
God will give you
Not only enthusiasm-waves,
But also success-sea.

4011.

The universal Oneness-Heart
Wants you to cry.
The transcendental Oneness-Soul
Wants your life to fly.

4012.

His heart has inherited
Forgiveness-Satisfaction
From God Himself.

4013.

His ego-life ended
Only when his oneness-heart
He offered to mankind
For its outer and inner progress.

4014.

Don't worry, don't worry!
Your heart will eventually win
In the battlefield of life
In spite of your mind.

4015.

God's Compassion can be seen
With man's possession,
But man's possession can never be seen
With God's Satisfaction-Delight.

4016.

The ups and downs of aspiration-kite
Are quite natural today.
But tomorrow the aspiration-kite
Must fly only high, higher, highest.

4017.

The heart believes
In endless education.
Therefore
Its teacher, the soul,
Is always ready
With its ever-contributing
Illumination.

4018.

For faith to mingle
With miracles
Is as easy
As God's granting
A Perfection-Smile.

4019.

I gazed and gazed
Upon the blue-white horizon
And watched a thought-free world
Entering into my heart's
   aspiration-cry.

4020.

What I want from God
Is a powerful Smile.
What God wants from me
Is a soulful cry.

4021.

A childish dream I used to have.
I used to see God losing to me
In cleverness-contest.
Now a childlike dream every night
   I have.
God and I play hide-and-seek
In God's Heart-Palace.

4022.

With my soul's adamantine
   certitude
I shall conquer
My life's stupid nothingness-
   pride.

4023.

Each aspiring heart
Is destined to sing
With tomorrow's dawn
In the Heart-Garden
Of the Absolute Supreme.

4024.

Undoubtedly
The mind is a road.
But while walking along
This road
There comes a time
When we realise
That this particular road
Goes nowhere.

4025.

If God has examined you,
Then you are bound to pass,
For He knows that if you fail,
It will be His loss,
And also
It will be His added endeavour
To make you perfect.

4026.

There is only one secret
In human life,
And that secret is:
God is not keeping
His Perfection-Satisfaction
All for Himself.
He is both secretly and openly
Giving away His Perfection-
    Satisfaction
To humanity.

4027.

The expansion of a seeker's heart
Is the Satisfaction of God
Not only here on earth
But also in Heaven.

4028.

Each undivine intention
Of the human mind
Eventually will meet with
    perdition.

4029.

The mind needs constant
    freshness,
The heart needs constant oneness,
The life needs constant newness.
Then only do we become
Conscious and helpful members
Of God's Family.

4030.

An innocence-life
Is always guided
By God's Perfection-bestowing
    Height.

4031.

God always treats you
As His dearest child.
But where is your heart
To feel it,
And where is your mind
To believe it?

4032.

God's Compassion-Eye
Has forgiven my life,
Saved my heart
And inspired my mind
To a new God-oriented life.

4033.

A simplicity-life
Is the satisfaction-smile
Of God's Beauty in man.

4034.

You are not responsible
For your neighbour's possessions,
But you are definitely responsible
For your neighbour's aspiration-cry
And dedication-smile.

4035.

My mind's silver desire
Is to become
As powerful as God.
My heart's golden desire
Is to become
An unconditionally surrendered breath
Of God's Satisfaction-Will.

4036.

Frustration-life
Is only a few feet ahead
Of disaster-tiger!

4037.

God is always eager and anxious
To trade His Compassion-Sun
For a prayer-flame of mine.

4038.

If you want to be
A choice instrument of God,
Then live always
In the prosperous vicinity of faith
And never
In the dangerous vicinity of doubt.

4039.

You are desiring
The heart of satisfaction.
Can you not see
That your body is already lost
Totally
In the temptation-valley?

4040.

God's Satisfaction-Home
May be far away from you.
Again, do you not realise
That your perfection-heart
Is also far away from God?

4041.

Either you become
God's alone,
Or you have to become
All yours.
There is no other alternative.

4042.

Yesterday I fought
With my doubtful and confusing
    mind.
Today I am fighting
With my imperfection-self.
Tomorrow God and I together
Shall celebrate my victory-life.

4043.

If you are boarding
Your self-transcendence-plane,
Then rest assured,
God's transcendental Heights
Will never be denied to you.

4044.

Your soul will never allow God
To lower the price
Of your life's divine satisfaction.

4045.

No human power
Can tie the soul,
For it wants only to be tied
By the divine power,
Love.

4046.

God right now does not want
A reality-partner.
He wants to be satisfied
Only with a dream-partner.

4047.

Who can resist
His heart's enthusiasm
To transform humanity's face
And perform divinity's dance
On earth-stage?

4048.

Insecurity,
You are not appreciated.
Impurity,
You are not appreciated.
Faith,
You are not only appreciated
But also admired.
Surrender,
You are not only appreciated
And admired,
But also adored.
Gratitude,
You are not only appreciated,
Admired and adored,
But also loved.

4049.

My conscious and constant
Need of God
Is a supreme secret.
This supreme secret neither God
   nor I
Want to share with anybody else.

4050.

God the Compassion
Does not believe in calculation.
Therefore
He does not want
His Calculator to work
At any time.

4051.

If you hold God
In your daily thoughts,
God will travel with you
All the time,
Not only physically
But also mentally.
He will travel with you physically
To strengthen you.
He will travel with you mentally
To illumine you.

4052.

Everything of God
I love deeply,
But His earth-visiting
Forgiveness-Feet
I love most.

4053.

To live a simple life
Is to live in wisdom-light.
To live a soulful life
Is to be inseparably one
With God's infinite Delight.

4054.

A mind of doubt
Is the fatal beginning
Of the seeker's self-destruction.

4055.

O my mind,
Do not be afraid
Of your soul's silence!
Your soul's silence-light
Is going to illumine
The undivine in you
And manifest
The divine in you.

4056.

God has given my heart
An eternal name:
Aspiration.
God has given me
An eternal name:
Surrender.

4057.

What is disobedience
If not a catastrophic experience
In a seeker's aspiration-life?

4058.

Ecstasy-explorers
Must climb up perfection-peaks
To become one with God's
Self-Transcendence-Satisfaction.

4059.

If you can cut down
Your mind's ingratitude-tree,
Then God will grant you
His Heart's Vastness-Property.

4060.

My Lord asks me to show Him
Only one soulful thing.
And what do I do?
In return I ask Him to give me
A good many fruitful things.

4061.

Two changes
Will make your vital better:
Ask your vital
To be more pure.
Ask your vital
To be less demanding.

4062.

Since your mind is always busy,
Can you not ask your heart
To be of help to you
In receiving God's infinite
Compassion-Light?

4063.

My mind's employer
Is doubt, the unknown.
My heart's employer
Is Delight, the Unknowable.

4064.

When God knocks
At my heart's door,
I immediately become faithful
To my heart's life.

4065.

These are the two messages
Of Heaven:
God is always for you.
You will eventually become
Another God.

4066.

My heart is not smart,
But my heart is always expert
In following God's Compassion-
    Eye
And God's Forgiveness-Heart.

4067.

Doubt has the audacity
To declare everything wrong
In God's entire creation.

4068.

The human in us
Does not love a loser.
The divine in us
Sympathises with a loser.
The Supreme in us
Is undoubtedly both the Winner
And the Loser.

4069.

His folded hands of humility
Are given the right
To take a short-cut
While running towards
Tomorrow's destination.

4070.

With your mind's dimly lit
Inspiration-lamp,
How can you hope to awaken
The aspiration-life of mankind?

4071.

Deep inside humanity's heart
I wish to see, admire, adore
And finally love
Only the silence-seekers.

4072.

Your absent-minded meditation
Can easily say "No"
To God's Compassion-Eye.

4073.

Alas,
His life is firmly seated
In failure,
Because he made friends
With disobedience-night.

4074.

O stupid ignorance,
Would you tell me,
Since when have you become
My boss?
My Boss, my only Boss,
Is my Beloved Supreme.

4075.

His mind has opened
A disobedience-school.
In that school
Everybody is getting
The chaos-diploma.

4076.

Look ahead.
What do you see?
Frustration!
Look behind.
What do you see?
Destruction!
Alas, you are in between
A frustration-bull
And a destruction-panther.

4077.

When disappointment strikes you
Powerfully,
There is only one way to escape,
And that way is to remember
How many times
And in how many ways
You have pleased your Beloved
    Supreme.

4078.

A swimmer in ignorance-sea
Will eventually become
A God-lover,
For no ignorance-sea-swimmer
Will have the capacity
To dislike God forever.

4079.

To be a conscious partner of God
Is not a difficult task,
For God's Vision-Eye
Every day
Inspires each human being
To be His closest partner.

4080.

If you have a brave heart,
Then you can have a new life.
If you have a new life,
Then you are bound
To feel the Heart and see the Face
Of a new God.
Who is that new God?
Your own transformed reality.

4081.

The music of the heart
Is the sweetness
That has a free access
To the all-embracing Oneness-
   Heart
Of God.

4082.

My old inner prayer was:
"God, give me the power to
   become great."
My new inner prayer is:
"My Lord, give me the power
To become an unconditional
   instrument
Of Yours."

4083.

Your heart-eye is the only eye
That can see
The perfection-beauty of Heaven
And the satisfaction-heart
Of the cosmic gods.

4084.

Every day God's God-Hour can
   strike.
But where is your conscious
And soulful willingness
To anchor your life-boat
In God's Delight-Harbour?

4085.

Don't worry about your heart-
   room!
Your daily meditation most gladly
And most satisfactorily
Will take care of it.

4086.

Even your mind's closed door
Will open up
As soon as it hears
God-Heart's Compassion-Knock.

4087.

Two enemies,
Life and death,
Both pray to God
For the same boon:
Immortality.

4088.

If your life lives
In a dark corner
Of your mind-room,
Then I can easily see
Your spiritual death
Right in your face.

4089.

From humanity,
When I expect anything,
My expectation is nothing but
A life-devouring experience.
From divinity,
When I expect anything,
My expectation is nothing other than
A life-illumining realisation.

4090.

When you are dealing with your mind,
You must be a sincere inspector.
When you are dealing with your heart,
You must be a sincere lover.

4091.

In your life of aspiration
You never need a tremendous mind.
What you need is a spacious heart.

4092.

Because of my self-styled guidance,
I am unable to arrive
At God's Golden Gate.

4093.

Because you hesitated
To call on God yesterday,
Today you are pitifully crying.
And if you hesitate
To call on God today,
Tomorrow you will unmistakably die!

4094.

There are two ways
To win forgiveness:
One way is to tell God,
"My Lord,
I shall not do it again!"
The other way is to ask God,
"My Lord,
Please show me the way
To live consciously in You
And for You."

4095.

Unless you ignore life's endless
   demands,
Your soul will not be able to make
A glorious beginning
In your God-manifestation-
   journey.

4096.

God's Compassion-Eye on me
Is for God's Satisfaction-Heart.
Indeed, today I am blessed
With this new vision-dawn
In my life of dedication.

4097.

Today my life
Is a winding experience-path
And my heart
Is a binding experience-path.
But I know tomorrow
My life shall be
A liberating realisation-journey
And my heart shall be
An immortalising realisation-
   journey.

4098.

Slowly and steadily
Your inner sun is rising.
That means God is blessingfully
   binding
Your entire existence
In a new way.

4099.

If you do not use
Your aspiration-wings
Daily,
You will not only displease God,
But also increase
Your destruction-flowing doubts
And fears.

4100.

My Lord,
I thank You deeply
For three daily miracles:
I love You only,
I need You only,
And I belong to You only.

4101.

Remember your first and foremost
Promise to God,
That you will become at once
The breath of God's Cry
And the life of God's Smile.

4102.

Don't argue with God.
Why do you forget
That He is much older than you
And therefore
He has much more experience
Than you have?

4103.

Even if you are a late arriver
At God's Blessing-Feast,
God does not mind.
You must always join
God's Blessing-Feast
When you are invited.

4104.

If you are
Completely awakened,
Then for you
There is but one way:
God's Way,
Only God's Way.

4105.

God will amaze you
By doing everything for you
Unconditionally,
And you will amaze God
Just by telling Him
That you will do one thing for
 Him
Unconditionally.

4106.

At long last
Wisdom-light has dawned
In my aspiration-heart:
I shall make my Beloved Supreme
My conscious and constant
Decision-Maker.

4107.

How much
Have I humbly done for God?
I do not know
And I do not want to know.
How much
God has compassionately done
For me
God does not want to know
Either.

4108.

Happiness left his heart
Because his mind
Deliberately embraced
The sighs of loneliness.

4109.

My Lord,
I have not been able
To please You,
True.
But I tell You
In all sincerity,
I have been all along
Meaning to please You.

4110.

Alas,
I am waiting for the inevitable
Realisation-day
Without giving a peak
   performance
In my aspiration-dedication-
   world.

4111.

Do you think only you
Are entitled to change
Your mind?
What is wrong if God also
Wants to change His Mind?

4112.

Consciously ally yourself
With God.
You will see
That God's Compassion-Eye
Will end the eclipse
Of your heart.

4113.

My heart has such compassion
For my mind
That it never criticises my mind
Even when it is totally out of tune
With my heart's God-songs.

4114.

When God visited you last night,
How is it
That you forgot to ask Him
To grant you
A flood of surrender-light?

4115.

He is competing
For his self-transcendence-
    trophies
After he has educated himself
At the university of surrender.

4116.

If you are not obedient
To your concentration-coach,
You will never be able
To reach your destination
As a victor.

4117.

Unless you have faith
In abundant measure,
Someday you may be paralysed
By suspicion-phantoms.

4118.

Alas,
I really do not want
To shuttle
Back and forth
From a mind of sound
To a heart of silence.

4119.

If your mind is anchored
In an agnostic abyss,
How will you ever be able
To bathe in the sea
Of gnostic light?

4120.

A self-giving heart-flower
Neither withers
Nor perishes
With the passage of time.

4121.

God has created
His Excellence-Delight in you.
How is it
That you are not using it
For yourself?

4122.

A bigger problem
Than the mind's non-acceptance
Of light
Is not visible on earth.

4123.

God hears
The soulful prayers of a seeker
Not only with great Readiness
But also with immediate Oneness.

4124.

The things that I do not know,
My Lord Supreme knows for me.
The things that He wants me to
   know
Are more than enough for me.

4125.

You do not need
A long preparation
For God the Peace
To enter into you.
Just cheerfully claim Him
As your own
As soon as He enters.

4126.

God's silence-messengers
Are those
Who are commissioned
By God Himself
To manifest Him most powerfully
On earth.

4127.

You will be defeated
In the battlefield of life
Unless you stop
Groaning and moaning
In your self-styled
Ignorance-sleep.

4128.

God will show you
The map to Heaven.
Just cease to be
A talking mind
And become
A self-giving heart.

4129.

I love your soul's
God-entrusted promises,
But I never like your life's
Opportunity-craving
   compromises.

4130.

I surrender to the Supreme
Not because I feel I am helpless,
But because I feel
His Oneness-Delight is something
I have all along been craving
In my own life.

4131.

A very sad case of unpreparedness
Tortured his entire being
When God came and stood before him
Uninvited.

4132.

You are slow
In turning to God.
I tell you,
This can never be
Your real capacity.

4133.

He who is a God-lover
Has already been entrusted
With faster-than-the-fastest speed
By God the Supreme Beloved.

4134.

To realise God
In His transcendental Heights,
Each seeker must have
A very long-range
Aspiration-programme.

4135.

If you do not break down
Your mind's resistance-wall,
Then yours will be
A dry and dust-filled life.

4136.

Good news for God:
Man loves Him.
Good news for man:
God needs him.

4137.

A life of failure
Is an oft-told story.
Neither God's Compassion
Nor man's aspiration
Wants to hear it.

4138.

If you have failed
In your heart's gratitude-run,
Remember
That there are other races to run.
Why not try
Your life's surrender-run
Immediately?
I am sure you will win it
Triumphantly!

4139.

You may see the sun set
On your yesterday's failures
If you want to.
But you must see the sun rise
On your today's determined
  effort.

4140.

God's Compassion
Only hires,
And even His Justice
Does not fire.

4141.

If you allow your vital and mind
To be hypnotised by desire-life,
There is nobody on earth
Who can liberate you
From this deplorable hypnotism.

4142.

Yes, it is true
That God is always busy.
But He is never too busy
To listen to your heart's cry.

4143.

My Lord,
My outer promotions
Have taken away all my
  aspiration.
Please give me an inner
  promotion
So that my aspiration and I
Will never part.

4144.

If it is really God's Road,
Then the Road itself
Will help you to run on it
Instead of standing or walking.

4145.

Alas,
My impurity-mind
Is always overweight.
Alas,
My gratitude-heart
Is always underweight.

4146.

If Heaven is not ready
To give you its blessingful love,
Then how do you think
Earth will be ready
To give you its powerful
   appreciation?

4147.

Because of your soul's
Oneness-surrender to God's Will,
God has allowed your soul
To cash His Satisfaction-Checks.

4148.

My life is homesick
For Heaven.
My heart is homesick
For God.
And I am homesick
For silence-sea.

4149.

There is still time
For my stupid mind
To unlearn
And for my sleeping heart
To learn.

4150.

If you scatter indecision-dust
Before you,
How can you speedily run
Towards your satisfaction-
   destination?

4151.

Because of your disobedience
Your mind cannot separate itself
From guilt.
Because of your disobedience
Your heart feels
That God lives without it.

4152.

You are your sick mind.
Therefore, you do not realise
That you are living
In the inferno of sweltering pride,
And nowhere else.

4153.

God's Compassion-River
Never runs dry.
This is a common experience
Of each and every passenger
In God's Golden Boat.

4154.

Desire-road
Is full of dead-end signs.
Aspiration-highway
Does not believe in a speed limit.

4155.

My mind's doubt-car
Had a very serious collision
With my heart's faith-train.

4156.

The shadow of sorrow
Descended upon his life
Right after he entered
Into a turbulent vital-sea.

4157.

In human life
Self-pity-prison-experience
Is common and universal.

4158.

If you have to whisper
In God's Ear,
Then whisper only one thing:
That you are going to please God
Unconditionally.

4159.

The human mind is scared to death
When it is asked
To tune in to God's Silence-Station.

4160.

If you really want to succeed
In your outer life
And proceed in your inner life,
Then keep your life's dedication-door
Wide open.

4161.

He was a favourite hero-soldier
Of the Supreme.
Therefore, he was invited to come
To Heaven's palace
Through Heaven's back door.

4162.

There shall come a time
When humanity's pride
Will be dwarfed
By its humility-giant.

4163.

Since the day I increased
My willingness-mileage,
God has given me the capacity
To completely ignore
Ignorance-glance.

4164.

Although he started
His spiritual journey
With a very poor background
In self-giving,
Now constant self-giving
And his life
Have become synonymous.

4165.

A gratitude-heart
Is only a very short distance away
From God-Victory.

4166.

An uncertainty-mind
Is immediately followed
By its worst possible failure-foe.

4167.

Because you trust God
In everything that you do and say,
You have God the Treasure
And God the Treasurer
At the same time
At your disposal.

4168.

The length of God's Smile
Shall always remain
An uncharted Vision-Reality
In God's Garden
Of Heaven-free Delight.

4169.

Remember your promise!
You are determined to break
Your mind's resistance-wall.

4170.

Soulfully you must step
Into your new future,
Where your expectation-life
Has completely surrendered
To God's Satisfaction-Delight
In God's own Way.

4171.

God's commitment is to give you
Everything that He has and is
Provided you and your heart
Become prayerful longings.

4172.

What can the poor human life do
When the death-hour arrives?
It has to lie hopeless and helpless
Before death's door.

4173.

You are waiting for God
To arrive.
But do you not think
That by going to God yourself
You can give God
A great surprise?

4174.

The ancient world's
Silence-light
Is still guiding the modern world
Of sickening suspicion-night.

4175.

How can you forget
That your life came to nothing
Because you treasured blindly
Your limitation-life?

4176.

If you are not well-prepared
For God's arrival,
No harm!
Just keep your heart's door
Wide open.
God will be satisfied.

4177.

Each God-thought
Eventually awakens a God-seeker
To God's transcendental Vision.

4178.

You have simply no idea
How sad you have made God
By allowing yourself to be hit
By the torpedo of self-doubt.

4179.

You can buy God back
With only one gift,
And that gift is
Your heart's gratitude-flower.

4180.

The hardest thing
For man to give up
Is his conscious feeling
Of his life's insecurity.

4181.

Now that you have learnt
To be occupied spiritually,
Nobody will see you floundering
In the outer life.

4182.

Any good thing,
Any divine dream,
Can never be hidden
From humanity's big eye.

4183.

I shall definitely
Cease to be sad,
For my sadness
Makes my Beloved Supreme mad.

4184.

Can I ever do this?
Can I ever say that I live
Only for God's Life
And God lives
Only for my heart?

4185.

The soul is all compassion,
But when it sees
That the mind has become
Total unwillingness
And the heart has become
Total cheerlessness,
Then the soul complains to God.

4186.

Nobody will accept you
In his aspiration-dedication-boat
If you are going to carry with you
All your ignorance-baggage.

4187.

If I cannot feel you on earth
Inside my heart,
Will I ever find you in Heaven
With my soul?

4188.

You have an outstanding mind.
But from your outstanding mind
I am not going to get
Anything soulful.
You have an astounding heart.
From your astounding heart
I shall not only get
Everything soulful
But also everything fruitful.

4189.

If you sow gratitude-seeds
Inside your heart,
Then definitely you will see
Dedication-flames
That will grow up and up
And eventually grow into
A perfection-sun.

4190.

Your soon-to-be-successful life
Will before long be
The only cause
Of your destruction-death.

4191.

In God's God-Manifestation-Army
Everybody has
A cheerful, powerful and fruitful
Volunteer-force.

4192.

Deliberately you have allowed
Confusion to stab you,
So it is absurd for illumination
To try to befriend you.

4193.

A God-realised life
Is the only satisfaction-fruit
Of God's Promise-Tree.

4194.

Why have you allowed your mind
To play host to uncomely
  thoughts?
Can you not see now
That ignorance-prince
Is intimidating you
To make you his intimate friend?

4195.

Imperfection's overdressed
Self-indulgence-ego
Has capsized his life-boat
Long before it was due
To reach its destination.

4196.

Humanity's thickening
Unwillingness-web
Is saddening the compassion-
  willingness
Of divinity.

4197.

If you are assisted
By your soul-assertion,
Then the complete revelation
Of your inner life
Cannot remain a far cry.

4198.

How can you ever wear
Victory's crown
When you keep your enthusiasm-
   flag
At half-mast?

4199.

Because you do not have
An iota of love for God,
Your future happiness-hope
And your mental hallucination-
   reality
Will always go together.

4200.

One thing I ask God:
Am I not His?
One thing I tell God:
I am all for Him.

4201.

God's golden Dreams
One by one
Have entered into my heart's
Aspiration-cry.

4202.

Even the cosmic gods
Are justly accused
Of envying the great awakening
Of superlative seekers.

4203.

When are you going
To see and feel
That your vital-tiger
Has completely devoured
Your heart-lamb?

4204.

My only capacity:
My Lord's constant
Compassion-Receptivity.

4205.

When are you going to stop
Existing like a useless human
   being?
When are you going to start
Living like a saint?

4206.

God the Compassion
Always comes before
God the Love.
This is my unmistakable
   realisation.

4207.

I want to live
Inside the rapture-palace
Of your heart
And not
Inside the torture-chamber
Of your mind.

4208.

I seem to remember
That I was once
A most favourite instrument
Of God.
Alas, those golden days
Are no more in my possession!

4209.

Far beyond my "Yes" and "No"
Is God's
Infinite Forgiveness-Light
For me.

4210.

What is faith?
Faith is obedience.
And what is obedience?
Obedience is
Conscious oneness-recognition
Of one's highest height.

4211.

My heart
Is a Heaven-blessed dream
And an earth-born reality.

4212.

If you pray for others,
God will definitely ask you
To claim His Infinity's Love
As your very own.

4213.

Nothing can you call your own,
For you have not become one,
Lovingly one,
Inseparably one,
With the Owner of everything.

4214.

Do you know
What my soul does?
My soul laughs and laughs
When I think ignorance-night
Is going to devour me.

4215.

O eye of my soul,
Do help me
To be as wide awake
As you are
All the time.

4216.

We can never love
God the Compassion
And God the Forgiveness
To excess.

4217.

Where will I ever find
A true friend
Who will help me
In awakening my aspiration-sun
Inside my heart's sky?

4218.

There is no turning back
Once you accept God
For God-Satisfaction's sake
And earth for God-Compassion's sake.

4219.

My Beloved Supreme
Offered me His All.
Alas, I foolishly declined it.
Now I have become a perfect stranger
Even to myself.

4220.

Something that money
Can never buy:
God's Satisfaction-Smile.

4221.

The human mind
Knows doubt as a destination.
But this destination
Is nothing but confusion
Mixed with illusion!

4222.

A wise seeker
Has a special kind of fear—
He is afraid of losing God.
Therefore
He does not do anything
Undivine.

4223.

His identity he will reveal
Not through the power
Of his mouth
But through the light
Of his heart.

4224.

You have recognised many things
In life,
But one thing
You have yet to recognise:
That you have betrayed yourself.

4225.

You do not pray,
You do not meditate
Regularly.
How can you then expect
Your heart's telephone line
To God's Heart
To work?

4226.

Unless you have a purity-life
And a sincerity-heart,
God will not keep you
On His Attendance List.

4227.

If you gaze and gaze
Down the road of nostalgia-
    pleasure,
You will arrive at nothing.

4228.

A doubting mind
And a strangling vital
Are two cunning agents
Of the dark forces in your life.

4229.

God is always anxious
To measure
Your self-transcendence-steps.

4230.

One noble thought
Can certainly conquer
The powerful strength
Of insecurity.

4231.

Always
It takes time,
Energy
And practice
To become a very special truth-seeker
And God-lover.

4232.

Your implicit faith in God
Is God's Satisfaction-Smile
In His Perfection-Vision-Reality.

4233.

If you do not compel
Your doubting mind
To starve to death,
How can you ever be happy?

4234.

I shall keep my Beloved Supreme
Unconditionally happy
Inside my heart's aspiration-flames.

4235.

My aspiration-heart
Longs to be one with God's creation
As a new friend,
An illumining brother
And a fulfilling soul.

4236.

As tomorrow and never
Are two neighbours,
Even so,
Now and forever
Are two neighbours.

4237.

If you do not force
Your doubts to retreat,
You will be forced
Not only to minimise
But also to diminish
Your heart's receptivity.

4238.

He has gone
Beyond, beyond, beyond
Virtue and vice.
Therefore
He has mastered the capacity
To leap over his ego's hurdles.

4239.

From the heart
Of his sweet sorrows
He is receiving
Nectar-peace.

4240.

The wise man's
Faithful and fulfilling friend
Is his own self-giving life.

4241.

His heart of devotion
And his life of surrender
Every day are accustomed
To running together
Towards their supreme
   destination.

4242.

Alas,
In spite of my heart's pitiful cry,
I find my life
In a dizzy whirlpool of despair.

4243.

Your attachment to pleasure-life
Is the cause of your losing
All your inner power of delight.

4244.

A true God-lover's mind
Must always learn
The language of his soul's
Silence-joy.

4245.

You have become blind
By your mental reasoning.
You have become lame
By not fulfilling
Your psychic awakening.

4246.

Even when your mind
Is only a little hungry,
You die to feed your mind.
But when your heart
Is literally starving,
You have no time
And no willingness
To feed your heart.

4247.

His heart's aspiration-cries
Are private matters
Between him and his Lord
   Supreme.

4248.

I am going to touch your feet,
Not because
You have done something very
    great,
But because
I see you clearly
Touching my Lord's Feet
Every day.

4249.

You do not have to walk
Down your mind's anxiety-alley.
You can easily walk along
Your heart's sunlit road.

4250.

Try to fool your jealousy-feelings
By pretending every day
To be a oneness-heart.
I tell you,
A day will come
When you will be freed
From your jealousy's division-
    world.

4251.

Every day try to practise
Your heart's gratitude-lesson
To lessen God's Burden.

4252.

Your mind should feel sorry
For its over-population
And your heart should feel sorry
For its under-population.

4253.

I may not know many things,
But of one thing
I am absolutely certain:
God will someday give me the
    capacity
To end my desire-game.

4254.

I feel sorry
That you have been bitten
So mercilessly
By the temptation-snake.
But I tell you,
Your heart's illumination-sun
Will someday cure you.

4255.

He who is conquered
By desire
Is immediately invited
By the temptation-life
Of hell.

4256.

Unless you have
Fierce determination-fire
Inside you,
Your mind's confusion
Will not be able to arrive
At any solution.

4257.

Unless you have the authority
To command your mind,
How are you going
To expand your heart?

4258.

I admire
Your untiring progress-march.
I love
God's Satisfaction-Delight
In the heart of your perfection-
  journey.

4259.

You must always keep
A discriminating eye
On your mind's thought-door.

4260.

I want to celebrate
God's Victory-Day.
My Lord wants to celebrate
My life's surrender-day.

4261.

Your mental life
Is blundering.
Your vital life
Is thundering.
Your psychic life
Is crying.

4262.

Where will it take you,
Your sincerity-life?
You want to know.
It will not only take you
To God's Palace,
But also place you
Inside His Satisfaction-Heart.

4263.

A doubtful mind
And a fearful heart
Are two danger signs.
Do not disregard
These two danger signs
In life.

4264.

Have no compassion
For ugly thought-flies.
As soon as you see them
Nearing you,
Brush them away!

4265.

Your mind's criticism-crimes
Have removed
Beauty's rainbow-dawn
From your heart.

4266.

Why suffer?
Can you not ask God
To grant you His Oneness-
    Delight?
I tell you,
He is all ready!

4267.

My faith in God
Has enormously helped me
To terminate my close
    relationship
With insecurity.

4268.

The dawn of my new life
Is helping me
To climb over
My unknown fear-mountain.

4269.

The day I surrendered
My life's division-ego-mind
To God's Compassion-Eye,
I became a passenger
In God's fast-sailing
Satisfaction-Boat.

4270.

Do
What makes you happy.
Become
What makes God happy.

4271.

Not only things human
But also things divine
Lose their fruitfulness
If they are not used.

4272.

To surrender to God
Is to hear God
Practising His Vision-Melody
In your aspiration-heart.

4273.

Bring your contradiction-mind
Only to God,
For He alone has the capacity
To grant you an illumination-mind
The way He has already given you
An illumination-soul.

4274.

My faith and I have decided
To inspire my doubt
To commit suicide
To lessen the world's confusion.

4275.

I have two new desires:
One is to serve
Divinity in humanity,
And the other is to love
Humanity in divinity.

4276.

In the garden of my heart's gratitude,
God is performing His supreme Role
Of watching me, loving me
And liberating me from ignorance-dream.

4277.

I am learning something important
About humility:
Humility is man's conscious
Divinity-oneness
With God's entire creation.

4278.

You must break the chains
Of your old thoughts
If you want your heart to reach out
And touch the Satisfaction-Tree
Of God's Life.

4279.

Gladness tells me
That time is faster
Than the fastest consciousness-
    plane.
Sadness tells me
That time is slower
Than the slowest inconscience-
    snake.

4280.

The seeker's aspiration-flames
Are bound to arise, shine
And touch the Saviour's
Salvation-Feet.

4281.

God gave you the mind
To transcend itself
And not to engage in
A completely complicated
    analysis.

4282.

He has kept a truth-protecting
    guard
On his mind's
Deplorably stupid carelessness.

4283.

What I need
Is an inspiration-voice
To call me back
To my aspiration-life.

4284.

What is integrity
If not the flowering
Of the soul's beauty
In the entire being?

4285.

You must not waste your time
In weakling hopes of happiness
Any more.
Always look for powerful hopes
And happiness will be all yours.

4286.

God does not mind
When you spy on Him,
But He does mind
When you spy on any creation-life
Of His.

4287.

He has thrown open
His hope-door
And compelled
His failure-life
To fall into
A deep oblivion-chasm.

4288.

The lovers of Infinity and Eternity
Are always instructed
By their inner teacher:
Faith.

4289.

This unaspiring body
Is weighing down my poor soul
Far beyond my imagination.

4290.

Your delinquent desires
Have unfortunately created
False confidence in you.

4291.

To distrust others at every
　moment
Is no inconsequential inner crime.
Indeed, it is a very serious crime!

4292.

Don't hide your doubts.
Illumine them for the benefit of
　the world.
The world will not only
Admire your mind
But also love your heart.

4293.

The agony of uncertainty
Is apt to frustrate
All human beings,
Either in the spiritual life
Or in the ordinary life.

4294.

For a human mind
To live inside a chaos-cave
Is not an unusual experience.

4295.

The clever mind
Observes.
The pure heart
Serves.

4296.

Unless you realise
That your earth-bound mind
Is not competent to realise God,
You will not become
A most intimate friend
Of your heart.

4297.

Mental developments
Quite often prove to have
Very shallow and shabby
   foundations.

4298.

If you are starving
For God,
How can the world's gossip-food
Ever satisfy you?

4299.

Your thirsty expectations
Are all ruined
Because your vital
Is a wall of stubbornness.

4300.

My Lord,
When You forgive me,
What happens, You know:
I not only feel Your Heartbeat
Inside my heart,
But I also feel
That Your Compassion-Universe
Is my salvation-universe.

4301.

When God came and told me
That He would make me
A perfect instrument of His,
I shared this good news
With my heart
Immediately.

4302.

If you are really afraid
Of your dry mind,
Then why do you not offer it
To God's Compassion-Eye?
He will transform your dry mind
Into His Vastness-Smile
And Calmness-Dance.

4303.

My Lord Supreme,
Is it too late for me
To please You?
My Lord Supreme,
Is it too late for me
To claim You?
My Lord Supreme,
Is it too late for You
To make me Your choicest
   instrument?

4304.

Do you not know
What is wrong with you?
I am telling you
What is wrong with you.
You do not allow God,
Your Inner Pilot,
To whisper in your ear
That you are a choice instrument
Of His.

4305.

My earth-bound life
May not be certain,
But my self-giving heart
Is certain.
And what else is certain?
My arrival at my God-ordained
Destination
At God's choice Hour.

4306.

My Lord Supreme,
My heart-vessel is filled
With Your Love.
What can I have,
What will I have
To fill Your Heart-Vessel?

4307.

God-success is attainable
On the strength of the seeker's
Heart-progress.

4308.

God has given you the capacity
To be His Dream-Wave
And kept for Himself the capacity
To be your Satisfaction-Shore.

4309.

My seeker-friend,
This time do not find fault
With God.
Just give Him a chance,
Only once,
To redesign your life.

4310.

You do not have to wait
For earthly fulfilment
To realise God.
To realise God
You do not have to wait
For anything.
Also, do not ask God
To wait for you.
Just keep your heart's door wide open
And let Him enter.
His Compassion-Presence
Is your earthly and Heavenly fulfilment
All at once.

4311.

For me there is no other way
To reach my goal
Than to claim God secretly
And openly
As my own, very own.

4312.

There is only one rule
For God-realisation:
When God the Referee
Starts the game,
Just play and play and play
And never ask Him when to stop.
If you can play continuously,
Sleeplessly and endlessly
While being observed
By your Beloved Supreme,
Then God-realisation is bound to dawn.

4313.

His mind lived
With success-illusion.
His heart lives
Only with progress-illumination.

4314.

How can you receive
Your Beloved Supreme
When you have not allowed
Your own heart to receive you?

4315.

If you are lost
In your mind-confusion,
Just mention soulfully only once
The Name of your sweetest Lord.
Not only will you come out
Of your mind-confusion,
But also your mind-confusion itself
Will be illumined.

4316.

What is temptation?
Temptation is something
That unconsciously helps
The divine within us
To conquer the human in us.

4317.

You will not be able to count
The number of times
You have delayed your meeting
With your Beloved Supreme.

4318.

Do not lock your problem-door.
Break asunder your problem-door
By listening to your soul's
Thunder-silence-voice.

4319.

When God came to you,
You forgot to ask Him
Where He kept
His Forgiveness-Delight.
Therefore
Today your entire being is miserable.

4320.

The idle cannot find God.
Therefore, God has to exert
Extra effort
To make the idle dynamic
So that God and they can enjoy
Mutual oneness-pride.

4321.

God has sown His Promise-Seeds
Inside you.
Now He expects you to grow into
Nothing other than
His Satisfaction-Fruits.

4322.

Selfless service
Keeps your faith in God
Sweeter than the sweetest
And makes your oneness-love
With God
Stronger than the strongest.

4323.

For years and years
You have begged God
   unconsciously
To fulfil your venom-desires.
Now for a fleeting day
Can you not consciously thank
   God
That He has not fulfilled
Your venom-desires
Out of His infinite Bounty?

4324.

God plays the role
Of the Satisfaction-Emperor
Only when He is able to address
An aspiring audience.

4325.

He wants to learn from you
How to become another God,
How to love God
And how to serve Him
Soulfully and unconditionally.

4326.

Unless you have
The willingness to transcend,
How can God grant you
His Satisfaction-Eye?

4327.

Alas,
Your mind's ignorance-island
Is surrounded by
Your helpless surrender-sea.

4328.

O my heart's silence-singer, sing!
How I wish I could learn
Some God-pleasing songs
From you.

4329.

When I played the role
Of a giver,
I did not know what to give
Or how to give.
Now that I am playing the role
Of a taker,
I not only know how to take
But also what to take.

4330.

An able man
Has confidence enough
To feel that his burdens
Cannot surpass his capacity.

4331.

My first mistake was
I did not love God
Unconditionally.
My last mistake was
I did not rectify
My first mistake.

4332.

Your mind wants
To deceive God.
Your heart longs
To receive God.
And you want God
To immortalise you
Either as a sinner or as a saint.

4333.

If you have a seeker's heart,
Then it is bound to vouch
For your soul's victory.

4334.

The mind's hesitation
And the soul's illumination
Can never be found together
In the same boat.

4335.

I must improve the accuracy
Of my heart's
Soulful aspiration-arrows.

4336.

Your mind's rising doubt-river
Must surrender to your heart's
Expanding faith-sea.

4337.

A humility-host
Has the unparalleled capacity
To soulfully bow
To any guest.

4338.

God has kept
His Compassion-Pillow
All ready.
Now where is your head?
Where is it?

4339.

His life's helplessness-cry
Melts even
The coldest heart.

4340.

Enough!
Do not stage any more
Your self-accusation-play.
The world is quite sick of it.

4341.

Even God,
Not to speak of human beings,
Does not want to walk
On your mind's slippery path.

4342.

Not your naked sword
But your surrender-cries
Will be able to awaken
His heart.

4343.

In the spiritual life
A surrender-life
Is the only source
Of a satisfaction-heart.

4344.

If you want to live
Under God's Protection-Canopy,
Then destroy the breath
Of your ego-prince.

4345.

How is it
That there is such a yawning gulf
Between you
And your heart's unswerving
    faith?

4346.

You want to know
Where your gratitude-heart is.
Alas, it has gone to dig
Its own grave.

4347.

It is not enough
To browse in God's Bookstore.
You must buy at least one book
To illumine your heart.

4348.

Who is the real culprit,
If not the strangling vital?
Who else,
If not the suspecting vital?

4349.

Prosperity
Has made my heart beautiful.
Adversity
Is making my life powerful.

4350.

You are a real saint
If you do not have the capacity
To delight in others' despair.

4351.

Unless you have totally forgotten
Your failure-past,
God is not going to invite you
To dine with Him.

4352.

Since your heart knows how
To hear God's Voice,
Can you not ask your mind, too,
To hear the Voice of God?

4353.

How can you expect
Anything divine and perfect
From a non-seeker's sterile life?

4354.

The divinity
Of a purity-heart
Has always to be sought
And invited.

4355.

His is the beautiful life-garden
That allows no weeds
To grow.

4356.

When he dived deep within,
He realised
That God's Silence-Heart
Is nothing other than
God's Thunder-Voice.

4357.

If you want to fly back
To your heart-nest,
Then be a conscious partner
Of your soul-bird.

4358.

You want me to tell you
What kind of sword you need
To slay your ignorance.
I wish to tell you
That you need only one sword,
And that is your heart's
Mountain-aspiration-cry,
Conscious and constant.

4359.

As it was you
Who allowed your life
To be infested with delusions,
Even so, it is you
Who can inspire your life
To be flooded with illumination.

4360.

To fly the Banner of the Supreme,
During the day I shall cry
With the cries of the Unknown
And at night I shall smile
With the smiles of the
   Unknowable.

4361.

His vision-eye
Leaves nothing unseen.
His compassion-heart
Leaves nothing untouched.
His forgiveness-oneness
Leaves nothing unillumined.

4362.

The other day my Beloved
   Supreme
Told me in secret
That when He put me on earth,
It was for His Amusement,
And when He puts me in Heaven,
It will be for His Enchantment.

4363.

The strength of dissatisfaction
Cannot be measured.
It defies everything inspiring,
Aspiring and illumining.

4364.

The joy of the heart
And the willingness of life
Shall eternally remain
   inseparable.

4365.

The outer failure
Quite often embodies
The beauty of inner fulfilment-
   necessities.

4366.

O seeker-friend of mine,
Pray daily, meditate daily.
Otherwise, you are bound to
   develop
A confidence-shattering fear
Deep inside you
That God-realisation
Is not meant for you.

4367.

You have come to tell God
That you are going to love Him.
God says to you,
"My son, if you have the capacity
To love Me,
Then I have the capacity
To follow you."

4368.

I can easily dare to imagine
Everything in God's entire
   creation,
But I am always afraid of
   imagining
Only one thing:
That God is really pleased with
   me.

4369.

If you have a mind,
Then make it fertile.
If you have a fertile mind,
Then make it fertile
With something totally new:
God's God-Will.

4370.

Time and again
I have seen my heart's sorrow
Serving my Beloved Supreme
Far beyond my imagination's
   flight.

4371.

He who has God's Satisfaction-
   Heart
Already has God's Compassion-
   Eye
As well.

4372.

No star
Ever wants to blossom
In your mind's
Tenebrous ego-sky.

4373.

Do not worry!
God Himself
Will keep a flawless record
Of your self-transcendence-cries.

4374.

I am learning something
Most important about delight.
Delight is the unparalleled
Transcendental Beauty
Of God's Satisfaction-Heart.

4375.

What God teaches you,
You have to prove to God
That you have learnt.

4376.

God needs you.
Therefore, He has forgotten
Everything else.
You want God.
Therefore, you have to forget
Everything else.

4377.

Do you see
What you are becoming?
You are undoubtedly becoming
Happier today
Than you were
The day before yesterday.

4378.

The Love-Sea of our Beloved
   Supreme
Invites all soulful seekers.
What for?
To swim sleeplessly,
Not to sink immediately.

4379.

Do you not think
It is high time for you
To worship another God
Than your ego-god?

4380.

You want to please God
In His own Way,
But you do not know how.
But do you not think
That God will give you
The capacity,
Since He has already given you
The aspiration
To please Him in His own Way?

4381.

You are such a fool!
You are devoting your life to the
   God
That you do not want to become
Instead of to the God
That you actually want to become.

4382.

Each God-beginning
Marks not a man-end
But God's Self-Transcendence.

4383.

If you are desperate
To realise God,
No, not even the most powerful
   titan
Can keep you separate
From God's Oneness-Smile
And Satisfaction-Dance.

4384.

A silence-seeker
Needs only the fragrance
Of his own self-giving heart
To enter the Heart-Garden
Of his Beloved Supreme.

4385.

If you are a soulful seeker
And if you enjoy wishful
   thinking,
Then God loves you powerfully
Along with your wishful God-
   thinking.

4386.

You commit Himalayan blunders
Almost every day.
But when God's swift Justice-Blow
Is upon you,
You do not want to accept it
As His Compassion-Touch.
Today's Justice-Blow of God
Is tomorrow's Illumination-
   Touch
For you.

4387.

You want to represent God,
But are you sure that God wants
To present you to the world
As His choice gift?

4388.

In my life-house
I have quite a few rooms
To live in,
But God wants to live with me
Only in my heart-room.

4389.

To misuse God's
Compassion-Smiles
Is to lose them
Forever.

4390.

A life of success
You have been.
Can you not prepare yourself
To be a heart of progress?

4391.

You want to know
What you should desire from God.
I am telling you to ask God
To free you from your desire-
 slavery.

4392.

You are miserable
Because you have
Deliberately abandoned
Your heart-child.

4393.

Before, he begged
For satisfaction-alms.
Now he is ready to be satisfied
Simply with aspiration-alms.

4394.

To see a doubt-free mind
He is prepared to go
To the farthest part
Of the world.

4395.

Not where I meet God
But when I meet God
Is of supreme importance
To me.

4396.

How can you fail God
When He Himself wants you to be
A passenger
In His Heart-Boat?

4397.

Disobedience,
The deadliest weapon,
Has destroyed the human in him
And ignored the divine in him.

4398.

If you disown your doubt-sky,
Then God will help you own
Your faith-sun.

4399.

Every day
My soul sings God-songs
For me and my heart,
And we are measurelessly
   enlightened
By them.

4400.

My Lord Supreme,
I have not realised You,
I may not realise You
In this lifetime.
But will You not do me
A big favour?
Will You not give me the capacity
To love You,
Only love You, only love You?

4401.

When God sends for you,
Be determined to be available
At your heart-home.

4402.

The faintest
Of the faraway whispers
Of your heart
God proudly hears.

4403.

My sterile self-torture
Is over.
I am now
My God's God-Rapture.

4404.

Every morning
His heart imports soulfulness
From Heaven.

4405.

Depression-culprit
Has shamelessly caused
His life's aspiration-drought.

4406.

Today
My soul is richly enjoying
The total collapse
Of my life's bondage-bridge.

4407.

Unless you shed
Your mind's selfishness-skin,
God is not going to give you
His Heart's Fulness-Smile.

4408.

The business-filled days
Of your desire-life
Have nothing to do with
God's Satisfaction-Heart.

4409.

Since God has no need
To understand me,
Why do I need
To understand God?

4410.

Every day
My mind's brooding
Hesitation-questions
Baffle me.

4411.

My aspiration-heart,
I adore you
Because you abhor
Lethargy's tenebrous night.

4412.

Right now
My heart desperately needs
Only one thing:
An island of hope.

4413.

Man's insecurity-life
And God's Emergency Room
Are constantly busy.

4414.

Pure is your heart,
Sweet is your faith.
No wonder
You can always smile!

4415.

Today
My soul's divinity-bird
And my heart's purity-bird
Are together on the wing.

4416.

How can you ever be
A perfect God-seeker
Unless you have developed
A top-quality heart-cry?

4417.

My Lord, do tell me
The God-honest truth!
Has anybody pleased You
Since the birth of Your creation?

4418.

You must dare to cross
Your heart's shaky
Insecurity-bridge
As fast as possible!

4419.

To a perfect God-lover
A life of temptation
Is a totally foreign language.

4420.

My mind always
Respectfully enters
My heart's purity-temple.

4421.

Do you want to discover God?
Then embark
On your love-expedition.

4422.

You are right.
Your spiritual inheritance
Is your soul's
God-manifestation-promise.

4423.

My Beloved Supreme
Does two things for me:
He simplifies my complexity-mind
And amplifies my purity-heart.

4424.

You must not repeat
Your deplorable mistakes
In the same uncontrollable way.

4425.

My love-deposits
In God's Heart-Bank
Give God infinite Delight.

4426.

Try to see and feel
That your imitation prayers
Have unthinkable limitations.

4427.

Because God Himself wants you,
He has transformed your tomorrow
Into His Today.

4428.

Who asked you to sleep
When God Himself came to you
And wanted to talk to you?

4429.

When perfection comes in,
My mind
Hesitates to welcome it,
And my heart
Jumps up with ecstasy!

4430.

Alas, how can I forgive myself
When I have allowed
My God-manifestation
To be a forgotten project?

4431.

Each good thought
Definitely marks the beginning
Of a new God-fulfilling dawn.

4432.

His eyes show me
An aspiration-mountain.
His life shows me
A dedication-fountain.

4433.

You can easily ease God's pain
By increasing a little more
Your heart's cry.

4434.

We can never get
The heart's spontaneous
    happiness
From the mind's rigid rituals.

4435.

You have to become
A simplified truth-seeker
Before you can become
A certified God-lover.

4436.

Soon your supreme Music Teacher
Will examine you
As you play on the kettledrum
Of delight.

4437.

Nothing was,
Nothing is
And nothing can ever be
Beyond my hope-mountain.

4438.

All you need to understand
Is this:
God does not want you
To try to understand Him.

4439.

Try to keep
Brave and wise company.
Stay with
God's dedication-troops.

4440.

My Heavenly dreams,
How absurd you are!
My earthly promises,
How useless you are!

4441.

A true God-lover
Is he who is always ready
With his heart's
Aspiring answer-cries.

4442.

You should be happy and proud
That you are not the producer
Of the world's criticism-voice.

4443.

As God's Face
And His Grace
Are inseparable,
Even if I want my heart
And my heart's cry
To be inseparable.

4444.

God loves me.
He loves my helpless heart
More.
He loves my surrender-life
Most.

4445.

My Lord was hungry.
Therefore
He devoured my ignorance-life.
I am hungry.
Therefore
I am devouring my Lord's
   Compassion-Eye.

4446.

I do not want to live
In the dust of my dead memories
Any more.

4447.

His self-transcending life
Works
At the aspiration-airport.

4448.

You are not
Your mind's misty haze.
You are
Your heart's God-loving
And God-pleasing dawn.

4449.

It is never too late
For any heart-sailor
To set out
On an inner voyage.

4450.

When I say
I know the world well,
Immediately I go out of tune
With God's cosmic Music.

4451.

Humility appears:
Pride surrenders
And disappears.

4452.

To feed your heart
Satisfactorily,
You have to strike your mind
Ruthlessly.

4453.

Meditation
Is the God-Touch
To end my life's
Teeming frictions.

4454.

I do not want to hear
Your vital's storm-stories.
I want to hear
Your heart's God-blossom-stories.

4455.

Eternity
Blessingfully invites
My life's fleeting time
To enter.

4456.

Unless you bury
Your disobedience-mind,
God is not going to invite you
To become a member
Of His inner Family.

4457.

My faith and I
Are desperately trying
To convince my doubts
To commit suicide
For their own good.

4458.

Stab your uncomely-thought-
    mind
With your soul's
Naked knife.

4459.

He who has a gratitude-heart
Will realise
That God's Delight in him
Is God's never-ending Beginning.

4460.

Your self-doubt-giant
Is no more.
Therefore, in front of you
You see none other than
The well-pleased God.

4461.

You cannot hide
Your real life
With a false humility-curtain.

4462.

Is there anybody
To whom God will not give
The needed capacity
To renew himself
If he sincerely wants to?

4463.

God the Supreme Pilot
Supremely enjoys
Your heart's vast silence-sky.

4464.

You must transcend your
    superiority
By replacing it
With your heart's oneness-
    divinity.

4465.

One school of thought says:
God is impartial.
Another school of thought says:
God is partial.
Yet another school of thought
    says:
God is neutral.

4466.

My Beloved Supreme,
Would You mind
Taking a new look
At my aspiration-heart?

4467.

Aspiration and dedication-
    workers
Only
Have the unparalleled skills
To build a stairway to God.

4468.

Your jealousy-mind
Wants to die.
Therefore
Your ecstasy-life
Can live forever.

4469.

Now that I dream
Of my unmistakable
Progress-paradise,
God loves me infinitely more.

4470.

If you can quote
From your soul's wisdom-light,
Then easily you will answer
Life's most difficult questions.

4471.

Two unfortunate losers:
Earth and Heaven.
Earth has lost its aspiration.
Heaven has lost its satisfaction.

4472.

O my mind,
How long will you remain
A vast reservoir
Of useless doubts?

4473.

It is useless to drag
Your mind's unwillingness-feet
Towards God's Compassion-Eye.

4474.

To think that you are impure
And to do nothing about it
Is as stupid
As floundering in the dark
Deliberately.

4475.

His promises run away
Even faster
Than his fleeting thoughts.

4476.

What my mind needs
Is a waveless sea.
What my heart needs
Is a cloudless sky.

4477.

My Lord Supreme has given me
Another chance
To change my ingratitude-heart.

4478.

My aspiration,
Like God's Compassion,
Will be eternal, infinite and
    immortal.

4479.

Because of your Heaven-blessed
Sincerity-heart,
Your life will not stray
From God's Path.

4480.

My hesitation is completely gone.
Therefore
My Lord Supreme has given me
Another chance to advance
    upward.

4481.

God-responsibility
Does not feel the necessity
Of entering into
Man's ingratitude-heart-room.

4482.

O my stupid mind,
When are you going to realise
That doubt is a forbidden food?

4483.

Pay no attention
To your past failure-life!
Then nobody will be able
To ridicule you.

4484.

What can I possibly give You,
My Lord,
To be worthy
Of Your Compassion-Eye?

4485.

You have wasted enough time!
Now muster all your courage
For a soulful and powerful
New beginning.

4486.

Give up your self-deception-life
First,
If you want to take up
God's Time.

4487.

I speak ill of humanity,
But I don't mean it.
It is just a bad habit—
Unintentional.

4488.

How can your soulless heart
Be loyal
To God's bountiful Eye?

4489.

Make God your Decision-Maker
If you want to become
A great performer
On the world-stage.

4490.

God is asking me
How many more years
I am going to keep
My heart's perfection-room
Unfurnished.

4491.

My mind is drawing
A wagon of fear.
Therefore
My life is compelled
To dance with failure.

4492.

God has a very special way
To spell "aspiration":
C-O-M-P-A-S-S-I-O-N.

4493.

My outer life
Shall never succeed
And my inner life
Shall never proceed
Unless I invent
A totally new surrender-way.

4494.

Go back
To your fond heart-country!
Your Beloved Supreme
Is eagerly waiting for you.

4495.

His God-hungry heart
Is never plagued
By world-hungry desires.

4496.

Negative thoughts
Have the daring spirit
To spread like wildfire.

4497.

No, not even my mind
Is going to be
In the same boat with you,
Since you are telling me
That God is somewhere else.

4498.

Give your heart aspiration.
This is what your heart needs.
Give your life illumination.
This is what your life deserves.

4499.

Your aspiration-life
Will eventually become
The deathless sunrise
Of God-Satisfaction.

4500.

Five all-completing words:
"Lord,
I love You only".

4501.

God unconditionally loves
Each and every human being.
Indeed, this is a divine mystery
That no human mind can ever fathom.

4502.

Death will not delay its arrival.
Therefore
Play your cosmic game
And complete it as soon as possible!

4503.

My Lord is thinking of me more
Because my love for Him
Is now flawless.

4504.

God has not chosen
Your doubtful mind
To serve Him.
He has chosen only
Your aspiring heart
To love Him,
Serve Him
And fulfil Him.

4505.

How long
Will you allow your heart
To remain discouraged?
Can you not energise your heart
To run faster than the fastest?

4506.

Do you seek none but God?
Then definitely
God loves you most.

4507.

God is sad
When He hears that you feel
There are divine things
In His creation
Which you cannot attain.

4508.

First you need the strength
To be faithful in your heart.
Then you need the strength
To be perfect in your life.

4509.

Alas,
My earthbound mind
Is suffering
From my heart's
Ingratitude-life.

4510.

You have strengthened
Your confidence in God.
That means
Your life has visibly become
God's Satisfaction-Light.

4511.

To please God in my own way
I go to God with empty hands.
To please God in God's own Way
I go to God with an empty heart.

4512.

Opportunity
Is going to touch your feet
If you are ready
To remain stationed carefully
In God's Heart.

4513.

He is his heart's
Secret tears.
He is his life's
Sacred mind.

4514.

You have been invited
To attend a cosmic dance
In Heaven.
That means you are far above
The attack of ignorance-lance.

4515.

When will the world-heart smile,
When?
The world-heart needs
   illumination.
When will the world-mind cry,
When?
The world-mind needs
   purification.

4516.

If you ceaselessly seek
A simplicity-life
And a purity-heart,
You will definitely expedite
Your God-journey.

4517.

Never be disappointed
If you see that your first steps
In your spiritual life
Are feeble.

4518.

Alas, he no longer appreciates
His aspiration-course.
Alas, he is completely obedient
To his false inner messages.

4519.

I live
Where Love divine lives,
And that is inside
My purity's heart-garden.

4520.

A doubting mind
Is an undeveloped
And unevolved state
Of consciousness-reality.

4521.

An aspiring life
Never forgets
God's Compassion-Light
And never regrets
Its past failures.

4522.

When I think of God,
I feel that God's Love for me
Is His unconditional Guarantee.

4523.

Do you not see
That your vital is more insistent
Than a swarm of insects
In disturbing and ruining
Your heart's poise?

4524.

God can be seen
Even by the poorest fool,
But not by the self-styled,
God-arguing
Intellectual giants.

4525.

If you do not have the courage
To be sincere,
How can you expect God
To be the Writer
Of your life-story?

4526.

God is not going to pass through
The thick wall
Of your disobedience-mind.
No, never!
You may wait for Eternity,
But all in vain.

4527.

True, your aspiration-elevator
Has come down
And touched the ground floor.
But you can easily bring it up
Once again
To the top floor.

4528.

God's biggest Headache
Is not my desire-life
But my unwillingness to accept
The aspiration-life.

4529.

I agree,
You can easily scale
My heart's aspiration-height.
But I tell you,
You can never scale
The whole height
Of my soulful life.

4530.

Hell speaks
Through your suspicion-mind.
Heaven speaks
Through your aspiration-heart.

4531.

Since you are drowning
In luxury-sea,
How can you be found
In God's Ecstasy-Ocean?

4532.

If you are a great God-lover,
Then every day
Your aspiration-heart
Needs a tune-up.

4533.

Wherever your heart goes,
Do not allow your jealous mind
To follow,
For your mind can do great harm
To your soul's perfection-beauty.

4534.

You have travelled far
And you have found nothing.
Why?
Because you have walked along
    the path
Of your doubting mind.

4535.

You fool!
Why are you still dragging
Your lifeless and useless
Vital-tiger
Along your soul's sunlit path?

4536.

My Lord Supreme,
May my heart's surrender-life
Blossom every day
At Your Compassion-Feet.

4537.

God has given me a new task.
He wants me to measure
Carefully and impartially
The depth of my self-giving heart.

4538.

My heart feels miserable
When it has to live
With its strangling vital
And its doubting mind
Inside the body-room.

4539.

Now that you have gone out
Of your heart's obedience-room,
You will be devoured by the tiger
Of your mind's doubt-forest.

4540.

Because you guard your heart
With your soul's illumination-
   power,
Yours will be the life
Of Himalayan triumph.

4541.

Since you yourself
Do not trust your mind,
Quite often your service-life
Is God's stupendous Satisfaction-
   Delight.
This is what God has been telling
   you
All the time.

4542.

To humiliate a fellow seeker
Is to ruin
One's own perfection-
   performance
On the life-stage.

4543.

I love and need God sleeplessly.
This realisation is possible
Only in my perfection-dreams.

4544.

God has given me a heart.
But alas,
I do not know how to teach my
   heart
To cry like an infant
For God's Compassion-Eye.

4545.

I am exceedingly proud of you!
At long last
You have brought your impurity-
   vital
Under control.

4546.

You do not have to be
The fastest starter.
Just be a starter!
You will, without fail,
Reach your destination-sun.

4547.

A true devotee knows
That inside his heart
Will always be found
The dance of his aspiration-
   sunbeams.

4548.

Indifference
Is the last resort
When a spiritual Master sees
That a particular seeker
Is an absolutely hopeless case.

4549.

A God-lover is he
Whose heart and life have become
A ceaselessly flowing
And self-giving river.

4550.

O my mind,
You can do something infinitely
   better
Than suspecting my purity-heart.

4551.

You do not want to know
How much affection, love and
   surrender
You gave to God.
Indeed, this is a clear sign
Of your progress.

4552.

It is unfair
To judge your life
Only by your today's
Deplorable performance.

4553.

Because you have shunned the
    company
Of your old friend,
Ignorance-night,
God is teaching you today
The Dance of His Beauty's Life.

4554.

Unless you shorten
Your life's frustration-line,
Your heart can never be happy.

4555.

Be careful!
Your inner progress
Is very fragile.
Carelessly
Do not destroy it!

4556.

Your aspiration-passport
To paradise
Has definitely expired.
You must renew it
As soon as possible
If you want a free access
To delight-world.

4557.

He lives inside
The citadel of purity.
Therefore
A life of divinity
Cannot remain a far cry.

4558.

If you sincerely mourn
Your vanished inner progress,
Then God will definitely give you
Another chance to become perfect
And remain perfect.

4559.

If you want to be
A choice instrument of God,
Then plant aspiration-dedication-
    virtues
In your soul's inner soil.

4560.

I can ignore everything
Except one thing:
The cry of my neglected heart.

4561.

You are longing for the birth
Of a brighter future.
Then do not be afraid
Of your daily
Spiritual struggle-hurdles.

4562.

Your new self
Is knocking at God's Liberation-
   Door.
Indeed,
This is your supreme
   achievement.

4563.

Mine is the aspiration-heart
That every day
Longs to sport
On my life's progress-mountain.

4564.

I shall see only two plants
In my garden of tomorrow:
My gratitude-heart-plant
And my surrender-life-plant.

4565.

Impurity
And its suffocating embrace
Can never be separated.

4566.

Each living breath of his
Is flourishing
In the rich soil of aspiration.

4567.

What is uncertainty?
It is the false dance
Of the mind's deplorable anxiety.

4568.

The sound-life
Has many, many questions.
The silence-life
Has not only the answers
But also the best answers.

4569.

The effulgence of Heaven
Is not for you,
For you have already fallen
Into the self-indulgence trap.

4570.

Now that you have dethroned
Your doubt-king,
You have a new king
Who will guide you
And satisfy you,
And that new king
Is your heart's faith.

4571.

I deeply admire your capacity
To transform the frustration-
   jungle
Into a satisfaction-garden.

4572.

Your insecurity-heart
Foolishly expects to be honoured
In the aspiration-academy.

4573.

You are cultivating
Your progress-plants.
Therefore, God has invited you
To board the satisfaction-plane.

4574.

Your aspiration-heart
Is the most adequate tranquilliser
To stop the trembling hand
Of fear.

4575.

When will you be exhausted
From your useless,
Excessive self-thought,
When?

4576.

If you shine from within,
You will never be attacked
By feeble human love.

4577.

I march only
In my heart's purity-parade
And my life's surrender-parade.

4578.

Now that you have thrown
Your doubt-ball
Far away,
Yours will be the heart that runs
From victory to victory.

4579.

To say that I shall not try
To be perfect
Any more
Is an unforgivable offence
Against God the Compassion.

4580.

Be quiet, O my mind!
God is now having a serious talk
With my surrender-heart
And my gratitude-life.

4581.

What will you accomplish
By treasuring yesterday's dreams?
You have to treasure
Only today's reality.

4582.

Alas, you do not realise
That your soul-bird is always
   ready
To shelter your heart
Under its beautiful and powerful
   wings.

4583.

Nobody is going to buy
Your mind's thought-fabric,
Nobody!
Everybody wants the adamantine
   will
Of your perfection-garden.

4584.

God's Compassion
And my aspiration
Have most cheerfully agreed
To become inseparably one.

4585.

The deadline was
The day before yesterday,
But God gave you
Another chance yesterday,
And today He is giving you
Still another chance
Out of His infinite Compassion.
This time do not disappoint Him!
Please Him in His own Way
For your immortal satisfaction.

4586.

It is indeed a great blessing
To take human birth.
It is indeed a greater satisfaction
When God can manifest Himself
Uninterrupted,
In His own Way,
In and through you.

4587.

Instead of illumining the world-
    heart,
He confuses the world-mind
When he tells the world
That he has lost
His God-realisation.

4588.

The hostile forces
Are untouchable!
This is what you have to convince
Your entire being.

4589.

The same old story!
You are nothing
But the dissatisfaction
Of your dark desire-life.

4590.

The greatest misery
In a seeker's life
Is when he finds it impossible
To give up his disobedience-life.

4591.

If you visit God's cosmic Vision-
    Garden,
Will you not enjoy
God's sacred Heart-Fragrance?

4592.

If you do not
Come to the aid of your soul
When it fights against ignorance-
    night,
Then you and your soul
Will be equal losers.

4593.

Where were you
When God so compassionately
Served His unconditional
    Delight-Meal?
Everybody else came.
Where were you?

4594.

Since you have the strongest desire
To be invited by God,
Then breathe in
By far the greatest prayer:
Patience-light.

4595.

Good news from Heaven:
Heaven will teach me
How to feel
God's Heart on earth.
Good news from earth:
Earth will teach me
How to touch
God's Feet in Heaven.

4596.

It is entirely your own fault
That you are deliberately avoiding
The inner struggle
To discipline your life.

4597.

Now that you have closed
Your mind's complaint-door,
Your heart's hunger
For God's Satisfaction-Feast
Is bound to increase.

4598.

A sincere mind
Dwells on God.
A pure heart
Dwells in God.

4599.

I have come back
To my heart-country,
And I am feeding myself
With my soul's
Selflessness-fragrance.

4600.

You have claimed God
As your very own.
This is indeed
God's greatest Satisfaction.

4601.

My Lord Supreme,
Do give my heart the capacity
To walk along
The path of silence-obedience
Always.

4602.

My dedication-life
Always wants my aspiration-heart
To have sovereign rights over it.

4603.

How can your life-tree
Be happy
When your mind's desire-wind
Is blowing very hard?

4604.

When the desire-wind blows,
Be extremely careful,
For your aspiration-plant
May helplessly die.

4605.

What really counts
In God's Eye
Is your cheerful and soulful
Willingness
And not your previous
Amazement-achievements.

4606.

He who gives his heart of love
And his life of satisfaction
To mankind
Can easily have free access
To God the Infinite.

4607.

Each obscure and impure thought
Has the capacity to make us feel
That our Compassion-Lord
Wants to remain a perfect
    stranger.

4608.

My soul tells my heart
That it will cheerfully and proudly
Carry all its messages
To the Lord Supreme.

4609.

O my stupid mind,
From now on
I shall never allow you
To be my decision-maker!

4610.

Say "Yes"
To God's Compassion-Heart
So that you can become one
With God's Perfection-Soul.

4611.

Why do you cherish
Your desire-life-slave
When you can cherish
Aspiration-mountain-king?

4612.

If you can possess yourself
And nobody else,
Then God's Vision-Satisfaction-
   Skies
Shall blossom inside you.

4613.

A good seeker never lives
On a borrowed inspiration-mind,
A borrowed aspiration-heart
Or a borrowed dedication-life.

4614.

My Lord Supreme,
In the morning
Do give me the capacity
To renounce everything.
In the evening
Do give me the capacity
To announce Your Victory
In and through my life.

4615.

What is easy?
To have soulful God-cries.
What is most difficult?
To feel that God loves you
No matter what you say and do.

4616.

The human mind
Teaches confusion.
The divine heart
Teaches illumination.
The Supreme Lord
Teaches Oneness-Satisfaction.

4617.

O gratitude,
Do not remain my God-hunger's
Rarest food.

4618.

If you allow the vital-thief
To steal your heart's God-
   treasures,
Then nobody will be there
To befriend you and your
   stupidity.

4619.

You must not delay!
You must achieve
As soon as possible,
Before your life fades away.

4620.

One thing I have learnt:
If I want to love God
Not only soulfully
But also unconditionally,
I surprisingly can.

4621.

If you can develop the capacity
To inspect your insecurity,
Security will come and befriend
   you.

4622.

Each child of hope
Is the glorious embodiment
Of God's Vision-Light.

4623.

To trust humanity
Is to feel
Divinity's closest oneness.

4624.

The body has to be always aware
That the soul
Is its most adorable guest.

4625.

My closing remarks
To this world:
I expected,
Therefore
I am disappointed.

4626.

This applies to you, too!
You must every day
Meditate on God
Soulfully plus unconditionally.

4627.

God does not want to be
   enthroned
Above my heart.
He desires to be enshrined
Inside my heart-temple.

4628.

Imagination
Has inspired him.
Aspiration
Has liberated him.
Realisation
Has immortalised him.

4629.

Because you have put your mind
On a strict diet,
Peace is fast approaching.

4630.

His giant ego
Can easily hide
His progress-dwarf.

4631.

It is beneath the dignity
Of a loving heart
To wear any disguise.

4632.

Because your heart suffers
From aspiration-deficiency,
Doubt will paralyse your mind.

4633.

Come and smile with me,
And then let us go
And attend the funeral
Of all our sorrows
Inside our heart-church.

4634.

His adamantine adherence
To truth
Has not only saved him
Time and again
But has also saved those
Who have implicit faith
In him.

4635.

Although mine
Is a most spacious life-palace,
I have no room
For ignorance-prince.

4636.

A silence-torch lights my way
The moment I long
To go beyond the domain
Of the mind.

4637.

Since you have descended
So successfully
The stairs of hell,
Can you not try to ascend
Cheerfully and bravely
The stairs of Heaven?

4638.

You may not know it,
But it is absolutely true
That God is extremely proud
Of your secret and sacred
Heart-tears.

4639.

He may not be a great soldier,
But he does always aspire
To be in the headquarters
Of the aspiration-army.

4640.

I am so proud
That God Himself has blessed you
With a self-control trophy.

4641.

Do at least one thing good
In this lifetime
Instead of only becoming
An encyclopaedia of good
   intentions.

4642.

When I mount
On the wings of my prayers,
God descends
On His love-winged Bird.

4643.

Now that I do not pray and
   meditate
Regularly,
I am forced to see a short circuit
In my heart's oneness-line
With God.

4644.

I am not going to surprise
The world
With my life's superlative glories,
But with my Lord's
Superlative Compassion-Stories.

4645.

God feels sad
That there is always
A great shortage
Of salvation-soldiers
In His Compassion-Army.

4646.

If you enjoy
Your limitation-poverty,
How is it that you mind
When the world scoffs at you?

4647.

Just because
God is His Compassion-Heart,
He does not mind
If His Compassion is misused
Every day by the masses
For millennia.

4648.

Who knocks at my door?
Neither my sleeping heart
Nor my suspecting mind
Wants to respond.

4649.

I shall never allow
My dedication-life
To be encased in inactivity.

4650.

Smite your self-doubt
Soundly
If you want God to plant
Faith-plants
Inside your heart
Cheerfully.

4651.

God's Compassion-Smile
Can easily transform
Your insecurity-heart
Into His own Security-Fort
In the wink of an eye.

4652.

If you want your aspiration-life
To make you happy,
Then immediately spurn
The hostile attacks
Of your depression-arrows.

4653.

Offer your aspiration-buds
To all.
God will grant you
His Satisfaction-Blossoms.

4654.

His heart's adamantine will
Wants to prove to him
That his mind's ego
Is not the centre of the universe.

4655.

Your mind is already so stupid.
Do not add more stupidity to it
By helping it to form
The habit of unhappiness!

4656.

Make all your rainbow-promises
Inside the sanctuary
Of your heart's silence
And nowhere else.

4657.

If you are sincere,
Omnipotence will guard you.
If you are pure,
Omniscience will guide you.

4658.

I know
If I become pure,
Absolutely pure,
My Lord Supreme
Will turn me into
His own melody-producing angel.

4659.

My determination,
Paired with God's Compassion,
Can easily smash the pride
Of impossibility.

4660.

Your mind's stupid neutrality-pride
Has destroyed
Your heart's spontaneous joy.

4661.

A man-written message:
God loves man
Only if he loves God.
A God-written message:
Man is loved by God
Unconditionally.

4662.

My heart feels
That God's personal Name
Is Forgiveness-Sun.
My mind thinks
That God's impersonal Name
Is Justice-Star.

4663.

If you lose your best friend,
Aspiration-bird,
Rest assured that your worst
    enemy,
Frustration-tiger,
Will devour you.

4664.

When dark thoughts appear,
God does not disappear.
He only watches and waits
To see if you are going to ask
The dark thoughts to disappear.

4665.

Frustration-plants grow
Most rapidly
In the desire-forest.

4666.

Each day is a golden opportunity
For those who believe
In the satisfaction-capacity
Of God the creation.

4667.

A desiring man
Is not a false man,
But each desire
In the spiritual life
Is nothing but
An unwanted unreality.

4668.

The insecurity-chaos
Of each human being
Is astonishingly confusing.

4669.

His is a sad experience:
From his old devotion
He came to learn
That God was the only One
Who could perfect his life.
From his new devotion
He thinks and feels
That he has to do everything
All by himself.

4670.

Truth can inspire you,
But it is God's Compassion-Light
That can and will liberate you.

4671.

Peace and satisfaction
On earth
Are two most precious
Hope-gifts.

4672.

Who called me?
God?
Then my heart and I are ready.
Who called me?
Man?
Then my doubting mind
And my suspecting vital
Are both ready.

4673.

Each night
God-dreams enlighten my sleep
And fulfil my heart's hunger-cry.

4674.

You must never suspect
Your sincerity,
For sincerity is the beginning
Of God-unfoldment in your life.

4675.

My heart is my Lord's
Compassion-Light-Victory.
My soul is my Lord's
Satisfaction-Delight-Victory.

4676.

You are a lover of doubting.
Therefore
You are found
In a speeding train of despair.

4677.

Give up all world-claims
If you want God to enchain you
With His Heart's golden Chain.

4678.

Do not fight with anybody.
But if you have to fight,
Then fight with God's
Forgiveness-Light,
For then you have
Nothing to lose.

4679.

If you do not want
To be aware
Of doubt's poison-presence
Inside your mind,
Who is going to take the trouble
Of making you aware?

4680.

My Lord,
How long am I going to keep
My heart's door
Stupidly open to ignorance-
    prince?

4681.

Every day I try and try
In vain
To swim in God's
Satisfaction-Pool.

4682.

O my mind,
In spite of your surly behaviour,
I see God-satisfaction-possibility
Inside of you.

4683.

Yesterday's world
Cried and cried.
Today's world
Is smiling and smiling.
Tomorrow's world
Will wonder and wonder.

4684.

His is the heart
That owns the beauty
Of sunlit silence.

4685.

His heart cries
Not for him,
But for his Lord's
Love-Manifestation.

4686.

God laughs and laughs
When He sees His seeker-child
Shoplifting
From His Compassion-
    Department Store.

4687.

Man and his stupidity
Will eventually be found
In the chasm of futility.

4688.

Yesterday
I breathed to hope.
Today
God is hoping to breathe
In me, through me.

4689.

One thing I will never
Want to have,
And that is the misery
Of a mistrust-miser.

4690.

Do you think
I should be willing
To be inside the long train
Of your excuses?

4691.

If you do the right thing,
Even if you become the target
Of wild criticism,
Your inner happiness
Will eventually prove to you
That God has always
Been pleased with you.

4692.

If he makes
The official announcement
Of his life's surrender,
Then his actual surrender
May remain a far cry.

4693.

To please the Supreme,
The human lips must express
Only what the divine heart
Soulfully desires.

4694.

If you do not appreciate
Your heart's satisfaction-sun,
This world
Is not going to help you,
And the higher world
Will never support you.

4695.

Because I allowed my mind
To guide my life,
Alas,
I am now nearing
A destruction-destination.

4696.

Do you not feed your mind
With your heart's compassion-
    concern
To illumine your mind's teeming
    doubts?

4697.

Your unguarded thought-world
Has completely shattered
Your heart's prosperity-peace.

4698.

Your self-deception
Has ruthlessly taken away from
    you
The power of your self-command.

4699.

When I swim in the silence-sea,
I see the blossoming
Of my heart's illumination-sun.

4700.

When your obedience-flute
And God's Satisfaction-Flute
Play together,
Earth and Heaven dance
Their ecstasy's dance.

4701.

Lightning-fast progress
You have made
Just because you have invoked
God's Forgiveness-Ocean
And His Compassion-Sky.

4702.

Your soul does not want
Your heart
To fall into the deep
Oblivion-chasm.

4703.

A moment's slackness
Can delay your heart's
Conscious oneness with God
Indefinitely.

4704.

You are such a fool!
You want to take a holiday
From reality-life.

4705.

You must realise
That your wisdom-reality
Is infinitely stronger
Than your ignorance-dream.

4706.

If you have the time
To think of God-manifestation,
Then you must have the time
To think of God-realisation first.

4707.

Meditate with greatest
   enthusiasm
If you want to make the fastest
   progress
In your aspiration-heart
And in your dedication-life.

4708.

There can be no
Dedication-garden
Without satisfaction-flowers.

4709.

Now that wisdom-light
Has dawned upon him,
He is immediately repairing
His doubt-created mind-damage.

4710.

If you can climb a little,
God will definitely help you
Climb His own
Transcendental Life-Tree.

4711.

My heart's willingness
Is my life's only official passport
To visit God's
Self-Transcendence-Kingdom.

4712.

You have now turned
Completely to God.
Therefore
God has given you
His Infinity's immortal Address.

4713.

Alas,
You have not fulfilled
Your promise.
Therefore
God's Hope-Seeds
Are all destroyed!

4714.

God's Justice-Scale
Will frighten you,
But His Compassion-Scale
Will only enlighten you.

4715.

You wanted to reach God
With your mind's brilliance.
You have badly failed.
There is another way
You can try to reach God:
With your heart's surrender-
  smile.

4716.

If you misuse opportunity,
All your blossoming hopes
Will before long be destroyed.

4717.

The mind's perfection
And the life's transformation
Are absolutely indispensable
In any human life.

4718.

Keep your heart
Always independent of your mind
So that God can share with you
His supreme Ecstasy.

4719.

My Lord was pleased
When He saw
Only one surrender-wave
In my life-sea.

4720.

It seems that my Lord
Has only one thing to do
Day in and day out:
Amplify my heart's aspiration-cry.

4721.

If you do not pay any attention
To your inner life's
Emergency signals,
You are bound to sink
In your outer life's
Destruction-sea.

4722.

If I have to choose
Between God's Grace and God's
  Love,
I will definitely choose God's
  Grace,
For I know perfectly well
That God's Love will follow God's
  Grace.

4723.

To please
Without being pleased in return:
This is an experience
That God gets every day
From His creation.

4724.

A fire-pure change of heart
Was the turning point
In his aspiration-life-career.

4725.

What has saved and illumined my life?
Not my possession-life,
But my cheerful surrender-breath
To my Lord's Will.

4726.

Everything in life will fade
Into insignificance-night
When God's Compassion-Light dawns
Upon your aspiration-life.

4727.

God-realisation
Is the final challenge,
But not
An unattainable challenge.

4728.

You are in search of something
To rely on.
Try your soul's
Illumination-sky!

4729.

If you have the courage to believe
That God loves you unconditionally,
Then you grant God the opportunity
To enjoy His infinite Satisfaction-Delight.

4730.

To meditate
Like a great seeker-soul,
What you need
Is a soulful child-heart.

4731.

If you are a true God-lover,
Then you will definitely feel
That your suffering-life
Is not desired by God.

4732.

Who gives me my heart-lessons
Daily?
Not man,
The self-styled knower,
But God,
The Supreme Lover.

4733.

Every day
Set a new goal,
Even if you have failed
To reach your previous goals.

4734.

If you have an inner cry,
Then you must never allow it to hide.
You must urge it to reveal itself
And touch God's Compassion-Heart.

4735.

My mind does not know
That it is being followed
By a frustration-panther.
My heart does not know
That it is being followed
By a peace-lamb.

4736.

If you can live
Inside your silence-heart,
Then you can easily establish
Your satisfaction-delight
For humanity to enjoy.

4737.

The sadness
Of an unfulfilled dream
Has prevented him from coming out
Of the dark doubt-room.

4738.

Alas,
I do not know
When my golden Boatman
Will arrive
With His golden Dream-Boat.

4739.

God is definitely
Counting on you.
For God's sake,
Don't disappoint Him!

4740.

Tame your vital-beast!
Otherwise, before long,
Your bellowing vital-beast
Will devour you.

4741.

It is you who have created
Your own misery
By arguing
With the divine in you
And by disobeying
The Supreme in you.

4742.

Just by avoiding the doubt-enemy
You cannot become happy.
You have to completely conquer
The doubt-enemy
Once and for all.

4743.

At long last,
I am so happy to hear,
The surrender-bells
Of my aspiration-life
Are tolling.

4744.

Do you know
That God is holding
A perfection-party?
I am sure
He is going to invite you.
Therefore
Be fully prepared
For His Invitation.

4745.

To improve your future
You must prove that you belong
To God's Compassion-Light
Alone.

4746.

Two momentous questions:
Does God, the Beloved Supreme,
Exist for me?
And do I, the God-seeker,
Exist for God?

4747.

Yes, you have seen
My body sleeping.
But have you not seen
That my heart is fully awake?

4748.

God wanted me to tell you
That you must not allow your mind
To house unwashed thoughts
Any more.

4749.

If you do not shorten
Your lethargy-hours,
You will not be able to lengthen
Your energy-days.

4750.

Ask your life
If its dedication
Is up-to-date.
Ask your heart
If its destination
Is up-to-date.
Ask yourself
If your oneness with God's Will
Is up-to-date.

4751.

If you have an inspiring past,
Then add to it your aspiring
    present
And finally,
Add to your past and present
Your surrendering future.

4752.

O Heaven,
Do allow me to try
Once more
To smile powerfully
With you.

4753.

A joyful God-seeker
Will definitely be able
To meet with God,
The playful Lover.

4754.

O smile of Heaven,
I am sorry to have missed you
    today.
But I assure you,
Tomorrow I am not going to miss
    you.

4755.

You want to know
Who he is.
He is his insatiable thirst
For his silence-meditation.

4756.

Two unexpected disasters:
God does not care for my needs.
I have forgotten God
The Compassion-Heart.

4757.

If you can be above
Your mind's demands,
You can easily command
Your soulless animal-life.

4758.

If you want to walk secretly
On God's sacred Pathway,
Then always sing
Your heart-songs.

4759.

If you are not ruthlessly strict
With your lethargy-life,
Then your heart's soul-education
Will never begin.

4760.

If you do not make yourself
Useful to God,
How can God ever make you
   fruitful
To please both Heaven and earth?

4761.

Every day try to sing
A newness-song.
Then you will not hear
The voice of world-illusion.

4762.

God has no ulterior motive
When He tells you
He will give you
His Heart's limitless Treasure
Unconditionally.

4763.

Because you are God's
Choice instrument,
He has given you the capacity
To replace the fleeting
With the everlasting.

4764.

Where do I stand?
I stand in between
My heart, the doer,
And my soul, the witness.

4765.

You call it your heart's
Gratitude-second.
God calls it His Life's
Satisfaction-Day.

4766.

God wants only one thing
From me:
He wants me to make my heart
The star of my earth-show.

4767.

Birthless is the soul's
Education-life.
Endless is the soul's
God-manifestation-life.

4768.

My purity-heart
Is the priceless gift
From my Absolute Beloved
   Supreme.

4769.

He and his aspiration-heart
Were both killed together
By his stupid mind's
Doubt-bullet.

4770.

If you are
Your doubt-destroying mind,
Then God will become
His self-giving Heart.

4771.

I am going to wash my mind
Every day.
Then my heart and I
Shall climb up
My life's perfection-tree.

4772.

The finite in me
Desires God the Infinite.
Indeed, this is my Lord's
Unrecognised miracle.

4773.

Whether you care for it
Or not,
Your soul will never stop
Its unconditional
Whispering guidance-light.

4774.

There is no such thing
As lasting defeat,
Since there is no such thing
As being unwanted by God.

4775.

The fool in me believes
In my mind's constant promises.
The wise man in me believes
In my Lord's self-giving Promise-
    Delight.

4776.

He who thinks that experience
Is not essential
Will not be recruited by Heaven
To become a hero-warrior
In its army.

4777.

Your aspiration-shrine
Is collapsing.
Your devotion-temple
Is crumbling.
Yet you expect to see
Satisfaction-duty
In your life.

4778.

Your inner life
Is unimaginably frail.
How can you then expect
To sail with God
In His Golden Boat?

4779.

Persistently
He has dismissed temptation.
Therefore
God is infinitely more pleased
With him
Than he can ever imagine.

4780.

Ask your heart-gardener
To sow only the seeds
Of God-Satisfaction.

4781.

The mind thinks
That flattery is most delicious.
The heart knows
That flattery is not at all
Nourishing.

4782.

I need only my heart's happiness
To cry sleeplessly
For God-manifestation
Here on earth.

4783.

You must satisfy God
Unconditionally.
Otherwise, your achievement
Will be far below
Your soul's expectation-light.

4784.

Never blame God!
He never asked you
To gamble away
Your heart's treasure-wealth
At the temptation-racetrack
Of your vital.

4785.

If you are a hero-seeker,
Then all your tomorrows
Will surrender to your today.

4786.

If you can spread
Your heart's redolent eagerness,
Then yours will be
God's Transformation-Touch.

4787.

God is dying for
Your longing heart
And not for
Your doubting mind.

4788.

God sometimes pretends
That He knows nothing
And He is as uncertain
As an ordinary human being.
This is the only way
He can expedite humanity's
    progress:
By descending to its own level
Of consciousness.

4789.

I gave God what I have
And what I am:
My willingness.
God is now giving me
What He has and what He is:
His Fulness.

4790.

The first and the last step
Must be taken
Soulfully and sleeplessly:
I love God.
I love God unconditionally.

4791.

Because you have given
Your undivided attention
To your God-life,
God is celebrating
The stupendous success
Of your outer life
And the momentous progress
Of your inner life.

4792.

He feels that there is always
A yawning gulf
Between the envisioned reality-life
And the fulfilled reality-breath.

4793.

The great thunder-sound
Of your mind's success-life
Definitely has nothing to do with
Your heart's progress-light.

4794.

God may accept your wish
If you do not want to become great.
But He will never accept your refusal
To become another God.

4795.

Accept only one challenge in life:
God-realisation.
All other challenges
Are worthless.

4796.

You must have
At least this much faith in God:
That He is going to solve
Your spiritual problems,
Only it may not be
At your choice hour.

4797.

Your chosen summit
And God's chosen summit for you
Are totally different.
You must aspire to reach
Only one summit:
Needless to say,
God's Perfection-Summit.

4798.

You are dreaming of
A peace-life
Without offering God
Your surrender-life!

4799.

I am now intensely inspired
In all my being
To sing only one song:
Self-improvement.

4800.

Mine is the heart
That desperately needs God's
    Love.
Mine is the life
That desperately needs God's
    Compassion.

4801.

Every morning I must realise
That I have the golden
    opportunity
Of an unused day before me
To use in a divine way.

4802.

God compassionately gave me
My eternal name:
Aspiration.
I unconditionally gave my Lord
His eternal Name:
Compassion.

4803.

On my heart's stage
I have had quite a few performers.
Nobody has satisfied me.
Therefore, I have invited
A totally new Performer:
My Beloved Supreme.

4804.

Do not fool yourself!
Do not try to convert falsehood
Into truth.
It is a thankless and useless task.
You simply cannot do it!

4805.

Man's Heaven-visiting hours
Depend on man's
Surrender-delight.
God's earth-visiting hours
Depend on God's
Unconditional Compassion.

4806.

In vain
God has been looking
For millennia
For His Vision-partner.

4807.

At long last
My life is able to board
My Lord's Forgiveness-Plane.

4808.

Insincerity,
You are not admired.
Impurity,
You are despised.
Ingratitude,
You should be hanged!

4809.

Yesterday I fought with God
With my impurity-breath.
Today I am dancing with God
With my purity-heart.

4810.

If you do not think much
Of God,
How do you expect
A Satisfaction-Letter
From God?

4811.

Now that I have cut down
My heart's ingratitude-tree,
God is opening His Heart-Door
Unconditionally
And will leave it open
Eternally.

4812.

Two changes
Will make your mind perfect:
Do not allow your mind
To be your teacher.
Do not allow your mind
To doubt you, your sincerity.

4813.

If you can be eager to receive
Blessings from God,
Then rest assured that God
Will be fond of granting you
His blessingful Favour.

4814.

God is really sad
When He sees that He is
Your second-best friend.
God is not happy
When He sees that He happens to be
Only your best friend.
God will be happy and proud
Of Himself and of you
Only when you consider Him to be
Your only Friend.

4815.

My grief and my sorrows
Flew away
When I received a Forgiveness-Letter
From my Beloved Supreme.

4816.

You have simply no idea
How selective God can be at times.
Therefore, I urge you to be
Perfect at every moment
In every way
Both in your outer life
And in your inner life.

4817.

If you cheerfully admit
Your teeming follies,
Then God the Compassion
And God the Satisfaction
Will not remain strangers to you.

4818.

If you demand instant realisation,
Then you will be compelled
To suffer the greatest defeat,
Both unimaginable and laughable,
If not unpardonable.

4819.

My mind often feels lost
When it sees
The purity, beauty and divinity
Of my heart.

4820.

You will never be able to climb
Perfection-peaks
Because of the catastrophic
   disobedience
Of your vital
In your aspiration-life.

4821.

Everybody needs an invitation
From God.
But impurity and insecurity
Do not care for
His formal Invitation.

4822.

Invite purity's life
On the strength of your sincerity.
Invite divinity's breath
On the strength of your purity-
   life.

4823.

You fool,
When are you going to unburden
Your stupid mind-donkey?

4824.

Wisdom-light is infinitely better
Than weak pride.
This is the unmistakable
   experience
Of all truth-seekers and God-
   lovers.

4825.

God wants to perfect your dream-
   life.
Can you not sit for a moment
Under His
Compassion-Protection-
   Illumination-Tree?

4826.

Poor anxiety
Has to live unwillingly
In the dangerous vicinity
Of doubt!

4827.

He was extremely happy
To trade his proud intelligence
For a soulful prayer.

4828.

God's Calculator
Is unlike ours.
It does not know
How to subtract.
It only adds and multiplies.
For whom?
For mankind.

4829.

Learn every day
A new way of living,
For that is the only way
You can please your Beloved
    Supreme
Most satisfactorily.

4830.

God's Satisfaction-Home
Is still quite far,
But it does definitely exist.

4831.

When he gave up
His aspiration-life,
He never thought
He would be totally lost
In the temptation-valley.

4832.

Why do you not trust God,
Only God,
When there are many people
    around you
Who can easily deceive you?
Why do you not trust yourself
When nobody is around you
And nobody is for you?

4833.

Alas, alas,
He is deliberately feeding
His aspiration-devouring doubt.

4834.

His heart's illumination-sun
Has at last put an end
To his close encounters
With his confusion-mind.

4835.

Your life of receptivity
Entirely depends on
Your heart's prayerful
    spontaneity.

4836.

You are such a fool!
Why did you allow your stupid
   mind
To be accepted into
The eyeless frustration-fraternity?

4837.

Yesterday
God selected him
To be man's most faithful servant.
Today
God is selecting him
To be His absolutely perfect
Representative on earth.

4838.

You can be my friend
Only if you want to become
An unconditional volunteer
To voice God's Victory
Sleeplessly.

4839.

Why do you want me to look
At your hesitation-mind
And frustration-vital?
Do you think I have nothing
   better to do?

4840.

You are such a fool!
Do you not see
That you are increasing
Your incarnations
By mixing with your stupid
   friends:
Desires!

4841.

Your leave of absence
From aspiration-school
Has turned your mind
Into a monkey
And your heart
Into a donkey.

4842.

Expectation-seeds grow into
Not only severe
But also chronic headaches.

4843.

Frustration-traveller
Is not allowed to walk alone.
He is forced to carry
Right on his shoulder
A grief-bag.

4844.

Heaven is always ready
To welcome hell into its house.
But hell, in its blind pride,
Finds it beneath its dignity
To accept Heaven's invitation.

4845.

He is at once chosen
By God's Satisfaction
And rejected
By humanity's hesitation.

4846.

He does not remember
That he unconsciously hid
A temptation-time-bomb
Inside his vital-closet.

4847.

The heart's willingness
Is always ready
To enjoy the company
Of cheerful lives.

4848.

Obedience knows
Many divine things.
Disobedience knows
Only one unpardonable thing:
God-denial.

4849.

Do not allow
Your mind's clouds
To hover over
Your heart's aspiration-tree.

4850.

Because you are so stupid,
You are cautiously approaching
Your own aspiration-heart.

4851.

His is the vastly untidy life
That is always engrossed
In confusing life-projects.

4852.

A seeker's heart-cry
And a seeker's life-smile
Are the two most delicious fruits
That his Beloved Supreme
Enjoys most.

4853.

O my mind,
Why didn't you tell me
That insecurity was desperately
   trying
To strangle you?
I could have prayed to my soul
To come to your rescue.

4854.

Each night
His aspiration-heart
Elopes
With God's Satisfaction-Heart.

4855.

Do not add more imperfection
To your mind:
Do not convince your mind
To belittle your heart's aspiration.

4856.

God is giving man
New work to do.
He does not want man
To mourn his fleeting breath
Any more.

4857.

Just because he allowed dimness
To cloud his mind yesterday,
Today darkness
Is enveloping his heart.

4858.

I am not the only one.
God, too, feels sad
To see the decay
Of your aspiring heart.

4859.

Because your faith is false,
You are failing
In your inner life
And you are imprisoning
Your outer life.

4860.

Do not refuse
God's three most significant Gifts:
His Compassion-Eye,
His Satisfaction-Heart,
His Oneness-Life.

4861.

Perhaps you have not
The slightest idea
What you have done:
You have damaged
God's Compassion-Crown.

4862.

Because of your heart's
Inner beauty,
Your life is able to claim God
As its very own.

4863.

God wants us to celebrate
The dying life of ignorance
And not to parade
The tortures of living death.

4864.

Insecurity has betrayed you.
This time guard yourself
With your universal oneness-
   heart.

4865.

Your mind may relax
On the clouds of illusion.
Your heart can relax
Only inside the heart
Of illumination-sun.

4866.

Every day God changes
His Fishing Rod,
For every day He has to catch
Ultramodern God-longing fish.

4867.

Because you have allowed your
   mind
To be encaged by insecurity,
Yours is a life of colossal failure.

4868.

Faith-flame I do not see
Inside him any more.
What I see in him
Is only doubt-smoke,
And this smoke
Is suffocating his aspiration-life.

4869.

If you do not live up to
Your spiritual standard,
Which is absolutely necessary,
Then do not blame God.
Blame your ill-fated life.

4870.

God could not understand
When he asked God
For a personal loan.
God said to him,
"The term 'loan' is not available
In My Heart-Dictionary.
Self-giving is the correct word
To be found in My Heart-
    Dictionary."

4871.

When your heart thinks for you,
You are safe,
For God is always pleased
With your purity-heart.

4872.

An unexpected inner cry
Has turned his life's frustration
Into a most powerful
Aspiration-delight.

4873.

A forced surrender
Is no surrender.
Eventually it will end
In a catastrophic revolt.

4874.

Your mind lives
In only one world,
But your heart can live
And does live
In many worlds at the same time
On the strength
Of its vast oneness-capacity.

4875.

My seeker-friend,
Do not lose heart.
There was a time
When I too was helplessly lost
In my mind's desire-life.

4876.

A purity-heart
Is his newly acquired
Inner treasure.

4877.

Man's ingratitude
And his failure
In the inner world
Are two inseparable friends.

4878.

Delay not, delay not!
You must replace
Your mind's old impurity-life
With your heart's new purity-life.

4879.

Desire-ship
Ultimately is bound to dock
At failure-landing.

4880.

You want to know where I live?
I tell you,
I lived, I live and I will forever live
In the powerful clasp of hope.

4881.

If you sing
With your dedication-life,
Then God will teach you
How to dance
With His Satisfaction-Heart.

4882.

If you are crying
Because of the loss
Of your imagination
And the unwanted appearance
Of frustration,
Then you are doing
Two absolutely perfect things.

4883.

When God was alone,
He definitely needed me
To be with Him.
Alas, why was I such a fool
That I would not be
His Vision-Reality-partner?

4884.

Death is forced to retire
When humanity aspires
For its inseparable oneness
With Immortality.

4885.

You have increased your hope-seeds.
That means eventually
You are going to collect
Countless satisfaction-fruits.

4886.

Do you want to be happy?
Then look at God's Compassion-
   Eye.
Do you want God to be happy?
Then feel God's Oneness-Heart.

4887.

Do you know that my future
Is the Eternal Now
And that my Eternal Now
Is God-Immortality's Satisfaction-
   Smile?

4888.

If you are shopping
For satisfaction-doll,
Then you must go
To aspiration-mall.

4889.

If you do not join
The faith-committee,
Then your self-doubt-demons
Will devour you.

4890.

His heart's
Flowering new enthusiasm
Has brought down God,
The complete Satisfaction-Heart.

4891.

Beyond my hopes,
Beyond my dreams,
Alas, alas,
Is my Lord's Satisfaction-Smile.

4892.

I am ready to weep
A fountain of gratitude-tears
If you can convince my mind
To come out of its doubt-prison.

4893.

His inner storm has cleared,
And now he is hearing
The song of perfection-life.

4894.

He is ready to tolerate
Everything undivine in himself
Except one thing:
His mind's devouring doubts.

4895.

Why are you moving
From one country to another
To find peace?
The sea of peace
Is just inside
Your mind's silence-sky.

4896.

You talk
To prove that you are right.
He talks
To prove that he exists.
I talk
To prove that I belong to God,
Only God.

4897.

I travelled with God.
He loved me
Not because
I am a man of capacity,
But because
I have a heart of enthusiasm.

4898.

Nothing can bind the soul.
And also,
Nothing can prevent the soul
From illumining the lower worlds
At God's choice Hour.

4899.

I begged God to lower the price
Of my God-realisation.
Believe it or not,
He immediately agreed.
What is more, He lowered it
Far beyond my imagination!

4900.

My mind's silver dream
Is to be as great as God.
My heart's golden dream
Is to become an aspiration-flame
Of God's transcendental Sun.

4901.

My Lord,
You have given me
The capacity to cry.
My Lord,
You have given me
The capacity to smile.
Now please give me the capacity
To have purity inside my cry
And beauty inside my smile.

4902.

If you want to be
The possessor of happiness,
Then you have to become
The cheerful renouncer of
    possessions,
If so is the Will of God.

4903.

Your heart of implicit faith
Has the capacity
To increase God's Inspiration-Joy
For a better creation.

4904.

Many times
God has given you the
    opportunity
To prove to the world
That you are His choice
    instrument.
Alas, you are afraid
That you are not going to succeed!

4905.

If you are going
To see God today,
Then please tell Him
That although the world
Does not want me
And does not need me,
It is not allowing me
To go and see Him.

4906.

If you do not have
An inspiration-mind,
You will not be able to appreciate
The beauty of God the creation.
If you do not have
An aspiration-heart,
You will not be able to adore
The Divinity of God the Creator.

4907.

He who wants
To be appreciated by God
Desires a mind of sound.
He who wants
To love God in God's own Way
Desires a heart of silence.

4908.

Search for the source
Of your smile.
You will see that the Source
Is God's own Aspiration-Cry.

4909.

Every human being
Has a special capacity
To create troubles for himself
In season and out of season.

4910.

If you are suspicious
Of your friends,
You will be forced to destroy
Your purity-heart and oneness-
    life.

4911.

If you can make
A spiritual comeback,
You will definitely have a way
To win Forgiveness-Light from
    God.

4912.

His life has given him
An unforgettable experience:
The futility of austerities.

4913.

God the Compassion
Gives us the opportunity.
Man the determination
Has to choose
The right thing to do.

4914.

Each aspiration-second
Is a fast God-approaching day.
Indeed,
This is a supreme experience
In a seeker's life.

4915.

Wherever You go, my Lord
    Supreme,
Do not forget
To give me the capacity
To follow You
Not only cheerfully, but also
    selflessly.

4916.

If you are the Buddha of today,
Why do I not see
Your compassion-eye?
If you are the Christ of today,
Why do I not feel
Your forgiveness-heart?
If you are the Krishna of today,
Why do I not see
Your life's ecstasy-dance?

4917.

Your sincerity
And your determination
Must not only fight with your ego
But also conquer it
Once and for all.

4918.

If you fan the fires of temptation,
There will be no way for you
To receive help
Either from Heaven's
    Compassion-Eye
Or from earth's consolation-heart.

4919.

You have started quickly.
Now you have to run fast,
Very fast.
So that you can reach
Your destination-shore
Sooner than you can possibly
    imagine.

4920.

If you want to walk
Along the road of Immortality,
Then you must not allow
Your immortal life-faults
To accompany you.

4921.

An insincere life
Is bound to experience
The unexpected collapse
Of its aspiration-edifice.

4922.

God has promised you
That He will meet your needs
Alas, He forgot to tell you
That He will meet only your real
    needs.

4923.

He is extremely happy
Because he has become
The marriage of his heart's love
And his life's service.

4924.

Good things are never easy:
To think of God soulfully,
To love God devotedly,
To surrender to God
   unconditionally.

4925.

His indifference
To the world's praise and insults
Has made his heart
A garden of God-Beauty.

4926.

The lion-pride of his vital
Was destroyed
By the thunder-voice of his soul.

4927.

He prayed to God
For God's Compassion-Light.
God's Compassion-Light
Secretly prevented him
From catching the temptation-
   train.

4928.

Every day
God takes your picture
With His Compassion-Camera
And develops it
With His Forgiveness-Light.

4929.

Alas, I did not know
That I had to pay
Such a heavy debt
To my unconscious past.

4930.

Your surrender-acceptance
Of God's Will
Has created a new hope
For the entire world.

4931.

Your gratitude-heart
Is your soul's most valuable
    treasure,
And this treasure can never be
    stolen
By anybody.

4932.

Cultivate your oneness-crop.
God will come to bless you
With His Infinity's Satisfaction-
    Dance.

4933.

If you do not cross
Your mind's hesitation-bridge,
You will never be able to reach
Your heart's illumination-shore.

4934.

His heart was playing
On his soul's golden sweetness-
    flute.
Therefore
His life became
His divinity's heart-shrine.

4935.

If you know
How to love God's creation,
God will teach you
How to live exactly the way He
    lives
In His Satisfaction-Delight.

4936.

Death is running away from your
    life
Because
You have placed your heart-flower
At God's Compassion-Feet.

4937.

I cannot blame God
If He refuses to see me,
Since I am persistently and
    endlessly
Studying ignorance-courses.

4938.

Each moonrise inspires me
To become beautiful.
Each sunrise creates in me
A beautiful perfection-promise.

4939.

I want to live forever
Where I am living now:
On the summit
Of my hope-mountain.

4940.

Faith
Is your life-preserver.
Surrender
Is your life-fulfiller.

4941.

When he lives
In his heart's faith-room,
He lives everywhere.
When he lives
In his mind's doubt-room,
He lives nowhere.

4942.

His clever nature has taught him
How to be consciously oblivious
Of his disobedience-life.

4943.

Definitely
God is your Aspiration-Friend
And not
Your destruction-friend.

4944.

I do not have to go anywhere else
To see you fall.
Your impurity-eyes have already announced
Your life's deplorable fall.

4945.

God's Heart-Room
Is vaster than the vastest,
Yet He does not allow any doubt
To live inside His Heart.

4946.

Who will be your mentor?
He who has the capacity
And is the capacity
To convince you
That your heart's beauty
Will become tomorrow
Your life's divinity.

4947.

Every day make friends with hope
If you want to fulfil
All your God-promises
Here on earth
Before Heaven invites you.

4948.

A mind of uncertainty
Damages the seeker's
Heart-purity-plant.

4949.

What were you doing
With your aspiration-life
When God came to you
To grant you His Satisfaction-
 Smile?

4950.

It seems humanity's
Perfect satisfaction-temple
Will always remain
Under construction.

4951.

His heart-fort
Was destroyed
By his own
Giant impurity-mind.

4952.

No flattery,
However delightful,
Can charm a true seeker
Of the Infinite Light
Even for a fleeting second,
For he has already escaped
The snare of temptation.

4953.

I was born
In God's immortal Dream-Boat,
And God is now steering His Boat
Cheerfully and proudly
To His immortal Reality-Shore.

4954.

O world, do not bind me,
Do not blind me!
Just let me return
To my heart's aspiration-home.

4955.

Unless you break
Your mind's indifference-shell,
You will not be able to spell
Your life's satisfaction-smile.

4956.

If you do not allow it,
No human being will be able
To close the iron gate
On your life's freedom-light.

4957.

If you avoid a collision
With your aggressive past,
You will easily be able to have
A progressive present
And also a progressive future.

4958.

Your frustration-blanket
Is supposed to be discarded,
Not used to cover
Your entire body, vital and mind.

4959.

God has not given you
Your depression-life.
Why, then, do you ask Him to
   carry
Your self-made depression-life?

4960.

My heart,
I am extremely sorry to see
That you are suffering
From my mind's voracious
   impurity-tiger.

4961.

Enthusiasm
Rules his inner world.
Determination
Rules his outer world.
Therefore
Happiness has become
His real name.

4962.

Love arrived at God's Gate
Not only on time,
But also before everybody else.
Hatred came only to miss
   everything,
Long after God had gone back
Into His Heart-Room.

4963.

Feed your possibilities
With your sleepless heart.
You will definitely win
In the battlefield of life.

4964.

Unless you shield your mind
With your purity-breath,
Your life will die
Long before it reaches its
   destination.

4965.

Your heart may not dare
To display its force
Against your mind,
But it can and it must,
If you want to see your soul
Happy.

4966.

I am happy
Not because
I have seen the Face of God,
Not because
I have felt the Heart of God,
But because
God is happy with His creation-
   child.

4967.

Simplicity saves my mind.
Sincerity illumines my heart.
Purity liberates my life.
Divinity immortalises my world.

4968.

To me
A life of expectation
Is nothing short of
A satisfaction-devouring
   experience.

4969.

Because you are
A sincere inspector
Of your life,
Your experience-path
Is not winding.

4970.

If you are marching
With ignorance-night,
You will never be able to value
The power of your life's self-
   control.

4971.

Because he hides
His division-impurity-life
Not only from others
But also from himself,
He does not know
What the heart's oneness-delight
   is.

4972.

Can you not see
That your aspiration-lamp
Has no flame in it?
Are you so blind?

4973.

One dynamic and profound action
Can easily nullify
All negative and evil theories.

4974.

Your heart is now in silence.
That means
Your life is soon going to be happy.

4975.

You have tamed your angry vital-tiger
With your heart's God-hunger.
You have done
A supremely beautiful thing.

4976.

Under your sentinel-eyes,
How do you allow your vital
To destroy
Your soul's beauty-garden?

4977.

Before you dare to sit
On the top of truth-mountain,
You must sit
At the foot of God's Love-Tree.

4978.

Leave nothing for tomorrow.
If today God does not
Come to you,
How can or why should God
Come to you tomorrow?

4979.

God does not believe
In any secrets,
Either in His Life
Or in His creation's life,
For each secret
Destroys the spontaneous blossom
Of vision's reality.

4980.

I sowed the seed
Of my life's perfection-plant
Inside my Lord's Heart.
My Lord has sowed the seed
Of His Satisfaction-Tree
Inside my aspiration-heart.

4981.

Sound and silence
Never care for each other.
Therefore, they do not know why
They are asked by God
To live together.

4982.

His life is lost
Between two opposing armies:
His mind's "No"
And his heart's "Yes".

4983.

It is you who have to choose
Between your heart's
Aspiration-fire
And your life's
Frustration-ash.

4984.

God Himself
Wants to orchestrate your life's
    symphony,
But you want to take the glory
Of orchestrating your life's
    symphony.
Therefore
Do not blame God
For your deplorable performance.

4985.

You simply cannot imagine
How proud God is of you
For your faith-sword
And surrender-shield.

4986.

Every day God loves to predict
Your progress-smile.
But you have sealed
Your ignorance-ears.
Therefore, you do not hear
God's Predictions.

4987.

If your life is sheltered
In God's Compassion-Grove,
Nobody will be able
To challenge you
Or capture your heart's
Aspiration-breath.

4988.

Take the oneness-initiative
If you want to offer to the world
Your heart's fulness-embrace.

4989.

I no more see the trouble-bridge
On my life's turbulent river,
For God has built a bridge
With His Compassion-Light.

4990.

If you have
An uncluttered mind-room,
Then your life will never see
The face of doom.

4991.

How long
Will you foolishly stay
With your mind,
The joy-killer?
From now on
Stay with your heart,
The builder!

4992.

Where is the difference
Between the joy-giver and the enjoyer?
No difference, none!
My heart is the indisputable witness.

4993.

Temptation's cleverly close companion
Is frustration.
Frustration's cleverly close companion
Is destruction.

4994.

Life
Can be made stronger
Than death
If man learns
Carefully and unmistakably
The language of love.

4995.

Why do you have to think
Of living tomorrow
Satisfactorily?
Have you lived today
Properly?

4996.

To be absolutely perfect,
Gather your soul's dreams
Before your life asks you
To take part in God's
Perfection-blossoming Scheme.

4997.

Claiming,
And not begging,
Is the language of God-
 Satisfaction
On earth.

4998.

If you bow daily
To your heart's purity-altar,
Then your life will be flooded
With God's Vision-Stars.

4999.

Heaven is not really far away from
 you.
But every day
Your desire-life is forcing you
To stay farther and farther away
From Heaven.

5000.

True,
I do not know
How great God is
And how good God is,
But I do know
That He will bless me
With His Greatness-Height
And He will embrace me
With His Goodness-Depth.

5001.

Like your heart,
You can be happy
Only when you ask God
How things can be done
In God's own Way.

5002.

Do not forget
That God does not cherish
Your inferiority feelings,
Just as He does not cherish
The superiority feelings of others.

5003.

One tiny insignificant word,
Doubt,
Has the capacity to ruin
The poise of the entire world.

5004.

Our oldest friend,
Love,
Tells us and shows us
That it can be our eternal friend.

5005.

If you give to mankind
Your life's gifts
With a careless hand,
Mankind is not going to appreciate
Your gifts
And is not going to derive
Any benefit from them.

5006.

If you really have concern
For someone,
You can never hide
The stupendous power
Of your concern.

5007.

Remember your promise to God:
You will break all the resistance
Of your doubtful and harmful mind.

5008.

The person with the ultimate power
Knows that without love
His life is dry and dust-filled.

5009.

Disappointment does not touch him,
For every day
God grants his heart
A new appointment.

5010.

Be careful of the past!
It has the power
To powerfully control
Not only the present
But also the entire future.

5011.

His mind's impurity-thoughts
And his heart's purity-will
Are in perpetual conflict.

5012.

Can I really live without
God's constant Compassion
And Forgiveness?
This question requires
My immediate answer.

5013.

A strange invitation has arrived
From the world unknown.
A sinner and a saint are invited
Together,
And they will be served together.

5014.

The immensity of self-offering
Is the perfection-beauty
Of a divine being.

5015.

If you want to satisfy
Any wish of yours,
Then keep in mind
Your ancient promise:
God-manifestation will be
Your life-breath.

5016.

A brave soldier always knows
That to achieve something great
And to become something good,
Now
Is always the best time.

5017.

When I enter into the vital world,
I hear nothing but bad news.
When I enter into the mental
    world,
I hear nothing but sad news.
When I enter into the psychic
    world,
I get the happiest news:
My Beloved Lord Supreme is all
    ready
To play with me.

5018.

If you think of God,
Pray to God
And love God soulfully,
Then you are bound to become
A possessor of marvellous secrets
And fantastic stories
From the other world.

5019.

There is only one disaster ahead:
Your total failure
Due to your
Wilful unwillingness.

5020.

You have anchored your heart
In the infinite Love of God.
Therefore
You do not have to worry
About anything
In the world of dreams
Or in the world of realities.

5021.

If you are a money-minded seeker,
Then you will not be blessed
With God's Satisfaction-Smile,
Even in your dreams.

5022.

A life of temptation
Compels you to stumble.
When you stumble,
Your vital is displayed to the outer
   world
With your unconscious
   frustration-frown.

5023.

Try hard to obey the unknown.
Otherwise, the Unknowable
Will be extremely strict
With your life.

5024.

God wants you to be
A liberated soul.
But it seems that
You do not want anything more
Than to become a frustrated
   seeker.

5025.

You are proud of your
Confessed insecurities.
But I shall be proud of you
Only if you invite your soul
To be your God-security.

5026.

Your doubting mind is laughing
At imminent disasters.
Alas, your mind does not realise
That it has already reached
The highest height of stupidity.

5027.

Do you know
What God has taught him?
God has taught him
Secretly, sacredly,
   compassionately
And unmistakably
How to forgive
His own unforgivable life.

5028.

O my proud mind,
May death invite you
To its deathless party!

5029.

The moonrise heralds
His heart's purity.
The sunrise heralds
His life's beauty.

5030.

How can your foggy mind
Appreciate
The vision-illumination
Of your soul?

5031.

My unparalleled inheritance
From God:
A gratitude-heart
And a surrender-life.

5032.

God's Smile will be available
Only when your attachment-cries
Are nowhere to be seen.

5033.

My Lord Supreme has to visit
A few places this morning.
Therefore
He has left His Fragrance-Smile
In my heart.

5034.

Who will save the world?
Not a king, not a diplomat—
No, nobody except one person,
And he is
The unconditional God-lover.

5035.

I always admire
Your detachment-heart.
I always dislike
Your indifference-eye.

5036.

When there is no difference
Between you and your heart's
Meditation-sea,
God will grant you
His Peace-Empire.

5037.

He thinks that he is too poor,
And his poverty is not allowing him
To think of God.
You think that you are too rich,
And therefore your riches
Are not allowing you
To think of God.
I think that I am neither poor nor rich.
Therefore God the Compassion
Has given me the capacity
To become man the aspiration.

5038.

Poor God has been suffering
Right from the day
He created this world.
Therefore
We must not make complaints to God
Against any human being
And add to His countless problems.

5039.

My mind wants to be
With the new generation
Of truth-seekers.
My heart longs to be
With the new generation
Of God-lovers.
And I aspire to be
With the new generation
Of world-transformers.

5040.

When bad thoughts come to you,
Grab them and place them
In front of God's Destruction-Eye.
When good thoughts come to you,
Carry them gently and place them
At God's Compassion-Feet.

5041.

In vain
Your mind wants to be admired
By offering to the world
False aspiration-coin.

5042.

If your mind is confined
All the time
To stupid curiosity,
Then it will never
Be able to arrive
At divinity's ecstasy-palace.

5043.

Attachment precedes
Wild frustration.
This is an undeniable
Human experience.

5044.

Do not foresee
A frightening future.
Believe only
In an ever-enlightening present.

5045.

Why have you allowed your life
To be enchained
By your absolutely useless
Idleness-body?

5046.

Each time he meditates soulfully,
He sees a new helicopter-heart
Flying up into Infinity's Delight-
   sky.

5047.

Before temptation touches your
   mind,
Run with your heart
Towards God's Compassion-
   Destination.

5048.

When I met God in the morning,
He immediately gave me
A clear vision
Of His Eternity's Road.

5049.

Pray soulfully,
Pray sleeplessly.
God is bound to hear
Even your faint
And faltering prayer.

5050.

The most difficult thing on earth
For a human being to feel
Is that yesterday's misdeeds
Are the cause of today's suffering.

5051.

The human mind not only has
   suspicion
In abundant measure,
But also is eager to pour
   suspicion-night
Into the human heart.

5052.

My Lord Supreme,
If You do not want to forgive me,
I shall not mind,
But please, please forgive
My daily false prayers.

5053.

I cannot master
Even my own mind.
How can I then expect to govern
The unruly vital of the world?

5054.

My mind was ruined
By cleverness.
My heart was ruined
By helplessness.
My life was ruined
By unwillingness.

5055.

My Compassion-Lord
Has transformed my wisdom-thoughts
Into flaming prayers.

5056.

I am satisfied
Only when my meditation shows me
A flaming rainbow
Descending from the Vision-Eye
Of my Beloved Supreme.

5057.

I can easily open
My heart's new
Love-devotion-surrender-lock.

5058.

When I sing,
I sing with the beauty
Of the moon.
When I dance,
I dance with the divinity
Of the sun.
When I cry,
I cry with the helplessness
Of the world.

5059.

If you think that your mind
Is all preoccupied
And therefore
You cannot think of God,
Then God the Satisfaction
Is not meant for you.

5060.

I ceaselessly admire
Your purity-heart.
I sleeplessly adore
Your divinity-life.
I breathlessly love
Your inner immortality-cry.

5061.

Because you have a new heart,
You will be the possessor
Of new God-experiences.

5062.

The entire world is running —
Running either towards
God the Satisfaction
Or man the frustration.

5063.

My mind is not my worst enemy.
My worst enemy is my mind's
   unwillingness
To become inseparably one
With my purity-heart.

5064.

If you give from your heart,
Then your offering will be
Not only unimaginable
But also indisputable.

5065.

If you have regained faith,
That means
Fear and doubt have lost you
For good.

5066.

You are not your parrot-mind!
You are a strong partner
Of your inventor-soul.

5067.

You do not have to meet God
Halfway.
Just try to walk always
Towards God's Way.

5068.

My Lord Supreme,
Will You not make me the best
At least in one thing?
Will You not make me
The best forgiveness-customer of
   Yours?

5069.

If you are loyal
Only to God's Love,
Then happiness will be
Your only name
Within, without, below, above.

5070.

I must congratulate your mind
Wholeheartedly,
For it has passed far beyond
The vast doubt-territory.

5071.

I have measured my aspiration-
   heart
And my dedication-life
With my Lord's Compassion-
   Ruler.
Therefore, my entire being
Is completely fulfilled and
   satisfied.

5072.

His purity-life
Is lit
By his heart's
Beauty-moon.

5073.

I am not a fool!
I shall never march
In my vital's frustration-parade.

5074.

If you pray soulfully,
You will not be able
To expect the worst.
You can and you will
Only hope for the best.

5075.

God does not want you to crawl
On your hands and knees
To reach Him.
He just wants you to participate
In all His races.

5076.

My Lord tells me
That I need no other companion
Save and except
His Compassion-Smile.

5077.

Whatever his soulful heart
   touches
Immediately becomes
The most beautiful gold
To satisfy his Lord Supreme
In His own Way.

5078.

To believe news about God
From the mind-newspaper
Is to be at once
Deceived and frustrated.

5079.

True, God is not yet bored
With your life.
But you must not do anything
   unaspiring
Deliberately,
For that will bore Him
Immediately.

5080.

You may break all the promises
That you have made to humanity,
But never break even one promise
To God
If you want to unveil
God's Smile on earth
And reveal humanity's cry
In Heaven.

5081.

I do not believe in defeat.
I believe only in victory.
Whose victory?
Definitely not mine, but God's.

5082.

Even God-instruments are no
   exception.
They become useless
Like other instruments
When they rest too long.

5083.

Don't discuss,
Don't think,
Just do!

5084.

Don't dream!
Where is the time to dream?
Just become
What God wants you to become.

5085.

Do not listen to your vital!
It is anxious to tell you
Horrifying God-denying stories.

5086.

Because your heart is pure,
The heart of the world
Has become pure to you.

5087.

Your soulfully patient
Persistence-tears
Are bound to win
God's supreme Smiles.

5088.

What I never need
Is a doleful mind.
What I ever need
Is a soulful heart.

5089.

His meditation-dawn
Has purified the impurity
Of his mind's city.

5090.

How can you lose
In the battlefield of life
If you are already well-acquainted
With the real life in you:
Your heart's aspiration-cry?

5091.

You must be always ready for
   anything.
Who knows,
God may at any moment ask you
To become another God
To share His countless problems.

5092.

Be an artist of the soul.
Then every day
You will be able to paint
A positive picture
Of your desire-freed life.

5093.

Since you do not want
To be misled,
Why do you allow
Your mind to lead you?
Since you want
To be fed,
Why do you not allow
Your loving heart to feed you?

5094.

"I want to be happy,
But I do not know how."
This is humanity's
Regularly unfailing message.

5095.

My Lord, You are telling me
That You have all along
Been here with me.
But how is it
That I cannot recognise You?
Is it really possible
For me to ignore You?

5096.

Since you are well-acquainted
With your higher self,
You will be visited
By God's Satisfaction-Vision-Eye.

5097.

The end of your Heavenly journey
   is near,
If this is what you want.
The beginning of your
Self-transcending earthly journey
Can at any time start
The moment you are ready.

5098.

My Lord Supreme,
Your Forgiveness-Smile
Is the most important thing
That You eternally have for me,
Your weak seeker-son
And Your strong lover-friend.

5099.

You are the most pathetic seeker!
Only God, the most sympathetic
   Listener!
And no human being
Can be of any use to you.

5100.

My Lord Supreme,
My Beloved Absolute,
Please do not allow me to miss
The privilege
Of Your earthly physical Presence.

5101.

If you want to put meditation
Into action,
Then allow God's Love
To grasp every second
Of your life.

5102.

This body is impermanent,
But inside the body
The message of Eternity
And the love of Infinity abide,
And in time
They come to the fore.

5103.

An unconditional obedience
Can never be the mistake
Of human thinking.

5104.

Eternity's cry and Infinity's smile
Shall always triumph
Over every thing
And over every human being.

5105.

The truth that lies
Upward and inward
Can be carried into
The farthest Beyond.

5106.

You can learn much
Even from a beginner-seeker,
Provided purity is your heart
And sincerity is your life.

5107.

If you can have
Obedience, obedience, obedience,
Then you can have
A heart-home of peace.

5108.

My Lord Supreme wants me
To look for Him
In His Face first,
And then He wants me
To look for Him
In every face.

5109.

You do not need many Calls
From God.
Only one Call
Can awaken you, perfect you
And fulfil the divine
Within you.

5110.

He is always looking
For a secret victory,
But God is always looking
For a sacred victory for him.

5111.

If you are intent
On transformation-light,
Then never be out of
God's inner circle of Delight.

5112.

God promises
His Perfection.
Can you not promise
Your aspiration?

5113.

You are always in the habit
Of wishing.
When will you be in the habit
Of willing?

5114.

Unless your heart has
A free access to aspiration,
Your life will not have
A free access to perfection.

5115.

If you prolong the human in you
And delay the divine in you,
How can you succeed and proceed
In your aspiration and dedication-
    life?

5116.

Each aspiring heart
Is a new morning
In God's new World.

5117.

You are imprisoned
By the desire-life
Because
You have proved to be unfaithful
In your thought-life.

5118.

God is eagerly looking forward
To seeing the final funeral
Of your earth-bound desire-life.

5119.

Your life is in wild disorder.
Therefore
God will not grant you
A quiet heart-to-heart talk.

5120.

God is ready to wait and wait
Until I invite Him to sit
On my heart's love-throne.

5121.

To create a new universe,
What you need is
The beauty of prayer
And the majesty of meditation
Every day.

5122.

Unless you put an end
To the miseries
Of your doubting life,
Your mind will never be free
From inclement weather.

5123.

Only an unfamiliar God
Can tell you that God-realisation
Is not meant for you
In this lifetime.

5124.

Yesterday he lived
In his heart's dear hope.
Today he is living
In his mind's solitary sorrow.

5125.

Now that he wants to be
Inundated with his soul's
Wisdom-light,
He sees that his mind
Is nothing but an excessive
Knowledge-burden.

5126.

The failure of the desiring mind
Is the march
Of the soul's certainty.

5127.

Many thanks for the interview,
My Lord Supreme.
"Many thanks for your obedience,
My sweet child."

5128.

If you refuse to try,
That means you are deliberately
    ruining
A lifetime of opportunity.

5129.

If you declare
That you are a defeated life,
Then there can be nothing for you
Either in God's Heart
Or in God's Eye.

5130.

I looked in my heart
Only to discover
An unflinching enemy:
Insecurity.

5131.

If you take
God's Affection and Love
With thankfulness,
Then you will indisputably
    become
Both great and good.

5132.

If you have no eyes
To see God's Grace,
God's Face will always
Be denied to you.

5133.

Time and death can be beaten
By the aspiration-champion
Within you.

5134.

If you are wise,
Then you will always veto
Your mind's absurd resistances.

5135.

Why return to your old home?
Enter into your new home:
The home of sleepless
Service-light.

5136.

Too many souls
Are apt to procrastinate.
Therefore, this world of ours
Will never be able to see
God's Satisfaction-Smile
At God's own God-Hour.

5137.

I love to live
Only at one place,
And that place is
Where love eternally rules.

5138.

You are a man of no dreams.
Therefore
You do not have the authority
To ask God to hurry up.

5139.

If you are expert in diving
From the springboard of faith,
Then you will establish
The victory of your higher self
Over your lower self.

5140.

In your heart-garden
There are many love-plants.
Can you not give away
Some of these plants
To truth-seekers and God-lovers?

5141.

I shall take advice
Even from a failure-life,
But not from a despair-vital.

5142.

What is faith?
Faith is the unmistakable fulfiller
Of human hopes.

5143.

Each soulful prayer of yours
Has the capacity to help you
Soar far above the dust
Of your inner destruction-storm.

5144.

Your indifference to mankind
Will never lead you to God.
On the contrary,
It will take you away
Farther and farther from God.

5145.

Today you have realised
That you, too, need God.
Tomorrow you will realise
That God, too, needs you
To become another God.

5146.

My Lord Supreme,
Do give me the capacity
To look at You at every moment
And not just whenever I would like
To look at You.

5147.

Question-mongers surround us.
Answer-givers are not to be found
Either on earth or in Heaven.

5148.

If you have patience,
Then God's Compassion
Will find for you
Your misplaced excellence.

5149.

Because your inner confidence
Is more distant than
A fading star,
God is unable to give you
His Infinity's Smile.

5150.

O my intellectual mind-chains,
Because of you
I have lost my heart's love
And my life's joy.

5151.

Beyond the mind
And beyond the heart
Are his silver tears.
Beyond life
And beyond death
Is his golden smile.

5152.

O my heart,
Run into God's Vastness infinite.
O my soul,
Soar beyond, far beyond,
The skies of knowledge-light.

5153.

If you have a soul,
Then ask your soul to promise.
If you have a heart,
Then ask your heart to love.
If you have a life,
Then ask your life to become.

5154.

If you really want to become
A perfect disciple,
Then stamp out doubt
And bring in faith.

5155.

If you want to be
God's absolutely perfect
   instrument,
Then pray to God not to indulge
Even your innocent desires.
If you want to become
God's breathless pride,
Then become sleepless obedience.

5156.

At least God can rely on me
For one thing:
I shall not go
To ignorance-prince
To be his choice instrument.

5157.

If you want to unload
All your self-styled burdens,
Then long for wisdom-light today
And cry for satisfaction-delight tomorrow.

5158.

You can never be
An excellent inner player
If you do not participate
In God's Compassion-Tournament.

5159.

O my mind,
Nobody compelled you to suffer
From your jealousy-cancer.
O my heart,
Nobody compelled you to suffer
From your insecurity-thorn.

5160.

Unless you compete
In the realisation-race,
God will not grant you
Your life's transformation-trophy.

5161.

How to melt God's Heart:
Empty your earth-bound mind,
Fill your Heaven-free heart.

5162.

You can enjoy sleeplessly
God's Sweetness-Nectar
If you allow your heart to pray
For your soul-stirring dreams.

5163.

Now that you have destroyed
The shackles of the finite,
You will be able to sail
On the river that flows
Towards Infinity's ocean of Bliss.

5164.

God Himself has given him
The biggest hope.
Therefore
He cries and tries,
Tries and cries,
To be God's perfect instrument.

5165.

Never blame anybody,
For he who blames others
Knows what a slippery slope is.

5166.

Are you hopelessly tone-deaf?
If not,
Why are you not listening
To God's sleepless Compassion-
    Songs?

5167.

God is my constant Playmate.
Therefore
My heart is sailing directly
Towards His Silence-Home.

5168.

Forgiveness begins with God.
Aspiration begins with man.
God's Forgiveness and man's
    aspiration
Are both fortified
By God's supreme Light and
    Delight.

5169.

Every day you have to be
A sky of wisdom-light.
Every day you have to tiptoe
Past teeming, sleeping doubts.

5170.

Do you not see
What you have been doing?
You have been swinging
From branch to branch
On desire's vital-tree.

5171.

You call it disobedience.
I call it a birthless
And deathless
Destruction-experience.

5172.

If your old hopes
Have not satisfied you,
Then strive for new hopes —
Illumining and fulfilling hopes —
Which are taking birth every day
Inside your heart's aspiration-
    garden.

5173.

If you want to see
The hidden treasures of your heart
Then first see the Footprints of
    God
In your heart's purity-snow.

5174.

He who aspires
Soulfully and sleeplessly,
Definitely knows how to organise well
His ascent to Heaven.

5175.

When you breathe a pure prayer
To God,
Eternity's life-transforming cry
And Infinity's life-fulfilling smile
Become yours.

5176.

I said what I meant:
"My Lord is all Compassion."
I meant what I said:
"I shall definitely grow into
A perfect instrument of God."

5177.

O my stupid mind,
Do you know
What you have just said to me?
You have told me
That I have outgrown
My need for God.

5178.

It is a mistake to think
That unconditional obedience
Will always remain unavailable.

5179.

If you are shopping
In God's Store,
Then God's Compassion-Presence
You must try to buy first.

5180.

God may not want you to know
When He is coming.
But He does want you to know
That He definitely is coming.

5181.

Only an explorer of the dream-world
Can remember
God's Compassion-Sea
And return to
God's Satisfaction-Sky.

5182.

You have enjoyed
Centuries of sleep.
Can you not now try to wake
In your soul's Himalayan palace?

5183.

Allow not
Impurity and insecurity-thieves
To enter into you.
Every day use a new padlock
On your heart-door.

5184.

You are trying to flatter God.
You are trying and you will be
    trying
Forever in vain
To do an impossible task.

5185.

There can be no debate
Between God's Compassion-Eye
And man's aspiration-heart.
They sing the same song:
The song of satisfaction.

5186.

Surrendered love
Multiplied by gratitude-life
Equals
God's supreme Satisfaction.

5187.

There is death in his face
Because his heart's love-boat
Has no room for his God-
    manifesting soul.

5188.

Because he plays
God's favourite Game,
Smile within and smile without,
He is able to destroy
The bondage-shackles of the
    finite.

5189.

If I had waited another day,
Who knows?
Perhaps I would have more
Inspiration-mind and aspiration-
    heart
To walk along the road
Of God-realisation.

5190.

Your unfortunate friendship
With ignorance-night
Will never allow you to turn
Your desire-life
Into destruction-death.

5191.

Every day
If you take obedience-exercises,
Your inner life and your outer life
Will become two solid pillars
Of God's Palace.

5192.

When the cosmic gods meditate
In Heaven,
You can join them.
They will definitely be happy
If you do.
Do they have a special time
To meditate on special attributes
   of God?
Yes, they do!
In the small hours of the morning.

5193.

If you are my true friend,
Then prove it
By remaining beside me,
By speaking well of me
And by speaking ceaselessly for
   me.

5194.

Alas,
My faith in God
And my love of God
Have always been feeble.

5195.

Who can escape
The supreme duty of self-giving
In God's cosmic Play?

5196.

Unless your eyes can weep,
Unless your tears can smile,
Your life will remain
Imperfect on earth.

5197.

Return to your self
Before it is too late.
Do not knock at others'
Aspiration-hearts.

5198.

If you always ask
God's Benediction,
Then He will teach you
How to do your inner homework.

5199.

God is not baffled
By man's ignorance-night.
He just wants man
To carry the message
Of the future God.

5200.

My Lord,
Your Compassion-Forgiveness-
    Flood
Is my name.
This name will be
My salvation on earth
And Your Satisfaction in Heaven.

5201.

If your heart
Is one hundred per cent pure,
Then yours will be the life
Of sleeplessly unalloyed ecstasy.

5202.

God's Compassion-Heart
Has given him
A first-class
Sacred sainthood-life.

5203.

O my mind,
When I think of you,
I feel nothing but the torture
Of unhappiness.

5204.

You have done
Absolutely the right thing
By digging
Your self-discovery-tunnel.

5205.

The height
Of your heart-flight
Has liberated you
From your murky mind-muddle.

5206.

Do not play for a long time
With ignorance
Or you will one day be beheaded
By ignorance-guillotine.

5207.

What your mind needs
Is the beauty of liberation
And not the unconsciousness
Of hesitation.

5208.

Although his mind does not know
What is real and what is unreal,
His life's continuous zeal
Is for the real.

5209.

Be careful, be careful!
At any moment
Ignorance-dam can completely
    block
Your heart's life-river.

5210.

Eternity's aspiration-art
Is a work
Of divinity's heart.

5211.

The animal in him was caught
While trespassing
In his heart's love-empire.

5212.

It does not take much time
For God the Listener
To become God the Giver.

5213.

Your past failure-life
Is undoubtedly the prologue
To your future happy life.

5214.

A fantasy-filled life
Cannot go very far.
It can never arrive
At reality's door.

5215.

There was a time
When I enjoyed expectation-joy.
Alas, now I am forced
To take the bitter pills
Of frustration.

5216.

Take the oneness-step
And yours will be the life
Of supreme success.

5217.

Your life's conflicting loyalties
Are hypnotising
Your weak mind.

5218.

If you have
A good heart of love,
Then make it better
By transforming it
Into perfection-delight.

5219.

Because of his surrender-life,
Because of his purity-heart
He has won
The perfection-grand prix.

5220.

Each awakened soul
Has only one mission:
World-family reunion.

5221.

God has no private property.
His Property
Is for the hearts that love Him
And want to grow for Him.

5222.

What you need
At every moment
Is a prayer-cure
For your unaspiring heart.

5223.

Is there any day
When God is not anxious
To hear a "Hello" from you?

5224.

Do you know
What you have become?
You have become
Your life's vanity-tree.

5225.

If you can wholeheartedly fight
For God,
God will appreciate you
Far beyond your imagination.
Then you will not need
Self-flattering imaginations.

5226.

Questions asked by the mind
Can easily be answered by the heart.
Questions asked by the heart
Can rarely be answered by the mind.

5227.

Even he who aspires
Is not exempt from ignorance-tax
All the time.

5228.

He is expecting news
From a new world,
His heart-world.
God is definitely
Going to supply him
With new News.

5229.

His only aim in life
Is to join the army
Of Eternity's freedom-thoughts.

5230.

It is you who have to make the
   choice
Whether you are going to live
In your sacred meditation-temple
Or inside your mind's confusion-
   prison.

5231.

Yesterday
I heard God
Walking in my heart-garden.
Today
I am seeing God
Walking in my heart-garden.
Tomorrow
God and I together
Will walk in my heart-garden.

5232.

You simply cannot imagine
How deeply I admire
Your silver faith
In your sun-bright future.

5233.

When will the world offer itself
To God?
The world will offer itself to God
Only when it realises
That it has nothing and is nothing
To be proud of.

5234.

Do you know why God is dancing?
God is dancing because
Your life's stupendous pretence-
   bubble
Has completely burst!

5235.

God's Perfection-Dream
Is definitely
Your heart's Heavenly heritage.

5236.

If you do not withdraw
The venom-shaft
Of your vital-impurity-arrow,
You will suffer
The most painful experience in life.

5237.

My concentration is always crushed
When my vital and my mind
Start enjoying
Useless marathon conversations.

5238.

Disappointment is tearing
At your heart
Because your life wants to embark
On a disobedience-career.

5239.

Aspiration
Is the absolute beginning
Of permanent
Emancipation.

5240.

A child's truth-filled eyes
I saw in him
Right from the day I became
His ardent admirer.

5241.

My aspiration-heart tells me
Only one thing:
God's Tears are more real
Than God Himself.

5242.

O error-torn humanity,
I have the heart
To sympathise with you.
Alas, what I need is the soul
To liberate you from making errors.

5243.

The final lesson
Of ignorance-life is:
You can live without God.

5244.

If you allow your mind
To be caught
In the currents of desire,
How can your soul
Fulfil its newness-hope
And its fulness-promise?

5245.

During the intellectual period
Of his life,
Not only his mind
But also his heart
Was empty of peace.

5246.

A heart of purity
Always has the capacity
To shine like the snow-white
And blue-gold peaks
Of aspiration-mountain.

5247.

A doubtful mind
Kills the beauty
Of the unknown.
A prayerful heart
Kindles the flames
Of the Unknowable.

5248.

My soul
Simply does not want to hear
That I have become so familiar
With earthly defeats.

5249.

Now I see why
You have so many confusion-
   arrows
Of self-doubt.
You have all along been living
Inside your tangled jungle-mind.

5250.

If you have a God-thirsty heart,
That means
God is all the time dreaming of
   you
In a very special way.

5251.

Because your life has become
A sleepless selflessness,
God will be teaching you
His Infinity's Fulness-Dance.

5252.

Your soulfulness-heart
And God's Illumination-Eye
Before long
Will greet each other.

5253.

Why do you not cut down
The forest of your wild desires,
If you really want to free yourself
From the stark frowns
Of this dark earth?

5254.

Who says
That you cannot conquer time?
Just try to satisfy
God's Compassion-Heart.
Lo, you have conquered
Eternity's immortal Time.

5255.

My heart's candlelight
And my life's hope-flames
Are going to show me the way
As I walk along
Eternity's God-Vision-Road.

5256.

The purity of the heart
Compelled the impurity of the mind
To renounce its plot
Against God-Satisfaction on earth.

5257.

Do you know what you are doing?
You are only enjoying
The fantasy of your pride.
Do you know what you can be?
You can be the hope and promise
Of your heart's Absolute.

5258.

Who am I?
I am my life's
Unfinished God-work.

5259.

His is an infallible animal instinct
To ruthlessly ruin
Others' flower-hearts.

5260.

You are always at war
With yourself.
Therefore, you are always forced
To show a sorrow-bowed head
To both Heaven and earth.

5261.

If you have a sincerity-mind
And a purity-heart,
Then you can never seek gold.
You can only seek God.

5262.

You are not the curse
Of your confusion-mind.
You are the blessing
Of your illumination-soul.

5263.

Can you mind your own business?
When did God ask you
To transform humanity's
   weaknesses?

5264.

All vital demonstrations
Are almost incurable diseases
In the seeker's inner life.

5265.

Mine is the aspiration-heart
That loves only one land:
The land of silence-delight.

5266.

In spite of our weakness-life
We can easily stand before God,
Because God is all Compassion.
But we cannot stand before Truth,
Because Truth is all justice.

5267.

As long as your mind indulges
In mountain-pride,
Your heart will not be able
To grant your mind
The ecstasy of God's Oneness-
   Delight.

5268.

Not an easy task
To remove
The body's heavy lethargy-load.
Not an easy task
To illumine
The mind's dark destruction-
   doubts.

5269.

God has already read
Your heart-poems.
Now either beg or force your mind
To read those precious poems.

5270.

God sleeplessly fights
Only on the heart-battlefield
Of His supremely chosen
Instrument-children
For their permanent victory
Over the abysmal abyss
Of ignorance-night.

5271.

A man of determination
Can easily prove to the world
That he is not a slave
To imperfection-monarch.

5272.

True,
I never spoke with God,
But every day
My heart of love speaks
With His Eye of Compassion
And my mind of impurity speaks
With His Heart of Forgiveness.

5273.

In oneness-love
The life of ego's demonstration-
    dance
Comes to a complete halt.

5274.

How will you recognise Heaven?
You will recognise Heaven
With your unconditional oneness-
    love
For the world.

5275.

My Lord,
Will You give me another chance
To please You?
"My child,
I can give you as many chances
As you not only need
But also want
To please Me in My own Way."

5276.

Who is inside me?
Ah, I see it is my Beloved Supreme.
Who is running ahead of me?
Ah, I see it is my Lord Absolute.

5277.

I want to prove to the world
That although my past was only
   mortal
My present and future
Will be absolutely immortal.

5278.

At the high tide of his earthly
   triumph,
He went to Heaven
With his heart's most soulful cry
To sit at God's Compassion-Feet.

5279.

O my mind,
Why do you blame God?
He has not forced you
To be an endless store
Of useless thoughts.

5280.

Either you have to draw
The picture of your self-
   perfection,
Or everybody else
Will continue taking the picture
Of your mind's deception-life.

5281.

When God turns your heart-tears
Into your life-smiles,
Your heart reaches Heaven's
Pinnacle-height.

5282.

Your purity-born aspiration
Will definitely be able to play
With God's Divinity-smiling Face.

5283.

Mine is a soulful hope-boat.
How can I have you,
O doubt-passenger,
In my boat?

5284.

Be careful
Of your absent-minded prayers.
They can easily cause
Very serious problems for you.

5285.

I have been asleep
All my life,
Yet I want to know
How close I am
To Heaven's gate.

5286.

There can be
No better start in life
Than to surrender your
   expectations
To God's Will.

5287.

At last!
I am so happy to see
Your sunrise-heart
And sunset-mind.

5288.

Simplicity is felicity.
Simplicity is God's Beauty
In its pristine form.

5289.

Am I a fool,
To enter into the desert
Of your desire-life?

5290.

You want to be satisfied
With your life-position,
But God wants you to be satisfied
With your life-disposition.

5291.

Fear is only a thought.
Courage is not only a thought
But also an adventure
To transform the unknown
Into a known reality.

5292.

For a fearless life
God is his
Perfection-vision,
God is his
Satisfaction-reality.

5293.

If your mind is in a collision
With your heart,
Everybody will know
That it is your mind
That wants to enjoy destruction.

5294.

What is failure?
It is something that, in vain,
Loves to be loved
By success.

5295.

Your prayers will transform your heart
And not alter God's Vision-Plan.
Therefore, why do you not continue
To do the right thing
For yourself?

5296.

Yesterday
My heart became
God's Vision-lover.
Today
God has made my heart
His Vision-interpreter.

5297.

Who says God has no desires?
God has desires
And His main Desire is
Humanity's constant progress.

5298.

If you want to live
Under the unclouded sun,
Then you must not allow
Your aspiration-heart
To sleep any longer.

5299.

If you do not have faith
Either in God's Compassion
Or in your own determination,
Then you will definitely become
An experienced loser
In the battlefield of your life.

5300.

My Lord Supreme,
Now that You have given me
The golden waves of Your Love-Sea,
How can I ask You for anything else?
I do not need anything more.

5301.

Every day
I play on a new heart-flute,
And every day
I surrender the melodies
To my Master-Musician,
My Beloved Supreme.

5302.

Doubt,
The captain of my mind-boat,
Has misguided my life
To utter destruction.

5303.

Never extinguish your heart-torch
If you want to see
The breath of illumination
In your mind-room.

5304.

My heart-consultant
Used to advise me
Compassionately,
Yet I made no progress.
Therefore, my heart-consultant
Is using a stronger weapon.
It is advising me
Unconditionally.

5305.

The petals of my heart-rose
I shall turn into
My life's gratitude-tears.

5306.

There is nothing
That cannot be done
Either here on earth
Or there in Heaven
By my soul's patience-sun.

5307.

The songs of my soul-bird
Can never be heard
By the restlessness
Of my mind-thoughts.

5308.

If you want to be
The strongest aspirant,
Then every day
You must go to the inner Doctor
For your heart's sincerity-check-up.

5309.

My love of my soul
Has abolished totally
My mind's sense of superiority.

5310.

Aspiration-flames
Reach realisation-sun.
Realisation-sun
Becomes an intimate friend
Of God's Self-Transcendence.

5311.

Self-doubt
Can be compared to
A ferocious, man-devouring
Tiger.

5312.

I have starved
My desire-thoughts.
Therefore
My aspiration-flames
Are climbing up very fast
And are about to touch
The Lotus-Feet
Of my Beloved Supreme.

5313.

My soulful prayer
Every day and every hour
Comes from the breath of Heaven.

5314.

Try to be
The eye of the cosmic gods,
And you will be found
In the lap of Infinity.

5315.

Do not remember
Your past years
If you want to climb up
A new aspiration-tree
And walk
In a new transcendence-field.

5316.

You have failed
In your aspiration-life
Precisely because
You allowed pride to rule
Your determination-mind.

5317.

A mind of doubt
Is the majestic monarch
Of humanity's life-confusing
   clouds.

5318.

Alas, I was preoccupied
With my mind-doubts.
Therefore
I could not save my heart-child
When it was drowning.

5319.

If your heart does not long for
A fully awakened wisdom-life,
Then you will, without fail, die
In a drowsy ignorance-night.

5320.

Three self-evident truths:
I love God.
God needs me.
God and I will never fail
Each other.

5321.

The moment you know
What God's Will is,
God will grant you
His own Freedom-Trumpet.

5322.

Once you know
That you are your life's silver
    dreams,
God will grant you
His Life's golden Visions.

5323.

Two are the gifts
Of man's sterling faith:
He cannot live
Without God's Satisfaction,
And God cannot live
Without his aspiration.

5324.

If you are ready
To ascend your heart's stairs,
Then do not allow
Your vital-dog to bark at you.

5325.

If you tell me
How you love God,
I will immediately tell you
Who you are.

5326.

My soul asks my heart
Every day
To take some peace-light
From my soul
And give it to my peaceless mind.

5327.

If you really have
A heart-house,
Can you not give
At least one room
Free of charge
To God?

5328.

You may not see
God the Justice,
But you are bound to see
God the Compassion
Walking every day
On every earth-road.

5329.

The doors of eternal Time
Will open only to those
Who possess the wisdom-light
Of ages.

5330.

Every day
Sail your heart-boat,
And every day
You will see that you are reaching
A new soul-destination.

5331.

In his life's
Aspiration-mansion
There is no room
For death.

5332.

If you do not love God,
Then who will?
If you fail to satisfy God,
Then I do not think
Anybody will succeed.

5333.

From mental collapse
To psychic collapse,
Your entire life
Has crumbled to dust!

5334.

There is no difference between
God and His Compassion,
As there is no difference between
My mind and my frustration.

5335.

Only God's Justice
Can speak of God's Forgiveness
With God's Authority.

5336.

His is the mind
That is always tired
Of living.
Again, his is the heart
That is always afraid
Of dying.

5337.

Unless you declare
Your ego's death,
God is not going to declare
The birth of His Satisfaction-Sun.

5338.

You think
That you are imperfect.
But I know
That perfection lives
Next door to your heart.

5339.

True, I do not know
What the world can give me,
But I do know
What the world should give me:
Its heart's oneness-love.

5340.

I always laugh at one thing:
That is,
My mind-philosopher's
Love-song.

5341.

His heart of sympathy
Is feeling sorry
That his unaspiring mind
Is marching towards death
Instead of marching towards
    perfection.

5342.

Although you have come
So late,
The cosmic gods are willing to
    hear
What you have to say.

5343.

When God reveals
His Plans,
Show your immediate eagerness
To manifest Him.

5344.

You are such a fool!
You always tamper with
God's Illumination-Messages.

5345.

Ups and downs
Always belong to
Humanity's perfection-seeking
   life.

5346.

His mind
Is indeed a world
That constantly needs direction
From his aspiration-heart.

5347.

When the mind wants to teach
   you,
You should try to see
That the lesson stops
Where and when the lesson
   begins.

5348.

A God-seeking heart
Will definitely have a life
Freed from all earthly turmoil.

5349.

The speedy retreat
Of discouragement-phantom
Is my most precious achievement
Today.

5350.

Today my mind's purity
And my heart's divinity
Are celebrating their joint victory.

5351.

Alas,
Inside my sealed heart
How can I ever see
The Face of my Compassion-Lord?

5352.

I am admiring
The waning of your destruction-
   night
And I am loving
The waxing of your aspiration-
   day.

5353.

If you have
A hesitation-heart,
Then you will be found
Someday
In the insecurity-mart.

5354.

A soulfully listening heart
My mind
Is constantly looking for.

5355.

In the morning
Every day
He writes "Welcome!"
On his life's purity-heart.

5356.

No more, no more I need
A paralysis-life.
I need a life
Of quick accomplishment.

5357.

Is there anybody
Who does not know the trickeries
Of wild attachment-life?

5358.

You may not remember,
But it was you who invoked God
To put you inside
The temptation-prison.

5359.

If you are firmly established
In your heart,
You will definitely be able
To plumb the depths
Of God's Heart.

5360.

The mind is not bad.
Just make it pure.
You will be able to enjoy
The purity-fragrance of truth.

5361.

This world of ours
Is wild and miserable.
Let us take shelter
In the arms of our soulful prayers.

5362.

Ignore your mind.
If you can do it,
Nobody will be able to force you
To abstain from Immortality's
    Delight.

5363.

Where life is pure,
Inspiration and aspiration
Are also pure.

5364.

My Lord, what shall I do
With the heart that You have
    given me
If You do not give me
Daily hopes to accompany it?

5365.

Every day
He and his life-transporting
Heart-cry
Get special invitations
From God.

5366.

Your hatred-weapon
Will wound you
Even before you have aimed it
At the target.

5367.

What is depression?
A strong undivine power
That destroys
The very breath of joy.

5368.

When you fear,
You create a phantom-hour
That cannot be obliterated.

5369.

I shall never invite ignorance
To come and play with me.
Indeed,
This is my sudden and immediate
But unchangeable decision.

5370.

One hour of faith-cultivation a day
Is enough to satisfy
A seeker's Inner Pilot.

5371.

I gaze and gaze
Over my life's pages,
Trying to transform
My dream-beauty
Into my reality-divinity.

5372.

If you allow your faith
To waver,
Then your life will immediately
Start lagging.

5373.

Although my life
Is always noisy,
God does not mind playing
His Silence-Song
Inside me.

5374.

That ancient day
When God created man,
He wanted His blossoming
    Infinity
To be loved
By His embracing Immortality.

5375.

It is not
That you do not know.
You do know
That your mind
Is a mountain of barren mistakes.

5376.

Inside my God-hungry heart
I always keep a sweet, soulful
And beautiful
God-manifestation-dream.

5377.

If you do not know
Which way your life-river should
    flow,
Then I ask you
To follow your heart's aspiration-
    boat.

5378.

Human love is not meant
For sweetness-smile.
Divine love is not meant
For bitterness-cry.

5379.

My mind,
Do you remember God?
He remembers you.
He said to me
That you will be happy
If you can remember Him
Occasionally.

5380.

Indeed,
You have done many things.
But you are not doing
The most important thing:
You are not leading a life
Worthy of God's Appreciation.

5381.

I really do not know
What has become of my
    satisfaction.
It is so distant
And so reluctant to visit me.

5382.

There shall come a time
When even the unconscious mind
And the subconscious vital
Will long for transformation-
    light.

5383.

His soul is extremely sad
Because his heart has become
A deserted shrine.

5384.

The seer-poet
Not only remains unappreciated,
But also is misunderstood
By the modern intellectual world.

5385.

If you want to eat
Supernatural food,
Then you must have
An unbreakable connection
With your aspiration's inner
    source.

5386.

Do you know
What the inner world does
Every morning?
It laughs and laughs
At your stupidity-mind.

5387.

It was once so easy to love you
Because you prayed and
    meditated
From sunrise to sunset.

5388.

I foolishly thought
That God would compassionately
Allow me
Not to give up my desire-life,
Since now I am doing well
In my aspiration-life.

5389.

Everything is possible
In the strong arms
Of soulful prayers.

5390.

Again I observe
My life's spiritual awakening.
Therefore, I am looking
For my heart's secret and sacred
    altar.

5391.

I really do not know
Why my mind
Spends so much time
In the company of doubt-fools.

5392.

I prayed to God
For a hiding place.
God has given me
A rising sun instead.

5393.

God always has
Time for you.
It is you who never want
To listen to Him.

5394.

I came to Your Lotus Feet,
My Lord,
With a helpless hope-heart
To be forgiven.

5395.

What gives life its value,
If not its inner cry
For self-transcendence?

5396.

As soon as you become
Your heart-life's cry,
God becomes
His Heart's Satisfaction-Smile.

5397.

If you follow the God-Road
To the end,
You will not only see God
But also become another God.

5398.

His mind of transformation
Has now become
The beauty of God's Satisfaction.

5399.

You are so callous and ungrateful!
Have you ever inquired
If God requires anything
From you?

5400.

If you are prepared
To give up everything else,
Then God will make you
The fulfilment of His Dream:
A perfection-God-child.

5401.

Peace
Is man's special oneness
With the Immortality
Of God's Love.

5402.

God always needs
The purity of our hearts
To run the world.

5403.

I am so proud of you
For having finally said good-bye
To your wild impurity-past.

5404.

You have no idea
How God cherishes
Your heart's
Snow-white hospitality.

5405.

He who serves the world
Undoubtedly manages
The vast world.

5406.

God I claim.
Therefore, my freedom-life
I proclaim.

5407.

Every morning
My heart weaves
A gratitude-garland
For my Beloved Supreme.

5408.

How will you succeed
In the battlefield of your life
If you do not subordinate
Your inordinate pride?

5409.

Please inform God
That your heart
Will never be indifferent
To God's beautiful creation.

5410.

God does not want you
To declare the independence
Of your mind's life.

5411.

When are you going
To see the world
From God's point of view?

5412.

Your faith is faltering.
Therefore
God is disappearing.

5413.

Peace-disturbers
Are frightening barkers
Without being dogs.

5414.

Your gratitude-heart
Is a great tribute
To God's Perfection-Promise.

5415.

True, you have not
Seen your soul,
But you have definitely Felt
your heart.
Now listen to your heart!

5416.

You need a soulful heart
To read
God's beautiful Handwriting.

5417.

Each blunder
Has the tremendous capacity
To tear man's heart
Asunder.

5418.

He knows nothing
About his optimistic heart.
He only knows
About his pessimistic mind.

5419.

If you nourish
Your inner purity,
Your outer divinity
Will flourish.

5420.

As long as my Beloved Supreme
Knows what I am going to be,
I do not have to worry.

5421.

There must be
A stronger power
Than my ceaseless stupidity.

5422.

His matchless goal
Is to set
A new aspiration-record
Every day.

5423.

Every morning
My Beloved Supreme
Breathes the prayer-perfume
Of my heart.

5424.

One sweet purity-breath
Means the most beautiful rose
In your heart-garden
Is definitely blossoming.

5425.

The loneliness
Of a desire-bound life
Is more dangerous
Than a naked knife.

5426.

The mind wants to become
A bold rival of God's Head.
The heart longs to become
A perfect instrument of God's
   Feet.

5427.

How can your life be satisfied
With small realities
If your heart has big dreams?

5428.

At last he has recognised
That he has had enough
Of desire-meal.

5429.

The heart's obedience
Paves the way
For the life's perfection.

5430.

There is only one thing faithful
In your life
And that is your doubt-dog.

5431.

Alas,
I do not know
When ignorance will become
   boring
To my mind.

5432.

When the mind starts listening
To God,
The loving heart starts dancing
For God.

5433.

I call it my obedience,
But God calls it
His Pride in me.

5434.

A God-lover is he
Who always feels
That the best is yet to come.

5435.

My open-heart policy:
Peace
At any price.

5436.

A genuine aspiration-heart
Can never miss
The heaven-bound express.

5437.

Purity is for those
Who desperately need
God the Beauty.

5438.

Implore the world-Lord
Today
If you want to explore His world
Tomorrow.

5439.

If you provoke
God the man,
How can you invoke
Man the God?

5440.

Because you fear loneliness,
God's Oneness-Loveliness
Always remains a far cry.

5441.

You do not need anybody else
To repair your broken heart.
That is God's job,
And He will gladly do it for you.

5442.

If you hesitate
To run forward,
You will be lost
In the tunnel of the past.

5443.

My Beloved Supreme
Still thinks
That my life needs a leash.

5444.

There is always
A reserved seat for him
In God's Satisfaction-Heart.

5445.

I am ready to introduce you
To God's Compassion-Eye
But not to His Satisfaction-Heart.

5446.

God is ready,
But your mind
Is still taking time
To be ready.

5447.

To clean up your mind,
Warm up your heart first,
For that is the correct way.

5448.

There is no such thing
As inevitability.
Therefore, I must always fight
To establish the divine within me.

5449.

If you want to extinguish
Your desire-life,
God will give you chance after
   chance
To achieve victory.

5450.

How much proof
Do you really want
That God does care for you
Unconditionally?

5451.

God is ready
To sponsor you.
Are you ready
To fight against ignorance-night?

5452.

A faith-plant
Has the capacity to challenge
A doubt-tree.

5453.

If you keep your mind
God-oriented,
Your life will not be frightened
By what it has done previously.

5454.

Every act of a God-lover
Reminds him
That God alone
Is the sleepless Performer.

5455.

Close your eyes
Not to imagine, but to feel,
That God's Compassion-Eye
Is playing
Inside your heart-garden.

5456.

Only a sincere seeker
Knows that God's Heart
Is in his heart,
And nowhere else.

5457.

He has stretched his empty hands
Towards Heaven.
Therefore, God's Pride in him
Has immensely increased.

5458.

Since you have stopped praying
For the wrong things,
The right things are automatically
Within your easy reach.

5459.

Soulful poise
Means a powerful life
Energised by the heart.

5460.

A genuine seeker
Will always have the capacity
To build a meditation-bridge
To Heaven.

5461.

Each human being
Is temporarily, not permanently,
Attached to this temptation-world.

5462.

You have to rely
On God's Promise first
Before you rely
On your life of hope.

5463.

A Smile from God today
Will illumine
Your tomorrow's doubt-life.

5464.

God the Compassion
Is so powerful.
Therefore
God the Justice
Cannot approach me.

5465.

Every day
Prepare yourself to fight
Against ignorance-night.
Otherwise
Your life will be
An agonising frustration.

5466.

The shortcomings
Of the attachment-life
Are no match for the perfection
Of a detachment-heart.

5467.

God loves you
To such an extent
That He even ignores
Your mind's widespread
   suspicion-night.

5468.

His prayerful life
Is the beauty
Of his heart's enlightenment-
   smile.

5469.

A heart-ache
Can definitely be cured
By the soul-medicine.

5470.

Rumours
Are quite often reluctant
To deliver good news.

5471.

If you can live
In the nest of your soul-bird,
You are bound to hear
God's Clarion Call.

5472.

If your heart has
Perfect poise,
Then your life will have
Crowning confidence.

5473.

Earth was laughing below,
Heaven was laughing above
When he declared
That he could do without God.

5474.

A life of doubt
Is nothing but
The doctrine of discouragement.

5475.

God's whispered Benediction
Has helped him reach
The pavilion of Heaven.

5476.

Believe me,
Once upon a time
I, too, was a weak seeker
Like you,
If not worse.

5477.

If you deliberately live
In the jungle of the mind's
   despair,
God is not going to hire you
To take care of His Heart-Garden.

5478.

He never thought
That God
Could ever be so important
In his life.

5479.

My Lord Supreme,
Will there ever be a time
When I shall be able
To make You proud of me?

5480.

An unguarded moment
Is the beginning
Of life's unmistakable death.

5481.

When the mind stops talking,
The heart starts dreaming
And life starts blossoming.

5482.

A heart-champion
Cheerfully meets
The teeming challenges
Of the desire-life.

5483.

Each soulful thought
Is a direct representative
Of your perfect illumination-soul.

5484.

To see the Compassion-Eye
Of God,
What you need
Is an open heart-window.

5485.

Even my soul admires
Your great long jump
From your mind
To your heart.

5486.

The key
To a sky-meditation
Is to become
A sea-aspiration.

5487.

My inner surrender gives me
Instant relief.
My outer smile gives me
Immediate belief.

5488.

I cannot afford to have
One thing in my life:
The sleep of lethargy.

5489.

He himself does not know
Why he always so willingly
    surrenders
To his lower vital attacks.

5490.

God does not want your aspiring
    heart
To be ruined.
So since you have made your
    doubting mind
Your best friend,
God has kept your aspiring heart
Inside His own.

5491.

You fool!
You want to rely on yourself,
Refusing God's Satisfaction-
    Hunger
In you.

5492.

Becoming a perfect instrument
Of God
Is so difficult
Because giving up
Is so easy.

5493.

Now that you have regained
Your old dependence on God,
You are bound to become
Once more happy.

5494.

God does not want
Your life to die.
He wants your heart
To live for Him.

5495.

You have seen so many times
That others have lost
In the battlefield of life
By thinking.
Why, then, do you indulge
In thinking?

5496.

Not the old heart of fear
But the new heart of courage only
Can give God a warm welcome.

5497.

To please God
I claim God the Creator.
To please God
I do not blame God the creation.

5498.

God has already arrived
To attend your mind's
Gorgeous funeral.

5499.

If you have
A sincere aspiration-heart,
You cannot be struck
By desire-lightning.

5500.

You do not have to know
Everything about everybody.
You just have to know
One thing about one person:
God's Love for you
Is unconditional.

5501.

The soulfulness-champion
Always wins
In all the inner races.

5502.

Pray to God to grant you
A failure-proof faith.
He will definitely
Grant you one.

5503.

Are you dancing
With God's Satisfaction
Or man's frustration?

5504.

Meditation
Is a staircase
To your own soul's world.

5505.

No compromise
With ignorance-night
If I need
God's Satisfaction-Delight.

5506.

Any deviation from truth
Means to lose
God's Perfection-Compassion.

5507.

Servers enter
Into God's Eye.
God enters
Into lovers' hearts.

5508.

One day you will realise
The devastating danger
Of your dark desire-life.

5509.

Yesterday I was crawling.
Today I am climbing.
Tomorrow God and I
Will be together dancing.

5510.

If you heed
The inner command,
God will feed
Your Eternity's hunger.

5511.

Impossible to live
With God's Justice,
Impossible to live
Without God's Compassion!

5512.

God has asked him
To bring his mind
Every day
To God's Compassion-Cleaner.

5513.

Imperfection
Is in remaining inactive.
Perfection
Is in moving forward,
Upward and inward.

5514.

He has vehemently denied
His allegiance
To the torture
Of his tyrant-mind.

5515.

My obedience-life
Simplifies and expedites
God's task.

5516.

Meditation
Is the only safeguard
Against frustration.

5517.

Do not allow your mind
To be scorched
By wild fantasy-flames.

5518.

Do not blame God!
Demand more
Of yourself.
Do not blame yourself!
Expect less
Of others.

5519.

To love the divine within you
Consciously
Is to free yourself
From the dire bondage
Of the past.

5520.

Nobody has forced you
To surrender
To your stupid thoughtlessness.

5521.

World-forsakers
Are definitely not
God-lovers.
In their self-styled renunciation
They are completely caught.

5522.

He is succeeding in escaping
From earth's time
And his own fate.

5523.

Man's pride
Is eternally at war
With his heart's love
For God.

5524.

My love of God
Has returned,
This time to win
Without fail.

5525.

An abiding purity-heart
Is a gigantic
Aspiration-achievement.

5526.

I do not care for
A prayer-rope.
I care only for
A meditation-elevator.

5527.

Frustration-flames
He was.
Destruction-fire
He now is.

5528.

If you do not develop
More purity in your heart,
Your spiritual life will be
Intensely frustrating.

5529.

He is possessed
By a self-pity-beggar
Inside him.

5530.

A reasoning mind fails
Because God Himself
Does not care for it.

5531.

If your aim is to reach
A higher plane,
Then low thoughts have no place
In your life.

5532.

My heart
Today wants to pray
Only for one thing:
Mountain-solitude.

5533.

God wants each human being
To be an unlimited supply
Of inner capacity.

5534.

God the Doctor
Will not keep you
For a long time
In His Waiting Room.

5535.

He easily forgets to remember
That once upon a time
He did love God unconditionally.

5536.

Why do you expect me
To believe
That I shall not be able
To realise God
In this life?
Why?

5537.

What you need
Is a faith-tide
To wash away
Your mind's teeming doubts.

5538.

Obedience
Is the perfection of the heart.
Obedience
Is the salvation of life.

5539.

Every day
Breathe new, fresh air
To transform
Your lethargy-surrendered life
Into a surge of dynamism-fire.

5540.

Alas,
For years I have been trying
To break
My mind's complication-chains.

5541.

Every day
My heart teaches my life
A new gratitude-song.

5542.

Your heart's purity
Can easily calm
Your storm-tossed mind.

5543.

What I love most
Is the sky-calm
Of my heart's self-offering.

5544.

Not because I needed,
But because I wanted,
Today I am a prisoner
Of attachment-night.

5545.

Forget all and start again!
Muster the courage
To become a perfect instrument
Of God.

5546.

He fearfully obeys
His self-doubt.
Yet everybody obeys him
Sleeplessly.

5547.

When will I find
God's Heart-Garden?
When?
When will God find
My mind-jungle?
When?

5548.

Although your life is paralysed
By impurity,
God has kept His Compassion-Eye
On your heart.

5549.

His unwillingness
To accept God's Will
Has enslaved his mind
Powerfully.

5550.

Every day
His life commutes
Between earth's helplessness
And Heaven's unwillingness.

5551.

From now on
Try to love God
With your heart's
Purity-flames
And not with your mind's
Impurity-fumes.

5552.

Because he is
A man of peace,
He is a member
Of God's inner Circle.

5553.

Cheerfulness and fearlessness
Have the capacity to equal
Perfection within
And
Satisfaction without.

5554.

Now that he has exhausted
Even his own expectations,
He is totally lost.

5555.

Every morning
God comes
To inspect your heart
And perfect your life.

5556.

Do you not see
That you are completely devoured
By your malicious mind
And your ferocious vital?

5557.

Do you not think
That it is high time for you
To demolish completely
Your mind's doubt-building?

5558.

Unless you awaken
Your dormant faith,
You are not going to feel
God's boundless Love for you.

5559.

Sacrifice yourself
Today
If you want to see perfection
Tomorrow
And if you want to become
    perfection
The day after.

5560.

You will be able to develop
Immediate purity
If you start living
Inside your heart-village.

5561.

Intensity-waves
Carry his mind far,
Very far.
Immensity-waves
Carry his heart far,
Very far.
Infinity-waves
Carry his life far,
Very far.

5562.

If you regularly do
Your inner speed-work,
Then your outer life
Will be most powerfully fruitful.

5563.

The wandering mind
Will never have the capacity
To have a lengthening heart.

5564.

Every day
Try to improve soulfully
The purity
Of your heart's aspiration-cry.

5565.

Because I am
A sincere well-wisher of yours,
I take the trouble
Of perfecting you
Every day.

5566.

In spite of
My desperate unwillingness,
My Lord Supreme has decided
To guide my life.

5567.

Because you are always
On God's side,
God goes to any length
To perfect you.

5568.

God has the capacity
To mend your broken heart,
But do you have
The eagerness and willingness
To come to God?

5569.

If you dare to smile
At God's Justice-Eye,
Then God will give you the
    capacity
To dance in the corridors
Of His eternal Time.

5570.

God is not going to defend
Your unjustifiable case,
Because you are pretending
To be a great seeker
Before innocent seekers.

5571.

If your heart
Is helpless,
Naturally your life
Will be useless.

5572.

What your heart needs
Every morning
Is a fragrant prayer-flower.

5573.

His mind is nothing
But a long list
Of limitations and imperfections.

5574.

At long last
His doubtful mind
Is forced to accept
Slow death.

5575.

Although ignorance-salesman
Every day knocks
At your heart-door,
Never open the door!

5576.

At the end of your mind's
Ignorance-tunnel,
God's Illumination-Chariot
Is waiting for you.

5577.

You are getting younger
And more beautiful,
Not because
You are praying and meditating
Every day,
But because
You are offering
Your experience-results
Cheerfully
To your Beloved Supreme.

5578.

My Lord,
Either give me the capacity
To please You in Your own Way,
Or give me the capacity
To end my life
Here and now.

5579.

At last, divinity-dreams
Have grown inside your heart.
Therefore
You are able to claim God
As your own, very own.

5580.

My mind's first choice
Is God's Compassion-Eye.
My heart's last choice
Is God's Forgiveness-Heart.

5581.

You have long been dedicated
To your desire-mind.
Can you not start devoting
    yourself
To your aspiration-heart?

5582.

God does not want you to browse
In the curiosity shop
Of this stupid world.

5583.

In the city of ignorance,
Doubt
Is the only currency.

5584.

If you use the torch
Of sincerity,
Your mind will have
A new name:
Clarity.

5585.

He does not have
The inner capacity
To build.
He does not have
The outer capacity
To explore.

5586.

Heaven gave him
Chance after chance
To illumine his earth-bound
   mind.
Yet, no iota of success
Do I notice in him.

5587.

To take refuge
Inside your doubting mind
Is nothing short of absurdity.

5588.

I shall no more waste
Heaven-sent moments.
I shall no more exploit
Earth-blossoming expectations.

5589.

The silence of your mouth
I like.
The silence of your mind
I simply adore.

5590.

God tells me that
I do not have to understand why
He and I love each other
Breathlessly.

5591.

He is spiritually
Paralysed
Because he has given up.

5592.

My Beloved Supreme,
I have failed time and again.
But I assure You,
This time I shall not
Fail You.

5593.

My soul needs
Only one thing
From God:
God-Satisfaction
In God's own Way.

5594.

You love God,
Yet you do not want
To come out of ignorance-tunnel.
How can I believe it!

5595.

Tell your insecurity to leave,
For it has already stayed
Inside your God-protected
Security-palace
Far longer than you expected.

5596.

Your life's speedometer
Is not doing anything special,
Except running very fast.

5597.

If you want to fix
This broken world,
Then sing the song
Of oneness-heart
And oneness-life
Soulfully and sleeplessly.

5598.

The most unnecessary fear
In God's entire creation is:
"I do not have the capacity
To please God in God's own Way."

5599.

You have to live
Either in your puny mind
Or in your giant heart.
Make your wise choice!

5600.

Exhale the dust
Of the past.
Inhale the fragrance
Of the future.

5601.

In my life of surrender,
Each step of my inner running
And each step of my outer
    running
I am offering, offering, offering
To my Lord Supreme.

5602.

When the physical consciousness
Is radiating the soul's light,
The vital and mind may become
   jealous.
But ultimately they will
   surrender,
And also turn to the soul.

5603.

Seeing the heart
Flooded with the soul's light,
The mind cursed itself:
"Oh, why am I so stupid!
Why do I not visit my soul
Every day?"

5604.

In this world we kill ourselves
All for outer success.
But there is another world
Where our happiness
Does not depend on outer results.

5605.

Impossibility is a mere word.
Such being the case,
Impossibility must surrender,
And it does surrender,
To the seeker's completely
   devoted oneness
With the Will of his Beloved
   Supreme.

5606.

Is your heart crying
To inspire others?
Then immediately start
Making tremendous progress
And creating stupendous
   improvement
In your own life.
Others are bound to see
A new radiance on your face
And obey you unconditionally.

5607.

The heart's intensity
Immediately becomes one
With God's Music.
But the dictator-mind
Wants to show off and prove
That it can have the same intensity
In a negative way
By destroying the heart's
Inner peace and delight.

5608.

O seeker,
How can you even think of leaving
The Supreme's Golden Boat
After staying so long
In your heart's only home?

5609.

To be a God-dreamer
What you need
Is a God-lover's heart
And a man-server's life.

5610.

Take a close look at yourself.
Your heart has travelled
Miles and miles
For a blessingful Smile from God.

5611.

Before God grants you
Your liberation,
You will have to pass
His purity-inspection.

5612.

God does not care for
Your millions of thoughts
And your millionaire-mind.
He cares only for
Your beauty's life
And your purity-heart.

5613.

Where are the world's peace-
 leaders?
They are all inside your hearts.
They are begging your minds
To open their doors
And keep them wide open
For God the man and man the God
To sport together.

5614.

What can God's Compassion do?
It can easily end
Your doubt-decade
And help you begin
Your aspiration-era.

5615.

God's omniscient Eye
Will guide you
Provided your aspiration-heart
Is not afraid
Of His omnipotent Hand.

5616.

It is always
Inside your ancient heart
That you can have
An ever-new harvest.

5617.

The outer day
Belongs to his devotion.
Therefore
He is divinely good.
The inner day
Belongs to his surrender.
Therefore
He is supremely perfect.

5618.

To aspire
For God's infinite Compassion-
    Light
Is to learn
The practicality-lesson
In God's inner School.

5619.

How can you ask God
To measure His Height
With an earthly measuring tape?
How can you?
And why should you?

5620.

God does not want to know
His own Height.
He just sings the Song
Of Self-Transcendence.

5621.

Now that you are
Spiritually awake,
You, and nobody else,
Will carry the Banner
Of the Lord Supreme.

5622.

Along with sincerity
Something else is needed
To take you to your goal
Faster than the fastest,
And the name of that something
Is intensity.

5623.

Let at least one member
Of your inner family
Listen all the time to the soul.
Its progress, happiness and
    satisfaction
Will immediately inspire
The other members to follow.

5624.

What an unfortunate seeker!
Not even one member
Of his inner family
Is fully convinced
That the soul is always right —
No, not even his heart!

5625.

My Lord Supreme,
I am aspiring to do something
    good.
Will You approve it, please?
My Lord Supreme,
I am desiring to do something
    bad.
Will You forgive me, please?

5626.

My Supreme Lord,
You are the Origin of everything.
Therefore
Ultimately, nothing can take place
Except through Your Will.
"True, My child, true.
But some things I approve of,
While others I only tolerate."

5627.

Before the race
They are all surrender.
They are praying for God's Victory.
But during the race
And after the race
They are thinking of
Nothing but their own victory!
I do not want you
To be in their company.

5628.

The cosmic gods and goddesses
Do not have to learn songs
By heart.
They just allow their divine
    capacity
Spontaneously to sing.

5629.

In my highest consciousness
No disturbance can breathe.
I can forgive the whole world.
I can even forgive myself,
For there I am
In God's Eternity.

5630.

The undivine may have won
An immediate victory,
But the ultimate Victory
Will always belong to God.

5631.

An inner defeat:
A great seeker has fallen
And lost his progress-chance
For this entire lifetime.
An inner victory:
The same seeker may return
To earth
With renewed aspiration
And more powerfully proceed
To a higher level than before.

5632.

If you can take everything
As God's Blessing,
Rest assured, you will always
    remain
At your highest height.

5633.

O purity, I love you,
For when you come forward
You create
Beauty's oneness
And divinity's fulness.

5634.

How to conquer fear?
With oneness within
And oneness without.
In oneness-light
There can be no fear.

5635.

O purity,
By the very sound of your name
Anything that is attacking me
Is weakened
And my own good qualities
Come to the fore.

5636.

Look around!
You will see so many things
To do for the world.
Dive deep within!
You will not only see
But also at once do
Many things for God.

5637.

In the world of aspiration
There are many roads,
But all the roads
Lead to the same Goal:
God, the Absolute Supreme.

5638.

The music of the heart,
The beauty of the soul
And the Divinity of God
Are inseparable.
This secret and sacred truth
Reveals itself
To the seeker-lovers of music.

5639.

Through each good action
I am carrying myself
Slowly but unmistakably
Towards my eternal Destination:
The Golden Shore of the Beyond.

5640.

Everything has to be done
On the basis of surrender.
Whatever we may do
Without surrender
Will remain utterly meaningless.

5641.

When I surrender my finite
    existence
To the infinite Consciousness,
Then my surrender is perfect,
For my lowest is surrendering
To my highest.

5642.

When I sing,
I know that I am singing
For the Supreme Singer.
When I play music,
I know that I am becoming one
With God the Supreme Musician.

5643.

You have a stubborn mind.
This is what I see.
You have an unborn heart.
This is also what I see.

5644.

When the seeker surrenders,
Then only
He becomes one with the Reality
He has been longing to reach.

5645.

Over the years
He has totally lost
His intense aspiration-flame.
But his own inmost sincerity
Still has the power
Once more to bring to the fore
The soulful inspiration and
    aspiration
That once upon a time
Started his spiritual journey.

5646.

He had an infallible vision:
The cosmic goddesses
Were so deeply moved
By the seekers' soulful singing
That they came and joined
The singers
And most powerfully sang
In and through their human
   voices.

5647.

I assure you,
Unlike the outer world,
The inner world is not asleep.
The inner world only watches and
   waits
For a little receptivity
From the outer world
So that it can pour and pour into it
Its unreserved blessings and love.

5648.

Once upon a time
You used to defeat ignorance-
   prince.
But now you are practising
Your surrender to ignorance.
Do you really think
That this kind of surrender
Is what your Beloved Supreme
Wanted from you?

5649.

Alas,
Where is my true
Aspiration-life?
Alas, alas,
When will I again
Pray and meditate
With my heart's utmost intensity?

5650.

O God-musician!
You are creating
An absolutely new world.
You are adding so much
Divine beauty and supreme
   majesty
To God's worlds of aspiration,
Dedication and manifestation.
Perhaps God only
Appreciates you adequately.

5651.

What else
Is my tremendous achievement,
O my Lord Supreme,
If not the manifestation
Of Your own supremely
   unparalleled
Compassion-Capacity?

5652.

Revive your old spiritual
　grandeur!
Even if your stone-heart
Does not feel it,
Your eyes are bound to see
That others are now lifting the
　burden
That once upon a time
You devotedly carried
For your Lord Supreme.

5653.

To have intensity
Without sincerity
Is like trying to reach
The Highest
By hook or by crook.
Success is just impossible.

5654.

You think that at the last moment
You will win the race.
But I am telling you,
Without tremendous inner
　intensity
How can you be sure
That you will even finish the race?

5655.

When your Master gives you
A private interview,
Remember that you are
Face to face
With God's own personal
　representative.

5656.

In your deep meditation
All is oneness.
Never allow division
Even to start,
Or soon it will take you
To the utter frustration
Of separativity-consciousness.

5657.

An undivine force came to attack.
It stood right in front of him!
But he challenged it
And conquered it
By invoking purity and light
From his Master
And from his own soul.

5658.

Before you go to sleep,
Do not forget to ask
For your Lord's Protection.
If your consciousness is high,
You will not have to worry
About unwanted nightmare-
   friends.

5659.

You are trying to fight with God.
But where is your capacity
And where is God's Capacity?
At the right moment
He will simply change your mind.
His Compassion-Light
Will be your Satisfaction-Delight.

5660.

My Lord,
You have entered into my heart
And made me feel
That we are all brothers and sisters
Of one world-family.
Now do enter into my mind
So it will act like the heart,
And I will not be able
To hurt others.

5661.

I am grateful to you,
My Master-Lord,
For when I cannot hear
My inner voice,
Your outer messages
Carry the voice of my own soul.

5662.

Easily you can hear
The voice of your Master.
Is his voice not inside
His books?
Is his voice not inside
His meditation?

5663.

O my body,
Do not suspect the soul,
Which has glowing faith in you
And infinite patience with you.
O my body,
Once you have full faith
In the soul,
You will no longer need the help
Of the vital, the mind
Or even the heart.
You will have your own free access
To the soul.

5664.

True, there was a time
When the mind and the vital
Were bitter rivals.
But now that their past rivalries
Are buried in oblivion,
Can they not become fellow
   travellers
In the search for God?

5665.

When he bragged about his past,
Some believed it and got
   inspiration
To become truly good.
If the result was nothing but
   truth,
Then who can say it was wrong
For him to tell lies?

5666.

The world is ruled
By human opinion.
Even one opinion
Has the strength
To divide the entire world.

5667.

O lethargy-prone seeker,
Spirituality you are separating
From your body, vital and mind.
But do not forget the Vedic times
When spiritual strength
And physical strength went
   together.
Once again
Spirituality has to be
In the physical and for the
   physical.

5668.

How I wish my heart
To remain always
Under the control of my soul,
So that every day my inspiration
Can soar beyond my belief,
And never will my service-offering
Become mechanical.

5669.

Insincere seekers
Will ask countless questions.
But those who soulfully hunger
For the Master's illumination
In silence only receive and receive.

5670.

To those who work very, very hard
In any field of life,
God will eventually give inner
   experiences —
Unimaginable and undeserved —
To tell them:
"Do not halt!
Do not stop here!
There is something infinitely
   higher,
Far beyond your present life."

5671.

You are working for name and
   fame
With the expectation
That they will make you
Outwardly happy.
He is praying and meditating
Without any expectation,
And he is already receiving
Abundant inner joy.

5672.

His unprecedented adventures
Offer tremendous confidence
To his seeker-brothers and sisters.
Why?
Because his great achievements
Are for his Beloved Supreme
   alone,
And for nobody else.

5673.

Right now we have to start,
Although insincerity is mixed
With our sincerity.
Eventually we will have pure
   sincerity
And ultimately we shall proceed
From illumining light
To more illumining light.
Right now we have to start.

5674.

The child believed
That his thief-father was a saint.
So right from the beginning
The son became good
And remained good,
Leading a saintly life
As he thought his father had.

5675.

Your Master's voice
Is inside your heart,
For your soul and your Master
Are always together.

5676.

I come from the Hindu family,
And perhaps you come from
The Christian family.
Although we live
In two different houses,
We can always come together
To share our ideas and ideals,
For together
We will be of greater service
To aspiring mankind.

5677.

God the Omnipotent
Created this universe.
Will He allow you or me
Or even the most hostile force
To destroy it?
Absurd!

5678.

God the Creator,
With His infinite Vision,
His infinite Light and Delight,
Has created us.
We are part of His universe.
This universe is His
Dream-Reality's Satisfaction-
    Delight.

5679.

How to minimise the strength
Of a hostile force?
Ignore it totally!
Feel that it is only a monkey
That is pinching and biting you.
Immediately you will be able
To reduce its strength
    considerably.

5680.

You say that the hostile forces
Have caused an atomic explosion
In the inner world.
But I say it was only a needle
That dropped to the ground.
I tell you, those undivine forces
Stand helpless before the
    Supreme in me.

5681.

When I pray and meditate,
When I soulfully sing
And even when I devotedly run,
I am following promise-roads
Taking me to my soul's eternal
    Home.

5682.

What else are a seeker's
Personal experiences
If not a solid reality
To help him
In his life of aspiration
And to lead him
To his Eternity's Beloved
  Supreme?

5683.

What you are
Is your heart's unknown capacity.
Someday you will be able
To use this capacity
To uncover your mind
And discover your God.

5684.

My Lord, please tell me,
Have I ever expressed
Real gratitude to You?
"My child, certainly you have!
Just remember the first time
You ever meditated with Me.
That was the first time
Of many."

5685.

When God sends for you,
Why do allow your mind
To carry your body away
Fast, very fast?

5686.

Do not forget
Your final prayer:
God-Satisfaction
And your perfection
Must dine together.

5687.

If you allow your mind
To enjoy endless questions,
Then you will be doomed to live
In a fathomless cave.

5688.

When he saw his previous height
He laughed and laughed,
For when he tried to measure it,
He realised that
It was lower than the lowest.

5689.

God's Concern-Branches
Are for your searching mind.
God's Compassion-Tree
Is for your aspiration-heart.
God's Blessing-Fruit
Is for your surrender-life.

5690.

Begin again and again
If you really want to win
God's Satisfaction-Heart again.

5691.

God's infinite Compassion-Light
Took full responsibility
For the breakdown
Of his useless computer-mind.

5692.

If you cannot carry the message
Of surrender-light
Inside your surrender-heart,
Then God will not grant you
The purity-insurance
Against world-temptation.

5693.

Once you have taken up
The spiritual life,
Do not give up!
If you give up,
The unnourished aspiration-heart
In you
Will be swept away
On a river of tears.

5694.

Study with your heart-tutor.
Your mind's desire-waves
Will not be able to disturb
Your life's powerful poise.

5695.

Your heart's perfection-step
Will, without fail,
Avoid the life-capturing trap.

5696.

God secretly laughs
At His own creation,
But openly and lovingly
He tells us to smile
At His creation.

5697.

When are you going to realise
That your godless life
Has definitely become a helpless raft
In the vast ignorance-sea?

5698.

Because you have become
The world's aspiration-tree,
God will grant you
His Vision's realisation-fruit.

5699.

It is almost an impossible task
For the human mind to arrive
At the self-discipline-harbour
With its cherished bondage-cargo.

5700.

Do not ask when
You will achieve God's Height.
You have already achieved it
On the strength of your oneness
With Him.
Just believe it,
That's all!

5701.

A true God-lover is he
Who every day celebrates
God's Compassion-Victory
In his life.

5702.

God told you
You are an unrevealed God.
You believed Him not.
Therefore
Both you and God
Are suffering.

5703.

Alas, is it my fate
That God-days slip away
While I remain
In ignorance-sleep?

5704.

Your heart brought
A very short-term aspiration
To God.
And now it wants
From God
A very long-term satisfaction!

5705.

When the age of reason ends,
The heart of peace
Will inundate the entire world.

5706.

His heart is trying
To do the impossible:
In one stroke
To transform
The world's long history of hatred
With its oneness-song.

5707.

God is faithful
To your heart.
Ask yourself if you are truthful
In your life.

5708.

Now that you have unchained
Your earthly dreams,
God will give you
His Heavenly Visions to treasure.

5709.

Unless you become
An unobstructed flood of self-offering,
God will forget to remember
Your heart's inner name.

5710.

You live in fear-apartment house.
Therefore, your life has become
Your heart's burning teardrops.

5711.

Alas, God won his heart
For five fleeting seconds,
Only to lose it
For an entire incarnation.

5712.

What you need
Is an ancient eye
And a modern heart
To see and appreciate
God's Beauty.

5713.

After a long time,
Today he has learnt to levitate
From his disproportionately
   heavy
Lethargy-life.

5714.

Unless you become
Your heart's friend,
How can God make you
His friend?

5715.

God came
To take away my fears.
I gave,
And also cleverly added
My ceaseless tears.

5716.

Doubt-earthquakes
Have destroyed your life-tower
Because you have not dug
The surrender-canal
For God's Love-Boat.

5717.

When you have offered
Your service to God,
How is it
That you have sent a bill
For your service?

5718.

In your inner life
It is good to eat
At least one thing:
Hope-bread.

5719.

The world's
Nightmare-complexity
Is a self-perpetuating
Ignorance-show.

5720.

You can easily outsmart
The cynics.
Just show them openly
What you have:
Your satisfaction-heart.

5721.

Earthly satisfaction
In any walk of life
Has always been
A truly transient reward.

5722.

Earth
Is my long imperfection-snare
And Heaven
Is my long-forgotten home.

5723.

If you do not have
The God-nearness-need,
Why should God come to you
To feed your inner heart
Or outer need?

5724.

What is surrender-light
If not giving God
Your earthly all
And Heavenly all?

5725.

Because you were a fool,
You did not evict
Your mind
From your heart-apartment.

5726.

You will always be buffeted
By gusts of insecurity
Because you did not accept
God's blessingful Invitation
To come to His Palace.

5727.

What can you possibly expect
From your mind
Which is already so fat
With indulgence-thoughts?

5728.

Yesterday
It was you who wanted
To keep your life-schedule empty.
Today
It is you again
Who are ready to lie
In your ingratitude-grave.

5729.

My Beloved Supreme,
How can my heart survive
Your powerful displeasure?
Do turn my life into
Your Oneness-Song.

5730.

If you want to work
In an aura of love,
Then invite your soul
Every morning
To enlighten your mind.

5731.

You will be able
To care for God
Only if you every day take
Aspiration-strength-vitamins.

5732.

If you are a genuine God-lover,
Then every day you must celebrate
God's Compassion
In your aspiration-dedication-life.

5733.

Without believing
What God tells you to do,
How can you tell the world
That you know who God is?

5734.

What is meditation
If not Eternity's infinite creation
In man for God?

5735.

You are an alien from Heaven
Not because
You do not pray and meditate
But because
You do not believe
In others' prayer and meditation.

5736.

My Lord Supreme,
My songs create tears
In Your Heart
And Your Songs create smiles
In my life.

5737.

God tells him,
"Please pay more attention
To Me in My children,
And not the other way around."

5738.

Every day he enjoys
A most special meal:
God's Forgiveness-Delight.

5739.

When madness becomes
Your life's only enemy,
Sadness becomes
Your soul's only enemy.

5740.

Never become lost
In your unaspiring past.
Do not become tired of knocking
At your heart's new door.

5741.

I do not want to see myself
As I actually am.
I want to see myself
Exactly the way
My Beloved Supreme sees me.

5742.

How can it be possible
For a mind-seeker
To learn the dance
Of a God-lover?

5743.

Do not cry, do not cry!
God has already given you
His Life's Compassion-Heart.

5744.

You are not tired
Of sleeping
And God is not tired
Of knocking
At your heart's door.

5745.

He who wants to manifest God
At times feels
That Eternity is too short.

5746.

God wants you to be a spectator
In His Cosmic Game,
But for that you must show God
What you have:
Your heart's surrender-smile.

5747.

He tells God,
"God, pay more attention to me."
God tells him,
"My son, show more affection to
   Me."

5748.

You gave up praying and meditating.
Therefore, today you have
An expired aspiration-passport.

5749.

My Lord Supreme,
I shall definitely be able to survive
Your Anger-Eye.
But I shall not be able to survive
Your Sorrow-Heart.

5750.

Countless rivals are there
For God's boundless Affection.
But is there anybody
Who is for God's
Unconditional manifestation?

5751.

You are such a fool!
You want to know
God's estimated time of arrival.
Do you not see
That God has already arrived?

5752.

If ever a deplorable fight takes place
Between earth's helpless cries
And Heaven's indifferent frowns,
I am sure God will help
Earth's helpless cries
To best Heaven's indifferent frowns.

5753.

A true hospital
Gladly welcomes the suffering world.
A true doctor
Immediately heals the suffering world.
A true nurse
Inseparably becomes one with
The suffering world.

5754.

How can God teach you
His God-Dance
If your heart does not feel
The necessity
To bleed for humanity's need?

5755.

I can never separate
Your desire-bound life
From your heart's
Ingratitude-grave.

5756.

Now that you have abandoned
Your obscure thought-world,
God's Sea of Peace will embrace
　you
With the swiftness of a
　thunderbolt.

5757.

Even though you are a prey
To impurity,
Do not forget to sleep
In God's Compassion-Camp
Every night.

5758.

Do not wait for the inner storm
To subside.
It will never subside on its own,
Never!

5759.

Only if you pray
In the small hours of the morning,
Will you be able to see
The morning sun's victory-
　delight.

5760.

God's Love
Has grasped his heart.
God's Compassion
Has grasped his eye.
God's Satisfaction
Has grasped his life.

5761.

He is always looking —
Looking for more sincerity,
More humility
And more dedication
In his life of aspiration.

5762.

What can meditation do?
It can stop the final victory
Of sorrow.

5763.

If you prolong
The animal in your human life,
Then you are bound to delay
The divine in your human life.

5764.

Give what you have
And what you are.
Then you will be blessed
With new mornings
In new worlds.

5765.

Can you not see
That you are imprisoned
By your desire-worlds
For your constant dissatisfaction?

5766.

Only the seekers
Of the infinite Truth
Will be blessed with the birth
Of a universal oneness-life.

5767.

God has always been taking
Good care of my heart.
Now I am trying to take
Good care of the dust
Of His Feet.

5768.

How do you expect to get
From me
My kindly affection
With your artificial aspiration?

5769.

You will always be crippled
By incapacity
Unless divinity
Is your first and foremost choice.

5770.

Yes, God gets angry.
Do you know why?
Because your mind is not hungry
For His Love and Oneness-Life.

5771.

The world's temptation-tricks
Are too swift
For man's eye to catch.

5772.

Your earthly years are not led
By your Heavenly wisdom-sun.
Therefore
How can God give you
A spotless surrender-satisfaction?

5773.

God is more than willing
To pay an exorbitant rent
Provided you give Him sole
   occupancy
Of your purity's heart-room.

5774.

Any self-transcendence-attempt
Will enable the seeker
To go beyond the circle
Of birth and death.

5775.

Each human being
Is swept away by his thought-
   waves.
Therefore, how can God's
Peace-Promise on earth
Be fulfilled?

5776.

He is always ready to feed
Your God-nearness-longing
And to illumine your aspiration-
   heart
And dedication-life.

5777.

How is it possible
That your aspiration-heart
Could not hear
God's courier's courage-call?

5778.

If you become
Your inspiration's dedication-life,
Then your satisfaction-soul
Cannot remain a far cry.

5779.

How can you be happy
Unless you daily
Examine and perfect
Your heart's aspiration-life?

5780.

To withstand ignorance-attack,
I have removed
All my old attachment-furniture
From my mind-room.

5781.

The instigation-boldness
Of your vital
And the hesitation-art
Of your mind
Have paralysed your aspiration-
  heart.

5782.

The latest arrival
At Heaven's gate
Is my life's
Gratitude-heart.

5783.

I can clearly see
That you have grown into
Your mind's clever capacity
To confuse your fellow travellers
In the spiritual life.

5784.

God is examining everyone.
Do not laugh!
You may be next!

5785.

Today I have discovered
Something most special;
Today I have discovered
Something unique:
God loves me infinitely more
Than I can ever love myself.

5786.

He who does not aspire soulfully
May make a serious blunder.
His mind may mistake psychic
  ecstasy
For vital lunacy.

5787.

There is no last chance
And no last hope
For you to see your soul's
Most familiar eye and face.

5788.

When I look at him
I see only one thing:
The same old familiar
Aspiration-heart.
When I look at you
I see only one thing:
The same old barren
Desire-face.

5789.

If you live inside your heart
For your soul,
Then for you to arrive at your goal
Will not be a difficult task.

5790.

He lives in God's
Forgiveness-Sun.
God lives in his
Surrender-sky.

5791.

If sadness
Is your only enemy,
Then why do you not ask
Oneness
To be your only friend?

5792.

If you are already an awakened
　　soul,
Then you must realise
That God has already given you
A supreme task to perform:
He wants you to work
For His Vision's world-blossoms.

5793.

What my heart sleeplessly needs
Is my soul's
Sleepless, tranquil faith
In my Beloved Supreme.

5794.

If you want to be
God's Compassion-Song,
Turn your life into
Your heart's aspiration-cries.

5795.

God does not mind
When you do not believe Him,
But He feels that someday
It will be a difficult task
For Him to console you.

5796.

If you have a vital
Which is a hotbed of desire,
How can you free yourself
From lifelong agony?

5797.

Does your mind ever tell you
That misfortune pursues you
Precisely because
Every day you drink
From desire-cup?

5798.

His is a birthless
And deathless search
For a nation of God-lovers.

5799.

Now that your aspiration-life
Shuns jealousy's ugly face,
You can easily discover
Your soul's delight-island.

5800.

My dedication-life
Needs the swiftness of a deer
To run at top speed.
My aspiration-life
Needs the soulfulness of a child
To run faster than the fastest.

5801.

You may not know,
But it is absolutely true:
With each heartbeat
Your heart is calling: "God, God!"
You may not hear it,
But God Himself definitely hears
Your heart's cry.

5802.

My Lord,
I am as old
As my mind's investigation.
Now, do make me as old
As my heart's aspiration.

5803.

You have weighed God
On your mind's scale.
Therefore
God is too heavy for you,
And it is simply impossible
For your mind to carry God.

5804.

If you are a genuine God-lover,
Then at every moment
Be prepared
For the coming God-Hour.

5805.

I do not need many places
To live in.
I need only one place,
And that place is
My Lord's Compassion-flooded
   Eye.

5806.

The God-Hour has arrived.
Are you ready
With your obedience-power?

5807.

A tiny tear can break
Not only a human heart
But also God's Universal Heart.

5808.

As a tree needs
All its countless branches,
Leaves and flowers,
Even so, the world needs
All its multifarious human
   capacities.
This is why God may give one
   thing
To one child of His,
But to another,
Something entirely different.

5809.

In the hour of danger
Ignorance I shall challenge,
I shall,
And thus re-establish
My soul's confidence-life in me.

5810.

Whenever you hear soulful music,
Become inseparably one with it
And feel that your soul
Is playing that very music
Only for you:
For your heart, for your mind,
For your vital and for your body.

5811.

O my heart,
When you assimilate the inner
   offering
Of spiritual music,
Which is beauty and divinity,
Do not forget to distribute
   everything
To my poor body, vital and mind.

5812.

In silence-light
The soul is playing
Its own divine music
For the total transformation
Of the body, vital, mind and heart.

5813.

Before entering
Into the world of sleep,
Listen to soulful music
Even for a few fleeting moments.
You definitely will be able
To go to the higher worlds
Without meditating.

5814.

Opportunity is the force
That helps us live
With the mountaintop-vision.

5815.

While listening to You sing,
Let me also do something, my
   Lord,
For You.
Let me start loving You more,
Infinitely more.

5816.

You do not have to search
For many things.
Just search for only one thing:
Your missing aspiration-heart.

5817.

What I need is not
A band of faithful souls.
What I need
Is a soulful cry from your heart.

5818.

Alas,
The road that lies
Between my aspiration
And God's Satisfaction
Is unimaginably long.

5819.

Your doubtful mind must halt
Before it can think
Of loving the Unknown.

5820.

I love the seeker in him
Deeply
Because his thirst
Is for the living God.

5821.

You are ignorant
Of peace.
That means
You are ignorant
Of God's Compassion.

5822.

If You are really my Lord,
Then every day
Write down Your Laws
In my aspiration-heart.

5823.

A gratitude-heart
Will unmistakably be invited
To God's Immortality-Feast.

5824.

Even to think of him
Is to have an inner glimpse
Of his unearthly beauty.

5825.

It seems
That your aspiration-life
Will never attain
Maturity's perfection-tree.

5826.

What is the difference
Between your oneness
And God's Fulness?
No difference!

5827.

At long last
He has come to realise
That his life has become
A withering flower
Of his teeming dreams.

5828.

You will not take a long time
To fill your heart
If you just empty your mind first.

5829.

How to melt God's Heart?
Just launder your life
With gratitude-soap.

5830.

What is God's favourite Game?
His favourite Game
Is His Satisfaction-Smile.

5831.

Unless you do your inner work,
Your faithless mind-dog
Will ceaselessly bark at you.

5832.

I run towards God.
My heart dives
Into God's Heart-Sea.
My soul soars
Beyond the boundaries
Of despair-night.

5833.

There is only one thing
That I see again and again
In my life,
And that is my Lord's
Compassion-Forgiveness-Flood.

5834.

If your heart is swimming
In the river of silver tears,
Then God-realisation cannot remain
A far cry.

5835.

Beyond life and death
Is his soul's
God-manifesting smile.

5836.

Misunderstanding-pain
Is not for the true truth-seeker
And God-lover.

5837.

I ask and ask and ask.
No answer
Is the only answer
I get from within.

5838.

God does not like it
When you go to Him
With whirlwinds of unwanted suggestions.

5839.

Each wrong thought
Is a new entrance
To destruction-death.

5840.

Each new Heaven-promise
Is the birth
Of a new God.

5841.

Each desire in itself
Is power.
Therefore, no desire
Is inconsequential.

5842.

If your heart aches
For the inner heights,
Then you will, without fail,
Be divinely perfect.

5843.

My heart has a special longing
For the aspiration-tree
Of silence-dream.

5844.

Expect thunder-admiration
Only from yourself
And from nobody else.

5845.

His heart was in love
With suffering.
Therefore
Even God's Compassion
Could not illumine him.

5846.

To love
Is to give soulfully.
To give
Is to become unmistakably.
To become
Is to please God in His own Way.

5847.

I am always grateful to my heart,
For it has given to God
All its glorious possessions —
Love, service and surrender —
So that God will readily accept
My body, vital and mind.

5848.

A seeker must know
That his faith
Is the treasure of treasures
That he must not lose.

5849.

A soul of silence-light
Is indeed
Sovereign on earth.

5850.

My heart's divine duty
Is to obey.
My life's supreme duty
Is to surrender.

5851.

Practise
The enlightenment-principle
And not
The excitement-principle.

5852.

Alas,
Why do I always think
That the world
Owes me something?
Why am I such a fool?

5853.

To reach your own mountain-top,
Quicken your heart's
Silver faith.

5854.

If you are a genuine seeker
Of the infinite Truth,
Then do not ask God to indulge
Even your so-called
Snow-white innocent desires.

5855.

My heart's love-boat
Has room even for those
Who are suffering
From jealousy-monster.

5856.

Be brave!
Make another bold attempt.
Do not allow yourself to be caught
By the hot tears
Of stark disappointment.

5857.

His heart's aspiration-cry
Can at any moment
Fling open the door
Of silence-light.

5858.

For a true seeker
There is only one way
To be happy:
By pleasing God,
His Beloved Supreme.

5859.

God has already
Cheerfully claimed and possessed
The strength of my inner love.

5860.

My heart of inner silence
Has destroyed
The strength of my outer violence.

5861.

When God was looking for him,
He was found in the ignorance-
    crowd
Of the mind.

5862.

How do you dare to drift
Outside the domain
Of your heart's
Beautiful and fruitful garden?

5863.

My purity-heart always reveals
My soul's hidden promise
To my life.

5864.

My faith
Is my beauty's strength
And my purity's length.

5865.

Stamp your heart
With a gratitude-smile.
You will really be perfect!

5866.

Alas, why do I allow
My mind-sorrows
To float on the tide
Of my heart's joy?

5867.

Every day, without fail,
God grants him
A silence-illumined appointment.

5868.

Because of your tremendous
Aspiration,
God has asked you to take
    possession
Of His Infinity.

5869.

You are perfect
Because you are selfless
In your prayerful heart
And soulful life.

5870.

Do not forget
That the road of the past
Is not only obscure
But also useless.

5871.

His heart is crying
To hear
The voice of silence-light.
His soul is crying
To become
God's Satisfaction-Delight.

5872.

You must realise
That there can be nothing
Whatsoever
Beyond the reach of your
    aspiration.

5873.

God definitely
Does not want you
To help the unworthy
To please Him.

5874.

A selfish life
Is forced to learn
What a desolate heart is.

5875.

The penalty
For disobedience
Is God's unavoidable
Withdrawal.

5876.

He who one-pointedly believes
Has already been chosen
To be supremely victorious.

5877.

Between the soul's illumination
And the heart's aspiration
Satisfaction shall always reign.

5878.

Are you willing to change?
If so,
God will come to you
Before long
With His Perfection-Eye
And His Satisfaction-Heart.

5879.

If your heart longs for
The purity-sky,
Then God will definitely
Appear before you
With His Divinity's Vision-Eye.

5880.

To lessen world tension
Each seeker-heart must feed
The peace-starving humanity.

5881.

God's Satisfaction-Eye
He wanted to find
In his ascetic cave.
Indeed, an impossible task!

5882.

A sincere seeker-heart
Knows perfectly well
That the human vital
Is most deplorable.

5883.

I sincerely feel sorry for him,
For he himself is afraid
Of walking along the track
Of his own mind-forest.

5884.

Alas,
Faith-medicine is not always
    available
To cure the mind's
Fatal doubt-disease.

5885.

How to be
A consistent peace-lover?
Just try the spiritual life,
Which has and is God,
The all-nourishing Peace.

5886.

I do not know
Who God is.
I do not want to know
What ignorance is.
I do not need to know
If I am a choice instrument
Of God.

5887.

If you do not want to fail
In your life-examination,
Then curtail your mind's
Conscious and unconscious
Proud wanderings.

5888.

If you do not limit
Your service-life,
God will not stop
His Manifestation-March
In you.

5889.

Do you not see
That your head is too high
For God's Compassion-Eye
To crown?

5890.

If you do not use
Your desire-fire-extinguisher,
You will always fail
In life's fulfilment-races.

5891.

He has sealed
The envelope of the past.
Therefore, in his heart-garden
The eternal love-flower
Is blossoming.

5892.

Why do you have to come
To a spiritual Master?
Because your aspiration-life
Always needs encouragement,
And this is the boon
That you can get
From a spiritual Master.

5893.

Do not take
Spiritual vacations
If you do not want
To be exiled
From ecstasy-kingdom.

5894.

Do you want to please God
Or do you want to please yourself?
If you claim to be a true seeker,
How can you be supremely happy
If the Person who created you
Is not happy?

5895.

Unless you are prepared
To cheerfully accept
God's Justice-Light,
How can you please God?

5896.

Only a heart of peace
Can enjoy
The supreme Friendship of God.

5897.

Purity's oneness-life
Is the world's
Transcendental hope.

5898.

He was faithful
To God's Compassion-Light.
Therefore
God made his life
Supremely beautiful.

5899.

Two promises of my life's
    morning:
Aspiration transcendental
And
Dedication universal.

5900.

O Lord, I do not wish
To keep anything for myself.
My entire being
I am offering at Your Feet.
You gave me
What You wanted to give.
I am giving You
What I now have become.

5901.

I live every moment
To please God.
God lives every moment
To illumine me.

5902.

Humanity's failure-cry
Is his partner
In his outer life.
Divinity's victory-smile
Is his partner
In his inner life.

5903.

Although
Yours is a desire-bound life,
God is inviting you
To sleep in His Compassion-
    Camp.

5904.

If your heart is truly bleeding
For humanity's need,
How can you have
Insecurity's ugly face?

5905.

If you want to discover
Delight-island,
Then be loyal
To your soul's royalty.

5906.

If you allow your dreams to die,
Then your life
Will run into the arms
Of destruction-night.

5907.

If you have a heart of faith,
Then only can you expect
To have access to perfection-light.

5908.

If you are always in the habit
Of desiring,
Then God cannot keep
His Himalayan Promise
To you.

5909.

If you are unfaithful
In thought,
Your heart will never be able
To arrive at the threshold
Of Heaven.

5910.

Your soulful prayers
And your powerful meditations
Will grant you
The all-seeing wakefulness
Inside sleep.

5911.

To reach your soul's highest
    height,
You must long for
A higher universe
Inside the heart of the Unknown.

5912.

He loves one thing
More than anything else
In his life,
And that is the daily majesty
Of his sublime meditations.

5913.

Alas, I did not know
That I would have to suffer so much
From the miseries
Of a doubting mind.

5914.

A heart of faith:
What is it
If not a sleeplessly luminous
Companion?

5915.

If you do not abandon
Your ignorance-thoughts,
Your life will be stranded
Without fail
On ignorance-island.

5916.

Every morning I sing and sing
In God's Compassion-Choir.
Therefore
God has given me the capacity
To run the fastest
Towards His golden Heart-Temple.

5917.

If you can think
Golden thoughts,
That means already
You have changed the winter weather
Of your mind.

5918.

Right now
You are a fallen god.
But do not give up
Your dear hope.
You will definitely once more become
The fully-risen God.

5919.

You have to voyage
From the familiar to the
   unfamiliar,
From the known to the Unknown,
From the knowable to the
   Unknowable.
Indeed,
This is the God-ordained way.

5920.

Make new inner friends:
Purity, humility and divinity Are
waiting for your invitation.

5921.

How can God ever deny
A truth-loving and world-serving
            soul?
         Impossible!

5922.

Today
You are an intruder in the inner
   world
With your doubting mind.
Tomorrow
You will have to live
Inside the forest of fears.

5923.

Is there anybody on earth
Who will not eventually see
The complete failure
Of the desiring mind?

5924.

His is a mind
Of uncertainty.
His is a life
Of insincerity.
But his heart
Is constantly longing for divinity
And nothing else.

5925.

Do not wait inactively
For progress-light,
Or you will always remain
A deplorable failure.

5926.

A God-lover is he
Who is an explorer
Of God's Vision-Worlds.

5927.

Each doubt
Is an unmistakable maker
Of humanity's incurable misery.

5928.

If you are a hero-seeker,
Then you must destroy the pride
Of obstacle-walls
Ahead of you.

5929.

If you think
That you are your own saviour,
Then why do you depend on
    others
To feed your exorbitant ego-life?

5930.

A stainless thought
Shortens your Heavenward
    journey
And makes God real
More than ever.

5931.

Nothing divine,
Nothing perfect,
Nothing worthwhile
Can ever be found ready-made.

5932.

Where is the difference
Between your life of hatred
And your mind of desire?

5933.

If you are lost
In your unaspiring past,
Who can give you
Your aspiring present?

5934.

Who am I,
If not a boatman
Whose boat is completely sunk
In the sea of life?

5935.

Do not be in a hurry.
God will definitely
Lengthen your time
If it is needed
For you to please Him
In His own Way.

5936.

If you are not willing
To make the needed soulful effort
Every day,
You will be forced to suffer
Spiritual starvation.

5937.

To be a superlative disciple,
You have to make friends
With faith
In your inner life
And with determination
In your outer life.

5938.

Who says
That the purification of the mind
Is an extremely severe task?
No,
The illumination of the heart
Is infinitely more difficult.

5939.

Every moment is the real time.
Every moment is the real God-
   Hour.
Every moment God comes
Only to go,
Because of my unwilling
   receptivity.

5940.

You hate your hope
Because your hope is never
   fulfilled.
But can you not
Go beyond your hope
And make friends with your
   heart's
Climbing flames?

5941.

To cross the borderline
Of imperfection
Is only the privilege
Of the pure.

5942.

Develop heart-power.
Why?
Because the power of the mind
Has now become obsolete.

5943.

Since you are walking
The peace-path,
Your mind will totally forget
That once upon a time
It was overcrowded with dark
   thoughts.

5944.

Look, look
What God has done for you!
He has unconditionally
   withdrawn
Your ignorance-death sentence.

5945.

A spark
From the heart's sacred fire
Can show you the way
To your soul's eternal peace.

5946.

Is it not unfair of you
To ask God to play
On your untuned life-strings?

5947.

Self-giving
Is an act of God-revelation.
But before that,
A seeker must be on the lookout
For God.

5948.

An impurity-mind
Illegally stays
Inside the heart
Of purity-life.

5949.

The human mind
Wants to know the truth.
The divine heart
Longs to embody
The Possessor of Truth:
God.

5950.

A heart of surrender
Is God's constant
And cheerful
Responsibility.

5951.

If you do not fulfil
Your outer obligations,
Your inner illumination
Will always remain a far cry.

5952.

You have all along resisted
Temptation.
Therefore
Transformation
Is knocking at your life's door.

5953.

First become
A seeker-flower,
If you long to become
A God-lover-fruit.

5954.

Only a heart
Of universal oneness
Can be freed
From the permanent ignorance-
   illness.

5955.

Do you know
That your mind's doubt-partner
Is trying to destroy
Your heart's oneness-friend:
Soul?

5956.

If you want to silence
The turbulent waves of your
   mind,
Then become inseparably one
With the vastness-smile of the sky.

5957.

Patience-light
Is the sleepless breath
Of my self-giving heart
For my Beloved Supreme.

5958.

To talk to God sleeplessly,
Try to open your soul's door.
If it is an impossible task,
Then open at least
Your heart's door.

5959.

If God's Heart can smile
Through every flower,
Can you not have a heart
That can cry with every leaf?

5960.

If you can have
A meditation-expanded life
And an ignorance-liberated heart,
Then you will be able to measure
The heights and depths
Of the Unknowable.

5961.

If you can penetrate your mind
With your soul's transcendental
   light,
Then you will be able to answer
The universal question easily:
"Who am I?"

5962.

Because God's Love-Sun shines
In each and every creation of His,
His Dream-Life is evolving
From mineral to man.

5963.

Because you are a problem-
   creator,
Your life's imperfection-crimes
Will never stop.

5964.

When the soul opens
Its all-seeing eye,
The heart desires to be
Its faithful employee.

5965.

The body
Always wants to sleep.
The vital
Always wants to fight.
The mind
Always wants to doubt.
The heart
Always wants to dream.
The soul
Always wants to witness.
The Supreme
Always wants to forgive and
   illumine.

5966.

If your life is not surcharged
With God's Compassion-Light,
Then your life will be poisoned
By ignorance-breath.

5967.

A feeble ant-fear:
This is what his desire-life
Has always been.

5968.

Your life's inner weather
Is always unpredictable
Because of the emotion-storms
Of your tormenting, impure vital.

5969.

He is all happiness
Because of the vision
Of a sweet, hope-filled tomorrow.

5970.

If you do not like
What you do for the world,
Then the beauty, perfection
And satisfaction of tomorrow
Will not knock
At your life's door.

5971.

Man in man
Is forcefully imprisoned.
God in man
Is cheerfully imprisoned.
Man in God
Enjoys an undeserved freedom.
God in God
Enjoys the Freedom of the
   Beyond.

5972.

God's supreme Will
Will lead you
Only after His infinite
   Compassion
Has decided to keep you
At your transcendental
   Destination.

5973.

He has kept
His silence-filled mind
Far above the grasp
Of this gossip-world.

5974.

I know it is an impossible task
For you
To cancel your teeming worries.
But you can, at least,
Try to postpone them!

5975.

You have tried today,
And you have failed.
But tomorrow you will not fail,
Because you are now begging God
To try for you.

5976.

If you speak to the world
About your failure
And get more satisfaction
From your failure-life
Than from your success-life,
That means your Inner Pilot
Has completely withdrawn from
   you.

5977.

You are not asked
To meet God halfway.
You are just asked
To come out of
Your tiny, dark mind-room.

5978.

Will you ever realise
That all your mistakes in life
Will be unmistakably followed
By God's Forgiveness?

5979.

Nobody can destroy you,
Nobody!
It is you alone
Who have the capacity
To destroy yourself
Through your own self-neglect.

5980.

The Fulness of God's Heart
Can abide in you
Only when you allow joy to reside
Inside your life-activities.

5981.

You do not belong
To your unfortunate failure-past.
You completely belong
To the happiness of tomorrow's
Vision-reality.

5982.

A heart of compassion
And a soul of forgiveness
Are by no means
Two unavoidable compromises.

5983.

You may not do the right things
Either in your inner life
Or in your outer life,
But you will be given every
   opportunity
To succeed in the outer life
And to proceed in the inner life.

5984.

Unless you realise
That your desire-life
Is nothing short of frustration-
   life,
How can God grant you
   aspiration-life
To please Him
In His Dream-filled creation?

5985.

God's Compassion-Delight
Is waiting and waiting
For you to succeed unmistakably
And to proceed unprecedentedly.

5986.

You serve devotedly:
This is your own experience.
You give joy to others:
This is not only your own
But also the universal experience.

5987.

The heart's simplicity
Shall always succeed
When and where
The mind's complexity fails.

5988.

Each negative thought
Has the capacity
To destroy immediately
Your life's happiness-core.

5989.

One God-Call
Can grant a seeker-heart
Fathomless satisfaction-delight.

5990.

When he meditates on earth,
He clearly sees
That Heaven does nothing for him.
When he meditates on Heaven,
He clearly sees
That earth has nothing to tell him.

5991.

Slowly and unmistakably
You are climbing
Your heart's gratitude-tree.

5992.

As long as fear owns
Your body, vital, mind and heart,
God will not invite you
To stand on His Platform
And speak.

5993.

Your doubt-balloon has burst.
Therefore
God is granting you
The Breath of His Nectar-Love.

5994.

I always cheerfully accept
The decree of my conscience-pilot
To save my mind
From doubt-catastrophes.

5995.

You do not know how to quit;
Therefore, I admire you.
Your mind does not know how to doubt;
Therefore, I admire your mind.
Your heart does not know how to fear;
Therefore, I admire your heart
Far beyond your imagination-light.

5996.

You have aspiration,
And this aspiration
Is nothing short of
God's Confidence-Delight
In you.

5997.

Unless you have secured your place
In the sacred temple of timeless time,
How will you appreciate
The Silence-Vision and sound-creation
Of God?

5998.

No matter how fleeting
Your smile is,
Your smile is the very beginning
Of your wisdom-light.

5999.

There is a special place
For your heart-confidence to glow,
And that special place
Is in the silence-cry
Of your meditation-mountain.

6000.

Courage powerfully grows,
Love soulfully grows,
Gratitude amazingly grows
When you share them
With the rest of the world.

6001.

God created a cry
Inside my heart
To love Him
More and more.
God created a smile
On my face
For Him to need me
More and more.

6002.

At last,
A moment of peace!
My doubting mind
Has surrendered
To my illumining heart.

6003.

A God-commissioned soul
Is always a fruitful mediator
Between earth and Heaven.

6004.

When hesitation whispers
In your ear,
Even God's Compassion
Flies away.

6005.

No distinction
Between your heart's minor
 disobedience
And your mind's major
 disobedience!
Disobedience is self-destructive
Everywhere.

6006.

As long as sincerity and purity
Linger on earth,
This world of ours
Will not be destroyed.

6007.

O insecurity-orphan,
Will you ever enjoy
Your soul's freedom-light?

6008.

He cannot separate
His helpless life
From his mind's
Fatal frustration.

6009.

Give the world
A moment of your concern.
God will always listen
To your heart's prayer.

6010.

O my mind,
You only know two things:
You know how to be
Unpardonably proud
And unthinkably loud.

6011.

At every moment
Your heart must try
To lose its earthly limits.

6012.

How will you ever
Climb up the confidence-tree
If you do not go
To your heart's aspiration-temple
Regularly?

6013.

Not politely,
But vehemently,
You must refuse all the time,
When your mind's doubts invite
    you.

6014.

The heart's purity-flower
Never fades.
The soul's divinity-tree
Never dies.

6015.

Your goals are high
Because of your soul.
Your consciousness is low
Because of your mind.

6016.

No, it is not possible
For any inner cry
To remain unheard.

6017.

God has been telling man
From time immemorial
That he is actually more
Than he appears.

6018.

Be wise!
Every day sacrifice
What you are
For what you can eventually
Become.

6019.

Man thinks
That his heart is waiting.
God knows
That His Eye is watching.

6020.

If you are fast asleep
In ignorance-bed,
Then rest assured that death's hour
Is upon you.

6021.

He who has wisdom,
Light and delight
Will never be caught
In the world's unhappiness-net.

6022.

No good heart
Will ever shirk any challenge,
For a good heart
Is braver than the bravest
When it has to manifest
Its Beloved Supreme on earth.

6023.

Yesterday's God-Compassion
And today's God-Love
Are dissolving all my problems,
Born and unborn.

6024.

Two rivers do not run dry:
The river of God's
Compassion-Life
And the river of God's
Forgiveness-Heart.

6025.

God wants every human being
To participate
In His Cosmic Theatre
Of time and space.

6026.

Every day
God is more than willing
To tune your out-of-tune
Body-instrument.
Just give Him the needed time.

6027.

If your heart
Can face the world unafraid,
Then your life-boat
Will reach Eternity's Shore.

6028.

Only a God-realised soul
Knows that it is quite possible
To conquer the relentless tide
Of desire.

6029.

Since God Himself
Is steering your life-boat,
The fetters of self-doubt
Can no longer exist.

6030.

A life
Of soulful faith
Is a native
Of Eternity.

6031.

To win
The aspiration-academy awards,
Accomplish first
The task for which you came
Into the world.

6032.

I do not want to be a slave
To the great Invisible,
But I wish to be a lover
Of the good Unknowable.

6033.

As soon as you acknowledge
The limits of knowledge,
You become a student
Of the soul's intuition-university.

6034.

If you are afraid
Of human problems,
How can you ever have
Divine solutions?

6035.

You can easily bear
The buffets of the world,
If every day you drink deeply
From Divinity's Nectar-Cup.

6036.

The heart's
Oneness-yearning
Is God's
Unrecognised hidden Power
In man.

6037.

O my seeker-friend,
Your perennial doubt-dilemma
   will last
Unless you take shelter
In the heart of your self-giving
   peace.

6038.

You must be strict
With your unruly mind,
For it is apt to run around
In confusion-circles.

6039.

If you yourself
Do not slow down
Your greed-speed,
Who will do it for you?
Nobody!

6040.

A soulful eye
Is bound to see
A fruitful world.

6041.

Long, long ago
God's Eye and my heart
Had a misunderstanding.
Now everything is totally
   resolved,
And both God and I
Are extremely pleased with each
   other.

6042.

Your heart's perfection-pictures
Can be taken
Only by God's self-giving
Illumination-Camera.

6043.

Do you want to be happy?
Then make your life
As soulfully simple
As sleeplessly breathing.

6044.

Every day you submit
To your own stupidity.
Therefore
Your soul's divinity does not
   knock
At your mind's door.

6045.

Your life will be changed,
Changed forever,
If you consciously take part
In God's love-fulfilling
Satisfaction-Drama.

6046.

When I inundate my life
With love,
I see deep inside me
The congress of giant souls.

6047.

The Compassion
Of my Beloved Supreme
Every day dries
My heart's surrender-tears.

6048.

I am waiting eagerly and
   sleeplessly
For the arrival
Of my Lord's Promise-Boat.

6049.

Aspiration-life and destruction-
   death
Can never be linked
In the same chain.

6050.

A soulfulness-heart
Can see and become
A oneness-life.

6051.

God's Compassion-Eye
And God's Satisfaction-Heart
Arrive only when invited.

6052.

Alas,
My prayers and my meditations
Have all become
Aching nights of despair.

6053.

His mind is the reservoir
Of positive thoughts.
Therefore, he never fails
In anything.

6054.

Because you doubt
God's Forgiveness,
God is no longer
Proud of you.

6055.

If you cling
To your ego-life,
Then God will definitely cling
To His withdrawal-life.

6056.

Your life is in full bloom today
Because you have removed
Your existence-life from bondage-clay.

6057.

God Himself is announcing
Your victory in Heaven,
For you have torn the ignorance-pages
From your life-book.

6058.

Do not seek a lesser goal.
If you do that,
Yours will be a life
Of sombre dole.

6059.

Whoever has told you
That your life will remain
Lost forever
In ignorance-vault
Is absolutely wrong.

6060.

Do you want to become
A searcher of truth?
Then I tell you,
You will never remain alone
Either in Heaven or on earth.

6061.

God lives
To give you everything.
God does not know
And will not know
How to give up.

6062.

If you are giving your life to God
Unconditionally,
Then it will not be long
Before God claims you
As His very own.

6063.

You can soar
Far beyond your life's struggle.
Just pray to God soulfully
To meditate for you.

6064.

God works for Eternity
To save humanity
From its unimaginable insanity.

6065.

Divinity
Is humanity's eternal heritage,
Believe it or not!

6066.

Is there any time
When the temptation-theatre
Is not shockingly overcrowded?

6067.

He does only one thing:
He daily walks along the road
Of the frustration-mind.

6068.

Doubt-train arrives
At the mind-station
Only when
It is not vehemently rejected.

6069.

Hold fast
To your life's obedience-tree
If you really want
A real God-manifestation-life.

6070.

Be always on time
For God's appointed Hour.
If not,
You will never be able
To come out of
Your mind's dark ego-cave.

6071.

One day you will believe
That God's Way is not only a
 better way,
But also the only way
To transform your entire life.

6072.

Hope-plant grows
Only after aspiration-seed
Has been sown.

6073.

The Master's compassion-eye
Will light your devotion-candle
Only at God's choice Hour.

6074.

If you are ready to reveal
God's Compassion,
Then only will God conceal
Your imperfections.

6075.

Never stop learning!
Never hesitate to ask!
God wants you to be a self-knower
More than anything else.

6076.

Like your heart,
Your mind, too,
Must learn how to dance
Sleeplessly
On the faith-floor.

6077.

Disaster fell unexpectedly
From the sky
Because when God's God-Hour
 struck,
You were not available.

6078.

God's Compassion-Eye
Is the source
Of my mind's thought-stopping
Incantation.

6079.

Each human being must know
That his prayer-life
And meditation-life
Are two most significant
Privileges.

6080.

If you do not take help
From your sky-climbing heart,
Then your life-descending mind
Will never stop.

6081.

If you want to expand
Your consciousness,
Then every day, at every moment,
Without fail,
Confront your life's ignorance-
   foe.

6082.

Just remember the day
You first met God.
How did you recognise Him?
You recognised Him
Because you became
Your life's surrender-soul.

6083.

Divinity's fulness-race
And humanity's oneness-race
Will be successful
Only when they need the Supreme
As their Compassion-Coach.

6084.

If you wear
Your heart's oneness-uniform,
Then God will inform the world
That you are His choicest
   instrument.

6085.

Until you realise
That your earthly life-car
Needs Heavenly aspiration-fuel,
You will not be able to see the Face
Of God's Satisfaction-Delight.

6086.

Here on earth
When you do not have
Any impure thoughts
On a particular day,
There in Heaven
God celebrates a special day.

6087.

Be not afraid of God.
Be always at your heart-home
So that you will meet God
When He compassionately calls
   on you.

6088.

If your mind
Is a disobedience-runner,
Then your life
Will definitely run
On a collision-course.

6089.

The sweet music
Of purity's soulful smile
Can create a God-dream
In human life.

6090.

If you keep your wisdom-light
To yourself,
You will never be able to please
    God
In His own Way.

6091.

I am telling you
Once and for all,
Nobody has the right to force you
To own defeat,
Nobody!

6092.

Why do you allow fear
To seize and freeze your heart?
Why do you allow doubt
To torture and conquer your
    mind?

6093.

My life reminds me
Of teeming struggles.
My heart reminds me
Of God's Salvation-Smile.

6094.

An aspiration-boat
Will eventually land
On the perfection-shore
Of satisfaction-delight.

6095.

No, you will not lose
Your existence-life for good
In the tide of temptation,
For God's Compassion
Is infinitely more powerful
Than your temptation-life.

6096.

God will show you the goal.
Can you not show Him
That you are most obedient
To your soul?

6097.

Time does not beckon me.
It is I who beckon time
To carry me
Beyond the limits of time.

6098.

His progress-life halted
The day he made friends
With his gossip-monger-mind.

6099.

Again and again I have told God
That I love Him deeply.
Again and again God has told me
That He needs me desperately.
Finally we have decided today
To trust each other.

6100.

What is human life
If not, right from the beginning,
A beautiful Vision-Flame of God?

6101.

In life
There are many questions,
But surrender to God's Will
Is the only answer.

6102.

Inseparable oneness means
A game of ignorance-
    transformation
In human life.

6103.

You must never forget
To guard your mind-door
Twenty-four hours a day.

6104.

A soulful cry
Embodies a magic wand
That opens every heart.

6105.

God appears
To be sleeping,
But He actually
Never sleeps.

6106.

Feed your heart
And make it strong
So that it can fight
Against your mind
And grant you
The supreme victory.

6107.

You want to be happy?
Then offer to God
Your heart's permanent
   invitation.

6108.

You can easily escape
Your mind's insecurity-jungle
Just by knocking
At your heart's oneness-door.

6109.

The fragrance of good thoughts
Will cut a path
Through your temptation-jungle.

6110.

Because your mind was occupied
With doubts,
God did not feel it necessary
To illumine your mind.

6111.

Just pray and pray!
God is more than ready
To listen
Even to your faint prayers.

6112.

Love your heart's wisdom-fire
More and more.
You will be able to kill
Your desire-life.

6113.

There are two experiences in life:
Gainful and painful.
My Lord Supreme,
Do give me the capacity
To be above these two experiences.

6114.

His heart's service-seeds
I saw yesterday.
Today I am seeing
His life's satisfaction-blossoms.

6115.

Be proud
Of your heart's aptitude.
Your mind's ineptitude
Will not be able to torment you.

6116.

The most difficult thing
In human life
Is to separate sweet expectation
From bitter frustration.

6117.

With your desire-life
You wanted to become
Spiritually tall.
It is impossible!
If you want to become
Spiritually tall,
You have to live
The life of aspiration.

6118.

What has brought you
To God's Golden Shore?
Not your capacity,
But your tender trust in God.

6119.

If you use your faith-key,
Easily
You will be able to unlock
Heaven's door.

6120.

My criminal mind
Has thrown doubts
Into my entire being.

6121.

Self-doubt
Is nothing short of
A seeker's inner treachery.

6122.

At long last
He is anxious to register
For the perfection-course
In his life's school.

6123.

Do not be a victim
To self-pity.
Self-pity is at once
The beginning and the end
Of life's uselessness.

6124.

God is not a dictator.
He is at once
An Inspirer
And a Liberator.

6125.

You worship success-idol.
I worship progress-pilgrim.
This is the difference
Between your mind and my heart.

6126.

The purity of dream
And the beauty of reality
Always go together
In the life of a true God-lover.

6127.

Nothing remains constant
In human life
But our constant desire
To transcend ourselves
So that we can eventually
Become one with God,
Who is both eternally changeless
And constantly changing.

6128.

Allow God's Heart
To announce your victory,
Or you will be forced
By your frustration-vital
To announce your defeat.

6129.

I shall launch my new career,
My heart's sleepless
And unconditionally self-giving
    career,
Tomorrow.

6130.

His is the life
That is sleeplessly longing
To be God-Eternity's
Perfection-climber.

6131.

I am glad that you have had
Your absolutely last
Doubt-destruction-dance.

6132.

There are some unfortunate
   human beings
Who are proud of their doubt-
   storms.
Alas, they do not know
That God will dissolve their
   doubt-storms
At His choice Hour.

6133.

Why do you allow your vital
To be always on the warpath?
Your vital should be controlled!
You must teach your vital
The song of volcano-
   determination.

6134.

God has already given you a tour
Of His Satisfaction-Heaven.
Now will you not give God a tour
Of your heart's aspiration-earth?

6135.

When are you going to see
That your insecurity-friend
Has robbed you
Totally and unmistakably?

6136.

There are two steps
To self-transformation:
I do not know,
And
I know because
My Beloved Supreme teaches me
How to know, what to know
And why to know.

6137.

If you live in your heart's
Humility-valley,
You will easily be able to climb
Your life's progress-tree.

6138.

Feed your mind with your soul's
Illumination-light-food.
You will be the happiest person
In God's entire creation.

6139.

Self-pity-tears
Are never meant
To please the Protection-Feet
And Satisfaction-Eye
Of God.

6140.

If you want to say farewell
To your wild frustration,
Then aspiration-abundance
Should be your real name,
Your only name.

6141.

God is never
Going to wipe away
Your stupid self-pity-tears.

6142.

The frustration-frowns
Of your vital
Can easily be conquered
By the aspiration-smile
Of your self-giving heart.

6143.

In the world of my self
I want to learn only
My humility's self-giving
Purity-song.

6144.

My meditation-life is not
My self-justification-life
On earth.
My meditation-life is
My God-satisfaction-life
Both on earth and in Heaven.

6145.

If you do not curtail
Your earthly roamings,
You will not be able to launch
The ship of perfection-light.

6146.

I do not feel the presence
Of my purity-heart.
Alas, that means I am not allowed
To live in the paradise of delight
Any more.

6147.

One single doubt is enough
To destroy man's purity-heart
And sincerity-life.

6148.

Do you know what actually
   happens
When you pray soulfully?
When you pray soulfully,
You start resembling
Your Beloved Supreme
More and more.

6149.

If your life contains
All artificial ingredients,
God will not be able to bless you
With His Infinity's natural
   Blessings.

6150.

In the spiritual life
The first-class compartment
Is the compartment of my soul-
   delight,
And the second-class
   compartment
Is the compartment of my heart-
   light.

6151.

Let bygones be bygones.
From today on
I shall be the perfect believer
Of God,
And then, before long,
I shall become an unconditional
   lover
Of God.

6152.

If you masquerade as a seeker,
Do you think God the Liberator
Will ever be pleased with you?

6153.

With all due respect
To earthly mental giants,
I must say
That I love only
Simple truth-seekers
And God-lovers.

6154.

A man of purity
Is the love-river
Of God-Eternity's
Self-giving Heart.

6155.

Why do you not just surrender?
You will see
That a life of surrender
Is the only way
To make you
Perfectly plus permanently happy.

6156.

A serious oversight:
My heart of aspiration
Forgot to claim God
As its very own.

6157.

Your mental brilliance
Is no match
For your psychic purity.
Remember this once and for all
If you want to succeed
In your spiritual life.

6158.

If you want to turn
Your mind's night
Into your heart's day,
Then do not pretend to love God,
But live in God persistently
And live for God only.

6159.

Do you need an earthly friend?
Don't mix with your mind's
   doubt.
Do you need a heavenly friend?
Then mix with your soul's
Heavenly promise.

6160.

A heart without aspiration
Is without fail
A totally lost voyager.

6161.

Mine is the heart
That brought me to God
Even much faster
Than my imagination's flight.

6162.

Look at your stupidity!
How can you surprise God
With your greatness?
Look at your stupidity!
You do not realise
That God is extremely pleased
With the purity, beauty and
   divinity
Of your goodness.

6163.

When you reach the final summit
Of your spiritual heights,
Both your friends and your
  enemies
Of the past
Will not only admire you
But also claim you
As their very own.

6164.

If you want to live
In a gratitude-world,
Then you must free yourself
From the temptation-world.

6165.

Unless you avoid
The company of despair,
You will not be able
To accompany
God the Satisfaction-Runner.

6166.

It may happen again!
Ignorance may knock you out.
Before it does,
You must become
A spiritual superman.

6167.

Someday
Your stupid mind
Will definitely realise
What the inner poverty is.

6168.

While you are in deep meditation,
Allow not any undivine thought
To enter into your mind,
For the intensity of that thought
Will be unmistakably unbearable.

6169.

Anything good,
I shall do it immediately.
Anything bad,
I shall tell myself, "Tomorrow."
By the Grace of the Lord Supreme
That tomorrow may never come!

6170.

No jealousy, no competition,
But determination
To sing the song of oneness
In the Fulness-Heart-Garden
Of God.

6171.

When others become jealous of
    you,
Be totally indifferent to them.
For cleverly and secretly
They are trying
Only to pull you down
Into their own darkness.

6172.

God is the divine Gardener.
Inside each flower-soul
He sees
His own new and unique Beauty.

6173.

What is peace?
Peace is to see God's Beauty.
What is perfection?
Perfection is to live
In God's Oneness-Home.

6174.

How to conquer jealousy?
Always think of God,
The Head of the family.
Will it not pain Him
If one child of His
Becomes jealous of another?

6175.

O my ordinary thoughts,
O my undivine, unhealthy
And uncomely thoughts,
During my meditation
If you knock at my mind's door,
This time I shall not open it,
For I know
That you will only misuse
The power of my meditation
To increase your own power.

6176.

We must separate
Our life's soulful songs
From our mind's depression-
    sighs.

6177.

God has
A very special Love for you
Because
You use your faith-map
Every day
In your life's inner journey.

6178.

You do not have to worry
About your heart-treasure.
God cheerfully and sleeplessly
Guards it for you.

6179.

An unlit mind
Is quite happy to live
Inside the blind limitation-cave.

6180.

No amount of information
Will help you
In your spiritual life.
No amount of explanation
Will help you
In your spiritual life.
No amount of elucidation
Will help you
In your spiritual life.
But an iota of aspiration
Is all you need
To be a complete success
In your spiritual life.

6181.

If you are ready
To close your mind
When it is needed,
If you are ready
To expose your vital
When it is needed,
Then God will be all ready
To revive your heart
When it is needed.

6182.

God's Satisfaction-Gift
He bestows
Only upon the sincerity
Of the aspiration-heart,
And nowhere else.

6183.

You are telling me
That you have nothing to do.
I am telling you
That you have not yet done
At least this particular thing:
You have not built a celestial home
For your Inner Pilot
Deep inside your heart.

6184.

Your heart must learn
How to renew soulfully every day
The splendour of your inner
    wealth.

6185.

My Beloved Lord Supreme,
Your Compassion-Eye
Unconditionally gives.
My aspiration-heart
Breathlessly receives.

6186.

If you deny your soul's silence,
You are definitely ignoring
God's Fragrance-Heart.

6187.

The hearts of true
Spiritual brothers and sisters
Together cry,
Together smile
And together live in oneness-
   home.

6188.

I cannot destroy
Your disobedience-night
With anything I have.
No, not even
With my soul's patience-sun.

6189.

This clamouring mind of yours
Has ruined the beauty
Of your heart's silence.

6190.

It is high time
For you to prepare yourself
To listen to God's Nectar-Melody
On His Flute.

6191.

Wherever he goes,
He has the wisdom-illumination
For a large collection
Of aspiration-hearts.

6192.

An aspiration-heart
Does not need an outer record,
For its very existence on earth
Is its supreme record.

6193.

Unless you become
The renouncer of expectation,
You cannot be
The possessor of peace.

6194.

Invoke new confidence
If you want your contribution
To your spiritual life
To be profound.

6195.

He is always found
Between his body's sleep
And his vital's argument.

6196.

His heart is blooming
In full glory
Because it is maintaining
Its glowing purity.

6197.

God's Secrets
Are only for those
Who are God-servers
In man.

6198.

We can arrive at perfection's gate
Only when we work together
Lovingly, untiringly and selflessly.

6199.

Can you not see
That your ignorance-family
Has made you blind?
Can you not see
That your ignorance-family
Has made you weak?
Why then do you have to remain
With your ignorance-family?

6200.

All calamities have come to an end.
All roads have come to an end.
No more shall I wander through life.
I hear my Lord Supreme
Knocking at my heart's door.

6201.

If you can open your heart
As a flower to the sun,
God will enfold you,
Your entire being,
In His universal Peace.

6202.

There are many things
A human being does
That surprise God,
But one thing amazes Him most:
When man ignores God,
His only Friend.

6203.

I see in you
A sorry-faced seeker
Because every day
You forget to fly
Your aspiration-kite.

6204.

If you deceive yourself
Every day,
Then God-discovery is indeed
A useless search.

6205.

God does not expect from you
At the very beginning
Mastery in anything,
But He does expect from you
In everything
Your soulful willingness.

6206.

Do you want to shine?
You can easily shine
Like the sun
In your self-offering
To God in man.

6207.

Hope and fear torture me
Most powerfully
While I am waiting
For God's Compassion-Call.

6208.

Your desire-dynamite
Will not only explode your life
But also destroy
Earth's strongest hope for you.

6209.

If you miss your flight
To Heaven,
You can never acquire
The supreme taste
For God's transcendental Truth.

6210.

Every day
Early in the morning
His soul's golden dream-secrets
Touch his slumbering eyes
And awaken them.

6211.

God's Protection-Boat
Always wants to stay near you.
Why do you swim away
To satisfy your stupid temptation-vital?

6212.

I never thought that God
Would have such a high opinion
   of me
While this world
Has such a low opinion of me.

6213.

Nobody compels you and your
   mind
To be caught in the teeming
   snares
Of tormenting doubts.
Nobody!

6214.

Unless you keep
Your consciousness-light-guard
On the alert,
Yours will be a life of failure,
Undoubtedly.

6215.

When will you ever realise
That shameless fear
Is hiding your beauty's face?

6216.

My heart's sweet surrender-smile
God always treasures
Far beyond my imagination's
   flight.

6217.

My Lord Supreme,
Your Peace leads me
And Your Satisfaction
Guides me.

6218.

If I place my fate
At Your Blessing-Feet,
I know I shall win
Your guiding Eye.

6219.

You do not have to write
Your heart's aspiration-epic.
God will do it.
You just become
Your life's surrender-plant.

6220.

You are sleeping.
Perhaps you will forever sleep.
Therefore
For you there is no need
To free yourself
From your mind's slavery.

6221.

If you exit
From your soul's land,
Then your heart will always remain
Away from the equanimity
Of God's Heart.

6222.

Now that all your ignorance-life
Is in the past tense,
God is granting you
His Infinity's Rainbow-Beauty.

6223.

Every day
Your God-love is accelerating.
That means
Every day God is making
An infinitely more significant Promise
In and through you
To mankind.

6224.

God's Compassion-Height
Saves me.
God's Justice-Light
Illumines me.

6225.

Time's tallest figure is he
Whose heart cries
For humanity's progress
And whose soul smiles
At Divinity's success.

6226.

One ancient question:
How can man free himself
From his expectation-snare?

6227.

Discard your list of grievances
Against yourself.
God wants you to live
In tomorrow's satisfaction-delight.

6228.

Even a beginner-seeker knows
That surrender
Is the ultimate approach
To God-Satisfaction.

6229.

You can try to have confidence
In your untried friends —
Especially your loving heart
And your illumining soul.

6230.

Every day breathe
A soulful prayer to God.
Then you can become
Sleeplessly faithful
To God's Vision-Light.

6231.

His mind is an expert
In evil thoughts.
Alas,
How can I tell this terrible secret
Even to his own heart?

6232.

The possessions of the soul
Are extremely powerful.
These possessions are:
Promise, confidence, perfection
And satisfaction.

6233.

You are always playing
With temptation-fire,
Yet you do not want to know
What danger truly is.

6234.

My Lord Supreme,
I have come to You
With my life's shattered hope-
 pieces.
I do not know when or why or how
My aspiration-cry
Has fallen fast asleep.

6235.

God will remain
A concealed Creator
If you do not look for Him
In His revealed creation.

6236.

Each human being
Is an unfortunate traveller
Chained by a desire-link
To the past.

6237.

You will be sorry
If you do not wake up
At God's choice Hour
To play
With God's Compassion-Eye.

6238.

The universal life of the soul
Begins in Heaven.
The transcendental life of the
   heart
Begins on earth.

6239.

If you refuse
To become a soulful seeker,
That means
You are ruining a lifetime
Of golden opportunities
To become another God.

6240.

If I had waited another day,
I am sure I would have seen
The transformation of man's face
Into the Perfection of God's Heart.

6241.

When God's Eye
Reaches into your heart,
Welcome it soulfully
And immediately.

6242.

Alas,
Nobody wants to recognise in me
My desperate need
For universal oneness.

6243.

If you take with thankfulness
What God gives you,
Then one day God will entrust you
With His Infinity's Fulness.

6244.

You are knocking
At the door of your heart.
That means
You have already achieved
A wonderful triumph
In your aspiration-life.

6245.

Dark shadows
That pass through our lives
Quite often unconsciously help us
To aspire for a luminous
    tomorrow.

6246.

I definitely did not even imagine
That my life would ever be special,
Either in God's Heart
Or in man's mind.

6247.

You need no special talents
To love God.
What you need is
A soulful heart-cry.

6248.

If you do not stay
Within God's calling distance,
How will God lead you
To His Mountain-Summit?

6249.

If you are willing
To slow down your greed-speed,
Then God will feed
Your entire being,
Within and without.

6250.

He was waiting
In all sincerity
For the arrival of inspiration.
Alas,
Inspiration has now
Turned into utter frustration!

6251.

Aspiration gradually ascends,
But if you value your aspiration,
Then needless to say
It swiftly ascends.

6252.

You can shorten the road
To Eternity,
If you can take everything
As divine
And every man
As a truth-seeker
And a God-lover.

6253.

Sleeplessly you should be careful
Of two thieves:
A fearful heart
And a doubting mind.

6254.

In the name of necessity,
Man enjoys a great friendship
With his desire-life.

6255.

How to shorten
The long road to Eternity?
Make friends with hope
And fly the banner of promise.

6256.

It is not your capacity
That has won the race
But the Grace of your Inner Pilot
That has won the race
All for you.

6257.

Unless God prunes
My life's aspiration-tree,
I do not see how
I will ever acquire
Realisation-fruit.

6258.

Fear and doubt,
Anxiety and frustration
Have always been strangers
In his heart-room.

6259.

Why are you crying?
Have you failed?
Why are you crying?
Is God displeased with you?
Why are you crying?
Does the world not need you?

6260.

Why are you smiling?
Have you passed
Your life-examination?
Why are you smiling?
Are you on the verge
Of God-realisation?

6261.

Although jealousy has crippled
   your mind,
Still there is time
For you to be cured.
Just try to respond
To your heart's Heaven-climbing
   cry.

6262.

My heart was extremely delighted
To see the last, dying desire-flame
Of my mind.

6263.

God tells me
That He will definitely
Be successful with me.
Therefore
He has been extending and
    extending
My life's transformation-deadline.

6264.

At the last moment
I had courage and wisdom enough
To cancel my reservation
On ignorance-plane.

6265.

Each concealed hope-bird
Must be transformed into
A revealed heart-flower.

6266.

When I cherish
My desire-life,
Hell celebrates
My utter stupidity.

6267.

Your self-importance
Is as fleeting
As a hopeless thought.

6268.

To hope for this world
Is nothing short of
A vanishing breath,
A hopeless pursuit.

6269.

Every day
I go to visit my body
In my mind's prison.
Every day
I go to visit my heart
In my soul's palace.

6270.

God is not answering
His inner Phone
Because you are cherishing
The conversations you have had
With your doubtful mind.

6271.

Your notorious mind tells you
That you do not need God.
Your uproarious vital tells you
That you are already another God.

6272.

Just because
Your heart-bird has flown
High above your mind's clouds,
God is granting you
The Silence, Beauty and Divinity
Of Eternity.

6273.

My Lord Supreme,
I am complete
Not even in Your Compassion-Eye,
But only in Your Forgiveness-Heart.

6274.

Do not abandon
Your golden hope-heart
If you really want to see
God's stupendous Pride in you.

6275.

A confusion-mind
And an imperfection-heart
Can never be separated.

6276.

If Heaven loves you,
Then Heaven will definitely
Grant you the capacity
To be its perfect slave.

6277.

If you are a true God-lover,
Then never will you dare to imagine
That you can ever outgrow your need
For God's Compassion-Light
And Forgiveness-Delight.

6278.

To conquer doubt
Is to conquer
The final, insurmountable
Mountain-obstacle.

6279.

If you do not
Put your meditation into action,
Then you will be running
With only one leg.

6280.

He who procrastinates
Cannot be a true member
Of God's God-Satisfaction-Family.

6281.

Why return
To your old earth-bound desire-home?
Can you not see
That your Heaven-free aspiration-home
Is awaiting your arrival?

6282.

If you do not veto
Your wild mind's constant resistance,
You will never be able to conquer
Time and death.

6283.

You do not need eyes
To see God's Compassion-Eye.
What you need is a loving heart
To sing the glory
Of God's Compassion-Eye.

6284.

You have got what you wanted:
The fulfilment of your desire-life.
But you have not got what you need:
The convincing and fulfilling delight
Of satisfaction.

6285.

Do not think
That God will ever give up on you.
He will wait for you
Throughout Eternity
Until He changes your doubting mind.

6286.

Forgive me, my Lord Supreme.
I have forgotten to thank You
For the interview.
"My child,
I am sorry that I have forgotten
To express My Satisfaction
In your acceptance of My Light."

6287.

If you are already
A good God-lover,
Then I do not have to tell you
To shut ignorance out of your life.

6288.

Your mind's climbing prayer
And your heart's glowing
   meditation
Can easily save you.
Your life need not remain
Forever paralysed
By helpless hopelessness.

6289.

If security is something
That you can easily unfold,
Insecurity is something
That you can bravely put away.

6290.

When I see the darkness
Of the human mind,
My silence-heart and I
Helplessly cry and cry.

6291.

Alas,
It seems that
A never-to-disappear depression
Has attacked your vital.

6292.

If a negative thought
Claims you as its victim,
Can you not immediately take
   shelter
In the embrace
Of a positive thought?

6293.

A stunning message from God:
"Man, take care of yourself
From now on!"

6294.

You fool!
Nobody has compelled you
To build your heart-nest
In the swamp of despair-night.

6295.

It is you who have allowed your mind
To be over-populated with worries.
Therefore, your faith in yourself
Every day is dwindling.

6296.

Alas,
I know where I am staying,
But I can't help staying
In the lifeless home of ignorance.

6297.

God is asking me
To do the right thing:
Instead of barking at His creation,
To love His creation.

6298.

No more ignorance-thoughts
Within and without!
God-thoughts have covered
The purity of my inner world
And the beauty of my outer world.

6299.

A longing heart
Unmistakably deserves satisfaction.
A self-giving life
Unquestionably deserves fulfilment.

6300.

God's Forgiveness-Feet,
No matter how high They are,
Always remain within easy reach
Of man's heart-prayers.

6301.

To see
A face of love
Is to feel
A heart of peace.

6302.

You know how to converse
With your heart.
Therefore
You and your aspiration-life
Are definitely pleasing
Your Beloved Supreme.

6303.

My Lord Supreme,
Your Heart beats
In my throbbing heart.
Therefore, all my questions,
Born and unborn,
Are answered.

6304.

O seeker,
The joy of your desire-life
Is nothing but your sorrow
Masked.

6305.

O my mind,
I pray to my Lord Supreme
To help you know
The sacred secrets
Of my soul.

6306.

My outer awakening
Is my deep dream-existence
In my Lord Supreme.

6307.

The inner heart
Can be made sweet, pure and
  perfect
Only with one thing:
The inner hunger.

6308.

The more desires you have,
The more helpless a puppet
You become
In the hands of ignorance-prince.

6309.

God does not want you
To remain alone.
He wants you to swim
With your heart's swift hope-river.

6310.

God will wait for you,
He will,
Although you are a worshipper
Of ignorance-night.

6311.

The inner disaster will strike
Without fail
If you are not already disgusted
With your life's insecurity-ant.

6312.

If you have a seeker's heart,
Then at the very mention
Of your Lord Supreme,
Your eyes of indifference
To the outer world of
   manifestation
Will be transformed into
A heart of sleepless concern.

6313.

One willing breath.
Lo,
The question of centuries
Is answered.

6314.

Centuries have rolled by,
Yet one question haunts him:
Does God know everything
Here on earth and there in
   Heaven?

6315.

God paints you
With your aspiration-life.
You paint yourself
With your desire-mind.

6316.

If you resign
From your God-appointed task,
Tomorrow's sorrow
Will knock at your heart's door
Powerfully today.

6317.

Your God-search
Is accelerating.
Therefore, God Himself
Is celebrating
Your graduation in Heaven.

6318.

God loves His unfinished
Vision-Eye
More than anything else.

6319.

Every day you must shed tears
For this poor earth
If you really care for
God the man.

6320.

God wants to write
Your aspiration-epic.
You just make friends
With your silence-mind.

6321.

Do not allow your heart,
Like your mind,
To be cramped
In life's insecurity-cage.

6322.

You want to save
The world at large.
Do you not see
That you have already become
Your mind's perfect and eternal slave?

6323.

I love and I need
Only one word
In God's Dictionary:
Forgiveness,
Sleepless forgiveness.

6324.

If you give your mind
All the time
Undue respect,
How do you expect your heart
To give you
Its soulful love?

6325.

Silence is not loved
By an ordinary man.
Sound is not loved
By an aspiring man.
But the soundless sound-life
And the soundless silence-life
Are loved
By a God-becoming man.

6326.

Human thoughts
Are mortal dreams,
But human self-giving
Is an immortal Reality.

6327.

Never wait passively
For progress-light,
For that is absolutely
The wrong approach.

6328.

A doubtful mind
And a fearful heart
Are the makers
Of endless miseries.

6329.

Satisfaction within
And satisfaction without
Come from the purity
Of inner aspiration
And from the beauty
Of outer dedication.

6330.

Hesitation
Is an unpardonable intruder
In the seeker's aspiration-world.

6331.

Today I am celebrating
The complete failure
Of my desire-mind.

6332.

Because you are a fool,
You have all along carried
Unnecessarily
An excessive ignorance-burden.

6333.

Too many souls
Love to procrastinate.
Again, too many souls
Want a quick liberation.

6334.

Why return to your old home,
Why?
A new home is waiting for you —
A home of perfection-light.

6335.

A slumbering life
Will definitely meet
With an inglorious defeat
At the end of its earthly sojourn.

6336.

He got
What he wanted,
Only to lose
His heart's Inner Pilot.

6337.

You have been knocking
At your mind's door.
Are you not tired of it?
Can you not ask your soul
To teach you how to knock
At your heart's door?

6338.

I know you have
An indisputably great mind.
But can you not prove to me
That you also have
An indisputably good heart?

6339.

A sincere seeker knows
That his aspiration-life
Is nothing short of
A lifetime opportunity
To realise God
And to become inseparably one
With God's Manifestation-Light
On earth.

6340.

Do not be baffled
By man's ignorance.
Just tell humanity
That God is not finished
With His creation-experience.

6341.

I have started dreaming
Of going back to my spiritual life,
For my present desire-life
Is like a pathless wood.

6342.

An impossible task:
To satisfy God
With your self-styled surrender.

6343.

You are hungry
For the rewards from Heaven,
But you are not willing to be one
With the earth's hunger-cry.

6344.

Because I am a slave
To my self-glory,
I am suffering from
A very high ignorance-fever.

6345.

Now that you have pleased God
In His own Way,
God has made a special reservation
For you to stay
In His celestial Heaven-Abode.

6346.

I have seen
Time and again,
My God, the Compassion-
　　Lifeguard,
Saving me from drowning
In ignorance-sea.

6347.

My heart-bird and soul-bird
In oneness fly
Towards the perfection-summit
Of Divinity.

6348.

He who claims God as his own,
Very own,
Is going to win
The soulful seeker award
Of Eternity.

6349.

Selfless service
Is man's visible love for God
In God-manifestation on earth.

6350.

Do not think
That you cannot do it.
Just think that God
Is definitely going to do it
In you, for you.

6351.

If you travel all the time
On the wings of hope,
And not
On the wings of determination,
You are not going to succeed
In the battlefield of life.

6352.

What good
Are all the multiple glories
Of the world
When you have lost
Your soul's smile?

6353.

God has lent you
His ready Heart.
Can you not lend Him
Your ready ear?

6354.

He has failed
In his search for God,
For he has allowed his mind
To be crushed
By the jaws of jealousy.

6355.

First place yourself
Before God's Compassion-Eye,
And then place yourself
At God's Transformation-Feet.

6356.

Follow your inner sun
While walking through
Your mind's ignorance-night.

6357.

If you can give up
Your earth-bound desire-life,
Then God will grant you
His Heart's Ecstasy-Empire.

6358.

Why do you not ask God
To drive your life-car?
He will not only drive you
Safely,
But also take you
To your satisfaction-destination
Swiftly.

6359.

Which master do you want?
The doubting mind.
Which master do you need?
The loving heart.

6360.

You have lost the inner race,
Not because you are slow,
But because you have been
    looking behind
All the time.

6361.

You hide
From God's Compassion-Light.
Therefore
You are the greatest fool
In God's entire creation!

6362.

Do you not see
That your ignorance-shadow
Is following you everywhere,
No matter where you go?

6363.

O my heart,
You have lost your inner key.
Therefore
You will not be able to open
Your life's realisation-door.

6364.

To reach
The pinnacle of perfection,
Every day try to compose
A God-pleasing, soulful song.

6365.

There shall come a time
When your life will definitely escape
From the torture of ignorance-night.
Soulfully wait for God's choice Hour.

6366.

Doubt, the aspiration-strangler,
Has finally been captured.
Therefore
I shall celebrate my God-victory
Inside my heart-garden.

6367.

You are all mind
And no heart.
Therefore, you are missing
Your soul.

6368.

In my heart's hour of need
I dived deep
And discovered
The eternal, self-illumining Sun.

6369.

You do not have to decide
Whether you should hide or abide.
Just cry with your heart,
Just smile with your soul.
In your soulful cry and powerful smile
All decisions will be made for you
By God Himself.

6370.

Do not allow insecurity
To kidnap your heart.
Sooner or later
You will definitely be blessed
With God-Vision.

6371.

His is a thankless heart
And his is a thoughtless mind.
What he enjoys
Is the pride
Of his little ego-possessions.

6372.

You are unloved and
   unremembered
Because
You do not want to participate
In God's Cosmic Play.

6373.

Your ignorance-era
Will come to an end
Because
Your sun-vast aspiration-life
Has just begun.

6374.

An impurity-thief
Has stolen all your joy.
God's Compassion invoke
To grant you His own
Universal Vision-Light.

6375.

Who says
God does not hear your prayers?
He does hear your prayers,
Provided they are
Your silence-prayers.

6376.

If you keep your heart-room clean
Every day,
God will force your mind
To sleep for good.

6377.

I do not know
Why I am crying
And for whom I am crying,
But I do know
Why I am smiling
And for whom I am smiling.
I am smiling to see
God's Compassion-Face.
I am smiling for God's
Satisfaction-Manifestation on
   earth.

6378.

You have fallen prey to impurity.
Your moment of colossal
    satisfaction
Has indisputably passed.

6379.

Because of his life's
Extraordinary transformation,
He is impervious
To all ignorance-attacks.

6380.

A life of meditation
Can be pleased
Only with one thing:
The ecstasy of the soul.

6381.

My aspiration-heart knows
How to cry for God.
My dedication-life knows
How to smile at man.

6382.

You must never think
That your life and heart
Are unprepared to meet with God.

6383.

Do you want to conquer
Your time-bound mind?
Then grow into
Your soul's patience-tree.

6384.

Do you want
To deserve God's Love?
Then serve God the man
In God's unfinished creation.

6385.

A bitter truth-pill
Has cured
His illness of millennia.

6386.

Alas,
Once to cry for God
Is not enough.
Alas,
One perfect soul on earth
Is not enough.

6387.

Your life
Is God's responsibility
If you care for
The divinity within you only.

6388.

If you are
An ordinary human being,
Then you will try to hide
From the world.
If you are
A special being,
Then you will try to abide
In God's Heart
For man's transformation-life.

6389.

Alas,
Purity has been hiding
For a long time
From the world's fearful eyes.

6390.

Time will not wait for you.
Do not waste your precious life
In searching for the best road.
Start walking along any road,
For eventually
All roads will lead you
To your goal.

6391.

First become the worshipper,
Then become the lover
And finally become the explorer
Of God's Vision-World.

6392.

You have begun
Your Eternity's journey
In Heaven.
Now you must continue it
Here on earth.

6393.

Because of his centuries
Of sleep,
He has forgotten to value
God-realisation.

6394.

Have new inner friends,
Especially your heart's purity
And your soul's divinity.

6395.

My heart tells my mind,
"O my searching mind,
Do not be satisfied
With your present achievement.
You want to love the Inner Pilot most,
But that is not enough.
You have to love
The Inner Pilot only."

6396.

He who is neutral
Cannot be
A promising and fulfilling soul
To God.

6397.

My mind thinks
God is beautiful
Because
My heart loves God.
My heart knows
God is beautiful
Because
My soul loves God.

6398.

There shall come a time
When your mind will be freed
From ignorance-fetters.
And then you will realise
That God is
A colossal Compassion-Heart.

6399.

If you are
A peace-supplier,
Then God will come to you
As a Supreme Lover.

6400.

If you are a seeker
Of silence-light,
Then God will grant you
An eternal dawn
In His universal Heart.

APPENDIX

POSTFACE

Publishing principles

This edition of *The works of Sri Chinmoy* aims to obey the Author's wish: scrupulous fidelity to his original words, use of typographical style by him selected, specific spelling choices, end placement of any editorial content (i.e. not written by Sri Chinmoy himself), particular treatment of some personal nouns in special cases, etc.

Textual accuracy

The text of this edition has been checked to ensure faithful accuracy to the originals. Although much effort has been put in proofreading and comparing different versions of the text, this print may still present a few lingering errors.

The Publisher would be grateful to be apprised of any mistypes via postal mail or facsimile, possibly with scan of the original page where the text is different. Please use original books only, specifying the year of publication. Online versions may be not as accurate and should not be considered authoritative.

Acknowledgements

The Publisher is very grateful to the late Professor Lambert and his équipe for his invaluable advice. For many decades Prof. Lambert conducted a small publishing house specialising in hand-made prints of philological edition of the classics. The standard of this edition would not have been the same without his scholarly advice.

The Publisher is also grateful to the international team of collaborators that spent countless hours proofreading and checking the current text against the originals.

Our deepest gratitude to Sri Chinmoy. His living presence can be felt breathing throughout his writings. It is such a privilege to be involved with his works, in any form.

Citation keys

Citation keys are used throughout *The works of Sri Chinmoy* to allow accurate cross-reference of texts across titles and editions. Examples: EA 13, ST 50000, UPA 7.

Sri Chinmoy Canon

We could not use better words than Professor Lambert's, who kindly offered the name *Sri Chinmoy Canon*:

> «By defining Sri Chinmoy's first editions as *editio princeps* we chose to follow classical scholarship criteria, not because we consider Sri Chinmoy's work antique, but because we believe it is among the few post ‹classical antiquity› works to rightly deserve to be considered a *classicus*, designating by that term *superiority*, *authority* and *perfection*.
>
> «The monumental work Sri Chinmoy is offering to mankind is awe-inspiring and supremely pre-eminent in proportions and quality. It is manifest that Sri Chinmoy's work — which we feel right to call *The Sri Chinmoy Canon* — will be of profound help and source of enlightenment to anyone seeking a higher wisdom, truth and reality supreme.»

[Translated from French by M. G.S.]

TABLE OF CONTENTS

TWENTY-SEVEN THOUSAND ASPIRATION-PLANTS	3
APPENDIX	835
POSTFACE	837
TABLE OF CONTENTS	841

*Composition typographique par imprimerie
Ab Academia Aoidon, Paris & Lyon.*

*Un grand merci à Prof Knuth pour
l'utilisation avancée de T_EX.*

A LYON, LE 13 NOVEMBRE LXXXVI Æ.G.

www.ingramcontent.com/pod-product-compliance
Lightning Source LLC
Chambersburg PA
CBHW030109240426
43661CB00031B/1351/J